D1174103

/3 25

WELLSPRINGS
OF
TORAH

WELLSPRINGS OF TORAH

An Anthology of Biblical Commentaries

by
RABBI ALEXANDER ZUSIA FRIEDMAN

Compiled and Edited
by
RABBI NISON ALPERT

Translated from the Original Yiddish
by
GERTRUDE HIRSCHLER

THE JUDAICA PRESS, INC.
NEW YORK ● 1980

Copyright © 1969 by
THE JUDAICA PRESS, INC.
NEW YORK, N.Y.

ALL RIGHTS RESERVED
INCLUDING THE RIGHT OF REPRODUCTION
IN WHOLE OR IN PART
IN ANY FORM

ISBN: 0–910818–04–5 HARD BOUND
ISBN: 0–910818–28–2 SOFT BOUND

First printing 1969
Second printing 1974
Third printing 1980

Manufactured in the United States of America

CONTENTS

PAGE

FOREWORD
by Nison L. Alpert vii

ALEXANDER ZUSIA FRIEDMAN
by Hillel Seidman xiii

THE BOOK OF GENESIS 3

THE BOOK OF EXODUS 105

THE BOOK OF LEVITICUS 199

THE BOOK OF NUMBERS 277

THE BOOK OF DEUTERONOMY 361

PASSOVER 477

SEFER HaMITZVOT 461

BIBLIOGRAPHY 523

המהדורה הזאת מוקדשת

לזכרו של הרב הגאון

ר' פנחס אלטר בן ר' יהודה ליב

הכהן שבשיביץ ז"ל

נפטר י"ט אלול תשכ"ד לפ"ק

THIS EDITION IS DEDICATED
TO THE MEMORY OF
PINCUS SHEBSHAIEVITZ
RABBI AND SCHOLAR
departed 19 Elul 5724

FOREWORD

The Jewish people are known as the "People of the Book" not because they gave the message of God to the world, nor even because of the paramount place they assigned to study. They acquired the title primarily because all the world could see that the people of Israel actually lived by the Book for which they were best known. To the Jewish people, the Torah is more than merely a code of law. It is a chronicle of its life, past, present and future.

Therefore, throughout the history of our people, the study of the Torah and the reading of its portions week after week has held a significant place in our way of life. To read it means to relive all the events of our past, to join, as it were, with our Patriarchs and with the Twelve Tribes, sharing their hopes and their sufferings. It means to identify with our brethren through the ages in our yearning for redemption, for the time when peace will reign supreme throughout the world and when all mankind will be filled with the love and understanding of God. To study the *sidrot* of the Five Books of Moses means to kindle anew for ourselves each week the light of the Word of God, and to gain renewed inspiration in our endeavor to emulate His ways and to lead lives of purity and holiness. To the Jew, to "learn" Torah means to climb a Jacob's ladder which, though it rests on earth, reaches up to Heaven.

In order to stimulate the interest of the masses who were not among the "learned in the Law", countless anthologies of commentaries and "midrashim" surrounding this record of the beginnings of our people have been published through the centuries. But few have been able to capture the spirit of the Torah, its commandments and its moral

vii

and ethical teachings as has the anthology *Der Torah Kval*, or *Wellsprings of the Torah*, which it is our privilege now to present to English-speaking Jewry for the first time.

Wellsprings of the Torah—which has already been translated into Hebrew under the title of *Ma'ane HaTorah*—was first published in Yiddish by Reb Alexander Zusia Friedman in Warsaw in 1937. A fine scholar with an encyclopedic knowledge of hundreds of Rabbinic commentaries and Hassidic sayings pertaining to the first five books of the Bible and to the excerpts from Prophetic literature which comprise the weekly *haftarot*, Rabbi Friedman was endowed not only with a rare understanding of the deeper meaning of Torah but also with the gift of discernment which enabled him to select those gems of Rabbinic and Hassidic lore that would have the most appeal to the Jewish reader, regardless of scholarly training.

Reading the commentaries, the wise sayings and the parables by sages over a span of time beginning with the Talmudic era and reaching over the Middle Ages down to the years immediately preceding the European holocaust, one is brought close to the wellsprings of the very life of our people. Selections from the writings and sermons of scholars dispersed all over the world, from Babylonia to Spain, from Poland to Canada, convey with straightforward clarity the character of the Jew through nearly two thousand years of exile.

Thrown into ghettos, persecuted, tortured and many times deprived of life itself, the Jew feared his Gentile neighbors beyond the walls within which he himself was confined, but he did not envy them. Through the ages, the Jew retained an unbroken spirit, coupled with a remarkable sense of humor and a good measure of faith in a better

future. And no matter how great the stress under which
the Jew was forced to fight for survival, the wellsprings of
Jewish creativity never ran dry. Commentaries on Biblical
and Prophetic literature, novellae on Talmudic law, and
philosophical and metaphysical treatises on Jewish wisdom
were written and gained wide audiences wherever Jews
found a temporary haven.

Wellsprings of the Torah provides the reader of today
with a portrait, as it were, of the saintly men of the spirit,
the teachers of the Law, and the *rebbes* of countless Jewish
communities, large and small, who ensured the survival of
Jewish creativity through the centuries. Arranged beneath
the appropriate verse from the Pentateuch and the *haftarot* accompanying each weekly portion, hundreds of comments, parables and sayings offer examples of the rare
combination of keen insight and profound love for their
brethren which distinguished the great teachers of the
Jewish people wherever they were scattered. While hardly any two of the scholars and rabbis represented in this
anthology are exactly alike with respect to background
or their approach to the sacred subject matter, the
message they convey is the same throughout. They admonish us not to lose faith and not to permit our own
character to be changed by the baseness that surrounds us
still, alas, in so many parts of the world. If only we will
study the Torah, they point out, we will come closer to our
Father in Heaven and at the same time gain a better understanding of our brethren everywhere. Only by serving
the Lord with gladness will we acquire true human dignity.
They bid us to be stern critics of our own conduct and of
our motives and to find pride and joy in observing the commandments with which God has honored us. Whether they

ix

were Hassidim or *mitnagdim*, whether they taught in Lithuania or Galicia, Hungary or Rumania, the men of Torah quoted in this volume were all inspired by the same Word which they made it their aim to interpret to future generations in a lucid fashion, simple enough for all to understand.

Wellsprings of the Torah found immediate acclaim in Jewish communities throughout Europe. Now, a little over a quarter-century later, Judaica Press has entrusted me with the sacred task of selecting from the original Yiddish edition those commentaries, interpretations, sayings and novellae whose meaning could be conveyed intact in the English idiom of today.

Thanks are due to Gertrude Hirschler, educator, writer and translator, who with keen perception and understanding carried out the exacting task of re-creating these selections in a form capable of providing inspiration for the men and women, young and old, who live in what is today the largest Jewish community of the world.

By way of a supplement, I have appended to Volume II a bibliography listing the works quoted, and brief biographical sketches of the authors represented in our anthology.

At the end of his preface to the original edition, Rabbi Friedman placed the Hebrew date of its completion, the year 5698 of the Creation of the World. In their conventional succession, the combination of Hebrew letters denoting that figure would spell TirTZaKH. These letters, read together, spell the Hebrew word for "thou wilt be murdered." Rabbi Friedman, therefore, altered the order of the letters to read TiRKHaTZ, meaning "thou shalt be cleansed." Alas, Rabbi Friedman was to experience the meaning of both these words in full. He was murdered by German soldiers, and his soul ascended to Heaven in the purity of heroic martyrdom.

May the English version of this anthology serve as his memorial for future generations.

Nison L. Alpert

ALEXANDER ZUSIA FRIEDMAN

By Hillel Seidman

Long before his thirtieth birthday, Alexander Zusia Friedman was already known and respected as one of the luminaries who led Orthodox Jewry in Poland during the era between the two World Wars. As secretary-general of the Agudath Israel movement of Poland, a position to which he was appointed when he was only twenty-eight, he was the spokesman of a powerful organization whose membership numbered into the tens of thousands and included some of the greatest spiritual leaders in the recent history of the Jewish people. A product and lifelong adherent of Hassidism, he came to Agudath Israel directly from the world of intensive Talmudic study. His was a happy blend of the warmth of Hassidism and the logic of Talmudic learning. He was an eloquent orator, articulate lecturer, capable administrator, forceful writer and inspiring teacher. And all these many gifts he placed unstintingly at the service of the Torah and of his people.

He was born in the town of Sochatchov, Poland, in 1897 (Av 11, 5697). His parents, like most of the Jews of the Polish countryside, were caught up in a never-ending struggle for the necessities of life. His father, Aaron Joshua Friedman, was the sexton of the town's synagogue. His mother sold groceries at markets in neighboring towns to supplement her husband's meager earnings.

Alexander was their only son. He was still very young when his parents first became aware of his unusual scholastic aptitude; he was able to recite the entire Book of Genesis from memory when he was only three years old. Alexander passed quickly from one teacher to the next until he was nine. At that point his teacher told his father that he had no more knowledge to impart to the boy and suggested that he be enrolled at the Yeshiva headed by the Hassidic Rebbe of Sochatchov. But the father, fearful that such advanced studies at so early an age would be too great a strain on the child, looked about for some other arrangement. It came to his attention that three wealthy Jews of the town, each blessed with a gifted son past the age of *bar mitzvah,* had jointly imported a Talmudic scholar from another city to teach their sons, paying him three roubles a week each — a munificent salary in those days — on condition that he take no other pupils. Aaron Joshua Friedman called on one of these men to inquire whether Zusia might join the three older boys in their studies, hastening to add, of course, that he would undertake to pay his share of the tuition. Delighted at the prospect of having the precocious nine-year-old study with their sons, the three fathers offered, instead, to pay the elder Friedman three roubles a week for giving the boys the opportunity to be inspired by Zusia's scholastic zeal and accomplishments. However, Aaron Joshua insisted on paying the teacher the same weekly tuition that each of the other fathers had been contributing — three roubles a week. Since this amount represented Aaron Joshua's entire weekly income, the family thenceforth lived solely on the mother's earnings.

At his *bar mitzvah* celebration, Zusia delivered a highly erudite Talmudic discourse to an audience which packed the House of Study and overflowed into the street outside. Among the invited guests were a number of noted rabbis, including no less a personage than Rabbi Abraham Bornstein, the Rebbe of Sochatchov.

After his *bar mitzvah,* Zusia enrolled at the Yeshiva of Sochatchov to continue his studies. In the summer of 1914 — when he was barely seventeen — he was betrothed to a girl from a small town nearby. The bride was neither wealthy nor of distinguished ancestry. Her father was a simple, hard-working man. But her mother was known far and wide for her piety and selflessness. She supported many needy Talmud scholars and went to work herself to help provide for her family's sustenance.

When World War I broke out, the Friedman family fled to Warsaw. In Warsaw, Zusia made the acquaintance of one Joel Schwarzstein, a wealthy watch dealer who delighted in testing the knowledge of Yeshiva students, rewarding anyone able to recite fifty folios of Talmud from memory with an expensive watch. Zusia was one of those to receive the gift, which he cherished for the rest of his life. He became a pupil of Rabbi Baruch Gelbart, a scholar of note and author of several learned treatises on Talmudic law. Rabbi Gelbart, a man of considerable means, offered to provide for the support of his promising student, a favor which Zusia, however, refused. It was during World War I, too, that Zusia first met Rabbi Dr. Emanuel Carlebach, a member of a distinguished rabbinical family in Germany, who was then stationed in Warsaw as a military chaplain while the city was under German occupation and had organized classes in Jewish studies for young refugees. Zusia Friedman also attended these lectures. It was his first contact with a representative of Western European Orthodoxy which, unlike the Orthodox of Eastern Europe, had not rejected secular culture and learning.

It was Rabbi Carlebach who, together with Rabbi Dr. Pinhas Kohn, helped organize a branch of Agudath Israel in Poland under the name Shlomei Emunei Israel.

Zusia was still quite young when he first became active in Agudath Israel or, more accurately, in *Tz'ire Agudath Israel,* its youth organization. He proved to be an effective speaker, a gifted writer and a capable organizer and rapidly rose in the movement's ranks. He became the leading figure in Tz'ire Agudath Israel, which eventually assumed a considerable share of the burden borne by the parent organization. Long after he had outgrown the youth organization and had moved on to wider areas of activity, thousands of "Tz'ire" members still regarded him as their trusted and admired leader and advisor.

In 1919 he attended the first country-wide conference of Poland's Agudath Israel, at which he delivered an inspiring address. Shortly thereafter he was named secretary of "Agudah" headquarters in Poland.

The leaders of the parent organization soon took him away from the youth movement. In 1925 he was appointed secretary-general of Agudath Israel of Poland. In this position, which he held until the end, he was charged with the task of bringing order to the work of the organization, supervising its accounts and its correspondence, and maintaining contact with local chapters throughout Poland and with Agudah branches in other countries. He took charge of all administrative details, planned agendas and took minutes of meetings. Conscientious and pains-taking as he was, he had little patience with those leaders who were so immersed in long-range objectives and affairs of note that they failed to appreciate the importance of detail and order in the day-to-day operations of the movement. Although he himself played an active part in the ideological and spiritual de-velopment of Agudath Israel, he did not consider administrative routine beneath his dignity.

Almost against his will, Alexander Zusia Friedman was thrust into the position of party leadership. He never assumed the airs of the professional politician. He was a scholar first and foremost, and it was his great scholarship which pervaded his whole being — his behavior, his manners, his speech, his think-ing and, indeed, his entire way of life. Earnest, simple and sincere, he was a friend especially to the young, with a ready eye and ear for the needs, the aspirations and the problems of youth.

Friedman was not a revolutionary in the conventional sense of the term — he was far too quiet and humble for that. Yet, by the sheer impact of his personality, he wrought an upheaval in the Jewish Community Council of Warsaw where he represented Agudath Israel, infusing into this small-scale Jewish parliament a true sense of Jewish peoplehood and an energy and vitality that had been sadly lacking before. He was elected to the Jewish Community Council of Warsaw three times — in 1926, in 1930 and again in 1936.

He was a master in the skills of oratory. His voice could be gentle and firm, caressing and impassioned at the same time. He was not an impromptu speaker who could rise and say whatever came to his mind at the moment. Imbued with a sense of mission and responsibility as the official spokesman of religious Jewry in Poland, he would prepare each address thoroughly, leaving nothing to chance, composing his speeches sentence by sentence, phrase by phrase and word by word in his own distinctive style. Yet he did not use words as ornaments or as poetic playthings. He was at least as much concerned with the content of his message as he was with its presentation. He always spoke briefly and to the point. He had no wish to impress audiences with his brilliance. His sole aim was to set forth his thoughts objectively and without wasting time.

When addressing mass meetings, on the other hand, he would deviate from his self-imposed restrictions and give free rein to his extraordinary rhetorical talent, inspiring and delighting his audiences with his genius for applying the sayings of the Sages — mainly comments on Biblical passages and especially on excerpts from the portion of the Torah read in the synagogue that week — to the issue under discussion. Years later, members of those audiences were still able to recall Friedman's speeches in detail. Friedman had a knack for presenting ideas in a manner simple enough for even young students to understand. He never subjected his listeners to ponderous ideological or political discourses. He drew his messages from the basic sources of Judaism which he would relate not to abstract ideas but to the day-to-day life and problems of the Jewish masses, to their needs, their strivings and their troubles.

The addresses he delivered before the international Congresses of the world Agudah movement between the two World Wars, from the first *K'nessiah Gedolah,* which met in Vienna in 1923, until the last before the Holocaust, which was held in Marienbad in 1937, were masterpieces in content and presentation. He impressed his audiences — which included religious leaders of world renown — not so much by spell-binding phrases as by the purity of heart, the genuine piety and the profound Jewish scholarship reflected in his every word.

Basically, Alexander Zusia Friedman was an educator, and it was to Jewish education that he devoted most of his time and effort. He could discern an educational purpose even in the purely political and administrative aspects of his work. When Agudath Israel won a political victory on the Jewish ticket in elections to the Polish *Sejm* (Parliament), he declared:

"I am even happier about the educational implications of the results of this election than I am about the actual number of members we will be able to send to Parliament. The fact that a quarter of a million Jews have identified themselves with the ideals of Agudath Israel to the extent of giving the movement their vote affords concrete proof to our pupils in the Yesode HaTorah Schools and to our Beth Jacob girls that they are not alone in their beliefs."

At a meeting of the Executive of the Agudah to discuss the qualifications of the party's candidates for the Polish Parliament,

Friedman spoke in support of the venerable Rabbi Aaron Lewin of Rzeshov.

"We must choose as our representative one who will appear in Parliament dressed in traditional rabbinic attire, his face framed in beard and *peyot,* with a skullcap on his head and the Hassidic *gartle* around his waist, so that our young people will see what sort of person we deem worthy of being honored by the community," he declared. "Just consider the educational impact of the image of a *Talmid Hacham* — a scholar of the Law, the author of weighty tomes on Aggadah and Halakhah, seated among the lawmakers of Poland and engaging Polish statesmen in debate on the rights of his people."

Alexander Zusia Friedman was a moving spirit behind every endeavor on behalf of religious education in Polish Jewry. He was the overall head of *Horeb* and of the Federation of Yesode HaTorah Schools. In addition, he was the chairman of Keren HaTorah, the educational fund-raising arm of Agudath Israel, a member of the National Executive of the Beth Jacob movement in Poland, and a director of the Beth Jacob Teachers' Seminary in Cracow. He was a founder of the Seminary for Religious Teachers at 6 Tvarda Street in Warsaw, which sought to raise not only the standards for teachers but also the status of the religious educator in the Jewish community. Not content with merely helping to organize the institution, he took an active part in its work, lecturing there as well as at the summer classes conducted for Beth Jacob teachers in Yordanow near Cracow.

Throughout the years, Friedman continued to be a pillar of Tz'ire Agudath Israel, of B'nos Agudath Israel (Agudah's organization for young girls) and of Po'ale Agudath Israel (the labor wing of the movement).

He founded and edited *Diglenu* (Our Banner), the first Hebrew-language periodical to be published by Agudath Israel. This journal, which appeared from 1919 to 1924, and again from 1930 to 1931, served as a guiding light for the youth movement and helped rear a generation of talented young writers. From 1936 to 1938 Friedman, together with Elimelekh Steuer and Hillel Seidman, edited *Darkeinu* (Our Path), the official organ of Agudath Israel in Poland.

Yet, journalism never captured Friedman's interest except to the extent to which it served to promote the cause of Jewish education. He had no desire to be a writer for the sake of writing. When he wrote for publication, he did so only when he felt that he had a message to bring to the attention of his readers. Written in simple, lucid language, his articles were convincing and to the point. Like his speech, his writings revealed the qualities of the man — his direct approach, his clarity of thought and logic.

On the debating platform, he was never anything but level-headed. His tactics in public forums were not designed to give prominence to his oratorical skills but solely to convince, to persuade, to explain and to teach. He weighed out each one of his words on the scale of Talmudic learning, for, first and foremost, he remained the selfless, devoted teacher.

Friedman never ceased to study. No matter how pressing his practical and political duties, he gave at least three hours of each day to the study of Talmud, of the decisions of the Codifiers and of the Biblical text itself. His "learning" was not a matter of cut-and-dried routines. He was the author of original works on several Talmudic tractates which he compiled and planned to publish under the title of *Avnei Ezel* (Guiding Stones). Unfortunately, the book was never published and the notes, save for those excerpts contained in *Wellsprings of Torah*, have been lost. He wrote a treatise of Halakhic responsa and carried on a learned dispute with Rabbi Menahem Zemba, a luminary among the Talmudic scholars of Poland between the two World Wars. He was the author of *K'riah LeIsha Yehudith,* a collection of Hebrew readings in religion for women which appeared in 1921, and of *Kesseph Mezukkak,* a book on Talmudic principles, which came out two years yater. He published a number of textbooks for religious schools, including *Iddish Loshen,* a primer in Yiddish, and a text on the *Sh'mone Esrei* (Eighteen Blessings).

He found time also to write many educational and ideological essays for the *Beth Jacob Monthly.* He even composed some Hebrew poems. One of these, *B'ne Papponia,* was printed in 1919 in *Der Yid,* Warsaw's Yiddish-language Orthodox weekly.

A book of Talmudic novellae which he completed in time for his fortieth birthday was never published, due to the outbreak of World War II.

The background of the book to which this biographical sketch serves as an introduction has been outlined in the introductory paragraphs written by Rabbi Nison L. Alpert.

The catastrophe which overtook Polish Jewry when the Germans invaded Poland in 1939 put Friedman's spiritual strength to the supreme test. For in addition to guiding the destinies of the movement to which he belonged heart and soul, he now became the leader of all of Warsaw's religious Jews.

On November 20, 1939, Friedman was taken into Nazi custody as a hostage along with twenty-one other Jewish leaders. The group was kept under arrest for a week and then released. I still remember standing at the gate of Danilovichevska Street Prison waiting for Friedman to come out. Finally, toward evening, he appeared. With hardly a glance at me, he darted off in the direction of his home. He had not had his *t'fillin* (phylacteries) with him in jail and so had been unable to put them on for a week. As a consequence, he was anxious to get home before nightfall lest he miss yet another day's opportunity to perform the commandment of donning the phylacteries. He later told me that he had never put on his *t'fillin* with greater exaltation than he had on that day after his release from the German prison.

During the first few months of German occupation, when the American Jewish Joint Distribution Committee (JDC) first began relief work in Poland, and the *Judenrat* (Jews' Council), under the chairmanship of Adam Cherniakov, did what it could to ease the distress of the Jews in Nazi-held Poland, Friedman emerged as the voice of religious Jewry, which had been the hardest hit. In addition to suffering more than most at the hands of the Nazis, the Orthodox Jews, particularly the rabbis, Talmudic scholars, yeshiva students, Beth Jacob teachers and religious instructors were the victims of discrimination by relief organizations led by non-religious individuals, many of whom had little sympathy for Orthodoxy. As the sole representative of Agudath Israel, and indeed of all religious Jewry, in the Jewish Community Council which advised the JDC, he vigorously insisted on equal treatment for Orthodox Jews. Aided by Eliezer Gershon Friedenson, Joseph Moshe Haber (chairman of the Jewish Community of Kalisz, who was then living in Warsaw), Abraham Meir Krongard, Abraham Mordecai Rogovy, David Shafran and Joel Ungar, Friedman set up a network of kosher soup kitchens to cater to the needs of observant Jews. As early as November 1939 Friedman had organized a large public soup kitchen in the building of the Beth Jacob School on Nalewki Street in Warsaw, where meals were prepared by three Beth Jacob teachers. Subsequently other soup kitchens were established elsewhere in the city. Run by young Agudah workers, they provided a gathering place for many Agudist writers. Thanks to the cooperation of David Guzsik, director of the JDC in Warsaw, Friedman managed to obtain special allocations from the United Fund for the Relief of Intellectuals, thus assuring the maintenance of the soup kitchen and of the Emergency Fund for the Relief of Needy Orthodox Jews, primarily rabbis, religious functionaries, yeshiva instructors and Talmudic scholars.

Even behind the walls of the Warsaw ghetto, Alexander Zusia Friedman never lost sight of what he considered the main task of Jewish leadership — to provide facilities for Jewish education. Forbidden by the occupation authorities to open schools in the ghetto, Friedman organized an underground network of religious schools, including a Yesode HaTorah School for boys, a Beth Jacob School for girls, a school for elementary Jewish instruction and three institutions for advanced Jewish studies. Disguised as kindergartens, health centers and public soup kitchens — the students were, in fact, provided with free meals — these schools were a place of refuge for thousands of children and adolescents and for hundreds of teachers.

When, in 1941, the occupation authorities extended official permission to the *Judenrat* to establish and operate schools, all these institutions emerged from hiding and began to receive financial support from the official Jewish community.

In February 1942, Adam Cherniakov, the chairman of the *Judenrat,* who held Friedman in high regard, set up a Religious Council which functioned independently of the *Judenrat* — a strictly secular body — to provide for the religious needs of the Jewish population under Friedman's chairmanship.

Despite their sufferings, the Jews of the Warsaw ghetto showed amazing vitality, upheld as they were by their faith in a better future.

ALEXANDER ZUSIA FRIEDMAN

Then, on July 22, 1942, the Eve of the Fast of Tisha B'Av, the Germans started their systematic slaughter of the Jews of the ghetto and began mass deportations to the death camps.

Among those deported were Friedman's wife and their only daughter, who had been born to her parents after eighteen years of marriage. I still recall the moving elegies in which the grieving husband and father mourned his loss.

In March 1943, Friedman received a Paraguayan passport through the good offices of Hayyim Israel Eis, a leader of Agudath Israel in neutral Switzerland. But the life-saving document came too late. Friedman was deported to the death camp of Travniki, Lublin District, where he was killed by the Germans in November 1943.

xxiv

WELLSPRINGS OF TORAH

GENESIS

THE BOOK OF GENESIS

בראשית

Weekly Portion of Bereshith (Genesis 1:1-6:8)

"In the beginning God created the heaven and the earth." (Gen. 1:1)

"In the beginning" — the first thing a Jew must know is that God created heaven and earth.

—*Rabbi Moses Leib of Sassov*

* * * *

The Sages relate (*Tractate Megillah 9*) that when the Elders translated the Scriptures for King Ptolemy, they rendered the first verse of the Book of Genesis as *"God* created, in the beginning . . ."

What was the reason for this textual alteration?

Actually, the change is in keeping with the rules of grammar, for the subject of the sentence should be at the beginning, as in "Reuben built a house." In this verse, too, "God", as the subject of the sentence, comes first.

But to the Jewish people it was no news that God had created the world. The Jews had become firm in their belief in the existence of God and in the constant renewal of the world when they went forth from Egypt, when the Red Sea was divided before their eyes, and again when they received the Law on Mount Sinai. Hence the intent of the original Scriptural text was not so much to imbue the Israelites with belief in Divine Creation as it was to narrate the chronological history of the origin of the world and all that dwells in it. Hence, actually, the word *bereshit* should be construed as the subject of the original Hebrew verse, implying that *"the first thing* which God created was the heaven and the earth."

But King Ptolemy was a heathen who first had to be given to understand that it was God Who had made the earth. For

3

this reason the translators in their rendering made "God" the subject of the first sentence and, as such, placed it first. "(It was) God (Who), in the beginning, created . . ."

—*Shemen Hamo'or*

* * * *

"And God called the light 'day' and the darkness He called 'night'
. . ." (Genesis 1:5)

> The Holy One, blessed be He, does not link His name with evil but only with good. Thus it is not written here "and God called the light day and the darkness God called night" but "and the darkness *He* called night."

—*Midrash*

Nothing evil ever comes forth from God, for even that which may seem evil to man is intended for a good purpose, either in order to let him receive his punishment in this world rather than in the next, or in order to have his reward in the world to come be greater than it would be otherwise. *"The Holy One, blessed be He, does not link His name with evil"*. All things that come from God are "good" so that there can be no "evil" with Him. It is only to man that they may seem "evil."

In this vein, it is written in the Midrash: "It is known to the Lord what is hidden in the darkness, the purpose and the deeper meaning of all the trouble, which is only goodness and light."

—*Ketav Sofer*

* * * *

". . . And there was evening and there was morning; one day."
(Genesis 1:5)

Scripture refers to the next day of Creation as the "second day." Why, then, does it call the first day *yom ehad,* "one day"?

Because the first day of Creation was different from all the other days. It was on a level entirely apart from the five days that followed. For what was created on that first day was that special "light" which was subsequently concealed, to be revealed only in the end of days, because the world was not deserving of such great light (*Gen. 1:3*). Had the Scriptural text read "the first day" it would have put that day on one level with all the other days, when in fact the first day of Creation was *"one day"*, unique in kind and degree.

—*Meshekh Hakhmah*

* * * *

". . . And (God) divided the waters which were beneath the firmament from the waters which were above the firmament, and it was so." (Genesis 1:8)

According to the Midrash, the comment "and it was good" was omitted here because the waters were divided from one another and division is not good.

But why, then, do we find the comment "and God saw that it was good" in connection with the fourth day of Creation, when God also made a division, this time between light and darkness? (*Genesis 1:18-19*)

Because the division between light and darkness, unlike that between the waters, was one between opposites, and it is permissible and even "good" to separate such opposites as light and darkness, since these two cannot exist together. But the waters belonged together, and it is not good to put asunder things that by right should be one.

This should teach us that men of like minds should unite and that any division among them is not good. But in the case of good and evil a clear-cut separation is not only permissible but actually "good".

—*Anon.*

* * * *

"And God said: 'Let us make man . . .'" (Genesis 1:26)

Although the angels did not assist Him in forming man, and although the use of the plural in this statement may give the heretics an excuse to rebel, yet the verse does not refrain from teaching the proper conduct and the virtue

5

of humility; namely, that the greater should consult and take permission from the smaller.

—*Rashi*

This explains the statement of the Sages that "he who is arrogant is as if he were worshipping idols" (*Sotah 4*). If a man considers himself better than the others he does not act in keeping with the spirit of God's declaration: "Let *us* make man", by which He taught us the way of humility, namely, that the greater should consult the smaller (as God consulted with the angels in making man). He who does not accept this interpretation of God's pronouncement obviously must think that it was meant to be construed literally as meaning that — Heaven forbid — there was more than one God who made the world. And this, of course, is idolatry.

—*Proshat Derakhim*

* * * *

(When He judges the kings) He likewise consults His Heavenly Council.

—*Rashi*

Even though the whole world was already complete, and the purpose of its creation was man, God stopped to deliberate and to reconsider His work. This should teach man that even after he has already completed a plan he should stop and reconsider before he proceeds, just as if he had only begun the work. The fact that he has already completed the task should not keep him from reconsidering it, even if such reconsideration would lead him to find that he must destroy it and begin all over again.

—*Musarist Writings*

* * * *

When the Holy One, blessed be He, proceeded to create man, Mercy said: "Let him be created, because he will dispense acts of loving-kindness." Truth argued: "Let him not be created, for he is made of falsehood." Justice said: "Let him be created." Peace said: "Let him not be created

because he is full of strife." What did the Holy One, blessed
be He, do? He took Truth and cast it down to the ground.

—Midrash

When Truth was cast down to the ground, Peace remained
the sole objector to man's creation, with Mercy and Justice both
in favor of the decision to make man.

Why did the Lord choose Truth, rather than Peace, the other
objector, to be cast to the ground?

Because not even a majority vote can stand up against Truth.
Even if both Justice and Mercy had favored man's creation, argu-
ing that he would practice justice and mercy, Truth would have
proceeded to prove that even his acts of justice and mercy would
be sham and falsehood. Peace, on the other hand, which argued
that man would be full of strife, could easily be made to give way
to a majority combination of Justice and Mercy. Hence Truth,
rather than Peace, was "cast to the ground."

—Ohel Torah,
Attributed to Rabbi Menahem Mendele of Kotzk

* * * *

"And God blessed the Seventh Day . . ." (Genesis 2:3)

He blessed it with the light of a man's countenance; the
light of a man's countenance during the week is not the
same as it is on the Sabbath.   *—Midrash*

According to Jewish law, the Seven Blessings of the Marriage Service may be repeated on the seven days of festivity following the wedding only at those meals where "a new face" is
present. On the Sabbath, however, the blessings may be recited
even if there is no "new face" among the guests.

Said the author of the treatise *Sefat Emet*:

"The Sabbath is exempt from the ruling because on the Sabbath the light of every Jew's contenance is transfigured. Thus, on
the Sabbath, each person would represent a 'new face' at the wedding festivities, because his face is not the same as it is during
the week."

"And (the serpent) said to the woman: 'Yea, has God said: You shall not eat of any tree of the garden?'" (Genesis 3:1)

It was one of the character traits of the first serpent on earth to seek to cool man's zeal for fulfilling the commandments of God, and to persuade him to disregard them.

The serpent said to Eve: "And what if God said that you must not eat of any tree of the garden? What harm can there be in disobeying just this once? Why be pious all the time?"

This approach, first tried by the serpent in the Garden of Eden, has been used by all inveiglers through history, to this very day.

> —*Attributed to Rabbi Isaac Meir Alter,*
> *the author of Hiddushei HaRIM*

* * * *

"And the serpent said to the woman: 'You shall not surely die . . .'" (Genesis 3:4)

> He pushed her to the tree until she touched it, and then he said to her: "Just as there is no death in touching it, so there is no death in eating it."
>
> —*Midrash*

What proof did the serpent cite that there was no death in merely touching the tree? The fact that he had made Eve touch the tree and she did not die immediately.

But had not God implied that death would come *"in the day that thou eatest of it"*? The day was still young. How could Eve be sure that she would not die that day?

Said the serpent: "You may eat of the fruit to your heart's content. If there is no death in touching it, there certainly will be no death in eating it. But even if you were to die after all for having touched the tree, you may eat of its fruit, because you can only die once, and you might as well enjoy yourself before."

This is the way of the Evil Impulse. Once he has caused man

to start on the road to sin, he says to him: "You see, you are lost already. So you might as well enjoy yourself."

—*Peninim Yekarim, attributed to the author of Bene Levi*

*   *   *   *

"And when the woman saw that the tree was good for food . . . she also gave (of its fruit) to her husband with her, and he ate." (Genesis 3:6)

> Why did the first man sin? Because he saw only two (things) instead of three.

—*Midrash*

This refers to the three things of which the Tannaite Akavia Ben Mahalalel speaks: "Reflect on three things and thou wilt not come into the grip of sin: know whence thou camest, whither thou art going and before whom thou art destined to render strict accounting" (*Ethics of the Fathers 3:1*).

Since the First Man was "a direct creation of the hand of the Holy One, blessed be He," he saw only two things — "whither he was going and before whom he was destined to render strict accounting — but he did not see the third: "whence thou camest — from a malodorous drop," and so he was led to sin.

—*Kol Dodi, attributed to*
Rabbi Elijah Solomon Zalman of Vilna

*   *   *   *

(And God said to man) "*. . . Hast thou eaten of the tree of which I commanded thee that thou shouldst not eat?"* (Genesis 3:11)

Alternative rendering: *"Hast thou eaten of the tree because I commanded thee that thou shouldst not eat?"*

Some may have a craving for forbidden food because it is good to eat. But there are others who have a craving for it not because it is good but for the very reason that it is forbidden, and who allow themselves to be persuaded by the evil impulse to eat it, as it is written: "Stolen waters are sweet" (*Prov. 9:17*).

The Lord said to the man: "Thou didst eat of the fruit of the Tree of Knowledge of Good and Evil not because thou considerest

9

the fruit to be good to eat, but only because I commanded thee that thou shouldst not eat of it."

The first man sought to justify his behavior, and replied: "The woman whom Thou gavest to be with me, she gave me of the tree, and I ate." To this the Midrash adds: "He meant: 'I ate and am still eating of it.' I ate of it not because Thou didst forbid it but only because the fruit was really good and I wanted to eat more of it."

—*Tifereth Shlomo, also Rabbi Abraham Samuel*
Benjamin Schreiber (Ketav Sofer)

* * * *

(*And God said to the serpent*) "*. . . and dust shalt thou eat all the days of thy life.*" (Genesis 3:14)

The Sages point out that, as a result of this curse; i.e. that he may only eat dust, the serpent finds food ready for him wherever he goes. Furthermore, it is written that "if a man sees a serpent in a dream, it means that his livelihood is assured" (*Tractate Berakhot 57*).

Wherein, then, does the curse lie?

The serpent's curse is that he had gone so far from the Godly way that God did not want him to turn heavenward for his food. All other creatures must search for their food, and there are times when they look up to the Lord for their sustenance (Cf. "The young lions roar after their prey and seek their food from God" — *Psalm 104:21*). But God wants no part of this serpent. Hence He says to him, in effect: "Here is all the food you want. Take it and get out of My sight."

—*Rabbi Isaac Meir Alter, in Hiddushei HaRIM*

* * * *

"*Unto the woman He said: 'I will greatly multiply thy pain and thy travail . . .*'" (Genesis 3:16)

> *Thy pain* — the trouble entailed in rearing children.
> *And thy travail* — the pain of confinement.

—*Rashi*

10

Why the reverse order? Does not the pain of confinement precede the troubles of child-rearing?

The reverse order implies still another curse with which Adam and Eve were punished for their sin. While the woman is still in the midst of the troubles entailed in the rearing of one child, she will become pregnant with the next, so that her pain will be great indeed.

God said to Eve: *"I will greatly multiply thy pain.* Thy pain will be a two-fold one. While thou wilt still be in the midst of the *pain,* the toil of rearing one child, *thy travail,* the pain of a new confinement, will already have begun."

—*Rabbi Hayyim of Volozhin*

*   *   *   *

". . . and thy desire shall be for thy husband, and he shall rule over thee." (Genesis 3:16)

A Hassidic saying: "When woman's desire is for her husband, he will rule over her, but if the man's desire is for his wife, she will rule over him instead."

*   *   *   *

". . . and He placed at the east of the Garden of Eden the Cherubim . . ." (Genesis 3:24)

Cherubim — angels of destruction.

—*Rashi*

The Cherubim on the Ark of the Covenant (*Exod. 25:20*) "spread out their wings on high, screening the Ark cover with their wings." To this, the Sages comment: "The Cherubim had the form of a child's face."

If a child is trained properly he may grow up to be like the Cherubim who guarded the Holy Ark. But if he does not receive the proper training, he will become like the Cherubim at the east of the Garden of Eden, who were angels of destruction.

—*Rabbi Moshe Mordecai Epstein*

*   *   *   *

11

"And in the course of time (literally "in the end of days") *it came to pass that Cain brought* (an offering) *of the fruit of the ground . . . and Abel also brought . . . and the Lord respected Abel and his offering."* (Genesis 4:3-4)

The expression "and it came to pass" — "in the end of days" implies grief. Cain brought his offering because he saw "the end of days," because he realized that the years of his life were coming to an end and he was grieved at the thought. Abel, on the other hand, brought his offering with joy and zest for life. He did it not because he felt he was about to die, but because he wanted to serve the Lord, and therefore "the Lord respected Abel and his offering."

—*Kol Simcha*

*　*　*　*

(And the Lord said to Cain) "*. . . If thou doest well, shall not* (*thy countenance*) *be lifted up? And if thou dost not do well, sin couches at the door . . ."* (Genesis 4:7)

When a man is in his own home he can easily adhere to his accustomed way of life. But once he crosses the threshold of his door and passes from his home into the street, his evil impulse will gain ground because he must now come to grips with obstacles that block the path of his loyalty to Judaism.

"Sin couches at the door" — the evil impulse lies in wait outside the door of your home, waiting for you to emerge so that he may take you unawares.

—*Rabbi Abraham Samuel Benjamin Schreiber (Ketav Sofer)*

*　*　*　*

". . . sin couches at the door, and its desire is for thee . . ." (Genesis 4:7)

The desires of a man depend on his station in life. A poor man wants no more than a penny or perhaps a piece of bread, and he remains standing humbly in front of the door of the one from whom he requests help. A man of more substance is more demanding; he does not wait outside but enters the house to ask for what he wants. A creditor who comes to collect a debt strides in boldly to demand his due. But the murderer who is not out for money but for a human life will be careful not to enter the home of his victim. Instead, he will waylay him on the highway or in the woods.

Scripture says that "sin couches at the door." It is true that the evil impulse remains humbly at the door of thy home like a beggar seeking alms from thee but in reality *its desire is for thee,* it is like a murderer who lies in wait for thee outside because he wants to take not thy alms but thy life.

—*Tifereth Shlomo*

*   *   *   *

"And the Lord said to Cain: 'Where is Abel, thy brother?' And he said: 'I do not know. Am I my brother's keeper?'" (Genesis 4:9)

What was the purpose of this exchange of question and answer? It almost seems as if God and Cain were seeking to make fools of each other. Did not Cain know that "all is revealed and known before Him"?

The dialogue served to fix the responsibility for Abel's death.

The Lord said to Cain: *"Where is Abel, thy brother?* Thou art responsible for him. It was within thy power to choose between right and wrong; hence thou art to blame for his death and art deserving of punishment."

Cain, however, was under the impression that since he had succeeded in killing Abel, his death must have been decreed by God Himself and he, Cain, was not to blame, since he had merely acted as an instrument to carry out the Divine plan. Therefore he replied: *"Am I my brother's keeper?* Thou, O Lord, art the Keeper of the world with all its creatures. ('No man so much as strikes his finger on earth except if it be ordained from Above' — *Hullin 7*). Hence it must have been Thy plan that I should kill him and I am not liable to punishment."

This is a grievous error, for whether a man does good or evil depends on his own free choice, which is not affected by Divine decree. God never forces the hand of man, and therefore man is held strictly accountable for all his actions.

—*Attributed to Rabbi Simcha Bunim of Przysucha*

* * * *

"And all the days that Adam lived were nine hundred and thirty years, and he died." (Genesis 5:5)

Are the words "that Adam lived" not redundant?

No, Scripture uses these words to point out that this was not the original life span allotted by God to Adam. According to the Sages, Adam was originally meant to live for a thousand years, for God had said to him that he would die "on the day" on which he would eat of the forbidden fruit, and in the sight of the Lord a thousand years are as one day. (Cf. "For a thousand years in Thy sight are but as yesterday when it is past" — *Psalm 90:4*). However, Adam gave away seventy years of his own allotted life span to King David who had no years at all to live. (*Midrash* and *Pirkei de-Rabbi Eliezer*).

"And all the days that Adam lived": Those are the years which Adam actually lived. The original plan had been that he was to live for another seventy years.

—*HaKetav VeHaKabbala*

* * * *

The Sages quote the above-cited passage to explain David's statement (Psalm 22:7) that *"I am a worm, and no man; a reproach of men and despised by the people."* Since the Hebrew term for "man" in general is *adam*, David's self-accusation is taken to mean that he considered himself a "reproach" or "disgrace" to Adam, the first man. "Adam gave me seventy years from his own life so that I might be able to accomplish something in this world, but I have not achieved anything on earth," David mourned. "Therefore I am ashamed to stand before Him."

* * * *

14

"And Enoch walked with God, and he was not, for God took him."
(Genesis 5:24)

> Enoch was a righteous man, but his mind was easily in-
> duced to turn from the righteous ways and to become
> wicked. He was therefore taken quickly, before his time.
>   *—Rashi*

Enoch kept aloof from his fellow-men and, consequently, he
did not instill any of his own righteousness into his generation.
God therefore feared that he might be corrupted by his contemporaries and become wicked, for "whoever leads the people to
righteousness, no sin shall occur through him" (*Sayings of the
Fathers 5:21*) but he who does not do so, preferring to keep to
himself, may be influenced by those around him to become evil.

It was because "Enoch walked with God", keeping aloof
from other men to serve God by himself, that "he was not, for
God took him." God took him before his time for fear that he
might be corrupted by the evil of the generation in which he lived.

—Attributed to Rabbi Moses Schreiber (Hatham Sofer)

*   *   *   *

"And Noah was five hundred years old, and Noah begat . . ." (Genesis 5:32)

The Sages say: "When the majority of a man's years have
passed without sin, he will sin no more" (*Yoma 39*). Accordingly, God waited until Noah had reached the age of five hundred
years — passing the halfway mark of the nine hundred fifty years
allotted to him as his life-span (*Gen. 9:28*) and it could be assumed that Noah would remain righteous — before He blessed
him with offspring. Similarly, He deferred the birth of Isaac
until Abraham had undergone circumcision, in order that Isaac
might be born in holiness.   *—Meshekh Hakhmah*

*   *   *   *

*"Hear, ye deaf, and look, ye blind, that you might see. Who is blind
but My servant? Or deaf as My messenger that I send? Who is so
blind as he who is wholehearted, and blind as the Lord's servant?"*
(Isaiah 42:18-19)

15

This passage is a rebuke to those righteous men who cleave to God and to the Torah in their own conduct, but pretend to be deaf and blind in order not to hear and see the evil done by their contemporaries, thus shirking their duty to rebuke them and seek ways in which to make them better.

To them, the prophet says: "True, you yourselves are whole-hearted in your effort to attain perfection in your own conduct. You are servants of the Lord; you may even be angels (*malakhi* — "My messenger" or "My angel"). Yet, if you refuse to see and hear the evil in the world about you, the sad state of neglect into which the observance of God's Law has fallen, you are blind and deaf. *Hear, ye deaf, and look, ye blind, that you might see.* It is not enough to be righteous yourselves. You must also be aware of the conduct of the others around you and seek ways to correct their errors."

—*Zavorei Shalal*

* * * *

"The Lord was pleased, for the sake of His righteousness, to make the Torah great and glorious." (Isaiah 42:21)

Elsewhere (11:9) Isaiah declares that in the end of days "the earth shall be full of the knowledge of the Lord, as the waters cover the sea."

According to the Sages, this statement should not be taken to mean that all men will have the same knowledge and the same ability to study, for how could a scholar, who has spent his life poring over the Law, ever be considered on one level with the ignoramus? Rather, all men will become "as the waters which cover the sea," which look uniform on the surface but conceal areas of varying depths beneath. All men will be filled with the knowledge of the Lord, but the knowledge of the scholars who have devoted their lives to the Torah will have greater depth than that of all the rest.

All this is implicit also in the verse from the Forty-second Chapter of Isaiah quoted above:

"The Lord was pleased, for the sake of His righteousness — when the Lord will cause the whole world to become righteous and impart knowledge to all men, *He will make the Torah great* so that all shall know it, *and glorious*; He will strengthen and deepen its knowledge even more in the minds of those who studied it in the past; He will cause the scholars to become even stronger in the Torah than they were before."

—Rabbi Hayyim Joseph David Azulai

*   *   *   *

Weekly Portion of Noah (Gen. 6:9-11:32)

"These are the generations (lit. "progeny") *of Noah. Noah was a righteous man . . ."* (Genesis 6:9)

The real progeny of the righteous are their good deeds.

—Rashi

Rashi means that the righteous regard their good deeds as their progeny.

R. Yaakov Yitzhak of Przysucha (1766-1814) used to say:

Every man says that he works and slaves only for his children so that they may grow up to become good Jews, well-versed in the Torah. But when the children are grown, the parents continue to insist that they have no time to think about their own education because they must attend to the training of their children.

Scripture points out that Noah regarded himself as a "child" in that sense of the word. *"These are the progeny of Noah"*. Noah was not content to devote all his time to the education of his children. He thought of his own personality, too, as a "child" who is in need of education and improvement. Thus, working to increase his own knowledge and to improve his own character, Noah become "a proper child" who understood that not only children, but also their parents, must serve the Lord.

—Beth Jacob by Rabbi Jacob Aaron of Alexander

* * * * *

". . . *Noah was in his generations a man righteous and wholehearted* . . ." (Genesis 6:9)

The Gemarah interprets the adjective *tamim*, "wholehearted" to mean "perfect in his ways" (*Avoda Zara 6*). Rashi renders it as "modest and humble in spirit."

Why should "wholeheartedness" or "perfection" be associated with the virtue of humility?

Because the Sages say that "if a man is arrogant, there is a blemish in him" (*Megillah 29*).

Thus, if arrogance is regarded as a defect, humility would naturally imply perfection.

—*Attributed to a Rabbi of Warsaw*

* * * *

"And the earth was corrupt before God and the earth was filled with violence." (Genesis 6:11)

When men are "corrupt before God"; i.e. corrupt in their relationship with God, lacking in the fear of God, the earth will be "filled with violence" between man and man, for where there is no fear of God, there also can be no humility.

—*Anon.*

* * * *

(*God said to Noah*) ". . . *for the earth is filled with violence through them* . . ." (Genesis 6:13)

> Their fate was sealed only on account of the robbery they committed.
>
> —*Rashi*

In a comment immediately preceding this statement, Rashi notes that their sin consisted in indecency and immorality. Why, then, does he state that their death was decreed only on account of the robbery of which they were guilty?

To indicate that if they would have possessed wealth acquired by legitimate means, God might have taken their wealth rather than their lives to punish them for their immorality.

According to the Sages, "the Merciful One does not decree

the death penalty immediately." God first punishes the sinner by
depriving him of his wealth; it is only in cases where this is of no
avail that He takes his life.

However, a man's wealth can be taken as atonement in place
of the death penalty only if he has acquired it by honest means.
Once he loses that wealth, it means that he has paid for his sin
by having been deprived of his possessions. But if he did not acquire his wealth by lawful means but by robbery, it is not his
property and its loss cannot be accepted as atonement to spare
him from the death penalty for his other sins.

Had the generation of the Flood been guilty only of indecency and immorality, God would not have destroyed them immediately but would first have punished them by stripping them
of their possessions. But since they had gained all their wealth
through robbery, it was not truly their own and could not be
accepted as atonement. Therefore the Lord decreed the death
penalty for them immediately, declaring that He would blot out
all men from the face of the earth.

—*Melo HaOmer*

* * * *

The same thought is expressed by the Prophet Jeremiah, who
declared that "so is he that gets riches and not by right; in the
midst of his days shall he leave them . . ." (*Jeremiah 17:11*). If
he acquired his possessions by dishonest means, he must pay with
his life for his other sins because riches amassed "not by right"
are not acceptable as atonement to redeem his soul.

—*Ibid.*

* * * *

"A light shalt thou make to the Ark . . ." (Genesis 6:16)

The Mishna uses the word *tebah* ("Ark") to denote the Ark
of the Law. Accordingly, *tebah* implies the word of Torah and
prayer which can save man from drowning in the flood of gross-
ness and materialism that has overrun the world.

19

The above verse, then, may be interpreted to mean that "thou shalt shed light upon the Word", i.e. that every teaching of Torah and prayer we utter must be lucid and clear to all.

—*Sefat Emet*

* * * *

"And take thou to thyself of all food that is eaten . . . and it shall be food for thee and for them." (Genesis 6:21)

The phrase "that is eaten" seems redundant. Moreover, the question may be asked how there could possibly have been sufficient space in the Ark to store a year's supply of food for all the persons, cattle, animals and birds gathered there.

It was to answer this question that the phrase "that is eaten" was inserted.

According to the Sages "of all the food that is eaten" refers to such quantities of food as can be eaten in one swallowing, namely, an amount the size of a hen's egg. (*Tractate Yoma 80*).

This would mean that the Ark could accommodate the food supply easily, for God commanded Noah to provide amounts of food no greater than the size of a hen's egg for each meal for all the men and beasts in the Ark. And God blessed the food, saying *"it shall be food for thee and for them,"*; i.e. the people and the animals will find even these small amounts sufficient and satisfactory food during their sojourn in the Ark.

—*Attributed to the Gaon of Vilna*

* * *

". . . and of beasts that are not clean . . ." (Genesis 7:8)

> Scripture employs a circumlocution of eight letters rather than use a crude expression.

—*Pesachim 3*

Why does Scripture not use this circumlocution ("not clean") in the many other pasages where the text plainly states "such and such shall be *unclean* . . ."

This passage in the Book of Genesis is a historical account and not a legal discussion. Hence the prohibition against using crude expressions applies here. But the other passages are laws specifying what is clean and what is not, and in setting forth laws and regulations one should not resort to euphemisms or circumlocutions but state clearly and forthrightly that " such and such is clean" and "such and such is unclean for you."

—*Based on Sayings of the Early Sages*

* * * *

"*. . . and Noah only was left . . .*" (Genesis 7:23)

Scripture does not say "and Noah, a righteous and wholehearted man, was left" but simply "Noah only was left." According to the Midrash, Noah, by doing nothing to persuade his contemporaries to mend their ways, was himself guilty of a sin. He who does not act to make others better descends to a lower level himself thereby.

When Noah found that he and his family were the only survivors of the Flood, he realized that he was Noah "only"; he was filled with a sense of inadequacy because he had done nothing to save the others from the fate which befell them.

—*Rabbi Meir Shapiro of Lublin*

* * * *

"*And the Lord smelled the sweet savor and the Lord said: 'I will not again curse the ground . . . for the imagination of man's heart is evil from his youth . . . while the earth remains, seedtime and harvest, and cold and heat, and summer and winter, and day and night shall not cease.'*" (Genesis 8:21-22)

It is written in the Mishna: "It is well to combine the study of the Law with some worldly occupation, for the combination of the two keeps sin out of the mind of man." (*Sayings of the Fathers 2:2*). Work and study pursued together tend to make man forget sin, whereas idleness is the mother of all sin and an empty mind leaves room for evil thoughts to thrive. As Maimonides put it: "Evil thoughts gain the upper hand only in a heart empty of words of Torah."

21

The generation of the Flood lived in idleness. They had no physical labor to do. According to the Midrash they needed to sow their fields only once to obtain crops for the next forty harvests. Besides, they did not have the Torah to occupy their minds. Hence they became corrupt and wanton. Therefore it is written: "And the Lord saw that the wickedness of man was great on the earth and that every imagination of the thoughts of his heart was only evil all the time . . . And the Lord said: 'I will blot out man whom I have created.'" (*Gen.* 6:5,7). For lack of work and cares, they drifted into sin and had to be destroyed.

But now God accepted the sweet savor of Noah's sacrifice and regretted the evil He had decreed. And He said: "I will not again curse man; I will not again seek to destroy man, for the impulses of his heart are evil from his youth; it is part of his nature. I have another plan. I will make his life on earth difficult so that he will be forced to labor mightily in order to survive. As long as the earth endures, he shall be compelled to reap, to harvest and to toil to provide for his needs from season to season. Once he will be forced to work day and night without respite, he will have little time for sin."

—*Kametz HaMinha*

*   *   *   *

Weekly Portion of Lekh Lekha (Genesis 12:1-17:27)
"Now the Lord God said to Abram: 'Get thee out of thy country, and from thy birthplace, and from thy father's house . . ." (Genesis 12:1)

"Thy country," "thy birthplace" and "thy father's house" allude to the three things of which it is written in the Sayings of the Fathers (3:1): "Reflect on three things and thou wilt not come into the grip of sin; know whence thou camest, where thou art going and before whom thou art destined to render strict accounting. *Whence thou camest* — from a malodorous drop. *Where thou art going* — to a place of dust, worms and moths.

And before Whom thou art destined to render strict accounting— before the supreme King of Kings, the Holy One, blessed be He."

"Thy country" (lit. "thy soil") alludes to the dust and soil into which you will be turned when you will go "to a place of dust, worms and moths."

"Thy birthplace" recalls your origin — "from a malodorous drop."

Remember also "thy father's house" — remember that you will have to come into the presence of your Father in Heaven and render strict accounting for your conduct "before the supreme King of Kings, the Holy One, blessed be He."

—Hashava LeTovah

* * * *

> The text reads *Lekh Lekha* (*"get thee* out") both here and in the section dealing with the binding of Isaac upon the altar of sacrifice. ("Take now thy son . . . and *get thee* into the land of Moriah and offer him there for a burnt-offering . . ." —*Genesis* 22:2). And we do not know which one of the two (is to be considered) a finer act, the former or the latter. The answer is that the second one (Abraham's going forth to sacrifice his son Isaac) is the finer.
>
> *—Midrash Rabba*

Why is Abraham's going forth to sacrifice his son considered a more significant and splendid act than his going forth to leave his father's house?

Because no matter what a man may have been able to do to come nearer to perfection in his own conduct, he has not fulfilled his life's task until he has succeeded in training his children also to be loyal and perfect in their faith so that they will be able to carry on his work after he is gone.

True, the command given Abraham to leave his birthplace and his father's house was a severe test of character, but it was intended only for his own improvement, to remove him from a corrupt environment and enable him to serve the Lord wholeheartedly. The second test, however — Abraham's readiness to offer up his only son as a sacrifice — gave proof that Abraham was willing also to mold the character of his offspring, imbuing Isaac with so much love for God that the youth was ready to go forth of his own free will to be offered up to the Lord. It was this second test of character that showed the true greatness and integrity of our father Abraham. Thus Abraham's second "going forth" was a finer act than the first.

—HaDrash VeHaEyun

* * * *

A similar thought is expressed by the Sages in Baba Kamma 97: "What was the coin of our father Abraham? An old man and an old woman on one side, and a young man and a young woman on the other."

The Talmud occasionally uses מטבע, the Hebrew term for "coin" to denote a teaching, a doctrine, a device or an "approach". According to the statement in Baba Kamma, then, the approach of our father Abraham consisted of a combination of two endeavors; to work upon his own growth in study and wisdom (symbolized by the old man and the old woman) and at the same time to see to the education of his offspring (symbolized by the young man and the young woman on the other side of the coin). Abraham's "going forth" from his father's house was for the former purpose; his "going forth" to offer up his son was meant to serve the latter.

—Ibid.

* * * *

"*. . . and be thou a blessing . . .*" (Genesis 12:2)
> They shall conclude the blessing with thee and not with them.

—Rashi

According to the Mishna (*Ethics of the Fathers 1:2*), "the world is based on three things — Torah, worship and loving-kindness."

24

These three pillars by which the world endures are recalled by the qualities of our three Patriarchs. Abraham personified loving-kindness; Isaac, who was ready to be offered up as a sacrifice to God, personified worship, and Jacob personified Torah, as is it written, "Jacob was a quiet man, dwelling in tents" (*Gen. 25:27*), meaning, "in the tents of study."

In the generations immediately preceding the coming of the Messiah, Torah and worship will have all but disappeared. Therefore the people of Israel will be redeemed solely for the sake of their righteousness and loving-kindness; as the prophet Isaiah put it: "Zion shall be redeemed with justice, and they shall return to her with righteousness" (*Isaiah 1:27*).

This is the meaning of Rashi's statement: "They shall conclude the blessing with thee." The blessing of redemption, the conclusion of exile, will come to pass only "with" (alternative rendering: "for the sake of") "thee", for the sake of thy loving-kindness, for there is little Torah and worship left in Israel.

—*Ohel Torah*

* * * *

"*. . . and I will bless thee, and make thy name great; and be thou a blessing.*" (Genesis 12:2)

When an ordinary man becomes rich and famous, he may become estranged from his less fortunate kinsmen and friends; he will keep aloof from them and make no effort to help them. As a result he will make enemies and many will curse him and wish him ill because they envy him.

Therefore God reassured Abraham, saying: "Even after I have made thy name great, thou wilt not make enemies but thou wilt be a blessing. Thou wilt continue to do good and therefore all will bless thee."

—*HaDrash VeHaEyun*

* * * *

25

"And I will bless those who bless thee, and him who curses thee I will curse. . ." (Genesis 12:3)

Why does the text not read: "And I will bless those who bless thee, and *I will curse him who curses thee"*?

To show that while "the Lord regards a good thought as equal to the deed", He "does not regard an evil thought as equal to an evil deed." Those who bless Abraham will be blessed for their good intention even before they demonstrate their friendship, but those who wish to curse him will be cursed only after they have put their evil desire into action, and not before.

—*K'lei Yakar*

* * * *

Why *"those* who bless thee" but *"him* who *curses thee"?*

When men will see that those who bless Abraham will be blesssed and that those who curse him will be cursed, many (as implied by the plural form) will join those who bless him because they, too, will want to be blessed, and only few (as implied by the singular form) will insist on cursing him, for no one wants to risk being afflicted with a curse.

—*Meshekh Hakhmah*

* * * *

"And Abraham took Sarai his wife . . . and the souls that they had gotten in Haran . . ." (Genesis 12:5)

The souls which Abraham had brought beneath the wings of the *Shekhina.* Abraham converted the men.

—*Rashi*

What became of these converts? Why is there no subsequent mention of them in the Biblical narrative?

When Abraham died, these converts did not want to follow Isaac, who took his father's place as their mentor. Having seen nothing but kindness — righteousness, mercy and hospitality — in the ways of Abraham, they could not get accustomed to the way of Isaac, which was characterized by militant heroism and the fear of God, and therefore they refused to accept the son as

26

their new master. As a result, they backslid into idolatry.

—*Attributed to Rabbi Hayyim Henoch of Aleksander*

*   *   *   *

"And he went on his journeys . . ." (Genesis 13:3)

> On his return, Abraham paid the debts which he had incurred previously.

—*Rashi*

Does this mean that Abraham was so improvident as to set out on his journeys without food or money so that he had to borrow money on the way? Who would have been willing to lend money to a passing wanderer?

Abraham's debts were not monetary in nature.

Wherever he went on his journeys, Abraham glorified the Name of the Lord, proclaiming that there was One Sole God in the universe Whom all men had to serve. In this manner he brought many people beneath the wings of the *Shekhina*. However, not all of those who heard him believed him, for they argued: "If Abraham is telling us the truth, why should the Lord allow so faithful a servant to journey through the world instead of giving him ample reward so that he could dwell in peace and quiet?"

Abraham was unable to answer these and similar questions at the time, for all the hardships he had suffered had been inflicted on him only to test him. It was this answer, which he could not give, that constituted the "debts" Abraham contracted on his journeys. Only now, when the miracle which the Lord had performed for Abraham in Egypt by striking Pharaoh with "great plagues" (*Gen. 12:17*) and permitting him to leave Egypt with great wealth ("and Abraham was very rich in cattle, in silver and in gold" — *Gen. 13:2*) had become common knowledge, could Abraham repay this debt by giving the proper answers to the questions he had had to leave unanswered before.

—*Rabbi of Kazimir*

*   *   *   *

27

"And there was a quarrel between the herdsmen of Abram's cattle and the herdsmen of Lot's cattle. And the Canaanite and the Perizzite dwelt in the land at that time." (Genesis 13:7)

This passage conveys in allegorical terms the importance of the proper religious training of our young.

According to the Sages "Jerusalem was destroyed solely because the people there neglected the education of their school children" (*Sabbath 119*). In a similar vein, the Midrash of the Book of Lamentations relates that when "her little ones went captive before the enemy, all her glory departed from the House of Zion."

It was due to the failure of the parents to train their young in the Law and in its observance that the Jewish people lost their home and strangers settled on the soil of the Land of Israel.

This is the thought expressed by the verse cited above: *"And there was a quarrel between the herdsmen of Abraham's cattle and the herdsmen of Lot's cattle.* Whenever Jews cannot agree on the care and training of their offspring; i.e. whether they should follow the way of Abraham, of whom it is written: '. . . *to the end that he may command his children and his household after him, that they may keep the way of the Lord, to do righteousness and justice . . .'* (Gen. 18:19), or the way of Lot who was drawn to "the evil and sinful men of Sodom," *the Canaanite and the Perizzite will dwell in the land.* As long as all Jews will not agree that there is no other alternative but the way of Abraham, the land of Israel will be ruled by alien peoples, for the Jews will not be worthy of dwelling there.

Therefore if the Jews will allow their children in the Land of Israel to be trained by "herdsmen of Lot," godless educators who teach them neither the Torah nor the faith of the Jewish people, they will not be able to keep the land of Israel.

—*Avnei Ezel*

* * * *

"And Abram said: 'Let there be no strife, I pray thee, between me and thee.'" (Genesis 13:8)

The quarrel, Abraham implied, had begun among the herdsmen, but if it were to be allowed to continue, it would eventually drive a wedge "between me and thee." This is the way of all quarrels. They begin among the followers but eventually involve the leaders as well.

—*Attributed to a Sage*

*   *   *   *

(Abraham said to Lot) "*. . . Separate thyself, I pray thee, from me . . .*" (Genesis 13:9)

Abraham was a man of tolerance and loving-kindness who invited even heathens into his home and gave them food and drink. However, when he saw Lot, his own kinsman, stray from the right path and draw near to the corruption of Sodom, he cried out to him, "Separate thyself, I pray thee, from me."

This teaches us that loving-kindness and love of man on the one hand, and loyalty to Judaism and the desire to keep aloof from evil on the other, should not be considered mutually exclusive.

—*Avnei Ezel*

*   *   *   *

"And the Lord said to Abram after Lot had separated from him . . ." (Genesis 13:14)

We are told that the Lord refused to communicate with Abram while the wicked Lot was still with him. Why, then, do we read elsewhere in the text that God appeared to Abram even when Lot was with him? The answer is that in those days Lot had still been righteous.

—*Rashi*

What, indeed, caused Lot to become so wicked?

The answer can be reasoned out easily enough. According to the Gemarah, one who comes from abroad to settle in the land of Israel rises to a higher level (*Ketuboth 5*), but it is well

29

known, too, that "he who is greater than his fellow man, his evil impulse grows accordingly," so that he must exert greater efforts than others to overcome it.

When Abram and his nephew Lot came to the Land of Canaan, Abram succeeded in overcoming his heightened evil impulse and so grew even greater in holiness than he had been before. But Lot was unable to conquer his evil impulse and hence became more wicked than he had been before entering the Land.

—*Melo HaOmer*

*   *   *   *

"*. . . Lift up now thine eyes, and look . . . for all the land which thou seest, to thee will I give it, and to thy seed forever.*" (Genesis 13:14-15)

This teaches us that the Land of Israel is holier than all other countries on earth even when it lies in ruins and alien peoples dwell in it, as it is written: "The eyes of the Lord thy God are always upon it, from the beginning of the year until the end of the year" (*Deut. 11:12*).

When Abraham looked about and saw the Canaanites still dwelling in the Promised Land, the Lord said to him:

"The land thou seest before thee seems no more than an ordinary tract of land settled by Canaanite tribes, but *lift up now thine eyes,* consider the Divine Providence which fills and guides the world, and then thou wilt understand that *all the land which thou seest, to thee will I give it,* that even now, when the Canaanite tribes still dwell on its soil, the land is holy and is destined to belong to thee and to thy descendants forever."

—*Meshekh Hakhmah*

*   *   *   *

"*. . . (Abram) led forth his trained men . . .*" (Genesis 14:14)

This refers to Eliezer whom Abraham had trained to observe the commandments. The term signifies introducing a person or thing for the first time to some particular oc-

30

cupation in which it is intended that he should remain. Cf. "Train up a child in the way he should go, and even when he is old, he will not depart from it." (*Proverbs* 22:6)

—*Rashi*

It is clear from this statement by Rashi that the training of a child is true training only if he will not depart from what he has been taught. Thus, merely teaching a child while he is small without seeing to it that he should remain a good Jew and a diligent student of the Law when he is older cannot be considered "training" in the proper sense of the word.

—*Rabbi Meir Shapiro of Lublin*

*   *   *   *

"And Abram said to the King of Sodom: 'I have lifted up my hand to the Lord . . . lest thou shouldst say: I have made Abram rich . . .'" (Genesis 14:22-23)
Alternative rendering: *" 'I have lifted up my hand to the Lord . . . lest it should say: I have made Abram rich.' "*

Abram had taken gifts from Pharaoh, but in the case of the King of Sodom, where the gifts would have been in the form of a tribute for the victory he, Abram, had wrought, he refused to accept anything, lest he should be tempted to think that he had earned the tribute by the strength of his own hand without the help of God — "lest it (his own hand) should say: I have made Abram rich."

Yad HaMelekh

*   *   *   *

". . . thy reward shall be very great . . . and Abram said: 'O Lord God, what wilt Thou give me, seeing that I go hence childless . . .'" (Genesis 15:1-2)

Why did Abraham wait until so late in life to pray for offspring?

Because he felt that at this stage he had accumulated so much merit that his luck might change.

According to the Sages (*Sabbath 153*), "Israel has no

luck," and elsewhere we read that, "the blessing of having children, life and sustenance depend not on merit but only on luck."

Abraham, aware that, according to the destiny ordained for him, he was not to have children, previously had not dared pray for offspring. But when the Lord had told him that "thy reward shall be very great", he realized that he had accumulated much merit during his long life and might therefore expect a change in his luck. Accordingly, he decided that he was now entitled to pray to the Lord to be given offspring. And indeed, God changed his luck, as Rashi notes to Verse 5: "*And He brought him outside* — This means that He removed him from the setting of his constellation — Abandon thy astrological speculations, for thou hast seen that according to thy constellation thou wert not destined to have children (but I am changing thy fortune so that thou wilt have numerous descendants)."

—*Melo HaOmer*

* * * *

"*. . . and he that shall be possessor of my house is Eliezer of Damascus . . .*" (Genesis 15:2)

> *Damascus (Dameshek)* — One who drew up and gave others a drink (*dole u-mashkah*) of the waters of instruction given by his teacher.

—*Rashi, after the Gemara*

According to Rashi's interpretation, this was Abraham's way of pointing out a serious shortcoming in Eliezer. Every great teacher in Israel has an approach of his own. Thus Abraham's way was that of loving-kindness; Isaac's device was "the fear of the Lord" and Jacob taught "truth" as the supreme principle. But Eliezer could only pass on to others the instruction he himself had received from his master and teacher, Abraham.

Therefore Abraham said to the Lord: "Eliezer has devised no original teachings. He can do no more than pass on what he has learned from me. That I can do myself. What good, then, would Eliezer be to me? If he has no teachings of his own to give, how could he take my place?"

—*MaHaRaM of Piltz*

* * * *

"And He brought him outside, and said: 'Look now toward heaven and count the stars . . . so shall thy seed be.' " (Genesis 15:5)

Seen from the earth, the stars look like tiny specks. Yet they are worlds in themselves, some even larger than our own earth. So, too, are the Jewish people. They may appear small and insignificant on earth, but in the sight of heaven they are great indeed and are considered as the pillar of all Creation.

—*Israel Ben Elizer Baal Shem Tov*

* * * *

Elevating him above the stars.

—*Rashi*

Only at a later point (Verse 12) are we told that the sun had set. Hence the meeting between God and Abraham must have taken place during the daytime, and the question arises how Abraham could have seen and counted the stars while the sun was still shining.

The answer is that God did not really expect Abraham to count the stars to see how numerous his seed would be. He did not intend to promise Abraham that his seed would be great in number. In fact, the Jews are the smallest among the peoples in that respect. Rather, the Lord's promise was that although the Jewish people would not be mighty in numbers as compared to the other nations, they would be endowed with spiritual qualities so great that they would act as teachers and guides for all the rest of humanity. All the nations would look to the people of Israel, for without the light spread by Israel, the world would sink into utter darkness.

The Lord said to Abraham:

"Look now towards heaven, while it is yet day and the sun

33

is shining, *and count the stars if thou art able to count them.* Of course thou wilt not be able to count them. The stars are in the sky, but thou canst not count them, for it is daytime, and the one great light of the sun eclipses the light of the millions and millions of stars in the heavens. Seest thou not then that virtues are more important than numbers? Behold, one great shining sun can be stronger than millions of stars."

And the Lord said to him:

"So shall thy seed be. Not like the stars, but like the sun. Thy descendants will be few and they will be vastly outnumbered by the other peoples of the world. But the one brilliant sun of Judaism will be strong enough to outshine the millions of the others nations. The spirit of Judaism, the light of its Torah, will stand invincible, outlasting all the many nations and their mighty armies."

—Kol Omer Kro

* * * *

"And he believed in the Lord, and he counted it to Him for righteousness." (Genesis 15:6)

Abraham believed in the Lord and he (Abraham) counted it to Him (God) for righteousness. Abraham regarded his very belief in the Lord as a favor bestowed upon him by the Lord in His righteousness, giving him even more cause to believe in Him.

—Avodat Yisrael

* * * *

"And also that nation, whom they shall serve, will I judge . . ." (Genesis 15:14).

If these two words *dan onokhi* ("will I judge") alone held the promise of the many wonders which were wrought at the time of the Exodus from Egypt, how many more miracles must surely come to pass at the time of redemption yet to be, concerning which Scripture brings such a multitude of references, promises and prophecies?

—R. Saadia Gaon

* * * *

34

Haphtarah Lekh Lekha (Isaiah 40:27 — 41:16)

"Why sayest thou, O Jacob, and speakest, O Israel: 'My way is hidden from the Lord, and my right is passed over from my God?' Hast thou not known? Hast thou not heard that the everlasting God, the Lord, the Creator of the ends of the earth . . . His discernment is beyond searching out." (Isaiah 40:27-28)

This passage deals with the problem of Divine omniscience as against freedom of choice.

Maimonides asked: How can Divine omniscience and human freedom of choice exist side by side? If God knows even before a man is created whether that man will be righteous or wicked, how can one say that man is free to choose his own path? With God knowing in advance what his choice will be, is the hand of men not forced?

Maimonides answers his own question as follows: Divine "knowledge" is entirely different from the knowledge known to man, and man cannot comprehend it any more than he can grasp the essence of God. As Isaiah (55:9) said: "For as the heavens are higher than earth, so are My ways higher than your ways, and My thoughts than your thoughts." Hence in a manner beyond our understanding, it is possible that, side by side with God's advance knowledge of all that men will do, man still has the power of free choice. (*Yad HaHazakah,* Chap. 5 of *Hilkhot Teshuva, Halakha 5*).

This same reasoning — question and answer — is conveyed also by the passage cited above. First, the question:

"Why sayest thou, O Jacob · · · 'My way is hidden from the Lord, and my right is passed over from my God.' Thou sayest either that 'my way is hidden from the Lord', that God has no advance knowledge of man's conduct, or that 'my right is passed over from my God,' that God must not judge the acts of man because man, bound by God's advance knowledge, has no freedom

of choice and so cannot be punished if he does wrong. Thou sayest that both these eventualities cannot exist side by side. Either 'my way is hidden from the Lord' or 'God cannot judge me.' "

This argument is followed by the answer:

"Hast thou not known? Hast thou not heard that the ever-lasting God, the Lord, the Creator of the ends of the earth . . . His discernment is beyond searching out? We are not capable of com-prehending His ways. How, then, could we expect to be able to understand the character of His knowledge which is such that it allows man full freedom of choice?"

—*Attributed to R. Elijah Ben Solomon Zalman,*
the Gaon of Vilna

* * * *

Weekly Portion of Vayyera (Genesis 18:1 — 22:24)
". . . as (Abraham) sat in the tent door in the heat of the day."
(Genesis 18:1)

From this verse the Sages inferred that Abraham is perpet-ually stationed at the gate of Gehenna, barring admittance to all those males who have been circumcised (*Erubin 19* and *Bere-shith Rabba 48*). They interpreted the verse as follows:

"As he sat" (the Hebrew verb is in the present tense): He is always sitting in the door of the tent where the wicked are being judged, a place which is denoted by the expression "the heat of the day," (Cf. Malachi 3:19: "For behold, the day comes, it burns as a furnace, and all the proud, and all that work wickedness, shall be stubble, *and the day that comes shall set them ablaze.*")

—*Rabbinic Literature*

* * * *

". . . and (Abraham) looked, and lo, three men stood over against him . . ." (Genesis 18:2)

> One to notify Sarah, and one to destroy Sodom, and one to heal Abraham, for no one of the angels performed more than one mission . . . but Raphael, the angel who had healed Abraham, went on from there to rescue Lot.

—*Rashi*

On the very day that he assumed the Rabbinate of Brody, Galicia, the famous Rabbi Solomon Kluger (1783-1869) was asked to serve as *sandak* (godfather) at the circumcision of an infant. Arriving at the parents' home, he learned that the father of the infant was dying and that according to a custom instituted in that city, circumcision in such a case would be deferred until after the death of the father so that the infant might be given the father's name. Rabbi Kluger, however, quickly called together a quorum of ten adult males and had the child circumcised at once. To the amazement of everyone, the child's father recovered, and the entire city was astir at the miracle that had come to pass.

Rabbi Kluger explained that he had based his action on his interpretation of the statement by Rashi cited above. Was there a lack of angels in heaven, he had asked himself, that the same angel who had the mission to heal Abraham had to be sent also to rescue Lot? The only explanation he could find was that Lot's merits had not been great enough to warrant the appointment of a special angel to rescue him, and so the angel who healed Abraham performed this additional task "on the way."

"It occurred to me," Rabbi Kluger said, "that the infant's father was being judged in Heaven and that his merits had not been found great enough to have the Prophet Elijah come down to earth just for the purpose of bringing him healing. But since Elijah is in attendance at all circumcisions, I had the infant circumcised at once, so that Elijah might come down immediately and bring healing to its father 'on the way.' "

*   *   *   *

"And (Abraham) said: . . . 'do not pass away, I pray thee, from thy servant.' " (Genesis 18:3)

> We learn from this that to extend hospitality is even more important than to receive the *Shekhina*.
>
> *—Sabbath* 127

Even the body of Abraham was so utterly dedicated to the

service of the Lord that his limbs would act of their own volition to do the will of their Maker. Hence, when Abraham felt his feet rise of themselves to rush to meet his guests, he knew that, according to the Law of God, hospitality took precedence even over receiving the *Shekhina*.

—*Rabbi Nathan ben Simeon Adler and also after*
Rabbi Meir of Przemysl

* * * *

"And Abraham hastened into the tent to Sarah and said: 'Make ready quickly three measures of fine meal...'" (Genesis 18:6)

The Torah teaches us that hospitality requires us to act quickly in order not to keep the hungry traveler waiting too long. The Sages (*Taanith 21*) relate that the Tannaite Nahum of Gimzo asked a poor traveler to wait while he unloaded his donkey, and the poor man collapsed and died of hunger in the meantime.

—*Avnei Ezel*

* * * *

Scripture first writes *kemakh* (ordinary meal) but then *solet* (fine meal). From this we learn that a woman looks on guests with a more grudging eye than a man.

—*Baba Metzia 87*

Maimonides taught that man should always take the middle course which, in this case, would be to be neither miserly nor extravagant. But one who is deficient in a virtue must go to the other extreme in order to attain the middle course

Abraham, who was exceedingly hospitable by nature, could choose the middle course and offer his guests cakes made from ordinary meal. But Sarah who, being a woman, was less hospitable, had to go to the extremes of generosity and hence had to take "fine" meal which was of better taste and quality than ordinary flour.

—*After the Rabbi of Lublin*

* * * *

"And Sarah laughed within herself, saying: 'After I have grown old shall I have the pleasure, my lord being old also?" And the Lord said to Abraham: 'Why did Sarah laugh . . .?' " (Genesis 18:12-13)

The Lord demanded an explanation from Abraham for Sarah's laughter, for if the wife does not behave as she should, the husband is to blame.

—Alshekh HaKodosh

*   *   *   *

"And the men rose up from there and looked out toward Sodom . . ." (Genesis 18:16)

What is the connotation of the expression "from there"?

To indicate the contrast between Abraham's hospitality and the evil of Sodom.

When the three angels saw Abraham's righteousness and hospitality and then thought of the evil of Sodom, their anger at Sodom became even greater than it had been before.

When the angels "rose up *from there*", from the house of Abraham where they had seen true righteousness, they *looked out toward Sodom*; i.e. they were strengthened in their view that Sodom had to be destroyed."   *—K'lei Hemda*

*   *   *   *

"Shall I hide from Abraham that which I am doing . . . for I have known him, to the end that he may command his children and his household after him, that they may keep the way of the Lord to do righteousness and justice . . ." (Genesis 18:17-19)

A good educator makes use of the happenings of daily life to inspire or reprove his students. Actual instances of reward for good deeds or punishment for evil provide him with impressive object lessons by means of which he can urge his students to avoid evil and to choose good instead.

Thus the destruction of Sodom provided Abraham with an excellent object lesson for his endeavors to teach men "to do righteousness and justice", for it was a visible demonstration of the results of evil and injustice.

Therefore the Lord said: *"Should I hide from Abraham that which I am doing?* Seeing that Abraham will *command his children and his household after him* and, indeed, teach his entire generation *to do righteousness and justice,* should I really hide from him My plan to destroy Sodom because of its sins? If I make it known to him in advance, it would only serve to help him in his holy endeavors, for then the people will not be able to argue that the fall of Sodom was nothing but an accident."

—*Avnei Ezel*

* * * *

"... that they may keep the way of the Lord to do righteousness and justice . . ." Genesis 18:19)

The "way of the Lord" must be kept, and not violated, not even in order "to do righteousness and justice." We must not imitate those of our charitable organizations which, in the name of charity, arrange affairs where the basic rules of modesty are blatantly flouted, for that is truly "committing a sin in order to fulfill a commandment". In doing "righteousness and justice" we must also "keep the way of the Lord."

—*Yalkut HaGershuni*

* * * *

"And (Lot) *said: 'Behold now, my lords, turn aside, I pray you, into your servant's house ..."* (Genesis 19:2)

Lot requested his visitors to enter "your servant's house."

Abraham, however, had said to his guests: ". . . do not pass away, I pray thee, from thy servant" (*Gen. 18:3*). He made no mention of his house, for when he would receive visitors, he would cease to think of himself as master of his house but place his home entirely at the disposal of his guests, regarding himself as nothing more than their servant.

—*Attributed to a Hassid*

* * * *

(The Sodomites said) *"This one fellow came in to sojourn and he will play the judge . . ."* (Genesis 19:9)

The reason why the Sodomites barred strangers from their city was their fear that those foreigners might eventually displace the natives from positions of authority and leadership. They said to Lot: "How can you expect us to admit two strangers when we know that only one fellow — yourself — came as a stranger to sojourn in our midst and now he already plays the judge. Think of what would happen if we were to open our gates to more foreigners. Why, they might take over our entire city."

—*Imrei Shofar*

* * * *

When Abimelech demanded of Abraham why he had lied to him, saying that Sarah was his sister, Abraham replied:
"Because I thought: 'Surely the fear of God is not in this place and they will slay me for my wife's sake.' " (Genesis 20:11)

Do not believe that even if a man does not fear the Lord he can still be noble and decent in his relationships with his fellow-men. Where fear of the Lord is lacking, human qualities cannot exist, and people will commit the grossest murder and inhumanity in order to gratify their lusts. Only faith in the Lord and the fear of Him will keep men from doing evil to their fellow-men.

—*Malbim*

* * * *

"And Sarah saw the son of Hagar . . . making sport." (Gen. 21:9)
Making sport: This means worshipping idols. According to another explanation the expression refers to immoral conduct. According to still another interpretation, it refers to murder. —*Rashi*

A little joking, a little fun may seem so harmless, yet such "sport" can lead to grave sin, including idolatry, immorality and murder. Some of the worst crimes had their beginning in seemingly harmless "sport."

—*Avnei Ezel*

* * * *

41

(Sarah said to Abraham) *"Cast out this bondwoman and her son . . ."*
(Genesis 21:10)

Sarah did not approve of Ishmael's behavior. But what objection did she have against Hagar?

She felt that if the son was bad, the mother could also not be good. Therefore she told Abraham: "Cast out this bondwoman *and her son*. The boy is her child, and if he is wicked, he is only following in the paths of his mother."

—Anon.

* * * *

(God said to Abraham): *"Take now thy son, thine only son, whom thou lovest . . ."* (Genesis 22:2)

God commanded Abraham to offer up Isaac with all the love he, the father, had for his son. Some men can bring themselves to be cruel, divesting themselves of all love for their children for the sake of the Lord. (*"Black as ravens* — these are the scholars of the Law who are like ravens in that they have no mercy on their children" — *Midrash Rabba* to *Song of Songs*). But Abraham was explicitly bidden to use all his strength to restrain — rather than to ignore — his love for Isaac and, in this state of mind, to offer him as a sacrifice to the Lord. Therein lay the significance of the test to which the Lord put Abraham.

—Hiddushei HaRIM

* * * *

". . . and he took in his hand the fire and the knife . . ." (Gen. 22:6)

In order to be strong enough to perform wholeheartedly the commandment to sacrifice his son, Abraham took with him two of the merits he had accumulated. The "fire" symbolized the burning oven into which he had cast himself to glorify the Lord. The "knife" signified his hospitality in which he would hurry to prepare food for passing travelers.

—Tifereth Jonathan

* * * *

"And the angel of the Lord called to him out of heaven . . ."
(Genesis 22:11)

Why was the order not to slaughter Isaac given by a mere angel, when the command to sacrifice him had been pronounced by God Himself?

To teach us that we must not obey anyone who commands us to harm a person, not even an angel, except the Lord alone. But when the command is to desist from doing harm, the word of an angel is sufficient.

—*Devash HaSadeh*

* * * *

"So Abraham returned to his young men . . ." (Genesis 22:19).

On Mount Moriah Abraham saw the true strength of the younger generation. He, Abraham, had received directly from God the commandment to sacrifice Isaac. Isaac had only heard it from his father, a human being like himself. Yet "they went both of them together" (22:6). Isaac went forth with the same zeal and determination as Abraham. When Abraham saw this spirit of devotion and self-sacrifice in his young son, he said to himself: "The old should associate more with the young" and he "returned to his young men."

—*Rabbi Menahem Mendel of Kotzk* (d. 1859)

* * * *

Haphtarah Vayyera (II Kings 4:1-37)
(The story of the widow's vessels).
"Now there cried a certain woman . . . to Elisha, saying: 'Thy servant my husband is dead : . . and the creditor has come to take my two children to be bondmen.' " (II Kings 4:1)

Why did the woman say: "Thy servant my husband is dead".

According to the Sages, the woman's husband was the prophet Obadiah, and the creditor was Jehoram, the son of King Ahab. Obadiah had borrowed money from Jehoram to provide food for the prophets of the Lord whom Jezebel had persecuted.

43

For this reason Jehoram now sought to take away the widow's two children to serve as slaves in his household.

Therefore the widow cried out to Elisha: *"Thy servant my husband is dead.* Only now is my husband, Obadiah,who feared the Lord, truly dead. Until this moment I had hoped that I would be able to raise his two children in his ways so that they might grow up to be God-fearing men. Then Obadiah would not have been lost forever, for his spirit would have survived in his children. (Cf. "He who has raised a son like himself is not regarded as dead" — *Baba Kamma 116*). But now that Jehoram will take our children to the royal court and train them in the corrupt ways of Ahab and Jezebel, my husband will truly cease to live because the children will not be able to carry on in his spirit. When the chain of tradition is broken, death has truly come."

—Avnei Ezel

* * * *

Weekly Portion of Hayye Sarah (Genesis 23:1 — 25:18)
"And the life of Sarah was one hundred years and twenty years and seven years . . ." (Genesis 23:1).

> At the age of one hundred she was like a woman of twenty as regards sin.

—Rashi

Scripture relates that Sarah always combined in her person the virtues of youth and those of old age. When she was only twenty years of age, she had the virtues of old age — calmness and moderation. But when she was one hundred years old, she was still blessed with the zeal, vitality and enthusiasm that are usually associated with a young woman of twenty.

—A Scholar

* * * *

". . . and Abraham came to mourn for Sarah . . ." (Genesis 23:2).
From where did he come? From Mount Moriah.
—Midrash

When Abraham wanted to rehearse the many virtues of his departed wife, he began with the story of the sacrifice of Isaac on Mount Moriah. The fact alone that she had succeeded in training her son to be willing to sacrifice his very life for God showed what manner of woman she had been.

This is the explanation of the statement quoted above from the Midrash:

"From where had Abraham come?" At what point did Abraham, in his eulogy, begin the story of Sarah's life? *From Mount Moriah* — with the event that took place on Mount Moriah, which gave him ample material for an eulogy.
—HaDrash VeHaEyun

*   *   *   *

(And the Hittites answered) *"Hear us, my Lord . . ."* (Gen. 23:6)

The Hittites addressed Abraham as "my lord" throughout the negotiations for a burial place for Sarah, but Abraham never referred to them in similar terms. He refrained from doing so because he had been the first to address God by this appellation. ("Before Abraham there had been no one to address the Holy One, blessed be He, as "Lord", until Abraham came and called Him Lord" — *Berakhot* 7). Having given the title of "Lord" to God, Abraham could no longer use it in addressing a mere man, not even out of courtesy.   *—Rabbi Joseph Josel Hurwitz*

*   *   *   *

". . . and Abraham weighed to Ephron the silver . . . current money with the merchant." (Genesis 23:16)

Who was "the merchant"?

A third party drawn into the transaction by Ephron, the original owner of the field in which the cave of Machpelah was situated.

Originally Ephron had been willing to give the field to Abraham as a gift. But in the end he decided to accept payment and asked a handsome amount for the field. Finidng it awkward to demand the price from Abraham, he designated a merchant to act as intermediary, to settle the financial part of the transaction. Naturally, the merchant did not hesitate to ask for proper payment in "conveniently-sized" currency.

—*Rabbi Ephraim Zalman Margolith of Brody*

* * * *

"And Abraham said to his servant, the elder of his house, who ruled over all that he had: 'Put, I pray thee, thy hand under my thigh . . ." (Genesis 24:2).

As a rule, a man who is approached for a loan makes careful inquiry about the borrower's credit and reliability before granting the request. Only after the borrower's willingness and ability to repay have been established beyond a doubt will the loan be extended. But in matters of religious observance, such as establishing whether meat that was bought is ritually pure or whether a pair of phylacteries is fit for ritual use, we are generally not so careful in our inquiries and are inclined to believe anyone who answers us in the affirmative.

Not so Abraham. Eliezer was "his servant, the elder of his house, who ruled over all that he had," Abraham trusted him with all his possessions and left all his business affairs to his management. But in matters involving religious observance, such as finding a suitable wife for his son Isaac, Abraham did not trust him unquestioningly but insisted that he swear a solemn oath before going on his mission: "Put, I pray thee, thy hand under my thigh."

—*Yalkut HaDrush*

* * * *

". . . that thou shalt take a wife for my son from among the daughters of the Canaanites . . ." (Genesis 24:3).

Abraham's own family had been idol-worshippers. What, then, made them better than the Canaanites?

The Canaanites tribes were morally corrupt — the Scriptures contain many references to the "abominations of the land of Canaan" — and moral corruption can be passed on from parent to child. Abraham's kin, on the other hand, were not corrupt; they were merely victims of error in that they worshipped *teraphim,* and error is not inheritable.

—*Abraham Bornstein*

*   *   *   *

"So let it come to pass that the maiden to whom I shall say: 'Let down thy pitcher, I pray thee, that I may drink,' and she will say: 'Drink, and I will give thy camels drink also,' let the same be the one whom Thou hast appointed for Thy servant, for Isaac . . ." (Genesis 24:14).

Eliezer wanted to put the maiden to the test to see not only whether she had good qualities but also whether she would use her virtues with wisdom and understanding.

Accordingly, he asked her to give him a drink of water from that pitcher with which the water was drawn up from the well. What, he wondered, would she do with the water that would be left in the pitcher after he had drunk from it? If she were to take it home, she would not be acting wisely, for it should occur to her that he might be ill and that it might be unsafe for others to drink the water that came in contact with his mouth. On the other hand, if she were to pour it out, it would be an insult to the stranger and would show that she was lacking in tact. The proper course for her to follow would be to say, "Drink, and I will give thy camels drink also." In this manner, there would be no insult to the stranger, nor would other people be exposed to danger by drinking water that might be contaminated. If she chose that alternative, it would be proof that she had not only good qualities but also sufficient intelligence to make the right decisions in unforeseen situations.

And it came to pass as Eliezer had hoped. The maiden said:

47

"I will draw for thy camels also, until they have done drinking (Gen. 24:19). Do not think that I will pour the remaining water into the trough for the camels just in order not to deal thee an insult. I really want the camels to have water. See, I will draw another pitcherful for them to make sure that they will have enough to drink." Thus did Rebecca perform an additional good deed in order to disguise her intention not to insult Eliezer.

—*Rabbi Joseph Dov Halevi Soloveitchik of Brisk*

* * * *

(Laban said to Eliezer) *"Come in . . . for I have cleared the house."* (Genesis 24:31)

I have cleared the house of idols.

—*Rashi*

Laban said to Eliezer: "I have even thrown out my own idols in order to get my hands on some money from your master in return for the hand of my sister Rebecca" (Rashi on Verse 29).

This is the way of Laban and his ilk. For a few coins of gold, they are willing to give away even their gods.

—*Rabbi Joseph Josel Hurwitz*

* * * *

(Eliezer said to Laban and Bethuel): *"And I came this day to the fountain . . ."* (Genesis 24:42).

Rabbi Acha said: "The ordinary conversation of the servants of the Patriarchs is more pleasing to God than even the Torah (study) of their children. For the chapter of Eliezer (the servant of Abraham) is repeated in the Scriptural account, while many important principles of the Law are derived only from the indirect indications given in the text."

—*Midrash Rabba*

Personal involvement in a situation may tempt a man to declare even vermin fit for consumption and to twist the meaning of the Law beyond recognition. The detailed account of the conversations of the servants of the Patriarchs teaches us how to keep selfish consideration from influencing our decisions, so that what is unclean should remain unclean in our eyes regardless of what we gain or lose thereby, even as Eliezer refused to allow his personal desire — that Isaac should marry his daughter and not Rebecca — to interfere with the mission he carried out on behalf of his master Abraham.

—Attributed to a Sage

*   *   *   *

". . . and they said to (Rebecca): 'Wilt thou go with this man?' And she said: 'I will go.' " (Genesis 24:58)

      Rebecca said: "I will go of my own accord even if you should not give your consent."

—Rashi

How could Rebecca have given such an insolent reply to her elders?

According to Rashi (Commentary to Verse 55) Bethuel, Rebecca's father, had refused to give his consent to her marriage and lost his life as a result. Thus Rebecca said to her family:

"I will have to go with him even if you should not give me your consent, because God will force you to let me go. You have seen what happened to my father because he refused to give his consent to my going with Eliezer. Would it not be better, then, if you would agree to let me go without delay?"

—Be'er Mayim Hayyim

*   *   *   *

"And they blessed Rebecca and said to her: 'Our sister, be thou the mother of thousands of ten thousands . . .' " (Genesis 24:60).

According to the Sages, children take after the mother's brother. Knowing this, Laban wanted his sister Rebecca to have a great many children, so that there might be many more men as evil as he in the world.

—Anon.

*   *   *   *

Weekly Portion of Toledoth (Genesis 25:19 — 28:9)
"And the children struggled together within (Rebecca) . . . and she went to inquire of the Lord." (Genesis 25:22)
> That He might tell her what would happen in the end.
> —*Rashi*

We are told that whenever Rebecca would pass by a house of study, Jacob would move convulsively in an effort to come forth, but whenever she would pass by a pagan temple, Esau would move convulsively, straining to emerge.

Now Rebecca thought that she was bearing only one child, and therefore she assumed that the convulsive movements she felt within her when she would pass by houses of study and heathen temples were indicative of the struggle between the good impulse and the evil impulse in the child she was to have. Sometimes, she thought, the evil urge won the day and the child would want to rush out to worship idols, and at other times the good inclination would gain the upper hand so that the child wanted to go forth to the house of study to learn the Law of God.

Naturally Rebecca was anxious to know "what would happen in the end"; she wanted to know the outcome of the inner struggle which she thought was taking place within her child. Good or evil — which of the two would strike the final blow and emerge as the victor?

Throughout his life, man must wage war against his evil inclination. Sometimes he will win; at other times the evil in him will gain the upper hand. But regardless of temporary reverses, he should see to it that he will be able to strike the final blow and thus emerge as the victor in the struggle.   —*Kol Simcha*

* * * *

". . . and they called his name Esau." (Genesis 25:25)
> Everyone called him thus.   —*Rashi*

Esau represents falsehood and deceit, while Jacob was truth personified. Of Esau we are told "and *they called* his name

Esau" because, unfortunately, deceit attracts many followers. Of Jacob, however, the Biblical account states "and his name was called Jacob," with the singular form of the statement indicating that truth has a much smaller number of adherents than falsehood.

—*Degel Mahane Ephraim*

*   *   *   *

"... *and* (Esau) *ate and drank, and rose up and went his way, and Esau despised his birthright."* (Genesis 25:34)

This is the way of Esau. He and his ilk are ready to give away their most sacred trust for a little food. When they are hungry they care little for their birthright or for worship, because their entire being is dominated by their craving for food and drink. Not so Jacob and those like him. Their senses are not ruled by the quest for food and drink. They acquire their birthright by industry and toil and thus gain predominance in matters of the spirit. At that point Esau becomes angry and claims that Jacob has deceived him. *"He has outwitted me these two times . . ."* (Gen. 27:36).

But we say to him: "Remember, O wicked Esau, that thou didst cast away thy birthright by thy own indolence and base cravings, and that Jacob earned the birthright by means of honest toil. He gained the birthright not through deceit, but through moderation in all the pleasure of the body, including eating and drinking."   —*Avnei Ezel*

*   *   *   *

"And Esau despised his birthright." We know that Esau began to make light of his birthright at an early age. It was Esau's attitude toward the sacred birthright that impelled Jacob to seek an opportunity to divest him of it.

From this we may learn that if we should see a sacred object such as a Scroll of the Law in the hands of a wicked man, the righteous are permitted to get it out of his hands by means of deceit, if need be.   —*Rabbi Judah HeHassid*

51

* * * *

"And (Isaac) *moved away from there, and dug another well, and they did not quarrel over it. And he called it Rehobot, for he said: 'For now the Lord has* made room *for us . . .' "* (Genesis 26:22).

The two wells (Esek and Sitnah) which were dug by Isaac's servants and which became objects of contention between the herdsmen of Gerar and those of Isaac may be taken allegorically to represent the two Temples which warring nations succeeded in destroying. The third well, *Rehobot,* which did not become an object of contention, symbolizes the Third Temple which will be built in days to come and which will never be attacked by enemy powers. When the Third Temple will rise in Jerusalem, the Children of Israel will live in "a broad expanse" and no nation will dare molest them.

—Nachmanides

* * * *

". . . and (Abimelech, Ahuzzath and Phicol) *departed from* (Isaac) *in peace."* (Genesis 26:31)
Alternative rendering: *". . . and they departed from Isaac at peace."*

Only heathens like Abimelech and his companions would be capable of that. Here they had been with Isaac; they had even been privileged to break bread with this righteous man, and then they departed from him completely at peace with themselves. When a Jew spends time with a righteous man, he is not at peace with himself, but crushed and contrite in spirit and can find no peace because his association with the righteous man has made him painfully aware of his own shortcomings.

—Rabbi Simcha Bunim of Przysucha

* * * *

"And it came to pass, that when Isaac was old and his eyes were dim . . ." (Genesis 27:1)

Abraham had cleansed his home of evil by driving his son

Ishmael away. He therefore enjoyed a peaceful old age and was privileged to welcome into his home a daughter-in-law such as Rebecca turned out to be. Isaac, however, did not send away his evil son Esau. Therefore his old age was marred by blindness which struck him when he saw the outrageous conduct of Esau and his heathen wives and found that Jacob had had to flee from home in order to save his life.

This teaches us that if we tolerate evil under our roof instead of driving it away, righteousness will be forced to flee from our dwelling-places.   —*Musarist Writings*

*   *   *   *

(Isaac said to Esau): *". . . take me venison and make me savory food, such as I love, and bring it to me . . . that my soul may bless thee before I die."* (Genesis 27:4)

Jacob blessed all his sons before he died, not just his first-born. Why, then, did Isaac want to bless Esau only?

Such was the decree from heaven. Had Isaac provided a separate blessing for Jacob, later generations would have argued that the Jewish people were worthy of these blessings only as long as they would be on the same high moral level as Jacob had been. Accordingly, the Lord ordained that Isaac should intend to give the blessing to Esau alone. Then it would be understood that the blessing would be applicable to the Jewish people at all times, even when they would sink very low indeed, for they could never become more evil than Esau.   —*Rabbi Isaac of Warka*

*   *   *   *

". . . and (Jacob) *said: 'The voice is Jacob's voice, but the hands are the hands of Esau.'"* (Genesis 27:22)

Alternative rendering: *"If Jacob's voice is faint, the hands will be the hands of Esau."*

> As long as the voice of Jacob will be heard in the synagogues and houses of study, the hand of Esau will not be able to rule over them.
>
> —*Midrash*

53

Note that the word *ha-kol* ("the voice") is spelled in the Hebrew text without the *vav*, and may therefore be read as *ha-kal*, meaning "light" or "faint." This is to teach us that whenever the voice of righteousness as symbolized by Jacob becomes faint, evil as embodied by the hands of Esau will gain control. But when the voice of Jacob gains full strength, (when *kal* becomes *kol* through the addition of the *vav*), the hands of Esau will no longer be in control.

—*Rabbi Elijah ben Solomon Zalman, the Gaon of Vilna*

* * * *

Haphtarah Toledoth (Malachi 1; 2:1-7)
"... *Yet you say: 'Wherein hast Thou loved us?' Was not Esau Jacob's brother, says the Lord, yet I loved Jacob, but I hated Esau* ..." (Malachi 1: 1-3)
Alternative rendering: "*Yet you say: 'For what reason shouldst Thou love us?' Was not Esau Jacob's brother, says the Lord, yet I loved Jacob, but I hated Esau* ..."

Even if the Children of Israel should sink so low as to seem unworthy of God's love, they still appear righteous and worthy of being loved as compared to the evil Esau.

This is the thought conveyed by Malachi:

"*Yet you say: For what reason shouldst Thou love us?* How could God love us, seeing that we have become unworthy of His love by reason of our wicked deeds? Then God will answer: "*Was not Esau Jacob's brother?* When I consider the conduct of your brother Esau, I must love you and hate Esau. However greatly you may have sinned, Esau is so much more evil than you that, compared to him, I must love you."

—*Ahavat Yonathan*

* * * *

54

Weekly Portion of Vayyetze (Genesis 28:10-32:3)
"And Jacob went out from Beersheba and went toward Haran."
(Genesis 28:10)

> This is intended to tell us that the departure of a righteous
> person from his city makes an impression . . . when he
> leaves it, its glory, splendor and beauty depart with him.
>   —*Rashi*

Whenever a person leaves the Holy Land, his departure is
described as a "going down" or "descent", for it is written that
"the Land of Israel is more exalted than any other country in the
world." Why, then, does the text cited above read "And Jacob
went out from Beersheba" and not "And Jacob *went down* . . ."?

In answer to our question, Rashi explains that when a righteous person leaves the Holy Land, "its glory, splendor and beauty
depart with him." The holiness of the land of Israel accompanied
Jacob on his journey abroad. As a matter of fact, Rashi relates
in his comment to Verse 17 that even Mount Moriah was moved
from its original place to Haran. Thus leaving the Land of Israel
actually was no "descent" for Jacob, for the glory of the Land,
which was purely spiritual in character, went abroad with him.
Wherever Jacob was, the Land of Israel was there also. Hence
the use of the expression "and Jacob went out" rather than "went
down" is justified.   —*Kedushat Levi*

*   *   *   *

"And he lighted upon the place . . ." (Genesis 28:11)

> Our Rabbis interpret the word *paga* ("and he lighted") to
> denote praying.   —*Rashi*

At a later point (Verse 20) we are explicitly told that Jacob
did indeed pray. He is quoted as saying: "If God will be with me
and will keep me . . . and give me bread to eat and clothing to
put on . . ." But what was the prayer he said (before he beheld the
vision described in Verses 12-15)?

Va-yifga ba-mokom ("and he lighted upon the place") may
also be rendered as "he prayed concerning the Omnipresent," with

ha-makom (lit. "the place") denoting Him Who is present in every place. Thus we know that before praying for the fulfillment of his personal wants (Verse 20), Jacob prayed in behalf of the glory of the Omnipresent, and for the Holy Temple which was to rise centuries later at the spot where Jacob spent the night on his way to Haran.

—*Tifereth Shlomo*

* * * *

To teach you that the road shrank beneath his feet.

—*Rashi*

When Jacob went forth to Haran, where he was to meet Rachel, whom he married, the road shrank beneath his feet, so that he arrived at his destination with speed. We are told that Eliezer, too, had this experience when he went forth to find a wife for Isaac.

This is to teach future generations that even exile and lack of means to give their children a proper dowry and support after marriage should not deter them from marrying off their sons and daughters at an early age. Let them trust in the Lord, for He will help them, even by miracle, should the need arise. The ground will rise up to meet them on the way so that they will be able to accomplish what they set out to do.

—*Bikkurei Aviv*

* * * *

"... *and behold a ladder set up on the ground, and the top of it reached to heaven* ..." (Genesis 28:12)

If a man regards himself as humble, "set up on the ground," then "his head will reach to heaven." God will consider him truly great. As the Holy Zohar puts it: "He who is small is actually great." Then, too, he will deserve to have "the Lord stand beside him," (Verse 13) to have the *Shekhina* hover over him, as it is written: "I dwell among the humble."

—*Orakh LeHayyim*

*   *   *   *

"And Jacob awoke . . . (and said) *'Surely the Lord is in this place, and I did not know it.' "* (Genesis 28:16)

According to the Midrash, Jacob's flight from his home to an alien land presaged the exile of the Jewish people. By revealing to him the vision of the ladder and the angels, the Lord meant to show to Jacob that even as this heavenly vision went with him into a strange land, so the sanctity of the Holy Temple would accompany the Jewish people into exile and would be built into the synagogues and houses of study which they would set up in the lands of their dispersion.

Jacob said: *"Surely the Lord is in this place*: I see now that the *Shekhina* will dwell in the midst of the people of Israel even here, in an alien land, *and I did not know it* — this I did not know before."

—*Melo HaOmer*

*   *   *   *

"How full of awe is this place! This is none other than the house of God, and this is the gate of heaven." (Genesis 28:17)

The Sages say: "Woe to him who has no dwelling place but makes himself a gate to the dwelling."

—*Sabbath* 31

The analogy: "He who has no dwelling place but makes himself a gate to the dwelling" describes one who studies the Law but does not fear the Lord. The Law is likened to a "gate" and the fear of the Lord is likened to the "dwelling place."

Jacob studied the Law for fourteen years at the School of Shem and Eber*. But he felt that he had not acquired the fear of the Lord until the time he had come to "this place."

---

* Son and great-grandson of Noah, respectively, who, acording to tradition, conducted the School at which the Patriarchs studied the Law.

He therefore exclaimed in amazement: *"How full of awe is this place.* This spot, where I first acquired the fear of the Lord, must be God's dwelling place. And *this* — my study of the Law in which I engaged until this day — *is the gate of heaven.* All my study and knowledge of the Law represent a mere gate on the way to heaven."

—Attributed to Rabbi Israel Eliezer Baal Shem Tov

* * * *

(And Jacob vowed): *"If God will be with me . . . and will give me bread to eat and clothing to put on . . ."* (Genesis 28:20)

Naturally, bread is meant to be eaten and clothing is meant to be put on. Is Jacob's statement not redundant?

Not at all. Jacob prayed not only for bread, but for good health to enjoy the bread, for there are many who have food in plenty but cannot eat because they are ill. He prayed not only for clothing, but for prosperity so that he should not have to pawn his garments, and for peace of mind so that he should be able to put them on.

—MaHaRSHaL of Lenchne

* * * *

". . . and of all that Thou shalt give me I will surely give the tenth part to Thee." (Genesis 28:22)

Said Jacob to the Lord: "Only that of which I am willing to give one-tenth to charity will remain truly mine, entrusted by Thee to me by virtue of my pledge to tithe it. Untithed wealth is not mine at all and I will not be able to keep it.

—Kametz HaMinha

Asser a'asrenu, the Hebrew expression for "I shall surely tithe" repeats the verb "to tithe" twice. This is the basis of the Rabbinic ordinance according to which the highest degree of charity is to give not just one-tenth but *two-tenths,* or one-fifth, of one's wealth to the poor. *—Anon.*

* * * *

58

(And Jacob said) *". . . it is not yet time that the cattle should be gathered together; water the sheep and go and feed them."* (Genesis 29:7)

Rabbi Meyer of Przemysl used to say:

"O Master of the Universe, if perchance *it is not yet time that the cattle should be gathered together,* that the Children of Israel should be gathered together and redeemed from their exile, I pray Thee, at least, to *water the sheep and go and feed them,* to let the Jews make a living so that they will have enough to eat and drink until the time is ripe for their deliverance."

*   *   *   *

". . . Jacob went near and rolled the stone from the mouth of the well . . ." (Genesis 29:10)

The strength of Jacob is truth, and truth enables man to roll even the heaviest of boulders of deceit and concealment from the well of living waters.   —*Rabbinic Literature*

*   *   *   *

". . . and (the seven years) *seemed to him only a few days, because of the love he had for her."* (Genesis 29:20)

Should not the reverse be true; i.e. that a day should seem to Jacob like years because of his love for Rachel?

The wording of this passage is meant to convey to us the profound spiritual nature of the love that bound Jacob and Rachel to one another. In a love based on physical desire, the lovers want the time of separation to pass quickly so that each day they are apart seems to them like a year. But in a spiritual love, devoid of self-seeking desire, such as that of Jacob and Rachel, the lovers do not care whether the object of their affection is near or far away. The spiritual love between Jacob and Rachel had already found fulfillment, and therefore seven years seemed to Jacob only a few days.

—*Abraham Joshua Heschel of Opatov*

*   *   *   *

"... and (Jacob) *loved Rachel more than Leah ..."* (Gen. 29:30)
    Alternative rendering: *"and* (Jacob) *loved Rachel by rea-*
son of (what she had done for) *Leah ..."*

Rachel was willing to sacrifice her own happiness for that of her sister Leah. In connection with Verse 22 of Chapter 30, Rashi relates that "(God) remembered it for her as a merit that she had transmitted the secret signs to her sister (Leah) and that she was greatly troubled lest she should fall to Esau's lot."

It was generally assumed that Esau and Jacob, the older and younger sons of Rebecca, would marry Leah and Rachel, the older and younger daughters of Laban, respectively. At first Leah wept constantly because she feared that, as the elder daughter of Laban, she would be given to Esau, Rebecca's first-born (Rashi's note to Chap. 29:17). But now Leah had been wed to Jacob, and Rachel had reason to fear that she would be married off to the evil Esau, for she did not know of Jacob's promise to work for another seven years in order to be able to marry her also. When she saw that Leah had been substituted for her at the wedding ceremony, she sacrificed her own happiness and jeopardized her share in the world to come by confiding to Leah the prearranged signs by which Jacob, the bridegroom, was meant to know he had been married to Rachel. She did this so that Leah should not be put to shame. And the Lord counted it as one of her merits that she had transmitted the secret signs to Leah, despite the fact that she, Rachel, knew that by helping her older sister accomplish this act of deceit and become the wife of Jacob, she increased the chances that she herself would be given to Esau.

As for Jacob, when he learned of her goodness and self-sacrifice, in which she disregarded her own happiness in order not to put her sister to shame, he grew to love her even more.

                                              —*Kedushat Levi*

*   *   *   *

(And Leah bore a son, and said): *"Now this time my husband will be joined to me, because I have borne him three sons . . ."* (Genesis 29:34)

The Commentary of the Elders gives the following odd explanation to this passage:

When a woman has one child, she holds it in both her arms. When the second infant arrives, she holds one in her right arm and the other in her left. But when there are three small children, her husband must help her hold them.

Thus, when Leah held her third son, she said: *"Now this time my husband will be joined to me*: Now my husband will have to help me, *because I have borne him three sons* and I cannot hold them all by myself."

*   *   *   *

'And (Leah) *conceived again, and bore a son, and she said: 'This time I will praise the Lord. Therefore she called his name Judah; and she left off bearing."* (Genesis 29:35)

> From the day the Holy One, blessed be He, created the world, there was no one who gave thanks to the Holy One, blessed be He, until Leah came. —*Berakhot 7*

The statement in Tractate Berakhot in connection with the above verse seems odd at first glance. Does not tradition tell us that the three Patriarchs instituted the daily prayers? How, then, can it be said that no one gave thanks to God before Leah?

The thanksgiving Leah offered to the Lord when Judah was born is not the same as that associated with the prayers of the three Patriarchs. The literal translation of the Hebrew word *hoda'ah* ("thanksgiving") used in the Biblical passage is "to acknowledge." The term implies a situation in which a person acknowledges that another person, whom he had previously thought to be wrong or unjust, had been right and just all along.

Such was the situation of Leah. First she had seen only unhappiness in her life. Feeling unwanted and unloved, she was convinced that the Lord had wronged her. But when she had

three sons, one after the other, she realized that her initial unhappiness had helped make her worthy to become the ancestress
of most of the tribes of the Children of Israel. She therefore said:
"This time I will praise the Lord, acknowledging that what I had
thought was evil and unjust was actually an act of Divine favor."

The Patriarchs and their families had cause many times to
praise the Lord, but they never had occasion to "acknowledge"
the wisdom of the Lord's ways as did Leah.

—Tiv Gittin

* * * *

*"And it came to pass when Rachel had borne Joseph, that Jacob
said to Laban: 'Send me away so that I may go to my own place
...'"* (Genesis 30:25)

> (It came to pass) after the birth of him who was to
> become Esau's adversary.
>
> *—Rashi*
>
> (Jacob made the request) because he knew that Esau
> would fall only by the hand of the sons of Rachel.
>
> *—Midrash Rabba*

Joseph, the son of Rachel, would be the one best fitted to
answer Esau when he clamors for vengance for Jacob's act of
deceit.

"Behold," Joseph could say to him, "my brothers did me
much more harm than Jacob did to thee. They sold me into
slavery. And yet I rewarded their evil with good."

This impressive argument should be sufficient to cause Esau
to "fall", ceding the victory to the Children of Israel.

—Anon.

* * * *

(God said to Laban) *"Take heed to thyself that thou speak not to
Jacob either good or bad."* (Genesis 31:24)

Said the Lord to Laban: "Do not attempt to discuss politics
with him, or to engage him in friendly talk with evil concealed in
thy words."

—Anon.

* * * *

(Laban said to Jacob) *"... Why didst thou flee secretly ... and didst not tell me, that I might have sent thee away with mirth and with songs, with tabret and with harp, and didst not allow me to kiss my sons and my daughters ... It is in the power of my hand to do you harm ..."* (Genesis 31:27-29)

First Laban talks of farewell parades, then of kissing his sons and daughters farewell, and in the same breath he cries out that it is in his power to do them harm. Is that the way of a good and loving father?

It is all quite in keeping with Laban's character. His farewell parades and demonstrations of love serve only to conceal his scheming to do evil to Jacob and his family.   —*Anon.*

* * * *

(Laban said to Jacob) *"The daughters are my daughters, and the children are my children ..."* (Genesis 31:43)

Laban said to Jacob: "Seeing that the daughters are mine, the children (i.e. thy sons) will be mine also."

Laban was right. If a man raises his daughters in the ways of evil as Laban did, he cannot expect that they, in turn, will bear good children. Their sons will be evil, because their mothers certainly will not raise them in the spirit of Jacob.

—*Anon.*

* * * *

"... And Jacob swore by the fear of his father Isaac." (Gen. 31:53) Alternative rendering: *"... And Jacob swore in fear of his father Isaac."*

Isaac had always taught Jacob not to take a vow unless absolutely necessary and if he had to take an oath, to do it with the reverence and respect proper in such cases. Hence when Jacob found himself compelled to take an oath, he did so filled with fear of his father Isaac, filled with reverence for the ideals his father had taught him.   —*Binah LeIttim*

* * * *

Haphtarah Vayyetze (Hosea 12:13 — 14:10)

". . . For the ways of the Lord are right, and the just walk therein, but transgressors stumble in them." (Hosea 14:10)

The wicked claim that God hates man and therefore burdened him with a heavy yoke in the form of commandments to deprive him of his freedom.

The fallacy of this view becomes obvious when we see how happy and content good people are to observe these commandments from which they gather strength for all their lives. Obviously, the only ones who find the commandments a burden are the wicked who have deliberately departed from the ways of the Lord, and if they find the Law burdensome, they have only themselves to blame.

The above may be illustrated by the following parable:

A wealthy man who was known far and wide for his hospitality arranged a great feast for passing travelers. He served them only the finest and most expensive foods. Yet one of the guests, a man who was not in good health, became seriously ill after having eaten heartily of the delicacies at his host's table. Outraged, he insisted that his host had wanted to poison his guests. But the host said to him: "Let us ask the other guests to find out whether the food agreed with them or not. I understand that you are not well. Therefore, if my food made you ill, you only have yourself to blame, since I prepared the meal for healthy people and not for the sick."

In a similar vein, Hosea declares:

"For the ways of the Lord are right, as proven by the fact that *the just walk therein* and live by them in contentment and happiness. *But transgressors stumble in them.* Those who regard these laws as burdens are transgressors, in whom the habit of sin is deeply rooted and to whom, therefore, the law of God is a stumbling-block that interferes with their way of life. But if this

is the way in which God's law affects them, they only have themselves to blame. The fault lies not in the character of the laws, but in the fact that these people are evil.

—*Kokhav MiYaakov*

*   *   *   *

Weekly Portion of Va-Yishlach (Genesis 32:4 — 36:43)
"And Jacob sent messengers before him to Esau his brother (commanding them to tell him): '. . . I have sojourned with Laban . . .'" (Genesis 32:4-5)

> *I have sojourned with Laban* — yet I observed the 613 commandments and did not learn any of his evil ways.*
>
> —*Rashi*

But Jacob added regretfully: "While I remained firm in my observance of the 613 commandments, I failed to learn from Laban to perform the commandments with the same dedication and zeal as he pursued his evil ways."

—*Meir Shapiro of Lublin*

Rabbi Isaac Meir Alter, author of the treatise *Hiddushei HaRIM,* was asked how he could account for the fact that the unbelievers were prospering. Why, the inquirer demanded, did their lies endure?

"The unbelievers," replied the Sage, "strive in behalf of falsehood, but with true dedication, while the believers strive on behalf of truth, but not with sufficient dedication."

*   *   *   *

"Then Jacob was greatly afraid and was distressed . . ." (Gen. 32:8)

Jacob was afraid of Esau. His distress, however, was due not to his fear of his brother, but to the thought that he should have dared fear anyone else but God.

For this reason he prayed: *"Deliver me, I pray Thee, from the hand of my brother, from the hand of Esau, for I fear him.* If I can still find it in my heart to be afraid of Esau, I know that I

---

* The total numerical value of the Hebrew letters *gimmel, resh, taph* and *yud* in *garti* — "I have sojourned" — is 613 (*TaRYaG*).

must still be far from perfect, and therefore I must pray Thee to deliver me." —*Orakh LeHayyim*

* * * *

(And Jacob said): *"I am not worthy of all the mercies and of all the truth which Thou hast shown to Thy servant . . . and now I am become two camps."* (Genesis 32:11)

A disciple of the wise must have within him an eighth of an eighth of pride. —*Sotah* 5

Although it is not good to be arrogant, a scholar must have an "eighth of an eighth" of pride in his character.

Why just "an eighth of an eighth"?

The Gaon of Vilna said: "The eighth portion of the Book of Genesis is the weekly portion of *Va-Yishlach* (Gen. 32:4 — 36:43) which deals with Jacob's encounter with Esau. The verse, "I am not worthy of all the mercies . . ." is the eighth verse of that weekly portion. This is to teach the scholar that even if he has just cause for pride in his scholastic accomplishments, even as Jacob said "and now I am become two camps", he must remember that his achievements are all mercies of God and realize that he is not worthy of such great mercies.

* * * *

"I am not worthy of all the mercies . . . for with my staff I passed over this Jordan, and now I am become two camps." (Gen. 32:11) Alternative rendering: *"I have grown small because of all the mercies . . ."*

Jacob said: "I have become small in my own eyes because of all the great mercies I have experienced. I have seen miracles, *for with my staff I passed over this Jordan.* These things should have taught me not to fear any man. Yet I find myself fearing Esau, *and now I am become two camps,* having divided my household into two camps out of fear. Hence I feel that I am very small indeed." —*Musarist Writings*

* * * *

"Deliver me, I pray Thee, from the hand of my brother, from the hand of Esau . . ." (Genesis 32:12)

The encounter with Esau could have had either of two outcomes, and Jacob feared the consequences of both. If Esau were to make war on his camp, there would be bloodshed. On the other hand, if Esau were to make peace with him, there was reason to fear that Esau and his men would become too intimate with Jacob and his household and would teach them their evil ways.

Therefore Jacob prayed to God to save him from two eventualities: "Deliver me *from the hand of my brother*: i.e. from becoming too intimate my evil brother, and *from the hand of Esau;* i.e. from the wickedness symbolized by the spirit of Esau."

And the Lord answered his prayer, for He saved Jacob not only from the wrath of Esau but also from too intimate involvement with him. (Cf. "So Esau returned that day on his way to Seir" — Gen. 34:16).

—Bet HaLevi

*   *   *   *

"And Esau said: 'I have enough, my brother . . ." (Gen. 33:9).
Alternative rendering: *"And Esau said: 'I have* much, *my brother . . ."*

Jacob urged the gifts on Esau, saying: ". . . because I have everything . . ." (Gen. 33:11). It will never occur to an Esau that he has "everything," for however much he may have, he will always want more. Jacob, on the other hand, "rejoices in his portion." However little a man of Jacob's character may possess, he will feel he has "everything" and desire nothing more.

—Attributed to a Sage

*   *   *   *

"And Jacob came in peace to the city of Shehem . . ." (Gen. 33:18)

The Hebrew letters in the word *shalem,* used here for "in peace" (lit. "whole"), form the initials of the Hebrew words *shem* (name), *lashon* (language) and *malbush* (dress). This is to teach us that despite his long association with Laban and his friendship — in the end — with Esau, Jacob remained "whole", clinging to his traditional Hebrew name, language and dress.

The "wholeness" or "integrity" of the Jew is measured by the extent to which he refuses to part with these three identifying characteristics of the Israelite.

—*Bnei Yissoskhor*

* * * *

"*. . . and* (Jacob) *encamped before the city.*" (Genesis 33:18)
   Rabbi Simeon said: It is a known maxim that Esau hates Jacob.

—*Rashi*

What does Rabbi Simeon mean by referring to Esau's hatred for Jacob as a "known maxim"?

There are people who are forever trying to find out reasons to justify the hatred of anti-Semites for the Jews. Practical experience, however, has shown that this hatred has no real cause and is not founded on logic or reasoning.

In some quarters the Jews are hated because they are supposed to be capitalists; in other circles they are persecuted because they are supposed to be Socialists. Some hate the Jews because they find them too gifted and too clever; others hate them because they consider them parasites and burdens on the rest of the population. Some accuse the Jews of religious fanaticism; others charge them with being radicals and spreading unbelief. Obviously, the Jews cannot possibly be guilty of all these things. Where, then, is the logic behind anti-Semitism?

Therefore Rabbi Simeon states: "*It is a known maxim that Esau hates Jacob.* The hatred of the anti-Semite for the Jew is a law unto itself, not founded on reasoning or motivation."

—*Rabbi Menahem Zemba of Warsaw*

* * * *

GENESIS   וישלח

(God commanded Jacob ". . . *and make there an altar to God, Who appeared to thee when thou didst flee from the face of Esau, thy brother."* (Genesis 35:1)

Alternative rendering: *"And make there an altar to God, Who appeared to thee* according to thy avoidance of *the face of Esau."*

A man's worthiness of receiving Divine revelation is determined by the extent to which he shuns evil.

—Zer Zahav, by Rabbi Wolf Landau

*   *   *   *

(Jacob said to his household): *"Put away the strange gods that are among you, and purify yourselves . . ."* (Genesis 35:2)

> The idols from the spoils of Shechem which you have in your possession.
>
> *—Rashi*

Jacob ordered the members of his household to discard the idols from the spoils they had acquired in Shechem, for a people could acquire the ways of an enemy even while they wage war upon him.   *—Musarist Writings*

*   *   *   *

"And let us arise and go up to Beth El, and I will make an altar there to God . . ." (Genesis 35:3)

This call follows the command to "put away the strange gods that are among you." And the Talmud (Sabbath 105) states: "What is a strange god which is inside the body of man? The evil inclination."

This teaches us that we must cleanse ourselves of the evil inclination before performing a positive commandment. It is only after we have removed the idols from our midst that we can build an altar and offer up sacrifices to the One God.

—Tifereth Shlomo

*   *   *   *

". . . the same is the pillar of Rachel's grave to this day." (Genesis 35:20)

The text does not read: "The same is the pillar of Rachel to this day," for Rachel herself did not need a monument. "One does

69

not rear monuments to the righteous, for their words are their memorial." Righteous men and women do not need pillars of stone to perpetuate their memory. Thus the pillar which Jacob set up was intended only as "the pillar of Rachel's grave," marking the site of the grave so that those of her descendants who might wish to visit the grave and pray there might know where it is.

—*Homat Esh*

*   *   *   *

Haphtarah Va-Yishlach (The Book of Obadiah)
"Thus says the Lord concerning Edom . . . Behold, I make thee small among the nations; thou art greatly despised. The pride of thy heart has beguiled thee . . ." (Verses 2-3)

When Edom is entrusted with the task of oppressing the Children of Israel and embittering their lives, he becomes boastful, thinking that God must regard him as a most important person. Actually, the fact that he is chosen to be the torturer and hangman of the Jewish people is proof how "small and greatly despised" Edom really is.

This may be likened to the story of a prince, the only son of a mighty king, who was adored by his father and petted by a household of devoted servants. One day the child became very ill and an evil-tasting medicine was prescribed to cure him. "I will be able to cure him," the court physician reassured the anxious father, "but I can do it only if neither the king nor his faithful servants will come into his son's presence. Instead, let the king appoint a cruel and wicked man who has neither regard nor understanding for the true nobility of the king's son and who will force the boy without mercy to take the bitter medicine and to adhere to the strict regimen which I will prescribe."

The evil man who was chosen for this task noted with pride that all the members of the royal household had been told to keep away from the prince and that he alone had been entrusted with the care of the king's son. Soon he began to boast of his importance and to regard himself as a great favorite at the court. But disillusionment was not long in coming, for he was eventually told: "It is only because you are so greatly despised, a stupid, cruel man entirely devoid of decency and compassion, that you were chosen to carry out this task. A fine and noble man would not be able to do the work for which you were hired. The king needs you only now to force his son to submit to the painful and unpleasant cure he must have if he is to recover. Once the prince is well, you will be dismissed from the king's court and sent back to the mean and despised among the people."

In the same vein the Prophet Obadiah said to Edom: *"The pride of thy heart has beguiled thee.* Thou art proud that thou hast been charged with the mission of oppressing the Children of Israel, but in truth, the fact that this task has been entrusted to thee is proof that *I have made thee small among the nations,* that *thou art greatly despised.* It was only because of thy cruelty, stupidity and heartlessness that thou wert chosen to take charge of the Children of Israel, to administer to them the punishment they must have in order to be cured of evil, while their loving Father in heaven must stay away and let thee do what must be done. But remember that in the end *I will bring thee down from hence,* says the Lord." (Verse 4)

—*Kokhav MiYaakov*

*   *   *   *

"For the violence done to thy brother Jacob shame shall cover thee . . ." (Verse 10)
Alternative rendering: *"For the violence of thy brother Jacob shame shall cover thee . . ."*

When an unruly lad comes to his father crying that his friend, who is known to be a quiet, well-behaved boy, has given him a beating, his father will say: "Let us go quickly and see how your friend is, for if he became sufficiently angry to strike you, you must have beaten him cruelly. I hope he is still alive."

In like manner, when an Esau protests that a Jacob has hurt him, that a Jewish boy has aimed a gun at him, or that a humble Jewish working-man has insulted his people, one may be sure that Esau first had tortured and oppressed Jacob so cruelly that even he, Esau, should be filled with shame at the thought.

The Lord says to Edom: *For the violence of thy brother Jacob shame shall cover thee.* How badly must thou have hurt him if thou, O evil Esau, didst succeed in driving even meek Jacob to resort to violence."

—Anon.

* * * *

Weekly Portion of VaYeshev (Genesis 37:1 — 40:23)
". . . and Joseph brought evil report of (his brothers) *to their father."* (Genesis 37:2)

Joseph did not actually bear tales of the conduct of his brothers to his father. But by his own conspicuous righteousness, he caused Jacob to be displeased with the conduct of his other children. If a father has one son whose conduct is exemplary, the shortcomings of his other sons will stand out all the more and he will punish them for not being as good as their brother.

Thus, although he was not guilty of tale-bearing or desirous of shaming his brothers, Joseph was punished because he should have performed his good deeds so quietly and unostentatiously that even his own father should not have noticed them.

—The Rabbi of Warka

* * * *

". . . they hated him and could not speak peaceably to him." (Gen. 37:4)

The brothers could not bear to hear Joseph speak to them so peaceably. "If you really think that we are sinners," they argued, "it would be your duty to hate us . (Cf. 'If one finds a sinful trait in his fellow-man one is duty-bound to hate him'.) Why, then, do you speak to us so kindly? Whatever your reason, O Joseph, you have sinned and are deserving of hatred. If you speak as you do because you know that we have really done no wrong, then you have sinned in that the evil reports you made about us were intentional slander. But if you know that we are evil men, you have sinned by not hating us as you should. Therefore, whatever your excuse, we are justified in hating you."

> —*Torat Moshe* (*R. Moses Schreiber*)

*   *   *   *

"*And* (Jacob) *said to him: 'Go now, see whether it is well with thy brothers . . .*" (Genesis 37:14)
Alternative rendering: "*Go now, see the peace* (shalom) *of thy brothers . . .*"

Jacob told Joseph to go and behold the integrity (*shelemuth,* from *shalom*) of his brothers, "Consider their virtues rather than their shortcomings," Jacob said to his son, "and thou wilt avoid strife and contention with them."

> —*Simcha Bunim of Przysucha*

Let everyone see the virtues of his fellow-men and not their faults.

> —*Prayer of Rabbi Elimelekh of Lizensk* (1717-1787)

*   *   *   *

". . . *and bring me back word . . .*" (Genesis 37:14)

Jacob knew that his other sons hated Joseph and he was afraid that they might do him harm. But he knew, also, that "agents sent out on a mission to perform a good deed will come to no harm." He therefore said to Joseph: "Come and I will *send thee* to them" (37:13), thus appointing him an agent to perform a good deed; namely, to do honor to his father by carrying out the latter's command to go and visit his brothers.

But then it occurred to Jacob that Joseph would be in danger on his return journey, for then his mission would have been completed. According to one view, "agents sent out on a mission to perform a good deed will come to no harm only in their going forth but not on their return." Jacob therefore explicitly commanded Joseph to "bring me back word" so that his return journey would be part of the errand on which his father had sent him.

—*Or HaHayyim*

*   *   *   *

"... and they ... cast him into the pit, and the pit was empty; there was no water in it." (Genesis 37:24)

Water it did not contain, but there were snakes and scorpions in it.

—*Rashi*

The water represents the Torah and the "snakes and scorpions" represent the agents of Satan who seek to gain control of man.

We know that the Torah is the only extant remedy against the evil impulse, as the Sages (Kiddushin 30) put it: "I created the evil impulse, and I created the Torah for the purpose of destroying it". Where there is no Torah, there is room for the agents of Satan.

This, then, is the thought which Rashi sought to convey in allegorical terms:

"*Water it did not contain;* there was no Torah. Therefore it is certain that *there were snakes and scorpions in it,* that the agents of evil which seek to harm man will be present and he will have no way of fighting them."

—*Avnei Ezel*

*   *   *   *

"*And they took Joseph's coat... and they dipped the coat in the blood.*" (Genesis 37:31)

It seems inconceivable that anyone should ever have suspected Jews of using human blood for their religious rituals. But it may be that these accusations were the punishment due them for the deceitful behavior of their remote ancestors who dipped Joseph's coat into the blood of a he-goat and then presented it to Jacob to identify as the coat of his favorite son.

—Rabbi Elhanan Wasserman

*   *   *   *

"And the Midianites sold him into Egypt . . ." (Genesis 37:36)

Just as Joseph was sold as a slave into Egypt because his brothers had envied him, so, years later, the Hebrews became slaves to the Egyptians because the Egyptians had envied them, saying: "Behold, the people of the Children of Israel are too many and too mighty for us" (Exod. 1:9). Indeed, all the slavery and oppression that the Jewish people had suffered in its long history were the result of envy on the part of the Gentiles.

—Commentary of Hiskuni

*   *   *   *

"And the Lord was with Joseph and he was a prosperous man, and he was in the house of his master the Egyptian." (Genesis 39:2)
Alternative rendering: *"And the Lord was with Joseph* when *he was a prosperous man, and* also when *he was in the house of his master, the Egyptian."*

There are people who can serve God only when they are poor. As soon as they grow wealthy, they forget Him. (Cf. "Jeshurun waxed fat and kicked" — Deut. 32:15).

Others serve the Lord as long as they lack for nothing, but as soon as they lose their wealth they act according to the adage that "poverty removes man from his intellect and from the knowledge of his Creator."

Joseph was not so. Scripture testifies that *"the Lord was with Joseph.* Joseph clung to his God when he was a *prosperous man* and also *when he was in the house of his master the Egyptian,* when he was no more than a humble slave at the home of Potiphar." Thus Joseph pased both tests — that of wealth as well as that of poverty.

—Tosafists, Daat Zekenim

*   *   *   *

"But (Joseph) *refused and said to his master's wife: 'Behold, my master, having me, does not know what is in the house . . . he is not greater in this house than I . . ."* (Genesis 39:8-9)

When someone tries to talk a man into sinning, the first thing he must do is refuse without going into details or engaging in debate on the reasons for his refusal. Only after having made it clear that he refuses to sin may he cite his reasons for refusing, as Joseph did (*"my master, having me, does not know what is in the house . . . he is not greater in this house than I . . . how can I do this great wickedness . . ."* and so forth.)

—*Sefat Emet*

* * * *

"And it came to pass on a certain day when (Joseph) *went into the house to do his work that she caught him . . ."* (Genesis 39:11-12).

Why was Joseph subjected to this test of character?

To see whether he was truly fit to become ruler over Egypt. By passing the test, he proved that he would be able to rule over that land of impurity and immorality without succumbing to its corrupting influence himself. —*Anon.*

* * * *

". . . and thou shalt give Pharaoh's cup into his hand, after the former manner when thou wast his butler." (Genesis 40:13)
Alternative rendering: *". . . and thou shalt give Pharaoh's cup into his hand, after the* original ruling *when thou wast his butler."*

What is the connection between "ruling" or "law" and a butler's services?

Actually, according to the law of Egypt, the butler had not committed a punishable crime. The chief baker, who had been put into prison becuse a pebble had been found in the pastry he had baked for Pharaoh, was guilty of a misdemeanor because, he had been negligent in sifting the flour. But the circumstance that a fly happened to fall into the wine the chief butler had poured for Pharaoh could not be construed as caused by any negligence on the part of the butler.

76

However, that Pharaoh should become angry with his chief butler and put him into prison was all part of God's plan to deliver Joseph. As the Midrash put it: "The Holy One, blessed be He, caused the master to be angry with his servants in order to bring about the deliverance of Joseph" so that Pharaoh had his chief butler imprisoned falsely.

But once the butler had promised to remember Joseph and the purpose of God had thus been fulfilled, the "original ruling" was reasserted, according to which the chief butler was not liable to punishment for what had happened to Pharaoh's wine.

—*Anon.·*

*   *   *   *

Haphtarah VaYeshev (Amos 2:6-3.8)
"You only have I known of all the families of the earth; therefore will I visit upon you all your iniquities." (Amos 3:2)

A dull student who is incapable of understanding his lessons will not be punished, because his teacher knows that in his case punishment would be to no avail. But a good student who possesses knowledge and the ability to learn and then refuses to study or laughs at his lessons will be punished severely.

In this vein the Lord says to His people: *"You only have I known;* I, the Lord, know you and the abilities you possess. Therefore, if you will not obey My commandments, I *will visit upon you all your iniquities,* and your punishment will be very severe."

—*Kokhav MiYaakov*

*   *   *   *

The reason why the Jewish people must suffer more than all the other nations, some of which are much more wicked and sinful than they, is that Israel is on a very high moral level. It was for the sake of the people of Israel that the world was created. The people of Israel were made to serve as the model for all of mankind, as the heart, as it were, for the entire world. Accordingly, a heavy responsibility has been placed upon them. If they sin, they actually mar Creation. Hence, even the mild transgressions they commit are liable to severe punishment.

—*Rabbinic Literature*

* * * *

Weekly Portion of Mi-Ketz (Genesis 41:1 — 44:17)
"And behold, seven other cows came up after them . . . and stood by the other cows . . . and the (lean) *cows ate up the seven well-favored and fat ones."* (Genesis 41:3-4)

Interpreting the "lean cows" as an allegorical representation of the evil inclination, the Sages base on this passage their statement that when the evil inclination comes to man, it acts like a transient at first, then like a guest, and finally like a master, ruling over him and his household.

The seven lean cows behaved toward the seven well-favored cows in the same manner as the evil inclination acts when it confronts man. At first, they "came up after them," slowly and inconspicuously. Then they "stood by" them like guests in their pasture, and finally they "ate them up" altogether.

—*Attributed to the author of Sefat Emet*

* * * *

"Then Pharaoh sent and called Joseph, and they brought him hastily out of the dungeon . . ." (Genesis 41:14)

The fact that Joseph was released from prison on Rosh Ha-Shana is of profound symbolic significance. There is in every Jew a spark of honesty and righteousness which never goes out and concerning which the Sages say: "A completely righteous man will never be swallowed up" (Megillah 6), meaning that the evil inclination will never be able to destroy this spark of decency. However, that spark, the "righteous Joseph" within us, is locked up all year long, imprisoned by the powers and appetites of the body. Only on Rosh HaShana, when the Jew casts aside his earthly desires and accepts the sovereignty of the Kingdom of Heaven, does our spark of righteousness emerge from its prison and stand revealed in all its glory.   —*Rabbinic Literature*

* * * *

(Pharaoh said to Joseph) *"And I told it to the magicians, but there was none among them who could declare it to me."* (Gen. 41:24)

Why did he not say "but there was none among them who *could interpret it for me*", as in the original account of Pharaoh's dream where we read (Verse 8) "but there was none who could interpret them to Pharaoh"?

Because it seemed to Pharaoh that the magicians had arrived at some sort of interpretation which they did not seem inclined to communicate to him.

The magicians interpreted Pharaoh's dreams in terms of events in his personal life rather than in terms of developments in his country. Thus, according to the Midrash, one of them said that Pharaoh would beget seven daughters and bury all seven, and another said that seven provinces would rise against him in rebellion. However, they were afraid to tell these unfavorable interpretations to the king.

Hence Pharaoh said to Joseph: *"And there was none among them who could declare it to me* aloud. They have an interpretation, but they keep discussing it among themselves in whispers. No one tells me anything."

—*K'lei Yakar*

*   *   *   *

"Now let Pharaoh seek out a man discreet and wise, and set him over the land of Egypt." (Genesis 41:33)

Let Pharaoh seek out such a man *now*. There would have been time for you to have the dream of the lean years seven years from now, at the end of the era of prosperity. But instead you were shown the lean years of famine now, far in advance. This was to give you time to choose a man "discreet and wise" who will begin to store up food while it is still available in plenty, against those lean years.

—*Rabbinic Literature*

*   *   *

79

"And Pharaoh said . . .'Can we find such a one as this, a man in whom the spirit of God is?' And Pharaoh said to Joseph: 'Seeing that God has shown thee all this, there is none so discreet and wise as thou.'" (Genesis 41:38-39)

Apparently even Pharoah understood that a man who is filled with the fear and knowledge of the Lord must also be "discreet and wise."

—Musarist Writings

*　*　*　*

"And Pharaoh called Joseph's name Zaphenath-Paneah, and he gave him as a wife Asenath, the daughter of Poti-phera, the priest of On . . ." (Genesis 41:45)

Zaphenath-Paneah — explainer of hidden things.

—Rashi

If *zaphenath* means "hidden things" and *paneah* means "explainer", should not the name read *Paneah-Zaphenath?*

The name is given in what seems the reverse order to show the reason why Joseph was found worthy to have the ability to discern hidden things; namely, that Joseph was exceedingly humble and kept his deeds of righteousness concealed so that they did not become immodestly conspicuous.

Zaphenath: It is because of conceals (his) deeds of righteousness, *Paneah*: that he is able to discover and explain hidden things.

—Sefat Emet

*　*　*　*

"And Joseph was the governor over the land; it was he who sold to all the people of the land." (Genesis 42:6)

Although he was governor over all of Egypt, he did not delegate the distribution of the produce to subordinate officials but supervised all the sales personally to make sure that no one would be cheated and to provide an example of how to practice the virtue of compassion in order to save the hungry.

—*Sifthei Kohen*

*   *   *   *

(And Joseph's brothers) *"... bowed down to him with their faces to the ground. And Joseph saw his brothers and he knew them, but he made himself a stranger to them ..."* (Genesis 42:6-7)

Defeat usually comes as a great grief to the loser. Thus Joseph knew what a humiliation it would be to his brothers if they were to learn that the lord before whom they were bowing "with their faces to the ground" was Joseph, whom they had ridiculed when he had told them of his dream that they would all bow down to him someday. It was in order to spare them this humiliation that Joseph did not make himself known to them immediately.

Scripture relates this fact in praise of the righteous Joseph. Another person in Joseph's position would have taken full advantage of this opportunity to have his revenge, to make the enemy truly feel his defeat. But Joseph did the opposite. When his brothers bowed down to him, he recognized them immediately, but he made himself a stranger to them in order to spare them the shame of defeat.

—*Kedushat Levi*

*   *   *   *

"... and (Joseph) *said to them: 'You are spies ...'* " (Gen. 42:9)

Of all crimes, why did Joseph accuse his brothers of espionage?

In order to prevent their making inquiries concerning the whereabouts of their brother Joseph. Joseph was afraid that his brothers, knowing that he had been sold into Egypt, might want to search for him, and particularly, he feared that they might note a resemblance between him and their brother Joseph as they remembered him. By accusing them of being spies, he effectively

81

barred all of Egypt's sources of information to them, for people suspected of espionage would not dare make inquiries about the ruler of the land to which they have come as strangers.

—*Rabbi Abraham Moshe of Przysucha*

* * * *

(Joseph said to his brothers) *"Do this, and live, for I fear God ..."* (Genesis 42:18)

Why should Joseph have boasted that he feared God?

In order to instill the fear of the Lord into his brothers so that they might be led to repent. When he told them that he feared God, they were gripped by fear and soon cried out: "We are truly guilty concerning our brother" (Verse 21.)

—*MaHaRaM of Amshinov*

* * * *

"And they said to one another: 'We are truly guilty concerning our brother, in that we saw the distress of his soul, when he besought us and we would not hear ..." (Genesis 42:21)

True, we did not commit a sin by selling Joseph, because that was his rightful due, but when he begged us to have compassion on him, we should have had mercy on him and we failed to do so.

—*Commentaries of Sforno and Malbim*

* * * *

"... therefore has this distress come upon us." (Gen. 42:22)

This punishment is retaliation. We wanted to murder Joseph because we knew that he would be the ancestor of sinful Jeroboam I* and we judged him by his descendants. Now we, too, are being judged by our descendants. Because our descendants will be spies in the wilderness, we are accused of being spies ourselves.

—*Melo HaOmer*

* * * *

---

* King of Israel.

82

(Jacob said to his sons) *"And (may) God Almighty give you mercy before the man . . ."* (Gen. 43:14)

According to the Sages (Sabbath 151) he who has pity on his fellow-creatures will find that Heaven will have pity on him in turn.

Jacob said to his sons:

"May God put mercy into your hearts so that you may have mercy on others, *before the man,* even before the Lord will cause the man to have mercy on you. This will insure the release of your other brother and of Benjamin, for if you yourselves will have mercy on your fellow-creatures, you, too, will receive mercy from heaven." —*Imrei Shofar*

* * * *

"And Joseph made haste, for his pity was deeply moved toward his brother . . . and he entered into his chamber and wept there . . . and he controlled himself and said: 'Set on bread.'" (Genesis 43:30-31)

Joseph symbolizes the righteous of future generations who would be moved with pity for the Jews because of their long and arduous exile which appears to stretch on and on without end. *And he entered into his chamber and wept there:* He forced his way into the secret chambers of the Lord and wept there. But there he learned that the time has not yet come for redemption, hence *he controlled himself,* for he was not permitted to hasten the end of the exile, *and said: Set on bread:* He prayed that, whatever their fate, the people of Israel might be given bread, at least, a modest living so that they might be able to endure the sufferings of their long exile. —*Tifereth Shlomo*

* * * *

"And portions were taken to (the brothers) *from before him, but Benjamin's portion was five times as much as any of theirs. And they drank and were merry with him."* (Genesis 43:34)

From the day they had sold Joseph they had not drunk wine . . . but on that day they drank wine.

—*Rashi*

They still did not know that the Egyptian lord before them was their brother Joseph. Therefore Joseph was still lost to them. Why, then, should they have drunk wine on that day?

They saw that Benjamin had received larger portions of food than they, and yet they were not jealous of him. Hence they realized that they had already ridded themselves of the sin of envy (*"and his brothers envied him . . ."* — Gen. 37:11) which had led them to sell Joseph into slavery, and consequently they felt that they might drink wine again.

—*Kav Hen*

The brothers were afraid that if they would not drink the wine, Joseph would accuse them again of being spies, refusing strong drink in order not to be led to divulge the secret information they had gathered.

—*Kehilat Yitzhak*

* * * *

Haphtarah MiKetz (I Kings 3:15 — 4:1)

"Then the King (Solomon) *said: 'The one says: This is my son that lives, and thy son is the dead. And the other says: No, thy son is the dead and my son is the living.' "* (I Kings 3:23)

King Solomon did not need to threaten to divide the living child in two to decide which mother had told the truth. He could discern the truth from the arguments advanced by the two women before him.

The first woman had said: *"This* is my son that lives." The other woman did not use the word "this" in reference to the living child and first spoke of the dead boy.

The woman who lied did not really want to be given the living child, for she had no desire to go through the troubles of raising a child which really was not hers at all. She was driven to her lie only by envy, not wanting the other woman to have a living

84

child. Thus, she actually did not substitute one child for the other, for she had no desire to take the living child to herself. All she sought to do was to come before the king and to tell him that the other woman had exchanged the children, giving her the dead child which she had murdered and taking the living child for herself. Thus the principal purpose of the untruthful woman was not to prove that the living child was hers, but to show that the dead child belonged to the other woman. The true mother of the living child, by contrast, clung to the living child, wanting not so much to prove that the dead child was the other woman's as to demonstrate that the living child was her own child.

Wise man that he was, King Solomon interpreted the testimony of the disputing parties as follows:

"The one woman says: *'This is my son that lives.'* She is holding the living child and points to it, saying: *'This* is my son that lives.' Her main point is to prove that this living child is indeed hers. The other woman, by contrast, begins her testimony with the statement: *'No, thy son is the dead,'* showing clearly that it is her main intention to prove that the dead child belongs to the other party. She does not want the woman to have a living child, but neither would *she* want to keep the living child if it were to be awarded to her . . ."

From this testimony of the two disputing parties it was clear to Solomon which of the women was the mother of the living child. It was only in order to make his verdict more plausible to the world that he commanded a sword to be brought with which to divide the living child into two parts. At this point, of course, the true mother of the living child, terrified lest her son lose his life, was willing to cede her child to the other woman, and the other woman, who was not at all concerned about the child's well-being, insisted that *'it shall be neither mine nor thine; divide it.'*

85

In this manner did King Solomon cause the others to behold the truth which he had already discerned through the testimony of the two women.

—Kokhav MiYaakov

* * * *

Weekly Portion of VaYiggash (Genesis 44:18 — 47:27)

"Then Judah came near to (Joseph) *and said: . . ."* (Gen. 44:18)

What argument could Judah now have used against Joseph? Had he himself not pronounced his own sentence, saying: *"Behold, we are my lord's bondmen, both we and also he in whose hand the cup is found"* (Gen. 44:16)? And Joseph had been kind enough to commute the sentence, saying: *"Far be it from me that I should do so; the man in whose hand the goblet is found shall be my bondman, but as for you, get up in peace to your father"* (Gen. 44:17). Why, then, should Judah now turn on Joseph in anger?

At first, Judah had believed that he and his brothers were about to receive their just punishment for having sold Joseph into slavery; namely, that they would be taken as slaves themselves. Therefore he had said: "What shall we say to my lord? What shall we speak? Or how shall we clear ourselves? God has found out the iniquity of thy servants" (Gen. 44:16), the iniquity being the sale of Joseph.

But now when Judah heard that Joseph was willing to let them all go free and wanted only Benjamin as a slave, he knew that this could not be a punishment for the sale of Joseph, for Benjamin had had no part in that deed. Therefore Judah was convinced that they were being punished on a false accusation, and he lashed out at Joseph in anger.

—R. Moses ben Hayyim Alshekh (1507-1600)

* * * *

". . . O my lord, let thy servant, I pray thee, speak a word in my lord's ears, and let not thy anger burn against thy servants, for thou

86

art even as Pharaoh." (Genesis 44:18)

> *"For thou are even as Pharaoh"* — "In my sight, thou art
> as important as the king himself." But a Midrashic explana-
> tion is as follows: "Thou wilt ultimately be stricken with
> leprosy for detaining Benjamin even as (thy ancestor)
> Pharaoh was stricken because he detained Sarah for one
> night." Another explanation: "Just as Pharaoh issues de-
> crees and then fails to carry them out, makes promises and
> then fails to fulfill them, so doest thou."
>
> —*Rashi*

Judah was an astute diplomat. The words he addressed to
Joseph — "for thou art even as Pharaoh" could be interpreted in
various ways. They could be taken as words of respect, meaning:
"Thou art as important in my eyes as Pharaoh himself." Or they
could be construed as a threat: "Thou wilt be stricken with leprosy just like that other Pharaoh before thee." Or else they could
be interpreted as an insult: "Just as Pharaoh issues decrees and
then fails to carry them out, so thou, too, art undependable."

Judah had in mind all three of these meanings, and it is as
if he had said to Joseph: "Interpret my words in any way thou
choosest, for all the interpretations would be equally correct."

—*Rabbi J. L. Graubart, Toronto*

* * * *

(Judah said to Joseph) *"My lord asked his servants, saying: 'Have
you a father . . .?'"* (Genesis 44:19)

You keep insisting, my lord, that the goblet is so precious to
you because "a man such as I will indeed divine" (Gen. 44:15).
If it is indeed true that the goblet tells you everything, why ask
me so many questions, unless the whole story is a lie and your
aim is simply to make false charges against us?

—*Mishna De R. Eliezer*

* * * *

"For how shall I go up to my father if the lad is not with me . . ."
(Genesis 44:34)

Let every Jew ask himself: "How will I be able, when the time comes, to appear before my Father in Heaven without being able to account for the years of my youth before Him?"

It therefore behooves us to make wise use of the years of our youth instead of squandering them in idleness and folly.

Then, too, let each Jewish father ask himself: "How will I be able to come before my Father in Heaven if my young children are not with me, if I have allowed them to drift away from me by letting them receive an education not in keeping with the traditions of Judaism?"   —*Commentators*

*   *   *   *

"And Joseph said to his brothers: 'I am Joseph. Is my father still alive?' And his brothers could not answer him, because they were frightened in his presence." (Genesis 45:3)

Abba Bar Delah, the Priest, said: "Woe to us because of the day of judgment and woe to us because of the day of rebuke. If the brothers of Joseph could not withstand the rebuke of the smallest in their family, what will become of us when the Lord will rebuke each of us according to his character?"

We are told that the brothers were badly frightened when Joseph made himself known to them. How could Joseph's words be construed as a rebuke to his brothers?

Actually the Hebrew term *tochacha* ("rebuke") implies the act of convincing or persuasion; i.e. of causing the person to whom the reproof is addressed to realize on his own that he has done wrong.

This is exactly what Joseph did when he made himself known to his brothers. By recalling to them the words they themselves had spoken, he convinced them that they had sinned. Judah had wanted to waken compassion in Joseph for his aged father, pleading that the old man would die of grief if Benjamin were not to return to him.

With this in mind, Joseph now said: "*I am Joseph,* the brother whom you sold into slavery. Is my father still alive? If it did not occur to you when you sold me into slavery that it would kill my father, why are you so worried about him now? If he managed to withstand the terrible grief you caused him when you took me away from him, he certainly will be able to survive even the loss of Benjamin."

Thus Joseph refuted the arguments of his brothers with their own words. Therein lay his rebuke and this is the reason why the brothers became so frightened that they were unable to answer him.

A similar rebuke will be administered to all men in days to come, and by none other than God Himself. Judgment Day, when all mankind will be judged, will also be a "Day of Rebuke" in which the Heavenly Judge will cause man to realize the wickedness of his ways.

"When you failed to give to charity," man will be told, "you pleaded the excuse that you had difficulties making ends meet. But if this was indeed so, how is it that you had enough money to spend on amusements and pleasures?"

In this manner will each man be reprimmanded "in accordance with his own deeds." God will reveal to him things hidden deep within himself, and then it will not be easy for him to find an excuse for his past conduct.

—*Bet Ha Levi*

*   *   *   *

"Hasten and go up to my father and tell him: 'Thus says thy son Joseph: God has made me lord of all Egypt . . .'" (Gen. 45:9)

Why should that have been such good news for Jacob?

The Hebrew *somani* ("has made me") may be rendered as *som ani* ("I have put"). Thus the message which Joseph actually sought to convey to his aged father was not that he, Joseph, had come to great power but that "I put the Lord over all of Egypt," that he, Joseph, had become the instrument to spread the ways of God so that God would become master of Egypt and over all the world.

—*The Rabbi of Rizhun*

* * * *

"*And* (Joseph) *fell upon his brother Benjamin's neck, and wept, and Benjamin wept upon his neck.*" (Genesis 45:14)

> *And he wept* — Joseph wept for the two Temples which were to be in the territory of the Tribe of Benjamin and would ultimately be laid in ruins, and Benjamin wept for the Tabernacle of Shilo which was to be in the territory of the Tribe of Joseph and would ultimately be destroyed.
>
> —*Rashi*

Why should the two brothers have wept at this hour of rejoicing, and why should each have wept over the other's misfortune rather than over his own?

Because they were both aware of the tragic consequences of hatred without just cause. We know that it was this evil of causeless hatred that bought about the destruction of the two Holy Temples of Jerusalem. When Joseph and Benjamin were reunited, they recalled that their separation had come about because of the causeless hatred of their brothers. Being endowed with prophetic vision, the two men thought of the calamities which would befall their descendants in days to come because of the same sin that had caused their own distress, and therefore thcy both wept.

Now the remedy for hatred without just cause is to strengthen the bonds of mutual affection to such an extent that the other's sorrow should cause one more pain than one's own. That was the reason why Joseph and Benjamin each wept over the calamity that was to befall the descendants of the other. Benjamin knew that the First Temple, which was to stand in the territory of his descendants, could not be built unless the Sanctuary in the territory of the Tribe of Joseph would first be destroyed. Yet he wept at the thought, for he would rather not have the Temples built in his tribal territory than to have the Sanctuary in the tribal land of Joseph be destroyed.

Such a love is great enough to act as a remedy for causeless hatred.
—*The Rabbi of Kazimir*

* * * *

"And to his father he sent . . . ten asses laden with the good things of Egypt . . ." (Genesis 45:23)

He sent him the old wine which old people like very much.
—*Rashi*

What was Joseph's purpose in sending this gift of wine to his aged father?

The gift was to set his father's mind at ease, conveying to his father in allegorical terms the message that, while to all outer appearances, he, Joseph, had adopted new ways, dressing and behaving like an Egyptian prince, he had not changed in mind and spirit. The outer trappings were new, but deep within his heart and soul, Joseph had maintained intact the tradition he had received from his father Jacob. (Cf. ". . . a new pitcher can be full of old wine" — *Ethics of the Fathers 4:27*).

All things that grow old spoil and become useless, except wine, which improves with age. Hence a gift of old wine conveys a message of encouragement to old people, reminding them that in some cases, old age can be a highly desirable quality.
—*Anon.*

One must remember, however, that wine improves with age only if it was good when it was new. If it was diluted with water when it was new, age only succeeds in turning it sour.

Similarly, whether or not old age improves a man depends on what he was like when he was young.
—*Rabbi Shelomo Alter*

* * * *

". . . and (Joseph) *fell on* (Jacob's) *neck . . ."* (Genesis 46:29)
> But Jacob did not fall on Joseph's neck, nor did he kiss
> him. According to our Rabbis, the reason was that he was
> reciting the *Shema.*   —*Rashi*

It is the way of the righteous that when they have the urge
to demonstrate affection for a dear one, they sink all their emotions into love for God. Thus, when Jacob first saw Joseph, and
his heart was filled with love for his favorite son from whom he
had been parted for so many years, he restrained his emotions
and, turning all his love to God, he recited the *Shema* and gave
all his thoughts to the commandment "and thou shalt love the
Lord thy God."

> —*Gur Aryeh, by Rabbi Judah Loew ben Bezalel,*
> *the MaHaRaL*

Jacob did not kiss Joseph at their reunion because he first
wanted to find out whether Joseph still was as he had been before,
and whether the corruption that was rife in Egypt had not led
him astray from the right path.

Whence did Jacob derive the strength to put aside his love
for his son and not to embrace him until he was sure that Joseph
was still walking in the ways of the Lord? From the *Shema,*
where it is written: "And thou shalt love the Lord thy God with
all thy heart, with all thy soul and with all thy might."

The love of God must take precedence over all other love,
and indeed, man must devote all his heart and all his soul to it.

When Jacob put aside his love for his son because he was not
yet certain whether Joseph was worthy of his affection, he was
only acting in the spirit of the declaration of faith and love of
God found in the *Shema.*   —*Avnei Ezel*

*   *   *   *

*"And Joseph made it a statute concerning the land of Egypt . . . that
Pharaoh should have the fifth; only the land of the priests alone did
not become Pharaoh's"* (Genesis 47:26)

Scripture relates this in order to teach the Children of Israel
that they must render gifts and tithes to the priests and Levites so
that the latter might be free to devote all their time to the worship
of the Lord. If even the Egyptians did not object to their pagan
priests' receiving their food from the nation's larders even at the
time of direst famine, it surely behooves the Children of Israel to
perform the same service willingly for their own priests who worship the true God.

—Don Isaac Abarbanel

*   *   *   *

Haphtarah VaYiggash (Ezekiel 37:15-28)

"And My servant David shall be king over them . . ." (Ezekiel 37:24)

In days to come all the Children of Israel will be moved to
repentance for their past sins so that they will be completely
cleansed of evil. But there will be some who will be ashamed to
repent because they know that they have sinned greatly and
often. At that time King David will be their guide and inspiration, teaching them that repentance can accomplish all things, as
the Sages put it: "David was considered worthy to perform this
deed only in order to teach the many how to repent."

—Ahavat Yonathan

*   *   *   *

Weekly Portion of VaYehi (Genesis 47:28 — 50:26)

"And Jacob lived in the land of Egypt . . ." (Genesis 47:28)

Why is this portion closed? Because Jacob wanted to reveal
to his sons the date of the end of days but his vision was
closed from him.

—Rashi

Why should Jacob have wanted to reveal the date of the end
of days to his sons?

Because exile is easier to bear if one knows in advance when
it will end. But God wanted Israel's exile to be difficult, and therefore He closed Jacob's vision from him so that the Children of

Israel should not learn the date of their final redemption.

—*Rabbi Simcha Bunim of Przysucha*

* * * *

(Jacob said to Joseph) *". . . deal kindly with me; do not bury me, I pray thee, in Egypt."* (Genesis 47:29)

The mercy shown to the dead is true mercy.

—*Rashi*

When dealing kindly with a person in life, one cannot know whether it was truly kindness, for many times that which one thinks is an act of mercy and kindness results in harm. But the mercy one shows to the dead is always true mercy because this is loving-kindness which the dead truly require and it therefore cannot possibly result in harm or evil.   —*Ohel Yaakov*

Hesed Shel Emeth — "True Mercy", the acts of mercy shown to the dead.

The word *Emeth* (truth) contains the letters *Aleph, Mem* and *Tav,* which are the initials of the Hebrew words *aron* (coffin) *mitah* (bier) and *tachrichin* (shrouds). These symbolize the acts of loving service which we must perform for the dead.

—*Midrash Talpioth*

* * * *

"And one told Jacob and said: 'Behold, thy son Joseph comes to thee.' And Jacob strengthened himself and sat upon the bed." (Genesis 48:2)

It is stated in Tractate Nedarim 39 that "anyone who visits a sick contemporary takes away one-sixtieth of his illness."

Now although Joseph was Jacob's son, he was considered his contemporary, for it is written that God had said: "All that I will show to Jacob I will also show to Joseph" (Rashi to Gen. 37:2). Therefore when Joseph came to visit Jacob, Jacob's illness was diminished by one-sixtieth and Jacob became strong enough to sit up on his bed.

—*Commentaries of Be'er Mayim Hayyim
and Alshekh HaKadosh*

* * * *

"And as for me, when I came from Paddan, Rachel died, to my sorrow . . ." (Genesis 48:7)

Why did Jacob speak to Joseph of Rachel now?

He wanted to admonish Joseph to fulfill the oath which he had sworn to him; i.e. that he would not bury him in Egypt. According to the Sages, Rachel had died because Jacob had sinned by neglecting to fulfill the vow he had taken.

—Meshekh Hakhmah

* * * *

"And Israel stretched out his right hand and laid it upon Ephraim's head . . . and his left hand upon Menasseh's head, guiding his hands wittingly, for Manasseh was the first-born." (Genesis 48:14)

He filled his hands with wisdom.

—Targum

Jacob had trained his limbs to such an extent that they were incapable of acting contrary to the will of God. Thus his hands placed themselves in this reverse position (left hand on the first-born and right hand on the younger) of their own accord, because it had been the will of God.

—Likutei Megodim

* * * *

"And he blessed Joseph and said . . ." (Genesis 48:15)

The blessing that follows was actually addressed not to Joseph but only to Joseph's two sons. Why, then, does Scripture say that Jacob blessed Joseph?

In order to show that there is no greater blessing for a father than the wish that his children should take after him and become good people. Hence Jacob's blessing to Manasseh and Ephraim "The angel who has redeemed me from all evil bless the lads and let my name be named in them and the name of my fathers, Abraham and Isaac" (Verse 16) is the greatest blessing Joseph, their father, could possibly have received.

—Rabbi Isaiah Horowitz, after Nachmanides

* * * *

95

"... and let them grow into a multitude in the midst of the earth." (Genesis 48:16)

Alternative rendering: *"... and let them multiply like fish in the midst of the land."*

There is no statement in the Scriptures to imply that the tribes of Ephraim and Manasseh should have been greater in numbers than any of the other tribes of Israel.

The blessing which Jacob gave to his two grandsons was to come true only "in the midst of the land," meaning the Land of Israel. It was only after their arrival in the Promised Land that they were to multiply like the fish in the sea. We know that this blessing did indeed come true, for Scripture (Joshua 17:14) tells us that even before the Land of Israel was apportioned among the various tribes, "the children of Joseph spoke to Joshua, saying: 'Why hast thou given me but one lot and one part for an inheritance, seeing I am a great people, forasmuch as the Lord has blessed me thus?' " And Joshua answered them: "If thou art a great people, get thee up to the forest and cut down for thyself there ..." (Joshua 17:15).

According to Baba Kamma 148, Joshua had commanded them to go into the woods so that the Evil Eye should not find them and do them harm, for it was nothing short of a miracle that the children of Joseph should have multiplied so greatly in so short a period.

—Adereth Eliyahu

* * * *

"By thee shall Israel bless, saying:'May God make thee as Ephraim and Manasseh ...'" (Genesis 48:20)

Why should Jacob have wanted all his descendants to bless their children with the example of Ephraim and Manasseh rather than with that of some other two of the Tribes of Israel?

Because the two young sons of Joseph had conducted them-

selves in accordance with the fundamental law of the Torah;
namely, that one should neither consider oneself greater than
another nor envy another. Even though Jacob had set Ephraim,
the younger son, before Manasseh, the first-born, Ephraim did
not become arrogant and Manasseh did not become jealous. Seeing this, Jacob expressed the hope that all the Children of Israel
would be like Ephraim and Manasseh, free of arrogance and envy.

—Igra DeKallah

*   *   *   *

"And Israel said to Joseph ... Moreover, I have given to thee one
portion above thy brothers, which I took out of the hand of the
Amorite with my sword and with my bow." (Genesis 48:22)

> *Which I took out of the hand of the Amorite with my*
> *sword and with my bow* — With my prayer and with my
> will.

—Targum

Why is the "bow" likened to prayer? Because just as the more
one tautens the bow the further the arrow will fly, so, too, the more
one applies his mind to his prayer with true devotion, the further
and higher will it soar into the heavens.

—Rabbi Menahem Mendel of Kotzk

*   *   *   *

"Assemble and hear, O sons of Jacob, and hearken to Israel, your
father." (Genesis 49:2)

The Patriarch's actual name, which had been given to him at
birth, was Jacob. Hence every Jew, regardless of the manner in
which he conducts himself, is regarded as a "son of Jacob" by
virtue of his descent from Jacob and of his being part of the Jewish nation.

The name Israel, however, was not given to Jacob until much
later in life, when he had attained the high moral level that made
him worthy of it (*"For thou hast striven with God and with men*
and hast prevailed" — Gen. 22:29). For this reason this name,
when applied to the Jewish people as a whole, signifies the high

moral level of the community of Israel as the spiritual heirs of Jacob.

A similar thought was expressed by Jacob, by way of an introduction to his last words to his children: *"Assemble and hear, O sons of Jacob.* To begin with, you are to unite as children of Jacob, all sharing one descent and nationality. But mere nationality ties are not enough. You must also *hearken to Israel, your father.* Every gathering of Jews must have as its purpose to strengthen the spirit of Judaism, so that the "sons of Jacob" may hear the voice of Israel, their father and, together with him, proclaim that "the Lord, our God, is One."

—Avnei Ezel

* * * *

"Simeon and Levi are brethren; weapons of violence their kinship. Let my soul not come into their council . . . for in their anger they slew men and in their self-will they lamed oxen." (Genesis 49:6)

> *They slew men*: This refers to Hamor and the people of Shehem (Gen. 34:1-31). *And they lamed an ox*: They wanted to exterminate Joseph. (Joseph is likened to a bullock in Deut. 33:17).
>
> *—Rashi*

What is the connection between the incident involving Hamor and Shehem and the sale of Joseph?

Jacob said to his sons Simeon and Levi: "I saw your anger when your sister was dishonored by Hamor and Shehem. At that time I did not know whether your wrath was motivated by sacred zeal or simply by lust for revenge and murder. I therefore bided my time until another occasion should arise for me to learn your true motivation. But then I saw how you dealt with your brother Joseph and that you would have found it an easy thing to remove him from this world. At that time I realized that in the case of Hamor and Shehem, too, you had been moved to action not by honest zeal but merely by base anger."

—Commentators

* * * *

98

"Judah ... stooped down, he couched as a lion ..." (Gen. 49:9)

Judah's outstanding quality is that even if he should fall and be bowed low, he still remains as firm and fearless as a lion. He does not succumb to despair, but readily admits his failure. By virtue of his repentance, he speedily rises again, even as Judah, the son of Jacob, was honest enough to admit his sin with his daughter-in-law Tamar (Gen. 38) and as a result Perez, one of the twins born of this relationship, became the forebear of the House of David from whom the Messiah will be descended.

—Rabbi Isaac Meir Alter

*   *   *   *

"For (Issachar) *saw a resting place, that it was good, and the land that it was pleasant, and he bowed his shoulder to bear ..."* (Gen. 49:15)

For he saw a resting place, that it was good: How can one attain true peace and rest? By *bowing his shoulder to bear;* i.e. by freely submitting to all that one is given to bear. Once one has acquired patience, one has also attained true peace.

—A Villager, quoted by Rabbi Isaac of Warka

*   *   *   *

Said the Sages: "If you do not want to suffer, then bear willingly whatever suffering you are given and you will not suffer. Accept and bear your sufferings, for if you will not, you will only suffer more."

*   *   *   *

"... and this is what their father spoke to them and blessed them, every one according to his blessing he blessed them." (Gen. 49:28)

Even Simeon and Levi received a blessing. The fact that Jacob cursed their anger and their wrath (Gen. 49:7) is a blessing in itself, for "no curse cleaves to him who is blessed." The circumstance that Jacob eradicated their two great shortcomings is actually the greatest blessing Simeon and Levi could have received.

—Kol Simcha

*   *   *   *

99

"And (the brothers) *sent a message to Joseph, saying . . . 'And now, we pray thee, forgive the transgression of the servants of the God of thy father . . .' "* (Genesis 50:16-17)

Although thy father dies, his God still lives.

—*Rashi*

The brothers believed that Joseph had refrained from punishing them while their father was still alive because he had not wanted to cause him grief. They therefore sent word to Joseph as follows: "Thy father is dead, but his God is still alive. If thou didst not want to cause thy father grief, thou certainly canst not grieve the Master of the Universe, Who is grieved by any suffering that comes to a son of Jacob."

—*Ateret Zvi*

* * * *

"And Joseph said to them: 'Fear not, for am I in the place of God? And as for me, you meant evil against me but God meant it for good . . .' " (Genesis 50:19-20)

Joseph said to his brothers: "Seeing that the evil you did to me resulted in a good thing, I would have to do to you, in return, such evil as would also eventually result in good. But what human being is there who would be able to prove what evil would result in good? Only God can do that, and *am I in the place of God?*"

—*Attributed to the Rabbi of Ostrowicze*

* * * *

Haftarah VaYehi (I Kings 2:1-12)

(David said to Solomon) *"I go the way of all the earth; be thou strong, therefore, and show thyself a man."* (1 Kings 2:2)

This is David's last will and testament, his charge to Solomon, his son and successor.

David must always say to himself: "I go the way of all the

100

earth;" he must always be aware of the end that awaits all men. "Then, surely," David says to his son, "thou wilt be strong and show thyself a man. Thou wilt be able to control thy evil inclination."

—*Zavore Shalal*

*   *   *   *

"But show kindness to the sons of Barzillai the Gileadite . . . for so they drew near to me when I fled from Absalom thy brother." (I Kings 50:7)

If the sons of Barzillai had dealt kindly with David, would it not have been Solomon's duty, rather than an act of special kindness on his part, to repay them in kind?

No, because the sons of Barzillai were only doing their duty.

According to the law, even a wealthy landowner, if he is on a journey and in need of food, is entitled to the gleanings from the corners of the fields, which are reserved for the poor. He has no obligation to give the field's owner anything in return because at the time he passed that field he was, to all intents and purposes, a hungry man in need of charity (Mishna Peah 5).

In the same manner, David in flight from Absalom had been entitled to benefit by the laws applicable to the poor. Hence the sons of Barzillai had the obligation to give him charity and were not deserving of a special reward for it. Therefore if Solomon repaid them for their act of charity, it would be a gesture of "kindness" and not the fulfillment of an obligation on the part of Solomon.

—*Rabbi Hayyim Joseph David Azulai*

*   *   *   *

WELLSPRINGS OF TORAH

EXODUS

EXODUS

שמות

Weekly Portion of Shemoth (Exodus 1:1-6:1)

"Now these are the names of the sons of Israel . . ." (Exodus 1:1)
To tell us that they are compared to the stars.

—*Rashi*

We Jews must know that the Lord loves us, and that even
as He made the stars to shine in the dark night. so He created the
Jewish people to spread His light to the darkest and lowliest
places on earth.

—*Sefat Emet*

* * * *

". . . every man came with his household . . ." (Exodus 1:1)

As a rule, when a man moves from a pious little village into
the big city where irreligion and immorality are rampant, he
himself, having been raised in the ways of Judaism from childhood, may remain unchanged, but his children will take to the
ways of the city and cast off their religion.

Scripture makes it a point to tell us that this was not so
in the case of the children of our patriarch Jacob. They had left
Canaan where they had led a pious and godly life and settled in
the unclean and godless land of Egypt. Yet they remained "every
man with his household." Their home life did not change and
the children remained close to the ways of their fathers and
mothers.

—*HaDrash VeHaEyun*

* * * *

"Now there arose a new king over Egypt who did not know Joseph."
(Exodus 1:8)

Had the new king known Joseph, his history and his past,
he would have known that all the attempts made to harm Joseph
— whether by his brothers or by Potiphar — actually led to his

rise to fame and good fortune, and he would have been afraid to oppress Joseph's descendants, the Hebrews, lest, by oppressing them, he would hasten their redemption and liberation.

—*Imrei Esh*

* * * *

"And it came to pass, because the midwives feared God, that he made them houses." (Exodus 1:21)

The pronoun "he" refers not to God but to Pharaoh. When Pharaoh saw that the midwives feared God, he realized that if they were to be permitted to go to the homes of the Hebrew mothers to deliver their babies, they would not carry out his order to kill all the male infants born of Hebrews. For this reason he set up maternity homes where all Hebrew mothers had to go to give birth. In this manner he could be sure that his orders would be carried out.

—*Malbim*

* * * *

"And Pharaoh charged all his people, saying: 'Every son that is born you shall throw into the river...'" (Exodus 1:22)

The Targum Onkelos renders this command as "Every son that is born *to Jewish people* you shall throw into the river."

Pharaoh purposely stated his decree in general terms, commanding that every child born in Egypt should be thrown into the river, for it would hardly have been proper for so highly civilized a nation as Egypt to discriminate so openly against the Hebrews. But the officials charged with the enforcement of the law had been told in confidence that it was applicable to Hebrew infants only.

—*Sihot Tzaddikim*

* * * *

"...and she put the child therein, and laid it in the flags by the river's edge." (Exodus 2:3)

Moses was born on the seventh day of Adar and his mother hid him for a period of three months (*Exodus 2:2*). Hence the day on which the infant Moses was placed into the river was the seventh day of Sivan. It was on the seventh of Sivan, too, that many years later, Moses was to receive the Law on Mount Sinai, and it was the merit of this great future task that brought about his miraculous rescue in infancy.

—Gemara, Tractate Sotah

* * * *

According to Rabbi Mordecai Benet (1753-1829) the Jewish custom to decorate the home on Shevuot (the festival commemorating the Giving of the Law) with green plants such as grow on river banks recalls the flags among which, that seventh day of Sivan, Yocheved laid the basket bearing her infant son.

* * * *

"And (Pharaoh's daughter) opened it, and saw it . . . and behold, a boy that was crying. And she . . . said: 'This is one of the Hebrews' children.' " (Exodus 2:6)

She did not hear him; she only *saw* him cry. This led her to realize that it must be a Hebrew infant, for only a Jew can weep without crying aloud.

—Rabbi Bunim of Otvotzk

* * * *

". . . and (Moses) saw an Egyptian smiting a Hebrew, one of his brethren. And he looked this way and that way, and when he saw that there was no man, he smote the Egyptian . . ." (Exod. 2:11-12)

With what did he slay him? According to one interpretation, he slew him with his bare fist. According to another interpretation, he slew him with a shovel, and still another interpretation has it that he slew him with the power of the Ineffable Name.

—Midrash

Some think that we can conquer our oppressors by mere main force. Others hold that we can overpower them with the tools we use for work. But the fact is that only with the help of the word of God and with faith in His Name can we overcome the many oppressors who smite us with their whips. Without the aid of the Ineffable Name, both the fist and the shovel are of no use.

—*Avnei Ezel*

* * * *

"*... And Moses feared and said: 'Surely the thing is known.'* " (Exodus 2:14)

At first, Moses did not understand why his people should suffer more than any other nation. But now, after his encounter with the two quarreling Hebrews (*2:13*), he knew the reason. In fact, seeing the slander and gossip that was rife among his people, he actually asked God (*3:11*) before the burning bush: "Who am I ... that I should bring forth the Children of Israel?" meaning "What merit do the Jews have to make them worthy of liberation?" This shows us that evil gossip, contention and slander nullify any merit a man might have.

—*Sefat Emet*

* * * *

"*And he said: 'Who made thee a ruler and judge over us?'* " (Exod. 2:14)

It is the way of wicked men that if someone comes and attempts to stop their evil conduct, they question his right and authority to do so and cry out: "Who appointed you a judge and authority over us?" But when it comes to fighting evil, each and every one of us has the right, and indeed the duty, to help all he can, for "in a place where there are no men, try thou to be a man."

—*Avnei Ezel*

* * * *

"*And* (the daughters of Jethro) *said: 'An Egyptian delivered us out of the hand of the shepherds ... and he said to his daughters: 'Where is he? ...'* " (Exodus 2:19-20)

—*Avnei Ezel*

Certainly, Jethro thought, a man who finds it in his heart to defend and to rescue people in distress cannot be an ordinary

108

Egyptian, even if he did look like one. It is really worth going out and looking at such an Egyptian.

—Avnei Ezel

*   *   *   *

"And God saw the Children of Israel, and God took cognizance of them (lit. "God knew them"). (Exodus 2:25)

God saw how the Children of Israel clung to their faith and how, despite the suffering and humiliation they had to endure, they had retained their Jewish traits, discarding neither their traditional dress nor their language. Therefore God "knew" them and resolved to deliver them.

—Attributed to a Tzaddik

*   *   *   *

"And (God) *said: . . . 'Put off thy shoes from thy feet, for the place on which thou standest is holy ground.' "* (Exodus 3:5)

As the shoe is to the foot, so the body is merely the outer garment of the human soul. Hence, in commanding Moses to remove his shoes, God meant to tell him: "If you wish to understand the ways of God and reach the level at which you will be able to behold the Revelation of God, you must first cast off the forces and urges of the body which conceal the soul within. Only then will you be able to attain to holiness."

—Malbim

*   *   *   *

"And Moses said to God: 'Who am I, that I should go to Pharaoh . . .' And He said: 'Certainly I will be with thee, and this shall be the token for thee, that I have sent thee. When thou hast brought forth the people out of Egypt, you shall serve God upon this mountain.' " (Exodus 3:11-12)

Moses, humble man that he was, did not consider himself, worthy of being the deliverer of the Jewish people and asked: "Who am I to do all this?"

Thereupon the Lord answered him that his very question was proof of his fitness for the task. *"And this —* this very question of yours: 'Who am I to do all this?' *shall be the token for thee,* that I have chosen thee to perform this task."

The Lord calls only on those who do not think highly of themselves. Thus, of all the mountains, He chose lowly Mount Sinai as the place on which to give the Law to the Children of Israel, for while the higher mountains boasted of their height, Mount Sinai remained little in its own eyes. It was for this reason that the Lord told Moses: *"When thou hast brought forth the people out of Egypt, you shall serve God upon this mountain.* The fact that I will give thee the Law on this mountain, on this small and lowly mountain, rather than on the mighty Hermon or Tabor, should be a sign for thee as well, to show thee that because thou, too, hast remained lowly and humble in thy own eyes, thou art worthy of being the deliverer of thy people."

—*Avnei Ezel*

Among the worthy and noted disciples of the Rabbi of Lublin there were two brothers. One enjoyed great respect and many *Hassidim* flocked to his home, while the other never had any visitors come to seek his counsel. One day, this man enviously asked his popular brother: "We are both equal in learning and good deeds, and we have both studied under one master. Why, then, should all the *Hassidim* crowd around you while no one ever comes to me?"

"Believe me, dear brother," the other replied. "I have often asked myself the same question. Why, really, should they all come to me and not to you? But I think that the answer may be found in the questions we ask. I do not understand why all the *Hassidim* should come to *me* of all people for advice, and you do not understand why they do *not* turn to you. There you have the reason why the *Hassidim* come to me rather than to you."

* * * *

"And I will give this people favor in the sight of the Egyptians. And it shall come to pass that when you go, you shall not go empty." (Exodus 3:21)

He who does not go "empty," devoid of knowledge of the Law, will find favor even in the sight of his enemies. Even his enemies must respect him for "if the Lord is pleased with the conduct of a man even his enemies must make peace with him."

—*Imrei Kohen*

* * * *

"And the Lord said to him: 'What is that in thy hand?' And he said: 'A rod.' And He said: 'Cast it on the ground.' And he cast it on the ground and it became a serpent and Moses fled from before it. And the Lord said to Moses: 'Put out thy hand and take it by the tail . . .'" (Exodus 4:2-4)

The Lord asked Moses: *"What is that in thy hand?* What power hast thou in thy hand to wield as the leader of Israel?" And Moses replied: *"A rod,"* implying that he would lead Israel with the rod of stern discipline. But then the Lord explained to him that rigid discipline is not the right way. Such a method turns into an insidious serpent, as it were; the people resent it, and eventually revolt against their leader. It was only when Moses "fled from before it," when he abandoned the stern approach entirely and resolved to lead his people with humility alone that the Lord said to him: *"Put out thy hand and take it by the tail.* There will be times when it will become necessary for thee to make use of the rod, when kindness must be reinforced with discipline, for without some discipline, no leadership can endure."

For this reason the Torah, while commanding the rulers in Israel not to be arrogant ("that his heart be not lifted up above his brethren"—*Deut. 17:20*), insists that no ruler may give up any part of the honor due him, "so that his fear may be upon thee."

—*Pardes Yosef*

* * * *

". . . and he put forth his hand and laid hold of it . . ." (Exod. 4:4)

The serpent symbolizes the evil impulse which induces man to do wrong. The Torah teaches us to "lay hold" of that evil impulse and use its strength for the good of Judaism, as the Sages put it: *"And thou shalt love the Lord thy God with all thy heart —* that means, with both thy impulses — good and evil." The evil forces at work within man must be altered and used in the service of God. The same thought is stressed also in the Ethics of the Fathers (*4:11*): "Who is strong? He who subdues his (evil) impulse." A hero is one who has conquered his evil impulse and made it serve good purposes. —*Pardes Yosef*

* * * *

". . . and he put his hand into his bosom, and . . . behold, his hand was leprous, as white as snow." (Exodus 4:6)

Man was made to act and to achieve, to work and to create. He who is negligent and too indolent to do what he should is as if he had wrought actual destruction ("he who is slack in his work is a brother to him who destroys"), for indolence bears the seeds of death and destruction. If the hand lies hidden "in the bosom" and does nothing, the result is leprosy, which is tantamount to death. But as soon as the hand is removed from there so that it may work and create, it will be restored to life, *"and it was turned again as his other flesh."* (*Exodus 4:7*)

—*Malbim*

* * * *

"And Moses said . . . 'I am slow of speech and of a slow tongue.'" (Exodus 4:10)

Moses was created a stammerer to make it known that the influence he wielded and the fact that he gave the Law to the Jewish people were not due to any talent of his but only to the spirit of prophetic vision with which he was endowed, for "the *Shekhina* spoke from within his throat."

—*RaN*

* * * *

"... Thus says the Lord: Israel is My son, My first-born." (Exodus 4:22)

The first-born son is given the distinction of receiving a double share of his father's inheritance since he was the son who first made him a father. Since the people of Israel is that nation which, by proclaiming the belief in God, in His Providence and in His almighty power, first caused God to be acknowledged as the Father of the Universe, it, too, can lay claim to the title and privileges of a "first-born son."

—*Meshekh Hakhmah*

*   *   *   *

"And it came to pass on the way at the lodging place that the Lord met (Moses) *and sought to kill him."* (Exodus 4:25)

According to the Sages, God intended to condemn Moses to death because, in his zeal immediately to carry out God's command that he go to Egypt, he had neglected to circumcise his infant son. We see, then, that, because of the unintentional neglect of only one Divine commandment, the deliverer of the Jewish people might have died and the whole plan of Israel's redemption come to naught. This should teach us that any work on behalf of the redemption of the people of Israel must be rooted in the strict observance of all the commandments of the Torah. For any plan of redemption, even that of the Redeemer himself, may be nullified by the neglect of no more then one commandment of the Torah.

—*Musarist Writings*

*   *   *   *

(Pharaoh commanded the taskmasters) *"You shall no longer give the people straw to make brick . . ."* (Exodus 5:7)

Why should Pharaoh have forbidden his taskmasters to supply the Hebrew slaves with the straw to make their bricks? If he wanted to make the work more difficult for them, could he not simply have required the Hebrews to produce greater quantities of bricks?

The point was that Pharaoh desired above all to embitter the lives of the Children of Israel. Knowing that worry and seemingly insurmountable problems were infinitely more harassing than even the hardest physical labor, he felt that the surest way to break the spirit of the Hebrews would be not to demand increased production from them but to tax them with the additional worry of how to procure the straw they needed for their work.

—*Rabbi Henoch of Alexander*

* * * *

(And Moses said to the Lord) *"Lord, wherefore hast Thou dealt ill with this people? Why is it that Thou hast sent me?"* (Exod. 5:22)

Rabbi Henoch of Alexander would use the following parable to explain this verse.

Once there was an ignorant villager who did not know how to prepare for the Passover Seder. In order to learn what had to be done, he told his wife to go to a neighbor, watch his preparations and then return home and tell him what she had seen. When the woman entered the neighbor's house, she came upon the neighbor beating his wife. She assumed that this was part of the preparations for the Seder. Afraid to report this to her husband, the woman did not go home but remained standing in the street. When she failed to return, her husband rushed out of the house in anger to look for her. Finding her walking up and down the street, he began to beat her mercilessly. "So you already know how to prepare the Passover Seder," the poor woman cried. "Why, then, did you have to send me to find out?"

In a similar vein, Moses asked of God: "Thou knewest well that Pharaoh would deal even more harshly with the people after my appearance before his throne. Why, then, didst Thou have to send me? If the people of Israel must be beaten before they can be redeemed, could that not have happened without my appearing before Pharaoh?"

* * * *

Haphtarah Shemoth (For Sephardim: *Jeremiah, Chapter 1 & 2*)

"But the Lord said to me: 'Say not, I am a child, for to whomever I will send thee, thou shalt go . . .'" (Jeremiah 1:7)

If a man arises and makes a statement in his own name he must be an acknowledged authority on his subject if he is to be heard. Age plays an important part here. A young person is not considered as important as an older man, and his words do not carry much weight. But if that person should speak not in his own name but as the messenger of a great and mighty king, it will not matter who he is. He will be heard whether he be young or old because the king whose messenger he is lends authority and importance to his words. Thus the Lord said to Jeremiah: *"To whomever I will send thee, thou shalt go as My messenger.* Therefore, *say not: 'I am a child'* for thy age is a matter of indifference. What thou thyself art is of no concern; what counts now is only Who is it that sends thee."

—*Malbim*

* * * *

". . . be not dismayed at them, lest I dismay thee before them." (Jeremiah 1:17)

If you remain strong and steadfast in the presence of an evil man, he will come to respect you. But if you should show dismay, if you should bend the knee and grovel before him, he will cease to respect you and tread upon you with his feet.

—*Anon.*

* * * *

(For Ashkenazim: *Isaiah 27:6-28:13 and 29:22,23*)

". . . For it is a people of no understanding; therefore He Who made them will not have compassion upon them . . ." (Isaiah 27:11)

From this verse the Sages deduce that "it is forbidden to

have compassion upon him who has no knowledge" (*Tractate Berakhot 33*).

Said Rabbi Isaac Meir Alter, the author of the treatise *Hiddushei HaRIM*: "A man of whom the Torah itself states that others may not have compassion on him is all the more pitiable. But how can we show our compassion, seeing that it is forbidden to have compassion on him? By imparting knowledge to him so that one may be permitted to have compassion on him."

* * * *

"And it shall come to pass in that day that a great horn shall be sounded; and they shall come who were lost in the land of Assyria and all those who were dispersed in the land of Egypt . . ." (Isaiah 17:13)

When the Messiah will come and gather all the people of Israel, all the lost and dispersed will return, those who were led astray by false, heretical views and ideas as well as those who were driven into exile because of their lusts and appetites which led them into corruption.

Assyria symbolizes godlessness and heresy, for Sennacherib, king of Assyria, worshipped his own strength and wisdom ("By the strength of my hand have I done it, and by my wisdom, for I am prudent" — *Isaiah 10:13*). Egypt betokens unbridled appetites and immorality.

This verse, then, implies that the great Return will include those who were "lost" on account of their godlessness (symbolized by Assyria) as well as those who were "dispersed" because of their immorality (represented by Egypt).

—*Avnei Ezel*

* * * *

"Whom shall one teach knowledge? And whom shall one make to understand the message? Those who are weaned from the milk, those who are drawn from the breasts?" (Isaiah 25:9)

The Sages say that since the destruction of the Temple the

gift of prophetic vision has been left to children and fools. When the Jews still dwelt in their own land, the gifts from heaven, both material and spiritual, went to the people and places truly worthy of receiving them. But since the Temple has been destroyed, this ceased to be so. Much rain is squandered on wastelands and spiritual inspiration, too, often does not come to the people who would be best fitted to receive it.

When the prophet says that knowledge and understanding will come to "those who are weaned from the milk," he means that they will not come to the people who would be able to put these qualities to the best use.

—Ahavat Yonathan

*   *   *   *

Weekly Portion of Va'Era (Exodus 6:2-9:35)
(God said to Moses)*". . . but by My Name YHVH I did not make Myself known to them."* (Exodus 6:3)

Alas for the lost who cannot be replaced.

—Rashi

The leaders of the Jewish community of a certain great city where few were learned in the Law were anxious to engage a certain great scholar to be their rabbi. Seeking to make the offer attractive to the sage, they told him that their community was entirely worthy of him. It was, they said, one of historic fame, for such great sages as Rabbi David ben Samuel Halevi (1586-1667), Abraham ben Hayyim (the author of the treatise *Mogen Abraham*) and Rabbi Akiba Eger were all buried in their city.

Eventually, however, the rabbi found out that Rabbi David ben Samuel Halevi was not buried in that city but in Lvov, that the grave of Rabbi Abraham ben Hayyim was in Kalisz and that the remains of Rabbi Akiba Eger lay in Posen.

"Why did you deceive me?" he demanded of the townsmen.

"Rabbi," they replied, "We did not deceive you. In Lvov there are still people who study the *Turei Zahav;* hence the author, Rabbi David ben Samuel Halevi, is not really buried there but still very much alive. In Kalisz, the Jews still pore over *Mogen Abraham;* hence its author, Rabbi Abraham ben Hayyim, too, cannot be said to be dead and buried. The same is true in Posen of the works of Rabbi Akiba Eger. But in our own city there is not even one man who studies any of the works of these great scholars, hence as far as we are concerned, they really are as dead and buried in this town."

This explains Rashi's statement: "Alas for the lost." Alas for those who have been so utterly lost that their words, thoughts and deeds have not been passed on to living heirs. They truly "cannot be replaced" and are indeed lost forever. But if a man has left disciples and spiritual heirs, even his death does not mean that we have lost him.

—*Shaar Bet Rabbim*

* * * *

"And moreover I have heard the groaning of the Children of Israel whom the Egyptians have enslaved . . ." (Exodus 6:5)

Said the Lord: "I have heard the groaning of the Children of Israel on account of their enslavement (*ma-avidim:* lit. "have enslaved"), for the Egyptians have enslaved not only their bodies but also their spirit. When the Children of Israel cried for help in their spiritual enslavement, the Lord had no other choice but to answer their plea for help.

—*Avnei Ezel*

* * * *

". . . and I will take you to Me as a people . . . and you shall know that I am the Lord . . ." (Exodus 6:7)

No human being can truly fathom the Divine, but the Jewish people can come to know the Lord through the light of the Torah and the commandments because "the Torah and the Holy One, blessed be He, are one." The fulfillment of God's promise to "take you to Me as a people," meaning that He will give them

118

the Torah, will make it possible for the Jewish people to "know that I am the Lord."

—*Kedushat Levi*

*   *   *   *

"*. . . and I will give it to you as a heritage . . .*" (Exodus 6:8)

The Hebrew term *morashah* for "heritage" occurs twice in the Five Books of Moses; in the above-cited verse in connection with the Land of Israel and again in Deut. 33:4 in connection with the Torah. ("The Torah which Moses commanded to us is a heritage of the community of Jacob.") This is to teach us that the heritage represented by the Land of Israel can remain ours only if we will conduct ourselves there in keeping with the statutes of the Torah. Without the Torah, the Land of Israel has no justification for survival, as it is written: "And He will give to them the lands of the nations *so that they may keep His statutes.*"

—*Yalkut Hadash*

*   *   *   *

(Moses said to the Lord) "*Behold, the Children of Israel have not hearkened unto me; how then shall Pharaoh hear me, who am of uncircumcised lips?*" (Exodus 6:11)

The Sages interpret the expression *avoda kasha* ("cruel bondage" — *Exodus 6:9*) to refer to idol worship, since the Hebrew word *avoda* — "work" or "bondage" can also denote "worship." They therefore interpret this expression as indicating that the Egyptians dragged the Israelites down to their paganism from which it is most difficult to break away. This, the Sages assert, was the reason why the Children of Israel could not, and did not hearken to the words of Moses.

If even the Israelites refused to listen to Moses for no other reason but that they had been seduced into idol worship, it stood to reason to expect that Pharaoh, who regarded himself as a divine being, certainly would not give him a hearing.

—*Torat Moshe*

*   *   *   *

As long as the Jews will refuse to listen to their leaders, the leaders will be ineffectual, because the leader derives all his power from the people in his charge. If the Children of Israel in Egypt would have listened to Moses, "his mouth would have been opened," he would have become articulate, and his words would have left an impression even on Pharaoh. But since the Children of Israel did not listen to him, Moses was "of uncircumcised lips" — he was unable to open his mouth to plead their cause effectively before Pharaoh.

—*Sefat Emet*

*　*　*　*

"And the Lord spoke to Moses and to Aaron, and gave them a charge to the Children of Israel . . ." (Exodus 6:13)

Even though the Children of Israel refused to listen, "for impatience of spirit and for cruel bondage" (*Exodus 6:9*), the Lord commanded Moses and Aaron to continue speaking to them. For the words of God must of necessity leave a profound impression; they may not take effect all at once, but eventually they must accomplish their purpose, for holy words can never be lost on man.

—*Sefat Emet*

*　*　*　*

"These are that Aaron and Moses to whom the Lord said . . . These are they who spoke to Pharaoh, King of Egypt . . . These are that Moses and Aaron." (Exodus 6:26-27)

Moses and Aaron were found worthy of attaining the highest level of holiness and of receiving the Divine gift of prophetic vision. And they remained on this high level ("that same Aaron and Moses") even after contact with so unclean a being as the heathen Pharaoh. Their holiness was so great that they could not be contaminated even by the corrupt atmosphere prevailing at the court of the King of Egypt.

—*Be'er Mayim Hayyim*

*　*　*　*

"When Pharaoh shall speak to you, saying: 'Show a wonder for you . . .'" (Exodus 7:9)

Why does the text not read, "Show a wonder *for them?*"

Rabbi Elimelekh of Lizensk (1717-1786) explained that this turn of speech shows the difference between false miracles, which are based on deception and magic, and true miracles, which derive from a Divine force. A false miracle is admired only by "them", by those who behold it as passive spectators. But a true miracle, wrought by God, is acknowledged as such even by those righteous men through whose action it comes to pass. By saying, "Show a wonder for *you*" God implied that the miracle Pharaoh would see would indeed be a true miracle. "The miracle which I will perform in his sight," said the Lord to Moses and Aaaron, "will seem a miracle even to *you,* the two righteous leaders through whom it will be brought to pass."

* * * *

". . . Take thy rod and cast it down before Pharaoh that it may become a serpent." (Exodus 7:9)

Environment has a profound influence on man. Even the most evil of men can improve when he comes into good and noble company. Conversely, even the best man can turn into a "serpent," a dangerous creature, if he is put into an environment where corruption predominates.

Moses sought to make Pharaoh understand that although they were hated and oppressed in Egypt to such a degree that they had lost all resemblance to human beings, the Jews could become the greatest and noblest among men if only they would be freed from the corrupt atmosphere of Egypt. To accomplish this end, Moses showed him the "rod of God", the rod on which the Ineffable Divine Name was engraved. This was the rod by means of which the greatest miracles of all were performed. When it was cast down before Pharaoh, i.e., when it was placed

121

into the environment of Pharaoh, it turned into a poisonous serpent, but as soon as Moses took hold of it, i.e., as soon as it returned to the immediate environment of Moses, it was transformed once again into a "rod of God." Such is the strength of the influence of environment on man.

—*Rabbi Meir Shapiro of Lublin*

* * * *

(Moses said to Pharaoh) *"Against what time shall I entreat* (the Lord) *for thee . . . and Moses cried out to the Lord concerning the frogs which He had brought upon Pharaoh."* (Exodus 8:5-8)

"Entreat" and "cry" are two of the ten expressions used in the Bible to denote prayer. The Sages taught that Egyptian oppression had sealed the lips of the Children of Israel so that they were unable to pray to the Lord. But the ten plagues, one by one, abolished Pharaoh's tyranny, thus unsealing the lips of the Israelites and enabling them to make use of all the expressions of prayer. Two of the ten plagues — the blood and the frogs — had already come to pass, restoring to the Israelites the use of the two expressions of prayer mentioned in the above verse.

—*Hiddushei HaRIM*

* * * *

"And Pharaoh called for Moses and Aaron and said: 'Go, sacrifice to your God in the land.' And Moses said: 'It is not right to do so . . . We will go three days' journey into the wilderness and sacrifice to the Lord our God . . .' " (Exodus 8:21-23)

Pharaoh was under the impression that even if one was deeply entangled in the corruption of Egypt and bound to "the land,' the earthly elements, one could proceed to worship God and to offer sacrifices to Him without prior spiritual preparations. But Moses explained to him that this is not the way of the Children of Israel. Before a Jew may go forth to worship the Lord and to offer sacrifices to Him, he must first move away from the corruption of which ancient Egypt was a symbol and cleanse himself of all earthly things. It is only after he has repented of

his sins and removed himself from evil that he may make his
offering to the Lord.

—*Shem MiShmuel, in the name of
the author of Avnei Nezer of Sohatchev*

* * * *

*"And the Lord said to Moses: 'Rise up early in the morning and
stand before Pharaoh . . .!"* (Exodus 9:13)

Being a man of great humility, Moses was accustomed to
bow to all men in greeting. Therefore the Lord found it necessary to command him explicitly to *"stand* before Pharaoh."
"When thou goest before Pharaoh," the Lord told Moses, "stand
erect before him and do not bow to him in greeting, for thou art
not to show him even the slightest sign of respect."

—*Or HaHayyim*

* * * *

*"He who feared the word of the Lord among the servants of Pha-
raoh made his servants and cattle flee into the houses."* (Exod. 9:20)
Alternative rendering: *"He who feared the word of the Lord* more
than *the servants of Pharaoh made his servants and his cattle flee
into the houses."*

Pharaoh's officers issued orders that no one should heed the
warnings of Moses concerning the hailstorm, but to leave all
sheep out in the fields. The Biblical narrative reports that those
ordinary Egyptians who feared the word of the Lord more than
that of the minions of Pharaoh caused their cattle to move "into
the houses." For this reason Moses subsequently said to Pharaoh:
"Some of thy people have shown their fear of the word of God,
but as for thee and thy servants, I know that you will not yet
fear the Lord God." *(Exodus 9:30)*

—*Meshekh Hakhmah*

Some have asked why the Egyptians were liable to punishment for having oppressed the Children of Israel. Was it not
decreed by God Himself that the Egyptians should oppress the
Israelites?

The answer is that the Egyptians did not oppress the Jews out of a desire to carry out God's decree but only out of wickedness and hatred. This was the reason why they were deserving of punishment.

At one point Pharaoh sought to justify his conduct, saying: "The Lord is righteous and (so am) I . . ." (*Exodus 9:27*), meaning that the Lord had been righteous in decreeing oppression for Israel and that he, Pharaoh, was righteous also because he had been motivated solely by the desire to carry out the decree. But Moses replied: *"But as for thee and thy servants, I know that you will not yet fear the Lord God.* I know that thou and thy servants oppressed the Children of Israel not because you feared the Lord, nor out of desire to fulfill His word, nor out of piety and fear of God, but only out of pure wickedness and cruelty. And for this reason you are deserving of punishment."

—*Torat Moshe*

* * * *

Haftarah Va'Era (Ezekiel, Chaps. 28-29)

"*. . . Behold, I am against thee, Pharaoh, King of Egypt . . .*" (*Ezekiel 29:3*)

Alternative rendering: "*Behold, I am* above *thee, Pharaoh, King of Egypt.*"

Pharaoh always boasted of being the mightiest absolute ruler on earth, with no one above him. In fact, he regarded himself as a deity, saying: "I do not know the Lord." Therefore the Lord said to him: "*Behold, I am above thee, Pharaoh, King of Egypt.* Know that I am thy master and can deal with thee as I see fit."

This may be likened to the case of a servant in a palace who boasts to a visitor that he is the sole owner of the palace, only to be interrupted by the coming of his master, who says to him: "Do not misrepresent your position. I am your master and

124

you are subject to my authority."

—*Kokhav MiYaakov*

*   *   *   *

"On that day will I cause a horn to shoot up from the House of Israel . . ." (Ezekiel 29:21)

The salvation of the people of Israel is like a shoot, which can sprout up only after the seed has rotted away and it would appear that no fruit could possibly come forth from it. In the same manner, salvation and renewed strength can come to Israel only after its fortunes have reached a low ebb and it would seem as if, God forbid, it were doomed to decay. This is the implication of Ezekiel's statement in the name of the Lord: "On that day will I cause a horn to shoot up for the House of Israel." The same thought is implicit also in the prayer which we recite daily as part of the Eighteen Blessings: "O King Who causest death and revivest and causest salvation to sprout forth." The sprouting of the "shoot" after it seemed to have rotted away symbolizes the eventual resurrection of the dead. It is proof that, even though the dead are turned into dust, they will all be restored to life at the appointed time.

—*Avnei Ezel*

*   *   *   *

Weekly Portion of Bo (Exodus 10:1-13:16)

"I have hardened (Pharaoh's)*heart . . . that I might show these My signs in the midst of them."* (Exodus 10:1)

By virtue of their exodus from Egypt, the Children of Israel were granted two such "signs"; namely, the Sabbath ("for it is a sign between Me and you" — *Exodus 31:16-17*) and the phylacteries ("thou shalt bind them for a sign upon thy hand" — *Deut. 6:4-9*). In either case, the Law specifies that these signs are intended to recall to us the exodus from Egypt. The Lord said: *". . . that I might show these My signs in the midst of them.* Through the miracles that come to pass at the time of the exodus,

I will give Israel My two signs — the Sabbath and the phylacteries."

—*Mo'or VoShomesh*

*   *   *   *

*"And that thou mayest tell in the ears of thy son, and of thy son's
son, what I have wrought upon Egypt . . . that you may know that
I am the Lord."* (Exodus 10:2)

Said the Lord to Israel: "If you will diligently impress the
greatness of God upon your children and grandchildren, you
yourselves will grow in strength of faith and in knowledge of the
Lord, and you will know that I am the Lord."

—*Toledoth Adam* (*Rabbi of Ostrova*)

*   *   *   *

*"And Moses said: 'We will go with our young and with our old . . .
for we must hold a feast to the Lord.' "* (Exodus 10:9)

"The reason why we must take our young with us," Moses
told Pharaoh, "is that we must hold a feast to the Lord, and how
could we rejoice or celebrate a holiday if we were to leave our
children behind in an alien land? Without our children, no joy
can be complete."

—*Shem MiShmuel*

*   *   *   *

*"And the Lord said to Moses: 'Stretch out thy hand . . . that there
may be darkness over the land of Egypt, darkness which may be
felt."* (Exodus 10:21)

Ordinary "darkness" is no phenomenon in itself but merely
the absence of light. When there is no light, it is dark. Darkness of
this sort has no existence in its own right and can be readily dispelled by the kindling of a light. But the darkness which came
over the land of Egypt was a phenomenon in its own right, so
real (Heb.: *mamash*) that it could be felt (*va-yomesh*) and could
not be dispelled by light.

—*Obadiah ben Jacob Sforno*

*   *   *   *

"They did not see one another, nor did any of them rise from his place . . ." (Exodus 10:23)

The worst darkness is that blindness in which one person will not "see another", refusing to look upon his misery and to help him. He who will not "see another" will himself become incapable of "rising from his place"; that is, of growth and development.

—*Hiddushei HaRIM*

This may also have been the thought of the Sages of the Midrash when they stated that the darkness which enveloped the land of Egypt was as thick as a golden *denar*. The pursuit of the golden *denar* makes men selfish so that they become unwilling and unable to "see" others and their needs.

—*Evnei Ezel*

*   *   *   *

"Our cattle also shall go with us . . . for thereof must we take to serve the Lord our God . . ." (Exodus 10:26)

Moses said to Pharaoh: "Our cattle will go with us of their own free will, for they are willing and ready to die in order to be offered up as sacrifices to the Lord."

The Sages related that the bullock which the Prophet Elijah wanted to offer as a sacrifice to the Lord on Mount Carmel (*I Kings 18:19-39*) ran to the altar of his own accord, while the bullock which the false prophets planned to slaughter on the altar of Baal refused to go. This should teach us the proper spirit in which to worship God. If even a dumb beast goes forth of its own accord to offer itself to the Lord, then we humans who, unlike the animal, are endowed with intelligence, should certainly do so of our own free will.

—*Malbim*

*   *   *   *

"When (Pharaoh) *shall let you go, he shall surely thrust you out from here altogether."*

God wanted no trace of the impurity of Egypt to remain with the Children of Israel. He therefore brought it about that they would be "thrust out" from there.

By literally expelling the Israelites from Egypt, Pharoah broke off all their ties with Egypt so that they no longer had any contact with the corruption in the land of their exile and could easily and speedily rise to the high moral level at which they would be worthy of the appelation "host of the Lord."

Had Pharaoh allowed them to depart in a spirit of peace and good will, a "clean break" in this sense would have been impossible.
—*Sefat Emet*

* * * *

"Speak now in the ears of the people and let them ask every man of his neighbor, and every woman of her neighbor, jewels of silver and jewels of gold." (Exodus 11:20)

> The Hebrew word *na,* which God employed in commanding Moses to speak to the people ("Speak *now*") is also an expression of entreaty. Here it means: "I entreat you to do that which will follow, so that Abraham, that righteous man, may not say: 'The prophecy that the Children of Israel should serve the Egyptians and that the Egyptians should afflict them, He permitted to be fulfilled, but the promise that, afterwards, they should go forth from Egypt with great substance, He did not fulfill for them.'"
> —*Rashi*

God's promise that "afterwards, they shall go forth with great substance" could be construed to refer to a higher, spiritual wealth, meaning that the Israelites were to take with them from Egypt not mere silver and gold but whatever sparks of goodness and holiness they might find among the Egyptians.

But then Abraham might have protested, saying: "The prophecy that the Children of Israel should serve the Egyptians and that the Egyptians should afflict them, God fulfilled in a very obvious manner so that every Israelite, even the simplest among them, could sense it. Therefore it is only right that the promise that 'afterwards, they shall go forth with great substance' should also come true not symbolically but literally so that every Israelite may be able to see the 'substance' with his own eyes."

It was out of these considerations that the Lord commanded the Children of Israel to ask their Egyptian neighbors for jewels of silver and gold to take with them when they left the land.

—*Sihot Tzaddikim*

*   *   *   *

"*. . . Moreover, the man Moses was very great in the land of Egypt, in the sight of Pharaoh's servants and in the sight of the people.*" (Exodus 11:3)

It is rare that a man should be accepted and respected in equal measure by the aristocracy and by the masses. In most cases a man who is popular with the masses will be hated by the higher society, and he who enjoys the respect of the upper classes will be disliked by the common people, for each class of society has its own standards and requirements.

What was so unusual about the personality of Moses was that he was respected not only by "Pharaoh's servants", Egypt's nobility, but also by the Egyptian masses.

—*HaDrash VeHaEyun*

*   *   *   *

"*But against any of the Children of Israel not a dog shall whet his tongue . . .*" (Exodus 11:7)

Through this statement the Bible means to tell us that the Children of Israel uprooted from their midst the vices of gossip and tale-bearing to which Moses had referred when he said concerning his slaying of the Egyptian taskmaster, "Surely the thing is known" (*Exodus 2:14*). For had the Children of Israel still indulged in these vices, they would have been subject to the penalty described by the Sages according to whom "anyone spreading evil gossip is deserving of being thrown to the dogs."

It is related in the Midrash that the Children of Israel had become so careful to avoid all tale-bearing that, for a period of a full twelve months, they could keep secret the Divine command that every man was to ask his Egyptian neighbors for jewels (*Exodus 11:2*) to take away with him from Egypt. They were able to keep this command from becoming prematurely known to the Egyptians only because they had truly exstirpated all tale-bearing from their midst. And it was for this reason that the Children of Israel were found worthy of redemption.

—Rabbi Mordecai Benet

* * * *

"This month shall be to you the beginning of months . . ." (Exodus 12:2)

The nations of the world build their calendar around the sun, while the Jewish people base theirs on the moon. This symbolizes the difference between the heathens and the Children of Israel. The heathens can survive only as long as the light shines upon them. As soon as darkness descends upon them they perish and disappear from the scene of history. But like the moon, which can shine even through the darkest night, the Jewish people can survive and spread light even in darkness.

—Sefat Emet

* * * *

". . . and you shall keep it a feast to the Lord; throughout your generations you shall keep it a feast by an ordinance forever." (Exodus 12:14)

If one considers the festival commemorating the exodus from Egypt as nothing more than the anniversary of liberation from physical oppression and slavery, it would be justifiable to argue that there was no sense in celebrating it as long as the Jewish people continue to be exiled and enslaved among the nations of the world.

But if the Exodus is understood in its proper meaning as the spiritual liberation of our people in which the Lord Himself led us forth from the corruption of Egypt, to take us to Himself as His people and to have His Presence rest upon us so that we became a holy nation, then it can be readily seen why the feast of Passover must be observed even while we are still in physical exile and suffering from persecution and oppression.

The Torah states: *"And you shall keep it a feast to the Lord. If you will celebrate this festival as a feast to the Lord,* as a Divinely-commanded feast marking the anniversary of Israel's spiritual liberation, then *you shall keep it a feast by an ordinance forever;* i.e. you will be able to observe it always, even through the worst periods of your exile."

—*Meshekh Hakhmah*

*   *   *   *

". . . but on the first day you shall put away leaven out of your houses, for whoever eats leavened bread from the first day until the seventh (of Passover), *that soul shall be cut off from Israel."* (Exodus 12:15)

Why, in the case of the prohibition of leaven, more than in the case of any other dietary prohibition, does the Torah specify that it must be destroyed and declared non-existent, and that it must "neither be seen nor found" in our homes?

The Early Sages give two reasons for this stringency. First, since one is accustomed to eating leaven all year long, it would be an easy thing to forget and partake of it also on Passover if any of it should remain in the home. Secondly, the Torah wants to make sure that the prohibition is strictly observed, for anyone who violates it is subject to the extreme penalty of *kareth,* "being cut off from his people."

This explanation is obvious from the text itself: *"But on the first day you shall put away leaven out of your houses.* Why must you do this? Because, to begin with, *everyone eats leavened bread* (the Hebrew *kol okhel hametz* may be rendered either as "whoever eats leavened bread" or as *"everyone eats leavened bread")* and secondly, *that soul shall be cut off from Israel;* whoever violates this prohibition is subject to the extreme penalty of *kareth."*

—*Nathan ben Simeon Hakohen Adler*

* * * *

"Then Moses called for all the elders of Israel and said to them: 'Draw out and take for yourselves lambs . . .' " (Exodus 12:21)

Alternative rendering: *"Draw out and* buy *for yourself lambs."* Ordinarily lambs, being objects of worship in Egypt, would not have been considered fit for use as a sacrifice to the Lord. For this reason the text specified *"Buy for yourselves lambs,"* meaning that the Children of Israel were to acquire the animals from the Egyptians through purchase. By agreeing to sell the lambs, the Egyptians would nullify the sacred status of these animals in their land, for according to Jewish law "a non-Jew who sells an idol (which he worships) is as if he had destroyed it."

—*Rabbi Eliezer Hakohen of Sochatchov*

* * * *

"And you shall take a bunch of hyssop and dip it into the blood that is in the basin, and strike the lintel and the two side-posts with the blood that is in the basin . . ." (Exodus 12:22)

This is to teach you that even if you should be as lowly as the hyssop which grows low on the ground, as long as you will be bound together into one united group, ready to give of your life-blood for Judaism, you will be able to *"strike* (lit.: reach) *the lintel";* you will be able to attain to high places.

—*Nehmad Mizahav, (Rabbi Yeheskiel of Kazimir)*

* * * *

"And the Lord said to Moses and Aaron: 'This is the ordinance of the Passover; no alien shall eat thereof." (Exodus 12:43)

An alien — any Israelite who has become an apostate.

—*Targum Onkelos*

In the *Kol Nidrei* which we recite on the Eve of the Day of Atonement, we declare that even sinners may participate in our fasting and our prayers. Why, then, should the Torah not permit the Jew who has become estranged from our people but wants to celebrate Passover with us to partake of the Paschal lamb?

Because of the considerations which motivate him. If a non-observant Jew — or even an apostate — feels impelled to join us in our fasting and weeping on the Day of Atonement, his intentions are obviously sincere and he must not be driven away. But as for the man who keeps away from our fasting and weeping and comes to us only on Passover to partake of the roast lamb we eat, it is plain that he wants to join us only in our feasting, and we can do without his kind. —*Pardes Yosef*

*   *   *   *

Haphtarah Bo (Jeremiah 46:13-28)

"But fear not, My servant Jacob, neither be dismayed, O Israel; for lo, I will save thee from afar . . ." (Jeremiah 46:27)

According to the Sages redemption will be hastened and will come before its appointed time if the Jewish people should repent of their sins. But they assure us that even if we should not repent of our sins, redemption will come in the end, although it will not then materialize before its appointed time.

Through His prophet, the Lord tells the Jewish people that they need not be afraid, because He will save them in due time even "from afar", even if they have drifted far away from Judaism and repentance.

The author of *Kedushat Levi* used to pray: "Master of the Universe, save Thy people while they are still Jews, for if Thou wilt tarry, Thou wilt have to redeem them as heathens."

Weekly Portion of Beshalakh (Exodus 13:17-17:16)
"... and the Children of Israel went up armed out of the land of Egypt, and Moses took the bones of Joseph with him ..." (Exodus 13:18-19)

The Children of Israel went forth armed. What were their weapons? The remains of Joseph, which they took with them, for the merit of a righteous man serves as a shield for his people and "the righteous are even greater in death than they were in life."

—*Torat Moshe*

The Hebrew term *atzmoth* (remains; lit. "bones") is related to *atzimuth*, the Hebrew for "personality" or "(good) character traits." Hence the verse can be interpreted to mean that Moses took "with him" the good qualities of Joseph, learning from Joseph's example how to lead a people and to keep it satisfied in times of hunger.

—*Torat HaMoreh VeHaTalmud*

* * * *

"And when Pharaoh drew nigh, the Children of Israel lifted up their eyes and behold, the Egyptians were marching after them ... and the Children of Israel cried out to the Lord." (Exodus 14:10)
Pharaoh drew Israel nigh to repentance.

—*Midrash*

The threat of annihilation at the hands of Pharaoh's host put the fear of the Lord into them.

The fact that it took Pharaoh and his host to make them repent struck dismay into the hearts of the Children of Israel, *and they cried out to the Lord* at the thought that they had repented only when they had beheld Pharaoh and his army in hot pursuit behind them.

—*Avnei Ezel*

* * * *

"... and behold, the Egyptians were marching after them ..."
(Exodus 14:10)

> (The Hebrew word for "were marching" is in the singular
> to show that the Egyptians were marching with one mind
> and as one man.   —*Rashi*

In the case of the Children of Israel, ("and there Israel encamped" — *Exodus 19:2*) Rashi comments "as one man and with
one mind"; the reverse of his statement that the Egyptians were
pursuing the Children of Israel "with one mind and as one man."

This reversal indicates that the Jews are by nature as "one
man" and their shortcoming is only that they still do not act "with
one mind." The other nations, by contrast, are disunited by nature, and it is only when they join "with one mind" in a concerted
effort for the sake of working for one cause that they become
"as one man."

—Abraham Bornstein

"The Lord will fight for you and you shall hold your peace." (Exod.
14:14)

> When the Children of Israel prepared to go forth from Egypt,
> they were required to perform a commandment; namely, to
> slaughter the Paschal lamb. But when they came to the Red Sea,
> they were not required to carry out any activity but only to re-
> main silent. This teaches us that when the spirit of self-sacrifice
> for the Lord is present, nothing else is needed. The strength and
> merit deriving from that spirit are more effective than any
> action.   —*Abraham Bornstein*

*   *   *   *

Rabbi Hayyim of Klausenburg explained that the Holy
Temple was built on Mount Moriah where Abraham had been
ready to sacrifice his son Isaac (rather than on Mount Sinai,
where the Law and the commandments had been given to the
Children of Israel) because on Mount Moriah a Jew was willing
and ready to be slaughtered at the command of God, and such

self-sacrificing devotion is greater than any other merit.

* * * *

"And the angel of God who went before the camp of Israel removed and went behind them ..." (Exodus 14:19)

When the Israelites are worthy of God's favor they are greater than even the holiest angels. At such times the angel who, by virtue of his holiness, ordinarily moves "before" them, remains "behind them," for they are greater than he.

—*Kedushat Levi*

* * * *

"... and the one did not come near the other all the night." (Exod. 14:20)

> The ministering angels wanted to sing a hymn. But the Holy One, blessed be He, said to them: "Do you wish to sing a hymn when the work of My hands has been drowned in the sea?"

—*Gemarah Erkhin*

When an operation is performed on a person who is dangerously ill, no hymns are sung, because the operation, although it is necessary, is always painful. Only when it has been successfully completed may we rejoice.

In this vein, God said to the ministering angels: "Now, when the work of My hands is being drowned in the sea, there is certainly no cause for rejoicing. It had to be done, for evil cannot go unpunished, but it is painful to Me and it would be wrong to sing hymns of praise now. Only after the operation has been completed, when the wicked have all been destroyed, may you rejoice at the victory won for justice and righteousness."

—*Yeshuat Malko, by Rabbi Israel Joshua Trunk of Kutno*

* * * *

"But the Children of Israel walked upon dry land in the midst of the sea ..." (Exodus 14:29)

Men are impressed only when they see events which are

clearly miraculous. They fail to realize that nature itself is a great miracle in which they can behold the greatness of the Guide and Creator of the Universe each day.

Only when they are confronted with an event that is obviously supernatural do they realize that the providence and the miracles of God are present even in everyday nature which we are so much inclined to take for granted.

This is the interpretation of the above-cited verse: "As for *the Children of Israel,* when they experienced the miracle that they could walk through the sea as on dry land, they became aware that *they walked upon dry land in the midst of the sea,* that even if they had been walking on dry land it would have been no less a miracle than if they had been walking through the midst of the sea."

—Rabbi Elimelekh of Lizensk

*   *   *   *

"This is my God, and I will glorify Him; my father's God, and I will exalt Him." (Exodus 15:2)

An alternative rendering is "This is my God, and I will make Him a habitation" (the Hebrew verb *anvehu* — "And I will glorify Him" is related to the noun *naveh* "habitation"). This means: "I will make a habitation for Him within my own being; I will sanctify and purify myself so that my body may become a dwelling place for the Holy Presence."

—Samson Raphael Hirsch

*   *   *   *

"And in the greatness of Thy excellency Thou overthrowest those who rise up against Thee; Thou sendest forth Thy wrath; it consumes them as stubble." (Exodus 15:7)

Thou art so great that it is not even fitting for Thee to fight against such base creatures, yet *Thou overthrowest those who rise up against Thee.* For it is not necessary for Thee to perform mighty acts for this purpose. *Thou sendest forth Thy wrath,* and

137

Thy wrath alone is sufficient to consume them. If a human being is wroth, he must act in order to destroy the object of his anger, but Thou needest do no more but remove Thy Providence from those who would rise up against Thee, and already they will be unable to survive.

—*Meshekh Hakhmah*

* * * *

"Thou hast guided them in Thy strength to Thy holy habitation." (Exodus 15:13)

Onkelos translates *nehalta* ("Thou hast guided them") in the meaning of "bearing" or "carrying", but he was not particular to translate it according to the Hebrew expression.

—*Rashi*

If the Targum rendered *nehalta* ("Thou hast guided them") as "Thou hast borne with them" it did so because all guidance involves patience and forebearance. A leader and guide must bear and forebear.

—*The Rabbi of Gur*

* * * *

"And Miriam the prophetess, the sister of Aaron, took a timbrel in her hand, and all the women went out after her with timbrels and with dances" (Exodus 15:21)

Miriam the prophetess so inspired the other women with her praises of the Holy One, blessed be He, that they all followed her and did likewise.

—*Rimzei D'Hokhmoso*

* * * *

". . . and the Lord showed him a tree and he cast it into the waters and the waters were made sweet . . ." (Exodus 15:25)

(The Lord) taught (to Moses) a word of the Torah, which is likened to the tree of life; namely, that the Lord uses the bitter to make the bitter sweet.

—*Midrash*

The scholar who engages in the study of the Torah to the

exclusion of all other pursuits has a bitter lot in that he has no material sustenance. The merchant who is constantly busy amassing material wealth is plagued by the bitter realization that he is allowing the things of the spirit to pass him by, and he cannot derive satisfaction from his toil because he lacks spiritual contentment. But if the merchant should support the scholar and provide for his needs, the bitterness in both their lives will be sweetened. The scholar will have sustenance and the merchant will derive spiritual satisfaction from having provided for him.

The "tree" is the Torah, the "tree of life to those who cleave to it," and it is through the study and support of Torah that the bitterness of life can be made sweet.

—*Torat Moshe*

*   *   *   *

"*. . . I will put none of the diseases upon thee which I have put upon the Egyptians, for I am the Lord Who heals thee.*" (Exod. 15:26)

A family doctor who is not paid by the visit but by annual retainer has nothing to gain when his patient is ill. The work for which he receives his retainer is the preservation of the health of the patient so that he should not become ill.

Similarly, the Lord is primarily concerned with guarding the health of our soul. This is the reason for all the commandments and statutes which He has given us. "I am the Lord, Who heals thee," He declared. "I am the physician at all times, not only when thou art ill. Therefore *I will put none of the diseases upon thee which I have put upon the Egyptians* but will give thee commandments to guard thy soul from illness."

—*Torat Moshe*

*   *   *   *

"*And when the Children of Israel saw it, they said to one another: 'What is it?' for they did not know what it was. And Moses said to them: 'It is the bread which the Lord has given you to eat.'*" (Exodus 16:11)

Alternative rendering: ". . . *they said to one another:* 'Who is he?' *for they did not know* who he *was* . . ."

Every Israelite who partook of the manna from heaven changed so greatly in appearance that the others were unable to recognize him. He was not the same as he had been before.

"*And . . . they said to one another:* 'Who is he?' Each would say of the other: 'Who is this? He is no longer the same man. He has taken on new spiritual dimensions.' *And Moses said to them: 'It is the bread!* . . . explaining to them that this change had been wrought by the bread from heaven of which they had partaken."

—*Rabbi Menahem Mendel of Rimanov*

* * * *

". . . *let every man abide in his place; let no man go out of his place* . . ." (Exodus 16:29)

Alternative rendering: ". . . *let every man abide* below *his place* . . ." (*tachtov* — "in his place" literally means "under him").

This means that it behooves every man to seat himself in a place lower than that due him according to his station. And "let no man go out of his place;" under no circumstances may he seat himself in a place higher than the one rightfully due him.

—*Rabbi Israel of Ruzhin*

* * * *

". . . *and because they tried the Lord, saying: 'Is the Lord among us or not?' Then came Amalek and fought with Israel in Rephidim.*" (Exodus 17:7-8)

> In Rephidim — because they became lax in the observance of the Torah. (*al she-rafu yedehem min haTorah*; lit. "because they removed their hands from the Torah.")
>
> —*Gemarah*

Neglect of and laxity in the observance of the Torah are an indication of the presence of evil thoughts such as the question: "Is the Lord among us or not?"

Doubt and lack of faith lead to laxity in the observance of the laws of the Torah. —*Malbim*

* * * *

140

*"And it came to pass when Moses held up his hand, that Israel pre-
vailed, and when he let down his hand, Amalek prevailed."* (Exodus 17:11)

> But could the hand of Moses wage a battle or lose a battle?
> This is rather to teach us that whenever the Children of
> Israel looked up and subjected their hearts to their Father
> in Heaven, they prevailed, but if not, they fell.
> —*Mishna, Rosh HaShanah* 29

If Moses knew that the Children of Israel would prevail only
as long as he would hold up his hand, why did he ever let his
hand down?

The hands of Moses were only as strong as his people were
steadfast. Whenever the Israelites turned their hearts to their
Father in Heaven, the hands of Moses were strengthened" (the
verb *mithgavrim*, "they prevailed"; lit. "they were strengthened"
in Rashi's statement refers not to the Children of Israel but to
the hands of Moses). Then Moses would be able to continue
holding up his hands. But whenever the Israelites turned their
hearts away from the Most High, the hands of Moses dropped.
This teaches us that the repentance and high resolves of a people
give strength to their leader, enabling him to act and pray to bring
them victory and salvation.

—*Sefat Emet*

*   *   *   *

Haphtarah Beshalakh (Judges 4:4-5:31)
*". . . but those who love Him be as the sun when he goes forth in his
might . . ."* (Judges 5:31)

> Of those who are insulted but do not return the insult, who
> hear their shame and do not retaliate, Scripture says:
> Those who love Him are as the sun when he goes forth in
> his might.   —*Tractate Gittin* 36

According to the Sages those who do not retaliate when they
are insulted and pay no attention when they are humiliated are
like the sun.

141

Actually, keeping silent in the face of insult and not reacting to humiliation is a virtue only when one's own honor is involved. This is what the Sages mean by the expression "they hear their shame", meaning their own, their personal shame. If one hears insults hurled at another person, of whom one knows that he is an honest man and a scholar, keeping silent is a sin.

In this respect, the sun showed conduct worthy of emulation.

We are told that when the world was first created, the moon, seeking to humiliate the sun, declared: "Two kings cannot have the same crown." The sun remained silent in the face of this insult to its dignity. But the Sages say that when Korah and his company revolted against Moses, the sun took up the fight for the honor of Moses, refusing to come forth and to spread its light over the world unless he who had insulted Moses would be punished. (*Tractate Nedarim 39*)

Hence those who "hear their own shame and do not reply" but are quick to defend the honor of other innocent persons are truly "like the sun when he goes forth in his might," for they show the same strength and steadfastness as the sun in the heavens.

—*Hadrash VeHaEyun*

* * * *

Weekly Portion of Yithro (Exodus 18:1-20:23)

"Now Jethro . . . heard . . ." (Exodus 18:1)

> What was the report which (Jethro) heard so that he came (to visit Moses)? The splitting of the Red Sea and the war with Amalek.
>
> —*Rashi*

Why did Jethro have to come to Moses? Could he not have become and remained a believer in God in his home?

He came because he was disturbed at the news that such a revelation of Divine Providence as the splitting of the Red Sea could be followed by a withdrawal of Divine favor such as the attack of the Amalekites. This report convinced him that one cannot understand the Law properly if one studies it by oneself. He realized that he must go and receive instruction from a teacher and that he must never cease to strive for the improvement of his character in order to be able to overcome the forces of evil which seek to blind man's eyes to truth and righteousness.

—Sihot Tzaddikim

*   *   *   *

"And Jethro . . . came . . . to Moses into the wilderness where he was encamped, at the mountain of God." (Exodus 18:5)

The place where Moses dwelt became a "mountain of God." It was through the presence of Moses that it became a dwelling-place for the *Shekhina*. A place is honored by the man who dwells there.

—Torat Moshe

*   *   *   *

"And he said to Moses: 'I, thy father-in-law Jethro, am coming to thee . . .'" (Exodus 18:6)

Go forth on my account.

—Mekhilta

What is meant by this statement in the Mekhilta?

Jethro asked Moses to "go forth", to descend a little, from his own high station, "on my account," for his sake, in order that he, Jethro, might be able to establish communion with him so that, when Moses would rise again to his lofty place, Jethro would rise with him.

This is what Jethro meant by the request: "Go forth on my account."

—Rabbi Menahem Mendel of Kotzk

*   *   *   *

"And Jethro rejoiced for all the goodness which the Lord had done to Israel, in that He had delivered them out of the hand of the Egyptians." (Exodus 18:9)

His flesh crept with horror. (The Hebrew *vayyihad* —
"and he rejoiced" is related to *hiddudim,* an expression
denoting prickling with horror.)

—*Rashi*

Jethro was stung with grief and horror at the thought that
the Egyptians did not mend their ways but had to be destroyed
because of their corruption.

—*Hiddushei HaRIM*

* * * *

*"And Moses said to his father-in-law: 'Because the people come to
me to inquire of God, when they have a matter, it comes to me, and
I judge between a man and his neighbor and I make known to them
the statutes of God ..."* (Exodus 18:15-16)

A leader in Israel has three tasks to fulfill. First, to pray
for any individual who is in trouble ("Because the people come
to me to inquire of God"); secondly, to act as arbitrator in financial disputes in accordance with the laws of the Torah ("and I
judge between a man and his neighbor"), and finally, to teach
his people about God and His law ("and I make known to them
the statutes of God.")

Since Moses had to discharge all these obligations single-
handedly, the people "stood about him from morning to evening." *(Exodus 18:14)*

—*Nachmanides*

* * * *

"When they have a matter, it comes to me ..." (Exodus 18:16)

Why does the text not read: "When they have a matter, *they
come* to me?"

Because Moses viewed each case as if the matter, rather than
the individuals involved, had come before him. This means that
he treated each "matter" impartially and objectively, without
regard to the personalities or other extraneous considerations
involved.

* * * *

"If thou shalt do this thing, and God commands thee so, then thou shalt be able to endure, and all this people also shall go to their place in peace." (Exodus 18:23)

The Sages term a compromise "peace" because in such an arrangement neither of the disputing parties emerges as the loser. However, according to Jewish law, a compromise can be made only in cases where the Court of Law has no clear directives as to how the Law of the Torah is to be applied. Once it is known to the Court "how the Law of the Torah is inclined" compromises are not permissible.

In view of this rule, Jethro said to Moses: "If you decide all legal questions single-handedly, you will not be able to arrange a compromise, for to you the Law is always abundantly clear. But if you will delegate some of the authority to lesser judges, it will be possible for them to arrange compromises because the Law will not always be clear to them, and then *all this people shall go to their places in peace*, they will be satisfied with the compromise arbitrated in their disputes."

—*Rabbi Hayyim Berlin*

* * * *

". . . the hard cases they brought to Moses, but every small matter they judged themselves." (Exodus 18:26)

Jethro said to Moses: "Every *great matter* they shall bring to thee" (*Exodus 18:22*) but the narrative states that "the *hard cases*" were brought to Moses. These two statements show the difference between the other nations and the Jewish people with regard to the settling of legal disputes. In other nations the importance of a case is made dependent on the amount of money involved. Thus litigation involving "great" amounts is assigned to a higher court of justice, while cases with smaller amounts at stake are left to lower courts. In Jewish religious law, on the other hand, the amount of money involved in a dispute is of no concern, for "the law concerning one penny is the same as that

145

concerning a hundred *maneh* (1 *maneh* — 150 common shek-els)." Instead, the importance of the case is determined by its difficulty. "Hard cases", more complex questions, are referred to judges more learned than those qualified to render judgment in less complicated disputes. Thus the Children of Israel brought "the hard cases" before Moses even when the dispute was not "great" in terms of the amount of money involved.

—*Rabbi Hayyim Berlin*

* * * *

"And when they were departed from Rephidim and had come to the wilderness of Sinai . . ." (Exodus 19:2)

How was it in the case of their arrival in the wilderness of Sinai? They were in a repentant mood. Thus, too, they set forth from Rephidim in a repentant mood.

—*Rashi*

Since the Israelites realized their weakness (they had become lax in the observance of the Torah) (for the meaning of Rephi-dim see Note to *Exodus 17:7-8*, p. 139) and were therefore discouraged and dejected, they gained strength from the thought that "they had come to the wilderness of Sinai," that they were on the way to Mount Sinai to receive the Law. It was the antici-pation of the great Revelation that gave them new courage and strength to face the tasks ahead.

—*Shem MiShmuel*

* * * *

". . . and there Israel encamped before the mountain. And Moses went up to God . . ." (Exodus 19:2-3)

If the people of Israel, united "as one man of one mind", can successfully confront the evil impulse, which is like a high mountain, then their leader, too, risen in Godliness ("and Moses went up to God").

—*HaDrash VeHaEyun*

* * * *

146

"Thus shalt thou say to the House of Jacob and tell the Children of Israel." (Exodus 19:3)

According to the Sages "the House of Jacob" refers to the women, who had to be taught the Law before the men because it was their task as mothers to educate their children in the Torah. Thus the command "and tell the *Children of Israel*" is construed as addressed to the women also because it is their duty to impart the Law and its commandments to the children of the people of Israel.

Said the Lord to Moses: *"Thus shalt thou say to the House of Jacob;* thou shalt tell it first to the women, because *she will tell it* (*ve-tagged* may mean either "thou shalt tell" or "she will tell") *to the Children of Israel."*

—*MaHarSHa, Tractate Sota*

*   *   *   *

"Now, therefore, if you will indeed hearken to My voice . . ." (Exodus 19:5)

Why did God wait until this point to admonish the Children of Israel to listen to His commandments?

Because it was only then that the Children of Israel were entirely free from the physical and mental enslavement to which the Egyptians had subjected them.

Man cannot truly accept the sovereignty of the kingdom of Heaven as long as he is in the service of human masters. Dependence on a fellow-man does not allow for complete faith in the Unity of God. Thus, according to the Jerusalem Talmud, Canaanite slaves in the land of Israel were exempt from reciting the *Shema*, the acknowledgement of the Unity of the Lord, because they had another master beside Him, and as long as they were beneath the yoke of the human master they could not fully accept the "yoke of the kingdom of Heaven."

Thus, too, the Lord did not demand complete obedience from the Children of Israel until they had left Egypt far behind them and had encamped before Mount Sinai. Only then did He say to them:

"I have removed you from the slavery of Egypt and have caused you to be higher than the Egyptians; I have borne you on eagles' wings (*Exodus 19:4*) so that now you no longer have any human master above you. Hence you are now in a position to accept the sovereignty of the Kingdom of Heaven and I expect you to hearken to My voice."

—*Shem MiShmuel*

* * * *

"...*for all the earth is Mine*..." (Exodus 19:5)

Said the Lord to the Children of Israel: "You will not be 'My own treasure' (*19:5*) only as long as all the other nations worship idols — that would be no great distinction. Your distinction lies in that even when the time will come when 'all the earth will be Mine,' when all the world will turn to Me and all the nations will acknowledge the sovereignty of God, you, the Children of Israel will still be My favorite people from among all the nations."

—*Yakar MiPoz*

* * * *

"*And the Lord said to Moses: 'Go to the people and sanctify them today and tomorrow.'*..." (Exodus 19:10)

Let their holiness persist not only "today," when they hear the law and God's other moral instructions, but even on the next day when they will go hence.

—*Pardes Yosef*

* * * *

"*And thou shalt set bounds to the people round about*..." (Exodus 19:12)

This is to teach us that a Jew must set bounds to himself and not delve too deeply into things Divine which are beyond his grasp. He should rather retain a simple, unquestioning faith.

—*Malbim*

* * * *

148

"And Moses brought forth the people, out of the camp, to meet God . . ." (Exodus 19:17)

According to Rabbi Isaac Meir Alter, the author of *Hiddushei HaRIM,* it is the task of the leader in Israel to remove his people from corruption and to bring them closer to holy things.

Moses fulfilled this task, for *"he brought forth the people out of the camp* of everyday life and caused them to rise *to meet God."*

—*The Rabbi of Gur*

* * * *

"And when the voice of the horn grew louder and louder, Moses spoke, and God answered him in a loud voice." (Exodus 19:19)

Why are the Hebrew verbs *yedabber* ("Moses *spoke*") and *yaanenu* ("and God *answered* him") in the future tense?

Because of the implications of this report for all the future generations.

Moses had added one day to the Divinely-ordained period of preparation and God had approved the change, so that the Divine Presence was not revealed upon the mountain until the third day. This shows the binding force of the Oral Tradition, indicating to us that whatever the Sages ordain becomes part of the Torah itself.

The sound of the Shofar, which, by request of Moses, was not heard until the third day, proclaimed that "whenever *Moses will speak,* and whenever a leader in Israel will speak after him, know that *God will answer him in a loud voice* — know that it is the voice of the Lord Himself, Who has given His approval to what the leader is commanding you to do."

—*HaDrash VeHaEyun*

* * * *

"I am the Lord thy God, Who brought thee out of the land of Egypt ..." (Exodus 20:2)

> I took you out so that you should accept the Kingdom of Heaven.

> —*Mekhilta*

This commandment was given in the singular ("I am the Lord *thy* God, Who brought *thee* . . .") because the knowledge of God and the ability to perceive the power and providence of the Creator of the Universe is not given to everyone in equal measure. Each individual understands these things in a manner commensurate with his mental and spiritual capacities, his knowledge of the Law and his work on behalf of Judaism, so that every man will have a different conception of the Lord Who has proclaimed Himself to be *his* God.

> —*Sifthei Kohen*

* * * *

"Thou shalt not take the Name of the Lord thy God in vain ..." (Exodus 20:7)
Alternative rendering: *'Thou shalt not* bear *the Name of the Lord thy God in vain ..."*

Thou shalt not carry the Name of God on thy person in a dishonest manner. This means: Thou shalt not pretend to be more honest and pious than thou really art.

> —*Or HaHayyim*

* * * *

"Remember the Sabbath Day to keep it holy." (Exodus 20:8)

> The two words "remember" and "keep" were spoken in one utterance.

> —*Rashi*

Rashi's statement is addressed to those who would make a distinction between "remembering" the Sabbath day and "keeping" it.

A poor man may find it an easy thing to "keep" the Sabbath because he has no business concerns which demand his attention and which would suffer if he did not attend to them on the Sabbath. But he may be remiss in "remembering" the Sabbath, because he lacks the money to honor the Sabbath by drinking wine and by partaking of good food. A wealthy man, on the other hand, may find it simple to "remember" the Sabbath with care, because he has more than enough money to buy food and drink to honor it, but he may not want to "keep" the Day of Rest for fear that he might suffer great financial losses by shutting down his factories and shops for a day.

Thus the Sages point out that the two commands "remember" and "keep" were said in one utterance and that therefore no distinction could be made between them. The wealthy man is duty-bound not only to "remember" the Sabbath. day but also to "keep" it. At the same time it is expected that he will not only help the poor man to "keep" the Sabbath but also, by financial assistance, enable him to "remember" it fittingly.

—*Maggid of Dubno*

*   *   *   *

"Six days shalt thou labor and do all thy work, but the Seventh Day is a Sabbath to the Lord thy God . . ." (Exodus 20:9-10)

The Hebrew verb *ta-avod* ("thou shalt labor") may also be rendered as "thou shalt *serve* (the Lord)." Hence the Fourth Commandment may be taken to convey a message as follows:

"Six days thou shalt serve the Lord by doing all thy work, but on the Seventh Day thou shalt serve Him by resting."

—*Rabbi Bahya ben Asher Ibn Halawa*
in the name of Maimonides

*   *   *   *

"Neither shalt thou go up by steps to My altar, that thy nakedness should not be exposed there." (Exodus 20:23)

Beyond its literal implications, this commandment symbolically reminds us that he who thinks highly of himself and boasts of his virtues (the Hebrew *maalot* — "steps" can be

151

rendered also as "virtues") will thereby cause his shortcomings to be exposed. For by his very arrogance, he reveals his foolishness and his faults.

—*Noam Elimelekh*

* * * *

Haphtarah Yithro (Isaiah 6, 7:6 and 9:5-6)
"*. . . Hear ye, indeed, but understand not, and see ye, indeed, but perceive not.*" (Isaiah 6:9)

In the beginning you must hear, even though you may not be able to understand, and see, even though you may be incapable of perceiving. For there is hope that those who are willing to "hear" and to "see" will gradually also come to "understand" and to "perceive", until, "understanding with their heart, they will return and be healed." (*Isaiah 6:10*). But if you will refuse to hear what you are told and to see what you are shown, there is no hope that you will ever come to understand and mend your ways.

—*Malbim*

You are to hearken to the commandments of God and not to seek at all costs to understand the reasons for them. For too great a desire to know the reasons for a commandment may lead you to neglect its observance and to disregard it until such time as you find a satisfactory reason for obeying it. The fact is that no one reason can be considered the basis for any of the commandments; the fundamental point to remember in the case of each commandment is that it is the will of the Lord.

—*Ahavat Yonathan*

* * * *

Weekly Portion of Mishpatim (Exodus 21:1-24:18)
"*Now these are the ordinances which thou shalt set before them.*" (Exodus 21:1)

What is the implication of the phrase "which thou shalt set *before them?*" It is that man must set the Divine ordinances "before himself." He must set aside his own person for the sake of these ordinances and give up his life for them, if necessary. He must view God's ordinances as taking precedence over his own life.

—*Kol Simcha*

*   *   *   *

Why is this section dealing with civil law placed immediately after that commanding the arrangements for the altar? To tell you that you should seat the Sanhedrin near the Temple.

—*Rashi*

Other nations regard the laws pertaining to the relations between man and his fellow-men not as religious observances but as social or civic duties which must be performed to preserve order in the land. The Jewish people, however, regard these civil ordinances as Divine commandments with a sanctity all their own. Just as the ritual of sacrifices constitutes the worship in the Temple, the observance of Jewish civil law represents the Jew's service of God in everyday life outside. For this reason it was only fitting that the Sanhedrin, Israel's Supreme Court of Law, should be seated close to the Holy Temple.

—*Avnei Ezel*

*   *   *   *

"*. . . and his master shall bore his ear though with an awl . . .*" (Exodus 21:6)

The ear which heard it said on Mount Sinai: "Thou shalt not steal" and then he goes forth and steals — let it be pierced.

—*Rashi*

Why should the ear be blamed if its owner does not obey the commandment which the ear heard?

Said Rabbi Isaac Meir Alter, author of *Hiddushei HaRIM*: "It is better not to hear at all than to disobey a commandment one has heard, for one who hears without the intention to obey

153

is deserving of the punishment of having his ear pierced."

Why should the earlobe be pierced?

Because it was not put to its intended use. If the ear heard a commandment proclaimed, but its owner did not take to heart what the ear perceived, that ear must have heard scornful language and lascivious talk of which even one drop is said to push away many words of Torah ("One drop of scorn shoves aside many words of the Law"). Now the soft earlobe was created for the purpose of stopping up the ear to keep it from hearing vulgar talk. Hence, if the ear was corrupted by vulgar speech it is obvious that the lobe was not put to its proper use. Therefore, "let it be pierced."

—*The Rabbi of Gur*

*   *   *   *

"And he who smites his father or his mother shall surely die, and he who steals a man and sells him . . . shall surely die." (Exodus 21:15, 16)

What is the connection between these two commandments?

The point made here is that even a child who is so wicked that he dares strike his own parents must not be kidnapped or sold into slavery, for the Torah does not countenance the sale of human beings into slavery, even in the case of children so utterly depraved.

—*Meshekh Hakhmah*

*   *   *   *

". . . and he shall cause him to be thoroughly healed." (Exodus 21:19)

This gives the physician permission to heal.

—*Rashi*

A sage of old was begged to pray for a sick man of whose life the doctors had already despaired. Said the sage: "The Torah gave the physicians permission to heal, but it did not permit them to despair of a man's life. They have no right to take any action for which they have no Divine authorization."

154

Rabbi Menahem Mendel of Kotzk used to say: "(The Hebrew expression) *unwitting resignation* implies that all resignation and despair stems from ignorance."

*   *   *   *

*"And if a man should smite his bondman or his bondwoman with a
rod, and he should die under his hand, he shall be punished. Not-
withstanding, if he survives a day or two, he shall not be punished . . ."*
(Exodus 21:20-21)

If a man beats his servant with a rod, he obviously intended
to do no more than discipline and correct him. Since such dis-
ciplining is within the master's rights, the law provides that if the
slave survives for a day or two, the master shall not be punished.
But if a man strikes his servant with a sword, or if he stones him,
it is clear that he is attacking the servant out of anger or lust for
revenge and hence he is liable to punishment even if the victim
should survive for many days.

         —Or HaHayyim, after Maimonides

*   *   *   *

"Eye for eye, tooth for tooth, hand for hand . . ." (Exodus 21:24)

First the crime is named, and then the punishment. Here,
too, the interpretation is as follows: *"Eye for eye —* if the aggres-
sor injured his victim's eye, he is obliged to make restitution for
the loss of the eye. *Tooth for tooth —* if he knocks out one of his
victim's teeth, he must make restitution for the loss of the tooth.
The Hebrew word *tachat* ("for") is frequently used in the Bible
in the sense of "substitute." It is therefore quite clear that what
is meant is not that whoever causes another to lose his eye should
have his own eye put out and so forth, but that he must make
financial restitution for the injury he has caused.

         —HaKetav VeHakabbalah

*   *   *   *

*"If a man delivers to his neighbor money or stuff to keep and it is
stolen out of the man's house, if the thief is found, he shall pay
double. If the thief is not found, then the master of the house shall*

155

come near to God . . ." (Exodus 22:6-7)

The term "a man" as used in this verse may refer not only to a man but even to God. ("The Lord is a man of war," *Exodus 15:3.*) Accordingly, the verse may be interpreted as follows:

"If God has given *to his neighbor* (lit. 'friend'); i.e. to a Jew (for every Jew is His friend) *money or stuff,* all the material and physical requirements he needs in order to live, *to keep,* so that he may keep them holy, *and it is stolen out of his house,* and if the Jew is wicked, abusing his limbs and squandering his money and thus desecrating them; *if the thief is found,* if, at the time of reckoning, that man, having failed to repent, is still found guilty, *he shall pay double,* he will receive a double punishment according to his crime(as it is written: 'That she has received from the hand of the Lord double for all her sins' — *Isaiah 40:2*). But *if the thief is not found,* if he is found innocent because he has repented, *then the master of the house shall come near to God,* the man will come closer to God, even closer than he had been before he had committed the transgression, for "even completely righteous men are not fit to stand in the place where repentant sinners may stand."

—Rabbi Moses Schreiber in the
name of Rabbi Nathan Adler

* * * *

"You shall not afflict any widow or fatherless child. If thou afflict them in any way, for if they cry at all to Me, I will surely hear their cry." (Exodus 22:21-22)

The Sages relate that when Penina, the other wife of Elkanah, harassed Hanna (*I Samuel, Chap. 1*), she insisted that she had done so with good intentions; namely, she thought that her taunting would make Hannah pray all the more fervently to the Lord to grant her offspring. Yet, Penina was punished so that all her own children died.

Thus, too, Scripture says: "Even if thou shouldst afflict the

widow or the fatherless child in order to make them cry to Me, with the good intention of making them pray more fervently, I still consider thy action a crime and I will hear their cry and punish thee." —*Elijah ben Solomon Zalman of Vilna*
(*the Gaon of Vilna*)

* * * *

"*If thou lend money to any of My people, even to the poor with thee, thou shalt not be to him as a creditor . . .*" (Exodus 22:24)
Alternative rendering: "*. . . even* when poverty is *with thee.*"

The commandment to give charity and to extend loans without charging interest applies even at times "when poverty is with thee." Even if you yourself are short of money you must still set aside part of what you have for the poor.

With regard to the verse "honor the Lord with thy wealth", the Sages say: "Read not *me-honekha* — 'with (or from) thy wealth' but *mi-geronekha* — 'from thy throat'." This means that you must give charity even if it means depriving your own stomach of food. —*Rabbi Shmelke of Nikolsburg*

* * * *

"*Thou shalt not revile God nor curse a ruler of thy people.*" (Exod. 22:27)

Unfortunately men are in the habit of finding fault with their leaders and of suspecting their motives. Indeed, some of the Children of Israel even suspected Moses of the most heinous crimes. Hence there is an explicit prohibition in the Torah against insulting or criticizing the prince or ruler who stands at the head of the people.

* * * *

"*And you shall be holy men to Me . . .*" (Exodus 22:30)

You shall be holy, but as *men*. You are to sanctify your human conduct, for that is the main holiness required of man. The Lord of the Universe has no lack of angels in heaven.

—*Rabbi Menahem Mendel of Kotzk*

* * * *

157

". . . do not put thy hand with the wicked to be an unrighteous witness" (Exodus 23:1)

Do not become too intimate with a wicked man, because you may thus cause him to rob others by his testimony. If you are known to be intimate with him, it will be assumed that he is an honest man and people will be inclined to believe his testimony even if it is actually false and calculated to cheat another person.

For instance, the Gemarah relates that if a man was seen talking in the street with the Amorah Rabbi Simeon Ben Lakish, people would trust that man with their money without first requesting a witness.

—*Torat Moshe*

*   *   *   *

". . . to turn according to a multitude . . . (Exodus 23:2)

In a case where the appropriate ruling is not clear cut and can be "turned" or viewed from various angles, the decision must be by majority vote. But in cases where there is no room for doubt, the decision is not subject to a vote. Therefore the Jewish people will never defer to the will or custom of the majority in matters of faith and religious observance.

—*Rabbi Moses Schreiber*

*   *   *   *

"If thou shouldst see the donkey of him who hates thee lying beneath its burden . . . thou shalt surely release it with him." (Exodus 23:5)

The good deed carries all the more weight if the donkey belongs to an enemy, because then the deed involves not only kindness to an animal but also the suppression of the evil impulse to hate.

But the enemy referred to in this verse cannot be construed as one whom one hates for personal reasons. After all, we know

158

that it is forbidden to hate a fellow-Jew. Some think that one is permitted to hate a fellow-Jew if one has seen him transgress a law of the Torah, because it is a commandment to hate such a person. However, in such cases there is always the danger that a hatred based on that commandment may eventually turn into a dislike motivated by personal considerations. For if I hate another, though with no sinful intent but solely in accordance with the commandment to hate the violator of the Law, he will come to hate me in return. His hatred for me, then, will be motivated not by the desire to fulfill a commandment but simply by personal dislike. In return, my own hatred for him will take on a personal character and the commandment will be forgotten.

Therefore the Torah, intending to make sure that hatred based on a commandment should not degenerate into a personal dislike, specified that one must give help to such an enemy when he is in trouble.

—Tosafoth Pesachim 117

*   *   *   *

"And thou shalt take no gift . . ." (Exodus 23:8)

A widow once came to Rabbi Joshua of Kutno and tearfully complained to him about a wrong done her by one of the townsmen. She asked the rabbi to arrange a hearing of the dispute in accordance with Jewish law.

Rabbi Joshua, however, refused to act as judge in her case. He pointed out that the term "gift" used by the Law with regard to such situations implies not only bribes of money but also tears. Tears, particularly those of a widow, can act as a powerful influence, preventing the judge from giving a fair hearing also to the other party in the dispute.

*   *   *   *

" . . .and the Feast of Ingathering at the end of the year . . ." (Exodus 23:16)

Why does this verse refer to the holiday as "the Feast of

Ingathering" instead of as "the Feast of Tabernacles" as it is termed in all the other Biblical passages where mention is made of it?

In order to answer this question, we must first understand the original purpose of the festival. The Gaon of Vilna was once asked why the feast of Succoth should be observed on the fifteenth day of Tishrei rather than during the month of Nissan when the Children of Israel had first gone out into the wilderness.

In reply, the Gaon pointed out that the original purpose of the festival was not to commemorate Israel's journey through the wilderness but to mark the anniversary of the reappearance of the "cloud of glory" above the Children of Israel. In the beginning there had been no need for a special festival to commemorate the cloud that hovered above the Israelites in the wilderness, just as there was no holiday to commemorate the manna which fell from heaven or the well of waters from which the people drank. But when the Children of Israel worshipped the Golden Calf, the Lord caused the cloud to disappear and the Children of Israel were left without protection. It was only after the Day of Atonement (the tenth day of the month of Tishrei), when God had forgiven Israel's sin, that the cloud reappeared. Since this is the event commemorated by the tabernacles in which we dwell on Succoth, the holiday is observed a few days after the Day of Atonement, in the month of Tishrei.

But this portion of the Book of Exodus deals with a time prior to the incident of the Golden Calf, when there still was no commandment to dwell in tabernacles to commemorate the reappearance of the cloud of glory. Hence the festival here is referred to as the Feast of Ingathering."

—Meshekh Hakhmah

*   *   *   *

"And you shall serve the Lord your God, and He will bless thy bread and thy water . . ." (Exodus 23:25)

Why does the text use the plural with reference to the Divine service ("and *you* shall serve"), but the singular with reference to the food (". . . and He will bless *thy* bread and *thy* water . . .")?

Said Rabbi Menahem Mendel of Kotzk: "When we worship God each individual may pray alone and in his own behalf, yet the prayers of the worshippers join together and become one public act of Divine service. But when we eat, even in company with a great many others, each individual still eats only for himself."

*   *   *   *

"And the appearance of the glory of the Lord was like devouring fire . . ." (Exodus 24:17)

If a Jew wants to know whether the Lord is pleased with his worship and whether he is really adding to the glory of God by his act, let him consider whether or not he is imbued with zeal and fiery inspiration. If God has caused him to be filled with enthusiasm and a longing to serve Him, it is proof that his worship has been accepted in heaven.

However, if he finds that he remains indifferent, it is a sign that his worship has not found favor in the eyes of the Lord.

"And the appearance (alternative rendering: '*proof*') *of the glory of the Lord,* the proof whether one's worship causes the glory of the Lord to appear before him, is whether one feels within himself a *devouring fire,* a yearning for God as fiery as the flame which burns upon the altar."   —*Kedushat Levi*

*   *   *   *

Haphtarah Mishpatim (Jeremiah 34:8-22 and 33:25-26)

"Thus says the Lord: 'If My covenant is not with day and night, if I have not appointed the ordinances of heaven and earth." (Jeremiah 33:25)

Alternative rendering: *"Thus says the Lord: 'If it were not for My covenant* (which is studied) *day and night, I would not have appointed the ordinances of heaven and earth."*

161

Were it not for the Law which the scholars study day and night, it would not be possible for nature ("the ordinances of heaven and earth") to survive. Thus those Jews who are constantly engaged in the study of the Law and seem to contribute nothing to worldly affairs actually do much more to ensure the world's survival than those who build houses and open shops.

Hence people who say that those who study the Law accomplish nothing thereby, that they study for their own pleasure without any profit to others, will not only be liable to punishment for heresy but, because they "give an interpretation of the Torah which is not in accordance with the Law," will also be counted among those who "have no portion in the world to come."

—*Sanhedrin* 99

* * * *

The laws of nature are universally accepted as facts which are not subject to debate even if they are beyond the grasp and understanding of man. Science seeks to shed light on the laws of nature and their mysteries, but no one will presume to say that they do not exist simply because he himself does not happen to understand them.

We must take the same attitude toward the laws of the Torah. They must be accepted as established truths not subject to doubt or debate even if they are beyond our understanding. We must make every effort to understand them, but our regard for them must not be made dependent on whether or not we succeed.

The Torah — "My covenant (which is studied) day and night" must be accepted like "the ordinances of heaven and earth" whose truth is not determined by whether or not they can be readily understood but which are accepted as facts which it is the mind's task to see to understand, not to decide whether or not to accept them.

—After Samson Raphael Hirsch

*   *   *   *

Weekly Portion of Terumah (Exodus 25:1-27:19)
"And the Lord spoke to Moses, saying: 'Speak to the Children of Israel, that they take for Me an offering . . ." (Exodus 25:1-2)
For me — for the glory of My Name.

—Rashi

Rabbi Isaac Meir Alter, the author of *Hiddushei HaRIM*, used to say:

"For me — for the glory of My Name. This means that you should not make the offering because you want your gifts to cause the *Shekhina* to dwell in your midst, but only 'for the glory of My Name', for no other reason but that it is the will of the Lord."

There is more merit in the resolve to obey the command of the Lord simply because it is His will that we do so than there is in any other high resolve, no matter how noble.

The Sages said that "the righteous value their money more than their bodies." How are we to understand this statement? Why should the righteous love money so much?

Rabbi Meir Shapiro of Lublin used to say:

"The righteous value money so greatly because they know how much can be accomplished with it. It can help revive the poor, support students of the Law and set up institutions of learning. These things could not be achieved by the strength of the body alone. This is the reason why the righteous value their money more than their bodies. Crude men, on the other hand, must love their bodies more than their money, because they use all their money to gratify their baser appetites."

Why does the text read ". . . that they *take for* Me an offering" instead of ". . . that they *give Me* an offering?"

Because actually man is in no position to "give" anything

to God. Whatever he has belongs to the Lord — "all of it is from Thee and it is only from Thy hand that we give to Thee." Only through the act of using his possessions for performing a good deed for the sake of God does man truly acquire them (the Sages said that it is by virtue of the blessing man recites when making use of a gift of God that "He gave the earth to the sons of man") and if he then makes a gift of these possessions to God it is as if he had given of his own property.

The foregoing was true also in the case of the *Terumah*. God asked the Israelites to "take for Him" an offering, implying that through the act of dedicating their possessions to the Lord they "take" or acquire it so that the property, which actually belongs to God, becomes as their own.

—*Malbim*

* * * *

It is written: "I have given you good doctrine (*lekah*), do not forsake My Torah." Do not abandon the merchandise (*mekach*) which I have given you.

—*Midrash*

You must think of the Torah as merchandise. A merchant never closes up shop because he has difficulty selling his merchandise, for he knows that once he closes up shop he will certainly be ruined. The same is true in the case of the Torah. Even if you should have difficulty studying the Torah you must not stop but continue the work, for once you cease to study you certainly will not be able to go on living.

—*Rabbi David of Kotzk*

* * * *

"... *of every man whose heart makes him willing you shall take My offering.*" (Exodus 25:2)

Actually, all the gold and silver on earth belong to the Lord, as it is written: "Mine is the silver, and Mine the gold, says the Lord." Hence, when man offers these things to the Lord, the gift he gives is not the wealth, because that is not really his to give away, but the willingness of his heart, the good intention that impelled him to make the offering. These qualities are truly his own, and he offers them to his God. But one who does not make his offering of silver and gold in this spirit really has given nothing, because the money is not his to give away and the spirit of willingness, which would have been the true gift, is lacking.

This is the meaning of the specification "of every man whose heart makes him willing": Only from him who gives with willingness of heart and with good intentions, *shall you take My offering.* Do not take anything from him whose heart does not make him willing to offer a gift to the Lord.

—Torat Moshe

*　*　·*　*

"*. . . gold and silver and brass.*" (Exodus 25:3)

Rabbi Moses Schreiber pointed out that the consonants of the three Hebrew words ZaHaV ("gold"), KeSePH ("silver") and NeCHoSHeTH ("brass") denote the days in the Jewish calendar on which the Law is read in the synagogues. *Zayin* (which has the numerical value of 7) stands for the Sabbath; *Hé* (which has the numerical value of 5) stands for Thursday, the fifth day of the week); *Beth* (which has the numerical value of 2), stands for Monday, the second day of the week. The Hebrew letter *Kaph* is the initial of *Kippur* (Day of Atonement); *Samekh* is the initial of Sukkoth (the Feast of Tabernacles); *Pheh* is the initial of Pessach (Passover). The letter *Nun* stands for *nerot* (lights; i.e. Hanukkah, the Feast of Lights); *CHeth* is for *Hodesh* (meaning the New Moon as well as *Rosh HaShana,* the New Year); *Shin* is for *Shevuot* (the Feast of Pentecost) and *Shemini Atzeret* (the Eighth Day of Solemn Assembly) and *Simhat Torah* (the Rejoicing of the Law), and *Tav* is for *taanith* (public fast days).

*　*　*　*

". . . and sealskins . . ." (Exodus 25:5)

> This species existed only at that time. It had many colors and therefore it is translated in the Targum (the Aramaic translation of the Bible) by *sasgona* because it delights and takes pride in its colors.

> —*Rashi*

The logical connection between the two statements in this passage from Rashi is to be understood in the following manner:

That various birds and animals mentioned in the Bible are designated by appelations in the (Aramaic) Targum different from those by which they are referred to in the original Biblical text is not surprising, for it is only natural that they should have other names in the Aramaic language than in the Hebrew in which the Bible was originally written. But the species *tehashim* (translated in English texts as "seals") was especially created for use in the building of the Tabernacle and was no longer extant in the days when Aramaic was the vernacular of the Jews. Hence it could not very well have been given an Aramaic designation. Why, then, does the Hebrew Biblical text refer to it as *tehashim* and the Aramaic Targum call it *sasgona?* According to Rashi, it must be that the appelation *sasgona* is not the name of the species but merely describe one of its characteristics "in that it delights and takes pride in its colors."

This explains the connection between Rashi's two statements. Since he begins by saying that the animal "existed only at that time (i.e., the time of the Tabernacle)," he adds that the appelation *sasgona* in the Aramaic translation is not the Aramaic name for the species but only denotes one of the animal's striking characteristics.

> —*Rabbi Joshua Leib Diskin*

* * * *

"And let them make Me a sanctuary, that I may dwell among them." (Exodus 25:8)

Alternative rendering: *"And let them make Me a sanctuary, that I may dwell* within *them."*

Should not the text read: "And let them make Me a sanctuary, that I may dwell within *it* (i.e., the sanctuary)?"

The explanation "that I may dwell within them" refers to
the Jewish people, and implies that it is the duty of each and every
one of the Children of Israel to make a sanctuary within his own
heart, a place in which the Holy Presence may dwell. If all the
Jews build such a tabernacle within their hearts, the Lord will
dwell within the heart of each and every one of them.

—Moses ben Hayyim Alshekh

For this reason, too, the text specifies "Accordingly . . . so
shall you make it" (*Exodus 25:9*). To this, Rashi comments:
"This means 'for all the generations to come' because such a
sanctuary, built within the hearts of men, can be reared at any
time and in any age.

—Malbim

The author of *Sefat Emet* expressed a similar thought in
his interpretation of Psalm 132, Verses 3 and 4: ("Surely I will
not come into the tent of my house, nor go up into the bed that
is spread for me; I will not give sleep to my eyes, nor slumber to
my eyelids until I find out a place for the Lord, a dwelling place
for the Mighty One of Jacob.")

King David prayed that he would find out a dwelling place
for the Lord, as it were, by performing these four physical acts:
i.e., coming into the tent of his house, going to bed, giving sleep
to his eyes and giving slumber to his eyelids. He wanted to perform all these everyday physical activities with pure intentions
and for the sake of Heaven so that they would rear a sanctuary
for the glory of God; i.e., that they would consecrate his life and
hallow it to the Lord.

*   *   *   *

"And they shall make an ark ... two cubits and a half shall be its length, and a cubit and a half its breadth, and a cubit and a half its height." (Exodus 25:10)

The measurements of the Ark of the Law are given in fractional figures (two and a half and one and a half), rather than in whole figures to remind scholars of the Law that even they still have not attained perfection and "wholeness" in their knowledge.

—*Nathan ben Simeon HaKohen Adler*

* * * *

"The staves shall be in the rings of the Ark; they shall not be taken from it." (Exodus 25:15)

According to the Sages, the Ark denotes the "crown of the Torah," implying that anyone who so desires can acquire the Law for himself by study (which is likened to a "crown"). For this reason the text (*Exodus 25:10*) reads "and *they* shall make an ark" rather than *"thou* shalt make an ark."

But even as the Ark had to have staves by which it could be transported from place to place, so the students of the Law must have supporters who can provide them with sustenance. Accordingly, the Torah specifies that the staves of the Ark must be kept in the rings at all times and must never be removed from there, to teach us in symbolic terms that those who provide the sustenance for students of the Law must never withdraw their support, not even for one moment, for without their aid the scholars would not be able to continue their studies.   —*Alshekh*

* * * *

"And thou shalt make two cherubim of gold ..." (Exodus 25:18)

The Sages relate that the cherubim had the form of a child's face. Thus the two cherubim upon the Ark were to remind him who would study the Law that he must be like a child in two respects; he must accept the authority of the Law like an obedient child who has not yet begun to study, and he must be pure and innocent of sin like a child.   —*Nahal Kedumim*

* * * *

168

"And the cherubim shall spread out their wings on high, screening the ark cover with their wings . . ." (Exodus 25:20)

The cherubim on the Ark containing the Law had the form of a child's face, implying that the study of the Law in which children engage in the *heder* serves as a shield of merit for the entire community of Israel, protecting it from evil ("screening the ark cover with their wings").

The Sages said: "The world survives only by the merit of the children in the house of study, as it is written: 'Out of the mouth of babes and sucklings hast Thou founded strength because of Thine adversaries, that Thou mightest silence the enemy and the avenger.' (*Psalm 8:3*)"

—*Tzror HaMor*

*   *   *   *

". . . with their faces one to another . . ." (Exodus 25:20)
     And one text says: "And their faces to the House." How so? One way if they do the will of the Omnipresent, and the other way if they will not do the will of the Omnipresent.
          —*Tractate Baba Bathra*

In seeking to do the will of the Omnipresent, "the face of each man must be turned to the other"; i.e., the individual must think not only of himself but also of his fellow-Jew. He must take care that his brother should also remain true to Judaism, and that his brother's child, too, should be able to study the Law. If a person's "face is turned to the house," if he thinks only of the spiritual needs of his own house, it is proof that he is not doing the will of the Omnipresent.

—*Pardes Yosef*

*   *   *   *

". . . and in the Ark thou shalt put the testimony . . ." (Exod. 25:21)
     He should first put the Testimony into it and only afterwards should he put the cover on it for the first time.
          —*Rashi*

169

If you want to take the Law unto yourself you must first become "an ark of pure gold," a person free of sin and impurity. As long as your body is not pure, you cannot employ it as a receptacle for the Law. Only after that can you add "the cover with the cherubim" and come closer to heaven. Only then "shall the cherubim spread out their wings on high." (*Exodus 25:20*)

—*Hashava LeTovah*

* * * *

"And thou shalt make a candlestick of pure gold . . . its globes and its flowers shall be of one piece with it." (Exodus 25:31)

There are reformers who draw on commentaries and illustrations from non-Jewish literature or on the works of Jewish heretics in order to explain a passage in the Bible. The specification in the Torah that even the decorations and ornaments of the *menorah*, the candlestick which symbolizes the Torah, should be of one piece with the candlestick was meant to teach us in symbolic terms that all explanations of Biblical passages should be taken from sacred literature and not "grafted" onto the holy text from alien sources.

—*Torat Moshe*

* * * *

"And thou shalt make the boards for the Tabernacle of acacia wood, standing up." (Exodus 26:15)

> The world was unworthy to have the use of cedars, and they (the cedars) were created solely for the Tabernacle and subsequently for the Temple.

> —*Midrash*

Cedarwood, which is very hard, symbolizes firmness and toughness ("man should always be tender as a reed and not hard as a cedar"). The character trait of hardness should not exist in the world at all except for use for those holy purposes symbolized by the Tabernacle and the Temple. In such matters firmness and inflexibility are imperative, because these qualities will guard us against the influence of scoffers and keep us from being lured away from the path of Judaism by instigators and seducers.

—Avnei Ezel

*   *   *   *

"...twenty boards for the south side southward." (Exodus 26:18)
The Hebrew word KeReSH ("board") spells SHeKeR
("falsehood") in reverse.

In other words, if you succeed in "reversing" falsehood you
will achieve the highest level of holiness — you will be worthy of
becoming a part of the Sanctuary.

—Noam Elimelekh

*   *   *

Haphtarah Terumah (I Kings 5:26-6:13)
*"As for this house which thou art building, if thou wilt walk in My
statutes and execute My ordinances and keep all My commandments..."* (I Kings 6:12)
Said the Lord to King Solomon:
"Do not think that the house which thou hast built becomes
a Holy Temple just because thou hast made generous use of gold
and silver in its construction. Only *if thou wilt walk in My statutes and execute My ordinances* canst thou build a place in which
the *Shekhina* will dwell and thus turn that place into a Holy
Temple."

"My statutes and ordinances" — these, and not silver and
gold, are the true building materials for the Temple. If Israel has
these materials, it can have a Holy Temple even though the visible
edifice has been destroyed, and we have the assurance from God
that He shall *"dwell therein among the Children of Israel and
will not forsake My people Israel."*

—Kokhav MiYaakov

*   *   *   *

Weekly Portion of Tetzaveh (Exodus 27:20-30:10)
*"And thou shalt command the Children of Israel that they bring to
thee pure olive oil..."* (Exodus 27:20)

171

Israel is likened to an olive which yields up its oil only when it is crushed, for Israel reveals its true virtues only when it is made to suffer.

The Jews are also likened to oil which never mixes with any other liquid but always remains on top, for the Jews always remain above the other nations and never mingle with them.

It is remarkable that although they have had to suffer torture and oppression, the Jews have remained on a level high above that of their oppressors and steadfastly refused to mingle with them.

— *Tzror HaMor*

*   *   *   *

"... *beaten for the light* ..." (Exodus 27:20)

If you want to reprove a person — to "beat him", as it were, to make him feel crushed and contrite, you must do it not to humiliate him but "for the light"; i.e., in order to light his path and to show him the right way.

— *Rabbi Yehiel of Aleksander*

*   *   *   *

"*beaten for the light to cause a lamp to burn continually.*" (Exodus 27:20)

If the light of the Torah is to burn continually, you must kindle it in such a manner that it should remain aglow forever, an eternal flame to brighten even the dark night of spiritual decline and the humiliation of exile.

— *Rabbinic Literature*

*   *   *   *

"*And bring thou near to thee Aaron thy brother* ..." (Exod. 28:1)

Why is it written: "Had not Thy law been my delight, I would have perished in my affliction (Paslm 119:92)?" Because when the Holy One, blessed be He, said to Moses: "And bring thou near to thee Aaron thy brother," Moses was displeased, but God said to him: "The Torah was Mine and I gave it to thee. Had it not been for the Torah, I would have destroyed My world." — *Midrash*

God appointed Aaron, and not Moses, to the office of High Priest, because the work of bringing the people, including sinners, closer to the Lord required a leader who would be closer to the people than Moses. Due to the high moral level he had attained, Moses was too far removed from the people, and just as it is useless to engage a great Talmudic scholar to teach a small child who has yet to learn the Hebrew alphabet, so Moses would not have made a good High Priest for the Children of Israel.

When God told Moses the reason why he could not become High Priest, He gave him to understand that he was disqualified solely because of the high spiritual level he had attained.

The Lord said to Moses:

"When I gave My Law to the Jewish people, I did not instruct them in it Myself because they were too remote from Godly things to be able to receive the instruction from Me directly. For this reason I appointed you, a mortal, to accept the Law and to teach it to the people. Likewise, when I want a High Priest to atone for the sins of the people and bring them closer to Me, you, Moses, cannot perform this task because you are too far above them. Hence I have given the office to your brother Aaron, who is on a lower rung than you and thus closer to the people than you are."

—*Ohel Yaakov*

*   *   *   *

"And thou shalt make holy garments for Aaron thy brother for splendor and for beauty. And thou shalt speak to all that are of wise heart . . . that they make Aaron's garments to sanctify him that he may minister to Me in the priestly office." (Exodus 28:2-3)

Ordinary people tend to honor only those who are dressed in beautiful garments. For this reason God commanded Moses to tell the Children of Israel that the priestly robes were to be made "for splendor and for beauty"; that is, to enhance the dignity of the holders of priestly office. But to those who were "of wise heart", who would understand the deeper significance of the priestly robes, Moses was to say that they were to make the garments "to sanctify him that He may minister to Me"; that is, not only to lend added dignity and splendor to the persons of the priests but to sanctify the priests the better to serve the Lord.

—*Rabbi Simon Schreiber of Cracow*

* * * *

"Six of their names on the one stone . . ." (Exodus 28:10)

According to the Jerusalem Talmud (Tractate Sotah, section beginning with *Elu Ne'emrin*) the name of the Tribe of Benjamin was divided between two of the stones in the ephod with the syllable *Ben* engraved on the one stone, and *Yamin* on the other. The name was divided between the two "shoulders" of the ephod. That is why, in the blessing of Moses (*Deut. 33:12*) it is said of Benjamin: "And he dwells between his shoulders."

—*Meshekh Hakhmah*

* * * *

". . . And the fourth row a beryl and an onyx and a jasper . . ." (Exodus 28:20)

According to the Sages (Jacob Ben Asher—1269-1340) the jasper was the stone of the Tribe of Benjamin.

An incident took place in connection with this stone which should teach us the importance of the commandment to honor one's father. The Gemarah (Jerusalem Talmud, Tractate Peah) relates that one day the jasper fell off the priestly breastplate, and it was known that only one man, Doma ben Nethina, a Gentile, had a stone fit to replace it. However, when this man was asked for the stone, he explained that his father, who had the key to the chest in which the jasper was kept, was asleep and that he would not disturb his sleep for this purpose. Thus he missed an opportunity to make a great deal of money This incident is frequently cited as an example of how children should honor their parents.

Why was it ordained that of all the gems on the ephod, the stone of the tribe of Benjamin should be the one to help demonstrate a lesson in the honor due a father from his son? Because Benjamin, the son of Jacob, had been perfect in his observance of the law to honor his father, for he had not had a part in the sale of Joseph and hence had no share in the blame for the grief this act caused his father.

—*Anon.*

* * * *

"... *and Aaron shall bear the judgment of the Children of Israel upon his heart before the Lord continually.*" (Exodus 28:30)

Aaron the High Priest was to represent in his person the heart of the Jewish people. Thus, even as the heart is the first organ to feel any pain that strikes the body, so Aaron felt the sufferings of every Jew and would pray for him.

This is the interpretation of the verse quoted above:

"*And Aaron shall bear the judgment of the Children of Israel* ('judgment' implying punishment, those decrees which entail suffering) *upon his heart;* he shall wear the 'breastplate of judgment' over his heart to show that whenever suffering will come to the Children of Israel, their pain will be very close to his heart and he will pray to the Lord to annul the evil decree."

—*Be'er Mayim Hayyim*

* * * *

" ... *and it shall always be upon his forehead that they may be accepted before the Lord.*" (Exodus 28:28)

"The Gold Plate atones for the sin of insolence." (*Tractate Erkhin 16*)

Scripture teaches the leader in Israel that when insolence and disregard of authority are rampant everywhere, he, the true leader of his people, must continue to bear with pride his Divinelybestowed crown upon which is written, like the engraving on a signet, "Holy to the Lord." This will serve as a counterbalance for all the insolence in this world, an acceptable atonement before the Lord.   *Rabbi Y. Lipschitz of Kalisz*

*   *   *   *

"The one lamb thou shalt offer in the morning, and the other lamb thou shalt offer at dusk." (Exodus 29:39)

Man must endeavor to serve the Lord in the morning as well as at the dusk of life, in youth as well as in old age. In youth, the body is healthy and strong, and man is in full possession of his vigor and energy. However, his mental faculties are still not fully matured. In old age, his mental faculties are mature, but his physical strength has declined.

Accordingly, the morning sacrifice should remind man to accept the sovereignty of the kingdom of heaven at the time when the sun of his own life is on the rise and not to allow himself to be led astray by the follies of this world. The sacrifice which he is required to offer at dusk, by the same token, should teach him that even when the sun of his life is about to set he must not grow lax in his endeavors but must gather new strength by continuing to serve the Lord.   —*HaDrash VeHaEyun*

*   *   *   *

Haphtarah Tetzaveh (Ezekiel 43:10-27)

"...show the House to the house of Israel so that they may be ashamed of their iniquities . . ." (Ezekiel 43:10)

Alternative rendering: "Rebuke Israel with *the House so that they may be ashamed . . ."*

Said the Lord to the Prophet Ezekiel: "Tell the people of Israel that you have already seen in a vision the future Temple complete with all its appointments, and that only their sins delay its completion. Then they will be ashamed of their iniquities and repent of their sins."   —*Malbim*

*   *   *   *

176

"And if they are ashamed of all that they have done, make known to them the form of the House and the fashion thereof . . . and write it in their sight that they may keep the whole form thereof . . ."
(Ezekiel 43:11)

We read in the Book of Lamentations (Chapter 2, Verse 8) that "the Lord has purposed to destroy the wall of the daughter of Zion; He has stretched out the line; He has not withdrawn His hand from destroying."

This is interpreted to mean that the Third Temple, which will rise in the Land of Israel in days to come, was ready in heaven even before the Second Temple was destroyed.

The reasoning which leads to this interpretation proceeds as follows:

What does the text mean by stating that the Lord planned to destroy the wall of Zion and did not withdraw His hand and at the same time saying that "He has stretched out the line," an act associated with building rather than with the razing of a house?

The Rabbi of Ger said: "According to Jewish law it is forbidden to destroy a synagogue before another has been built to take its place. The Midrashim relate that even God fulfills the laws of the Torah. It is obvious then that God could have permitted the destruction of the Temple only if a new Temple was ready in heaven to replace it at the appointed time."

Hence the thought of the verse cited from the Book of Lamentations is as follows:

"The Lord has purposed to destroy the wall of the daughter of Zion, but He could not carry out this plan until He had first *stretched out the line* to plan the future Temple. Only after that did He *not withdraw His hand from destroying;* only then could He proceed with the destruction of the old Temple."

*   *   *   *

". . . that they may keep the whole form thereof, and all the ordinances thereof, and do them." (Ezekiel 43:11)

The people of Israel must be so firm in their faith in the coming of the Messiah that they must make themselves thoroughly familiar with the plans and the "whole form" of the Temple, so that even if the Messiah should appear the very next day they should be able to start building the Temple at once.

If they will truly be so firm in their faith in the coming of the Messiah, if they will *"keep the whole form* (of the Temple) *and all the ordinances thereof"*, they will be found worthy of "doing them", of carrying out all the ordinances in practice in the building of the new Temple.

—*Rabbi Yom Tov Lipmann Heller*

* * * *

Weekly Portion of Ki Thissa (Exodus 30:11-34:35)

"And the Lord spoke to Moses, saying: 'When thou takest the sum of the Children of Israel, according to their number, then they shall give every man a ransom for his soul . . .'" (Exodus 30:11-12)
Alternative rendering: *"And the Lord spoke to Moses, saying: 'When thou* appointest the head *of the Children of Israel . . .'"*

The Lord said to Moses:

"When thou wilt appoint a leader and head of the Children of Israel, thou shalt choose only a man who is willing to sacrifice himself as a ransom for his people if need be."

—*Rabbi Moses ben Hayyim Alshekh*

* * * *

"This they shall give, every one that passes among them, that are numbered, from twenty years old and upward . . ." (Exod. 30:13-14)
Rabbi Meir said: "The Holy One, blessed be He, drew forth a coin of fire from beneath the Throne of Glory and showed it to Moses, saying: 'In this manner shall they give it.' "

—*Midrash Tanhuma*

178

In spending money, one must remember that the coin of gold or silver is like a fire. Fire can burn and destroy, but if it is put to proper use, it can give warmth and do much good. The same is true of the coin. If it is spent for good causes, such as charity and free loans to the deserving needy, it can be of great benefit to mankind, but if it should be squandered for evil purposes it can cause ruin and damage like fire that is allowed to burn untended.

—Noam Elimelekh

*   *   *   *

"... and thou shalt put (the laver) between the Tent of Meeting and the altar and thou shalt put water there." (Exodus 30:18)

Why does the Scriptural text read shamah ("there") and not bo ("therein" or '"into it')?

Because the important thing is not the vessel in which the water is contained but the place in which the vessel is set up.

According to Scriptural specifications, the water for the ritual laving of hands and feet in the Tabernacle did not have to be kept in a laver of brass, but could be taken from any holy vessel employed in the Divine service. The law specifies only the place in which the laving was to be performed; namely, somewhere between the Tent of Meeting and the altar.

Thus the text reads "and thou shalt put water there", meaning, "thou shalt put the water into the place appointed by law but the vessel in which it is kept need not necessarily be a laver made of brass."

—Meshekh Hakhmah

*   *   *   *

"See, I have called by name Bezalel the son of Uri ... to devise skillful works ..." (lit. "intentions" or "thoughts") (Exod. 31:1, 4)

Since makhshavot (skillful works) may be rendered literally as "thoughts" or "intentions" this passage can be construed to imply that Bezalel knew the intentions of everyone who con-

179

tributed gifts for the building of the Tabernacle, and he devised a use for each gift, from the feed for the cattle drawing the wagons to the Holy of Holies itself, in accordance with the purity of the donor's intentions in making the gift. Thus gifts entirely untainted by ulterior motivations such as pride or ambition on the part of their donor would be placed into the most sacred vessels of the Sanctuary.

—*Sihot Tzaddikim*

* * * *

"Verily you shall keep My Sabbaths . . ." (Exodus 31:13)
> (The Hebrew word *akh* — "verily") may be construed as excepting the Sabbath from the days on which the work of the Tabernacle may be done.

—*Rashi*

Nachmanides asks: "If the expression *akh* implies a narrowing qualification, it would have to set limits to the sanctity of the Sabbath, but is not this passage intended to magnify the importance of the Sabbath by indicating that one may not even work on the construction of the Tabernacle on the Sabbath?"

The answer is as follows:

Scripture frequently employs the expression *akh* to indicate a modification of what has been said before (as in "let them be married to whom they think best; *but only* into the family of the tribe of their father shall they be married" — *Num. 36:6;* or in "Rise up, go with them, *but only* the word which I speak to thee, that thou shalt do" — *Num. 22:30*).

In this passage, too, *akh* denotes a modification of what has gone before; i.e., that the Sanctuary which has been discussed in detail in the passages immediately preceding will indeed be a true dwelling place of the Holy Presence *"but only* if you shall keep My Sabbaths."* This implies that "if you will not keep My Sabbath, all the work will have been done in vain." Hence, if the observance of the Sabbath is an essential prerequisite for the sanctity of the

Tabernacle, it stands to reason that the Sabbath takes precedence over the work connected with the construction of the Tabernacle, and no such work may be done on the Sabbath.

—*Shem MiShmuel*

*   *   *   *

"... *every one who profanes* (the Sabbath) *shall surely be put to death, for whoever does any work on it, that soul shall be cut off from among his people.*" (Exodus 31:14)

Why should the violation of the Sabbath be subject to the death penalty? Does not the law explicitly state that the saving of a human life takes precedence over the observance of the Sabbath? Would this not imply that no Jew should ever be put to death for the sake of the Sabbath?

The answer lies in the Scriptural statement quoted above. We are told that "whoever does any work on (the Sabbath) shall be cut off from his people." Thus, when a Jew wilfully profanes the Sabbath, his soul is cut off from its very roots. Through his act of desecration he has already become as one who has been put to death, one whose life no longer has any meaning. Hence the law concerning the precedence of human life over the Sabbath is not applicable in his case.   —*The Rabbi of Miedzieboz*

*   *   *   *

"... *to observe the Sabbath throughout their generations* ..." (Exodus 31:16)

Le-dorotham ("throughout their generations") is spelled without the *vav*. Hence it may be read *le-dirotham* ("throughout their dwelling places").

When the Sabbath enters and the dwelling place of the Jewish home is ready to receive it, if the Sabbath table is set and the lights have been kindled, the *Shekhina* says: "I will dwell here with you." But if the home is not properly prepared for the Sabbath, He says: "This is no dwelling-place of Israel."

—*Yalkut Reubeni*

*   *   *   *

"It is a sign between Me and the Children of Israel forever..." (Exodus 31:17)

The Sabbath is the sign, the identifying mark, of the Jew. Just as the sign on the door of a home indicates who lives inside, so the Sabbath is a sign marking the place where a Jew dwells. Likewise, the shop that is closed on the Sabbath is marked as a Jewish enterprise. But if, heaven forbid, that shop should be open on the Sabbath, the mark indicates the reverse.

—*Haphetz Hayyim*

* * * *

"And it came to pass as soon as he came near the camp that he saw the calf and the dancing and Moses' anger waxed hot and he cast the Tablets out of his hands..." (Exodus 32:19)

Moses had already been informed by God on Mount Sinai that the Children of Israel in the camp below had made for themselves a golden calf to worship as their god. Why, then, should the sight of the calf have been such a shock to him?

When he had first learned the news, Moses still hoped that he would succeed in bringing the people to repent so that he would be able to give them the Tablets of the Law. But when he saw "the dancing," when he actually beheld the Children of Israel dancing around their idol, rejoicing in their sin, he despaired of ever being able to make them mend their ways, and "he cast the Tablets out of his hands."

—*Obadiah ben Jacob Sforno*

* * * *

The Holy Books convey a similar thought in their interpretation of Deut. 28:47; "*... because thou didst not serve the Lord thy God with joy.*" The principal reason for the punishment to be inflicted on the people of Israel will be that they did not serve the Lord their God, and went so far as to perpetrate this sin of omission "with joy." They were actually glad that they were doing evil.

* * * *

". . . and he broke them . . ." (Exodus 32:19)

> Moses said: "But the whole Torah is here and all the Israelites are apostates. How could I possibly give it to them?"
>
> —*Rashi*

When Moses first learned from the Lord that "thy people have dealt corruptly" (*Exodus 32:7*) he thought that the Israelites had merely been led astray and were imitating the pagan rituals of the other nations, and was confident that they would soon realize their error and return to the ways of truth.

But when he came down from the mountain, he saw that the Children of Israel had not adopted the false gods of some other nation but had actually made an idol of their own. They had done it "in the camp," disguised in the trappings of Judaism. They used the same altar *(". . . and he built an altar before it . . ."* — Exodus 22:5) and recited the same prayers *("This is thy god, O Israel, which brought thee up out of the land of Egypt"* — Exodus 22:4); everything was the same, except that the god they worshipped was not the Lord but a golden calf.

When Moses saw all this, he cried out in despair: *"But the whole Torah is here;* it would appear as if they were keeping all the laws of the Torah, *and* (yet) *all the Israelites are apostates.* They disguise their apostasy in the trappings of the Torah. What else, then, is there left for me to do but break the Tablets which I have brought down with me for them from Mount Sinai?"

> —*Pardes Yosef*

*   *   *   *

"And Moses returned to the Lord and said: 'Oh, this people have sinned a great sin . . .'" (Exodus 32:31)

If Moses intended to pray to the Lord in order to obtain forgiveness for the people of Israel, why did he stress the enormity of their sin?

In order to emphasize their repentance. Acknowledgement of the the full extent of one's sin is the basic prerequisite for true repentance. He who is truly repentant seeks neither excuses nor extenuating circumstances for his conduct but is contrite and filled with remorse.

Adam's repentance for his sin in the Garden of Eden was of no avail because he pleaded as an excuse " the woman whom Thou gavest to be with me" (*Genesis 3:12*).

Moses, desiring to have the repentance of his people accepted by God, said: *"Oh, this people have sinned a great sin.* They freely admit that they were guilty of a great sin. They neither seek excuses for their behavior nor do they attempt to justify it. They are filled with remorse and truly repent of their sin. For this reason, O Lord, they are deserving of Thy forgiveness."

—*Nehmad MiZahav, by the Rabbi of Kazimir*

* * * *

"Yet now, if Thou wilt forgive their sin — and if not, blot me, I pray Thee, out of Thy book . . ." (Exodus 32:32)

Alternative rendering: *"Yet now, whether Thou wilt forgive their sin, or not, blot me, I pray Thee, out of Thy book . . ."*

Moses said to the Lord: "In either case, blot me, I pray Thee, out of Thy book. If Thou art willing to forgive them if they have someone to suffer for their sins, I am willing to serve as their instrument of atonement. And if Thou shouldst not be willing to forgive them, why, then, I have nothing left for which to live."

—*K'lei Yakar*

* * * *

"Now Moses used to take the tent and to pitch it outside the camp . . . And it came to pass that every one who sought the Lord went out to the Tent of Meeting which was outside the camp." (Exodus 33:7)

Scripture does not say: "Every one who sought Moses" but "every one who sought the Lord" because he who calls on his teacher is as if he were calling on the Holy Presence.

—*Jerusalem Talmud, Erubin 85*

In the Holy Zohar to the Weekly Portion of *Bo* (*Exodus 10:1-13:16*) we read: "Let all your males look upon the face of the Master, the Lord. What is the 'face of the Master, the Lord'? The face of Rabbi Simeon Bar Yohai."

This statement seems strange at first glance, but can be readily understood in the light of the passages from the Jerusalem Talmud quoted above. It conveys the thought that just as we were commanded to make pilgrimages to Jerusalem on the Festivals to pay our respects to the Holy Presence, so, today, we must call on our Rabbi on the Holidays because "he who calls on his teacher is as if he were calling on the Holy Presence." Why did the Zohar single out Simeon Bar Yohai from among all the rabbis whose names it could have cited at this place? Because Simeon Bar Yohai was the greatest teacher of the Law in his generation.

—*HaDrash VeHaEyun*

*   *   *   *

"And the Lord said: 'Behold, there is a place by Me, and thou shalt stand upon the rock. And it shall come to pass, while My glory passes by, that I will put thee in the cleft of the rock . . ." (Exodus 33:21-22)

Rabbi Meir Shapiro of Lublin used to say:

"Thus did the Lord instruct the leader in Israel: '*Behold, there is a place by Me;* there comes a time at which My honor is at stake. Then *thou shalt stand upon the rock,* tall and erect and firm as a rock to defend the honor of the Lord. But *when My glory has passed by,* when that moment has passed and the issue under debate is purely personal and of secondary importance, then thou shalt stand *in the cleft of the rock,* hidden and humble.' "

*   *   *   *

'. . . and thou shalt see My back, but My face shall not be seen." (Exodus 33:23)

Alternative rendering: "*. . . and thou shalt see* (My ways) *afterwards, but* (they) *shall not be seen before."*

Frequently we do not understand the purpose of events in

185

history and in our lives at the time they come to pass. Only afterwards, with the passing of time, do the meaning of these events and the purpose of Providence in bringing them to pass become clear to us.

This is implied in the Scriptural text: "And thou shalt see *achorai* ("My back", but lit. "after Me"). Only after the events have come to pass will you understand the ways of Providence, *ufonai* ("My face"; but lit. "before Me"). Before the time has passed you will fail to see them."

—*Torat Moshe*

*   *   *   *

"... *Let the Lord, I pray thee, go in the midst of us, for it is a stiff-necked people, and pardon our iniquity and our sin* ..." (Exod. 34:9)

The Maggid of Dubno explained this passage by means of a parable:

A peddler was standing on a broad and elegant avenue with wooden spoons for sale. He remained there all day, hawking his wares, but he did not make a penny. Arriving home late at night with an empty purse, he told his sad tale to a friend. "Didn't you know that the people on that avenue use only silver spoons?" the friend demanded. "They're rich. They don't need your wooden spoons. Why not go to the Street of the Shoemakers? That's where you will make some sales."

In like manner did Moses speak to the Lord, after the Lord had shown him all the Divine attributes which He had "in stock" (mercy and grace, slowness to anger, readiness to forgive iniquity and transgression, and so forth — *Verses 5 and 7*). Moses said: "*Let the Lord go in the midst of us* — the people. The angels in heaven do not sin. They do not need Thy Divine attributes. It is only our world here below that is in need of them, for Israel '*is a stiffnecked people*'. Hence, O Lord, *pardon our iniquity.*"

*   *   *   *

". . . he put a veil on his face. But when Moses went in before the Lord that He might speak with him, he took off the veil until he came out . . ." (Exodus 34:33-34)

Moses was the humblest of all men. But he was also the leader and ruler of the Jewish people. He therefore had to conceal his humility behind a veil of sternness and dignity. But when he went in "before the Lord that He might speak with him," Moses removed the mask of majesty and stood before God in his true humility.   —*Akiba Eger*

*   *   *   *

Haphtarah Ki Thissa (I Kings 18:1-39)
"And Elijah came near to all the people and said: 'How long will you vacillate between two opinions? If the Lord is God, then follow Him; but if it is Baal, then follow him . . .'" (I Kings 18:21)

When a conflict breaks out between the believers and the unbelievers, every Jew must take a stand and decide which of the two opposing camps he will join. There is no way of remaining "neutral"; it is not possible to support both sides. Every individual must declare himself either as a follower of the Lord or — I beg to make a distinction — of Baal. Those who persist in "halting between two opinions" are much more dangerous than those who declare their support of Baal outright.

King Jerobeam I (*I Kings 11:26-14:20*) openly declared war on the Holy Temple, setting up golden calves as idols at Beth El and killing the pilgrims who journeyed to Jerusalem on the Festivals. Yet it was not during his reign that Israel was exiled. Exile came during the reign of Hoshea, the son of Elah (*II Kings 15:30*) who, according to the Talmud (end of Tractate Taanith) removed the guards whom Jerobeam had stationed on the highways, saying: "Let them go whatever way they please, either to Jerusalem (to worship the Lord) or to Beth El (to bow to the idols)." It was this inane "neutrality" of his that brought disaster to his people. He was the last ruler of the Kingdom of Israel, his

187

reign ending when Shalmaneser, King of Assyria, drove the tribes of Israel into exile (*II Kings 17:16*).

An avowed enemy, who can be fought, is not so dangerous as the "neutral" who "halts between two opinions" and whose vacillating attitude can plunge an entire people into ruin and exile.

—*Netzakh Yisrael*

* * * *

Weekly Portion of VaYakkhel (Exodus 35:1-38:20)
"And Moses assembled all the congregation of the Children of Israel and said to them: 'These are the words which the Lord has commanded that you should do them . . ." (Exodus 35:1)
Alternative rendering: *"These are the* things (*devarim* may mean either "words" or "things") *which the Lord has commanded that you should do them."*

These were the things that the Lord commanded Israel to do: to assemble, to gather together and always be united in heart and mind. Such is the will of the Lord.

—*Sifthei Tzaddikim*

However, peace and unity in Israel have meaning only if the Jewish people observes the commandments of the Torah, if unity brings about a strengthening of faith. A peace which does not attain this end has no value. Therefore the Sages say: "Great is the peace that is given to the righteous as their portion" and "great is the peace that is not given to the wicked as their portion" (*Yalkut Nasse*).

We read in the Biblical account that "Moses assembled all the congregation of the Children of Israel", thus commanding them to unite. But when they had done his bidding he told them at once that "these are the words which the Lord has commanded that you should do them," implying that unity had meaning only if it was accompanied by obedience to the laws of the Lord.

—*HaDrash VeHaEyun*

* * * *

"You shall kindle no fire throughout your habitation on the Sabbath day." (Exodus 35:3)

The Sabbath is a day of rest, on which the people have leisure to discuss communal affairs, to talk about their rabbis, cantors, slaughterers and sextons and to offer their comments on the way their institutions such as the Hebrew school and the ritual bath are run.

This is the reason why we are admonished explicitly: "You shall kindle no fire throughout your habitations on the Sabbath day. Do not mar your Sabbath rest by kindling fires of evil gossip and contention. This is not the purpose for which the Sabbath was given you. The Sabbath is not only a day of rest but also a day of moral sanctity."

—*SheLaH HaKodosh*

* * * *

"And let every wise-hearted man among you come, and make all that the Lord has commanded." (Exodus 35:10)

If you wish to perform a commandment, do it with dispatch. Wasting time on ingenious discussions may impede action. Hence the verse tells us: "Let him who is truly wise and anxious to fulfill the commandments of the Lord not waste too much time discussing them but set about at once to translate his resolve into action."

—*HaDrash VeHaEyun*

The greatest wisdom is not to be too wise, but to obey the command of the Lord without much speculation.

—*Pardes Yosef*

* * * *

"And Moses said to the Children of Israel: 'See, the Lord has called by name Bezalel the son of Uri the son of Hur of the tribe of Judah.'" (Exodus 35:30)

Why does the Biblical account go into such detail to stress the descent of Bezalel?

To show that the contributions the Israelites had given toward the construction of the sanctuary had already served to

189

atone for their worship of the Golden Calf. According to tradition, Hur, the grandfather of Bezalel, was killed by the Israelites when he refused to help make the Calf. Hence, if the Lord appointed a grandson of the martyred Hur to build the sanctuary for the Children of Israel, it was obvious that their sin had already been forgiven. For were this not so, Hur would have continued to act as their accuser in heaven and not spoken up in their defense, paving the way for the appointment of his own grandson for this hallowed task.

—Likutei Torah

A man can attain the level of selfless devotion only if he puts away all petty sophistry. This, too, is the reason why true self-sacrifice helps a man attain wisdom and understanding. The wisdom is given him to compensate him for the pseudo-intelligence he has cast aside.

Bezalel was endowed with wisdom and understanding because of the spirit of devotion and self-sacrifice shown by his ancestors. His grandfather Hur had allowed himself to be put to death rather than help the Children of Israel set up the Golden Calf, and the tribe of Judah, of which he was a member, had been the first to dash into the waves of the Red Sea at the Lord's command.

—Meshekh Hakhmah

* * * *

"And He has put in his heart that he may teach . . ." (Exod. 35:34)

Some scholars have a great deal of wisdom but keep it to themselves because they are either unwilling or unable to impart it to others. Hence the Torah found it necessary to stress that Bezalel and Oholiab had been endowed with both the ability and the will "to teach" and communicate their skill and knowledge to those willing to learn.

—Ibn Ezra

* * * *

190

". . . And they still brought to him free-will offerings every morning." (Exodus 35:3)

There are communal workers who feel that by virtue of their activity in behalf of their cause they are exempt from making contributions to it. It is to warn against this mentality that the Biblical account tells us that "they," Bezalel and Oholiab, the men who did the actual building of the Sanctuary in the wilderness, did not consider themselves exempt from making donations for the purpose. Early in the morning, before beginning their work, they would hasten to Moses with their free-will offerings.

—*Imrei Shofar*

*   *   *   *

"And he made the laver of brass . . . of the mirrors of the serving women who did service at the door of the Tent of Meeting." (Exodus 35:8)

Why were the mirrors of the women chosen particularly for the brass laver?

To serve as added inspiration to the priests who were to use the laver for cleansing their hands and feet before beginning the Temple service.

The ritual washing of hands and feet was to remind the priests that they must never tire in their ministrations but must bring ever-new strength and vigor to bear upon their work. The washing of hands and feet symbolizes renewed energy (Cf. Prov. 25:25: *"As cold water to a faint soul,* so is good news from a far country.")

Now the priests could hardly have had a better incentive than the knowledge that all classes of their people were supporting their work and that their activities served to strengthen faith even in circles that had seemed least likely to benefit from their endeavors.

The fact that there were among the Children of Israel pious women who were willing to give away their ornaments and even

191

their precious mirrors for the Sanctuary of God provided the priests with special incentive to carry on. These mirrors joined to form a laver that was truly fit to dispense to the priests the fresh and clear water symbolizing renewed vigor and inspiration.

—*Avnei Ezel*

* * * *

Haphtarah VaYakkhel (I Kings 7:13-26)
"And he set up the pillars at the porch of the Temple, and he set up the right pillar, and called its name Yachin, and he set up the left pillar, and called its name Boaz." (I Kings 7:21)

Yachin is a Hebrew term implying "establishment" or "preparation." The name *Boaz* is compounded of the Hebrew words *bo* — "in him" or "in it", and *oz*, "strength".

These two pillars had profound symbolic significance. The Sages say that "the evil urge of man is renewed each day, and unless the Holy One, blessed be He, is at his side, he cannot conquer it." But man will receive help from God only if he, for his part, girds himself to wage the good fight. If he makes no effort to do so, he cannot expect support from Above.

The message conveyed by the two great pillars at the Temple porch is as follows: "Only if there is *Yachin,* if man prepares himself and is willing to act to fight off the evil urge, will there be *Boaz,* sufficient strength in him to be able to carry on the struggle until he has won the final victory."

—*Rabbi Hayyim Joseph David Azulai*

* * * *

Weekly Portion of Pekude (Exodus 38:21-40:38)
"These are the accounts of the Tabernacle . . ." (Exodus 38:21)

Why did Moses not render the same detailed accounting for the gold used in the making of the Sanctuary as he did for the silver?

Because the gold was derived from voluntary donations while the silver consisted of the half-shekels which every Israelite had been commanded to pay. Moses felt that some of those who had made the compulsory contribution might become suspicious and demand an exact accounting of what had been done with their money, but that generous individuals who had made voluntary donations of gold would not be so petty as to insist on such a report.   *—Ahavat Yonathan*

But why, then, did Moses render detailed accounting for the brass as well? Was not the brass also a free-will offering? Because brass was the least valuable of the three metals contributed to the sanctuary, and Moses knew that those who give the least to charity are more insistent on getting detailed accounts of what was done with their contribution than those who give generously. Reluctant donors will devise all manner of arguments and insinuations to give them an excuse for not being more generous.

*   *   *   *

"... Even the tabernacle of testimony ..." (Exodus 38:21)

The Tabernacle itself, by its very existence, rendered testimony to the effect that the accounting had been honest and that there had been no embezzlement of funds. For had there been even the slightest misuse of funds, the Holy Presence certainly would not have revealed itself there.

—Malbim

*   *   *   *

"All the gold that was used for the work in all the work of the sanctuary ..." (Exodus 38:24)

Alternative reading: *"All the gold that was* made *for the work (assui* can be rendered as *made* or *used*) *in all the holy work ..."*

This implies that gold was put into the world only that man should use it for good and sacred purposes.

All the gold that was created was made only for "the work in all the holy work."

—Tiferet Yonathan

*   *   *   *

193

"...*a hundred sockets for the hundred talents, a talent for a socket.*"
(Exodus 38:27)

The number of sockets needed for the Sanctuary was one
hundred, the same number as that of the blessings which must
be recited daily. This implies that even as the sockets served as
the foundation of the Sanctuary, so the daily blessings represent
the foundations for the sanctity of the Jewish individual.

Adon, the Hebrew word for "socket", is related to *adon*,
the term for "master." Both the sockets and the blessings attest
to the fact that the Holy One, blessed be He, is the master of all
Creation.

—*Hiddushei HaRIM*

* * * *

"*And thou shalt anoint them as thou didst anoint their father . . .*"
(Exodus 40:15)

Why was it necessary to tell Moses to anoint the sons of
Aaron just as he had their father?

To signify to him the spirit in which he was to perform the
ceremony. Moses had not been jealous of the priestly sanctity
conferred upon his brother Aaron because he, Moses, had himself been prophet and king of his people and even fulfilled the
functions of a High Priest during the seven days of preparation
which preceded the Giving of the Law. But Moses might well
have resented the fact that his own children could not have been
raised to this lofty position. According to the Midrash, Moses
asked God to pass on his own qualities to his children, but the
Lord had refused his request. It was for this reason that the Lord
reminded Moses that when he would anoint Aaron's sons he must
do it with the same joy and eagerness as he had shown when con-
secrating their father.

—*Meshekh Hakhmah*

* * * *

Haphtarah Pekude (I Kings 6:51-8:21)

"And Solomon brought in the things which David, his father, had dedicated, the silver, and the gold, and the vessels, and put them in the treasuries of the house of the Lord." (I Kings 7:51)

David had left a great deal of silver and gold for the building of the Temple. But Solomon used only his own gold and silver, and had the treasures left by his father put into the Temple treasuries. Why did he do this?

Because he felt that it would not be fitting to use David's gold and silver for the building of the Temple. During the reign of David, the country had suffered famine for three years, but David, instead of using the gold and silver to bring relief to his hungry people, kept it for the construction of the Temple. This is the reason why Solomon refused to use it but put it aside instead.

This shows that to give food to the hungry is considered more important than to build the Holy Temple, and David's failure to act accordingly was counted as a sin.

*   *   *   *

195

WELLSPRINGS OF TORAH

LEVITICUS

LEVITICUS

ויקרא

Weekly Portion of Va-Yikra (Leviticus 1:1-5:26)
"And the Lord called to Moses..." (Leviticus 1:1)

Why is it customary to start the Jewish child's training in the Law with this portion, which deals wth the sacrifices?

To teach us that parents must be prepared to make great sacrifices in order to educate their children in the Law. Tuition must be paid even if it means skimping on other necessities, and parents must not concern themselves overly with the child's vocational training but dedicate all his early years to the study of the Law.

—*Avnei Ezel*

* * * *

"If his offering be a burned offering of the herd..." (Leviticus 1:3)

The thought always precedes the deed. For this reason the burned offering, which serves as an atonement for evil thoughts, is discussed in the Scriptures before all the other offerings.

—*Rabbenu Bahya*

* * * *

"...he shall bring it...that he may be accepted before the Lord." (Leviticus 1:3)

They press him until he says: "I wish to do it."

—*Rashi*

How can it be a free-will offering if the man making it must be *pressed* until he says: "I wish to do it"?

Maimonides answers this question as follows:

The concept of "pressing" applies only in cases where a man is pressed to perform an act other than a Divine commandment, for instance, to give a gift, or to sell some object. But if a man whose evil thought compels him to violate a com-

199

mandment or to commit a sin is constrained by another person to perform the commandment or to refrain from committing the sin, he cannot be said to be "pressed." On the contrary, he is regarded as one who has overcome the evil thought which "pressed" him to do wrong. For indeed, anyone who is truly a Jew has a desire to observe all the commandments and to keep away from sin, and it is only his evil inclination that "presses" him to wish to do evil. Hence, if he is "pressed" not to allow the evil inclination to dominate him, if he is belabored until the appetites of hs body grow weaker and his body, too, cries out: "I wish to do it," that is not "pressure" at all but no more than an improvement of his inner will so that he willingly does as he is commanded.

—*Maimonides, Mishne Torah, Hilkhot Gerushin,* Chap. 2

* * * *

"And he shall flay the burned offering and cut it into pieces." (Leviticus 1:6)

If a man thinks that he is a person of many virtues* and fears lest this make him arrogant, let him take all his good deeds and virtues and "cut them to pieces", examine them thoroughly and critically, and he will see that he is still far from perfection. Then he will know that all his virtues are still not true virtues by far.

* * * *

(A man offering fowl) *"... shall take away its crop with its feathers, and cast it beside the altar ..."* (Leviticus 1:16)

Because the bird feeds on what is stolen.

—*Rashi*

This Scriptural commandment concerning the offering of

"* *Oluh,* the Hebrew term for "burned offering" is related to *ma'alah,* the Hebrew for "virtue."

fowl, the poor man's sacrifice, teaches us that even poverty does not constitute a dispensation to put one's hands on money not one's own.

—*Alshekh Hakodosh*

* * * *

"And when any person brings a meal offering to the Lord . . ." (Leviticus 2:1)
Literal rendering: *"And when* a soul *brings a meal of offering to the Lord . . ."*

> Who is it that usually brings a meal offering? The poor man. The Holy One, blessed be He, says, as it were: "I will regard it from him as though he had brought *his very soul* as an offering."
>
> —*Rashi*

At first glance, it is difficult to understand why the term "soul" is used to refer to persons bringing a meal offering but not to describe individuals making burned offerings of fowl. Would it not be logical to assume that the flour, oil and frankincense which are needed for a meal offering cost much more than a turtle-dove or a young pigeon and that, therefore, an individual offering fowl would be poorer than one who brings a meal offering?

But Rabbi Moses Schreiber said: "If a man brings a meal offering, it is obvious that he does not even have the pennies that could buy a pigeon. Therefore he takes a little flour and a little oil from the produce he has gathered as the 'poor man's leavings' from the fields and offers it as a sacrifice, thus depriving himself of food he managed to scrape together for his own meals. This is a sacrifice that may be said to be considered as though 'he had brought his very soul as an offering.' "

—*Torat Moshe (R. Moses Schreiber)*

* * * *

201

"No meal offering which you shall bring to the Lord shall be made with leaven, for you shall cause no leaven, nor any honey, to smoke as an offering made by fire to the Lord." (Leviticus 2:11)

The old Rabbi of Kotzk used to say: "Let the sacrifices offered to the Lord be neither too sweet nor too sour. The spirit behind the sacrifice must be neither too crude nor too familiar."

* * * *

"If the anointed priest shall sin, so as to bring guilt on the people . . ." (Leviticus 4:3)

One who has been acknowledged as a leader must be even more careful than ordinary people not to fall into the trap of sin or even of error. For the masses are only too eager to point to him as their example when they sin, so that any sin of his — even one which he commits in error — may lead them to do evil on purpose.

—Jacob ben Jacob Moses of Lissa

* * * *

"And if any one (lit. 'any soul') *sins in that he hears the voice of adjuration, he being a witness, whether he has seen or known, if he does not utter it, then he shall bear his iniquity."* (Lev. 5:1)

And if any soul sins: If any person fails to perform his mission, although he has heard the *voice of adjuration* from heaven before he went down to earth, admonishing him to "be righteous and not evil", then if the Jew, *being a witness* attesting to the Kingdom of Heaven (Cf. "You are My witnesses" and, besides, he saw it on Mount Sinai and is aware of it, as is written: You have learned to know that the Lord is God; there is none else beside Him" — *Deut. 4:35*), *does not utter it,* if he does not recount this testimony and proclaims it by his own conduct and by his own deeds for all the world to see, then *he shall bear his iniquity;* he will bear sole responsibility for that sin of omission.

—Midrash

* * * *

Haphtarah VaYikra (Isaiah 43:21-44:23)

"The people which I formed for Myself, that they might tell of My praise. Yet thou hast not called upon Me, O Jacob . . ." (Isaiah 43:21-22)

God's complaint against the people of Israel may be illustrated by a parable as follows:

Shortly after his wedding, a young man went out to look for an article to sell. He came upon a market stall where nuts were being sold for four florins a pound. It occurred to him that since the shell comprised half of each nut, the customers paid two florins for half a pound of nutshells. Hence he came to think that he could go into business selling discarded nutshells, and get four florins for a whole pound of empty nutshells.

Taking a quantity of discarded nutshells, he stationed himself on the market place. Soon groups of passers-by gathered around his stall to laugh at the shopkeeper with the strange merchandise.

"Fool," they said to him. "People buy the shells only because of the nuts inside them. What good are empty nutshells?"

Similarly, Isaiah declares in the name of the Lord: *"The people which I have formed for Myself*: I have created this people with all its bodily urges and lusts, for the sole purpose *that they might tell of My praise.* That is the core, the fruit of My Creation. All of man's physical being is only a shell, a means through which this spiritual aim is to be achieved. But *thou hast not called upon Me, O Jacob*: Thou didst not call upon Me, but didst follow the desires of thy body instead, so that all that remains is the shell of thy body without the spiritual core. And what good are empty nutshells?"

—*Likutei Yekarim*

* * * *

Weekly Portion of Tzav (Leviticus 6:1-8:36)
"And the Lord spoke to Moses, saying: 'Command Aaron . . .'"
(Leviticus 6:1-2)

> The expression "command" always implies urging one to
> carry out a command, implying, too, that the command
> takes effect at once and is binding also on future genera-
> tions. Rabbi Simeon said: "Especially must Scripture urge
> the fulfillment of a command in cases involving financial
> loss."
> —*Rashi*

"Especially must Scripture urge the fulfillment of a command in cases involving financial loss." This admonition refers
particularly to the worst days of the Exile, when Jews are denied
nearly every opportunity to make a living and when we hardly
have a penny in our pockets to call our own. Such times constitute the most critical test of our loyalty to the Torah, for the
struggle for bare existence makes it difficult for us to observe
the laws of Judaism. For this reason, we must bend every effort
to muster sufficient strength to pass the test.

—*Sefat Emet*

*　*　*　*

> The expression "command" denotes encouragement in
> reference to the present and future generations.
> —*Rashi*

Since the commandment is binding on all future generations, its observance must be encouraged so that it should not
grow stale but will always be performed with zeal and vigor.
Hence we say in our prayers: "Happy are we and how goodly
is our portion." "And we say twice each day, with affection . . ."
We are happy to utter the *Shema;* and even though we recite
it twice each day, we do so each time with affection, with ever-
new delight, for it never grows stale but renews itself through
the ages.　*　*　*　*

According to the Sages (*Kiddushin 31*) "he who receives
a commandment and performs it is greater than one who re-

ceived no commandment and performs it," for it is more difficult to obey a commandment than to perform an act out of
one's own free will, without having received an explicit command. Hence the observance of a commandment must be given
considerable encouragement.

—Rabbi Menahem Mendel of Kotzk

*   *   *   *

*"...This is the law of the burned offering; it is that which goes
up* on its firewood upon the altar . . ."* (Leviticus 6:2)

> The words "this," "the" and "that" are qualifications. The
> Hebrew term for "qualifications" is synonymous with
> "narrowing" or "lowering."
>
> *—Gemara*

Olah, the Hebrew for burned offering, carries the connotation of ascent. The higher the moral level to which a person
rises, the more humble he must become.

For this reason the Law specifies that, in reciting the
Eighteen Blessings, a commoner need bow only twice, once when
he utters the first blessing and again when he ends the Blessings with "We thank Thee . . ." A High Priest, however, had
to bow after each of the blessings, and the king had to bow
at the beginning and remain in a bowed position throughout
the prayer.

The greater the person, the greater must be his striving to
remain humble before the Lord.

—Orakh LeHayyim

*   *   *   *

*"... it is that which goes up on its firewood upon the altar, all night
until the morning ..."* (Leviticus 6:2)

The letter *mem* in the Hebrew *mokedah* ("its firewood") is
small, to indicate that the fiery zeal of a Jew on behalf of his faith
must not be put on exhibit for all to see but should be kept deep

---

* Hebrew: *olah*

within the heart, away from the public eye.

—Atributed to Rabbi Menachem Mendel of Kotzk

* * * *

A similar explanation is attributed to still another sage in connection with the final clause of the above verse, "and the fire of the altar shall be kept burning thereby."

Bo, the Hebrew for "thereby", may also be rendered as "within" a person or thing. Hence this specification may be construed to mean that "the fire of the altar shall be kept burning *within him";* i.e., that the zeal of sacrifice is to be kept burning within the priest (Aaron and each of his priestly descendants) to whom the commandment was addressed.

* * * *

(In this connection) the Talmud (*Sukkoth 28*) relates that Hillel the Elder had eighty disciples, of whom Jonathan Ben Uziel was the greatest, and Yohanan Ben Zakkai — of whom it was said that there was nothing in Jewish law and lore that he had not studied — was the least significant. Now if the great Yohanan Ben Zakkai was the least significant of all of Hillel's disciples, what must the greatest scholar in the group have been like?

The Sages answer that Jonathan Ben Uziel would be consumed with such fiery zeal as he studied that any bird which happened to fly past him while he was poring over the Law would be burned to death (*Gemarah ibid.*).

If this was so, what of the master himself? Certainly, the greatness of Hillel was on a higher plane than that of any of his disciples. Hillel, too, studied with fiery zeal, yet no bird flying past him as he sat over his studies ever came to harm, for his greatness lay in the fact that the zeal was burning within his heart and was not outwardly obtrusive.

—Sefat Emet

* * * *

". . . and (he shall) *carry out the ashes outside the camp to a clean place."* (Leviticus 6:4)

Just as ashes can catch fire again, so even utter corruption, devoid of every spark of the Divine and hence "outside the camp", may change for the better. Since God "endeavors not to put aside an outcast" we must not discard the ashes of corruption in despair but put them away in a clean place. Perhaps they will glow again.

—*Beth Jacob, by the Rabbi of Isbicze*

* * * *

"And the fire upon the altar shall be kept burning thereby; it shall not go out; and the priest shall kindle wood on it every morning; and he shall lay the burnt-offering in order upon it, and shall make the peace offerings smoke thereon. Fire shall be kept burning on the altar continually; it shall not go out." (Leviticus 6:5-6)

In every Jew there flickers a spark of Divine fire that will never go out. But the leader, priest, prophet or scholar must feed that little spark with fiery oratory, and stir it up anew each morning, with regard to the duties of man toward his Maker — as symbolized by the *olah* — the burned offering which is burned up entirely and rises directly to heaven — and the duties of man to his fellow-men — as symbolized by the *shelomim,* the peace-offerings.

If the priests do this and kindle the sparks of the Divine in the hearts of the Jews they may be sure that the fire of God will burn continually upon the altar of Judaism and never go out.

—*Torat Moshe*

* * * *

"Fire shall be kept burning upon the altar continually; it shall not go out." (Leviticus 6:6)

It shall not go out, even when it travels.

—*Jerusalem Talmud* (Tractate Yoma 4:6)

As long as a man is in his home and carries on his everyday life among his relatives and friends, it is not so easy for him to stray from the straight path into sin. The discipline of daily living, coupled with the ever-watchful eyes of those around him, will keep him from improper conduct.

But when he travels, far from his home, the situation is entirely different. He meets only strangers; there is no one in whose presence he feels constrained to be circumspect, and many situations will arise to test him. At such times it is probable that he will go astray and take the path of evil.

We are therefore told by the Psalmist: "Happy is every one who fears the Lord, who walks in his ways" (*Ps. 128:1*). If "his" is taken to refer not to "the Lord" but to "every one," the meaning of the verse is "Happy is he who remains God-fearing (even) when he walks on his ways," when he is on a journey far from home. The true test of his fear of God is whether he will remain steadfast in his observance even when he is away from his usual environment.

This is the message Scripture and Talmud both seek to convey in the text quoted above:

Fire shall be kept burning upon the altar continually: The fire of the love and fear of God must be kept burning at all times upon the altar of the human heart, *and it shall not go out, even when it travels*: that Divine spark must not be permitted to go out even when the man is far from home.

If the flame of Judaism burns continually within a man's heart while he is at home, it will not die out even when he is abroad.

—*HaDrash VeHaEyun*

* * * *

"(the meal offering) *is most holy, as the sin-offering, and as the guilt-offering*." (Leviticus 6:10)

The meal offering is "most holy" because it is the poor man's offering and as such it is very precious to the Lord. But the sin-offering and the guilt-offering are also "most holy", for both are brought to demonstrate repentance, and repentant sinners, too, are very dear to the Lord, as it is said: "Even men of perfect righteousness cannot stand in the same place as repentant sinners."

—Don Isaac Abarbanel

*　*　*　*

"... the tenth part of an ephah of fine flour for a meal-offering perpetually ..." (Leviticus 6:13.)

An ordinary priest was obliged to bring a meal-offering only on the day of his induction into Temple service. The High Priest, however, had to bring one each day. For with a man on a higher spiritual level, every day must represent a new beginning, a renewal of zeal for the task he must accomplish. Thus, in the case of the High Priest, every day was a new "dedication" such as the ordinary priest experienced only on the day of his induction into office.

—From the Writings of a Sage

*　*　*　*

"But the earthen vessel wherein (the flesh of the sin-offering) is sodden shall be broken ..." (Leviticus 6:21)

This regulation applies to all sacrifices.

—Rashi

If, as Rashi explains, this regulation applies to every type of sacrifice, why is it mentioned only in connection with the sin-offering?

This is to teach us that, like the earthenware vessel that has absorbed some of the taste of food which may no longer be eaten (as the flesh of the sin-offering), so, too, the man who has sinned must be "broken", for only he who has a "broken" heart can be cleansed of past transgressions.

—K'lei Yakar

*　*　*　*

"If he offers it for a thanksgiving..." (Leviticus 7:12)

> All the sacrifices will be abolished except for the offerings
> of thanksgiving.   —*Midrash Tanhumah*

As for him who was fortunate enough never to have sinned
even in error so that he need not offer any other sacrifices, he
is duty-bound to make an offering of thanksgiving to demonstrate his gratitude to God for having protected him from sin.

—*Divrei Shaarei Hayyim*

* * * *

Haftarah Tzav (Jeremiah 7:21-8:3; 9:22-23)

*"For I spoke not to your fathers, nor commanded them ... concern-
ing burnt-offerings or sacrifices, but this thing I commanded them,
saying: Hearken unto My voice, and I shall be your God, and you
shall be My people and you shall walk in the way that I command
you ..."* (Jeremiah 7:22-23)

But did the Lord not command us to offer sacrifices?

The verse should be interpreted as follows:

*"For I spoke not to your fathers nor commanded them ...
concerning burnt-offerings* in the sense that they should be considered as ends in themselves. The purpose of My commandment concerning these sacrifices was that you should *hearken
unto My voice.* You must learn to do My will, so that the sacrifice should serve primarily as a symbol that you desire to please
God by doing His will, *that I shall be your God and you shall
be My People;* as a sign of the covenant between Israel and the
Lord, showing that He accepts gifts from them like a king who
accepts tribute from his subjects. *And you shall walk in the way
that I command you.* The purpose of your sacrifices is to remind you to walk only in the paths of the Lord and to forsake
the ways of evil. Hence, if you do not do My will, if you should
fail to acknowledge Me as your King and to walk in My ways,
and if you regard the sacrifices not as symbols fulfilling a purpose but as ends in themselves, then you are not acting in accordance with what I have said to your fathers." —*Malbim*

"Thus says the Lord: 'Let not the wise man glory in his wisdom, neither let the mighty man glory in his might, let not the rich man glory in his riches, but let him that glories glory in this, that he understands and knows Me . . ." (Jeremiah 9:22-23)

The wise, the mighty and the rich have no reason to glory in their wisdom, their might and their riches. *But let him that glories glory in this,* his willingness to make use of these attributes for the sake of Heaven, *to understand and to know Me.* Only when he uses them for this purpose can wisdom, might and riches be regarded as true virtues. If he does not make use of them to serve the Most High, however, these virtues are utterly meaningless and, in fact, should be considered as serious shortcomings.

—The Gaon of Vilna

* * * *

Weekly Portion of Shemini (Lev. 9:1-11:47)

". . . Take a he-goat for a sin-offering; and a calf, and a lamb, both of the first year, without blemish, for a burnt-offering." (Lev. 9:3)

> Why was Israel to bring more sacrifices than Aaron? He said to them: You have sinned in earlier times, as it is written: "And they (the brothers of Joseph) killed a he-goat (*Gen. 37:31*), and you have sinned in the end as it is written: "They have made for themselves a molten calf." (*Exodus 32:8*). And the he-goat will atone for the incident of (the brothers and) the he-goat, and the calf will atone for the incident of the (Golden) Calf."

—Torath Kohanim

Why did atonement have to be made at this point not only for the sin of the Golden Calf but also for the sale of Joseph?

The Midrash relates that the brothers had attempted to justify their cruelty to Joseph (selling him into slavery and then dipping his coat into the blood of a he-goat to make the aged Jacob think that Joseph had been killed) by claiming that, due to prophetic vision, they had known that one of Joseph's descendants would be King Jeroboam I who would erect golden calves in Beth El and cause the Israelites to sin. By destroying Joseph, they said, they wanted to prevent this calamity. Prior to the incident of the Golden Calf in the wilderness, this might have been acceptable as an excuse for what the brothers had sought to do to Joseph. But when the Children of Israel themselves built a golden calf long before the days of Jeroboam and thus showed that they themselves were willing to serve idols, the claim that the brothers had wanted to kill Joseph because they did not want Joseph to have a descendant who would erect golden calves ceased to be a valid excuse.

It was for this reason that at this point, when they had to bring a sin-offering to atone for the incident of the Golden Calf, the Children of Israel also had to atone for the sale of Joseph.

—*HaGahoth MaHarad*

* * * *

"And Moses said: 'This is the thing which the Lord commanded that you should do; that the glory of the Lord may appear to you.'" (Leviticus 9:6)

> You shall remove the evil impulse from your hearts and you shall all unite in awe, for even as He is One in His universe, so shall your worship be for Him alone.

—*Torath Kohanim*

Every commandment has countless deeper implications and meanings, and even those who are capable of discerning some of them must realize that whatever they know is still only a drop in the bucket as compared to the wealth of meaning inherent in any one of God's commands. It is therefore best to perform the commandment for no other reason but that the Lord bade us do it.

This, too, is the message of Moses to the Children of Israel: *"This is the thing which the Lord commanded:* Do it because it is what the Lord commanded you. Do not try to find other reasons, for you will never understand all its deeper implications. But if you will do it simply because it is the will of God, the *glory of God will appear to you.*"

—*Tifereth Shmuel*

*   *   *   *

"And Moses said to Aaron: 'Draw near to the altar ...'" (Lev. 9:7)
    Aaron was diffident and was afraid to go up there. Hence Moses said to him: "Why art thou diffident? It is for this purpose that thou wert chosen."

—*Rashi*

Moses explained to Aaron that he had been chosen because he was still ashamed of his participation in the making of the Golden Calf and still atoning for it. The Sages relate that following the incident, Aaron had put iron shackles around his loins and had gone from dwelling to dwelling to teach the Israelites to accept the sovereignty of the kingdom of Heaven. For this reason Moses felt that Aaron was the one best qualified to atone for the misdeeds of all the repentant sinners among the people of Israel.

—*Divrei Shaarei Hayyim*

*   *   *   *

"... and make atonement for thyself and for the people ..." (Leviticus 9:7)

According to the Sages anyone who causes another to be punished is regarded as a sinner. The Children of Israel had forced Aaron to make the Golden Calf, and thus caused him to be punished. Therefore, in addition to their own great sin, the Children of Israel bore partial guilt also for the sin of Aaron. Hence the atonement for Aaron was an atonement also for the sin of the Israelites to the extent that they contributed to the sin of Aaron.

Accordingly, Moses said to Aaron: *"Draw near to the altar and offer thy sin-offering and thy burnt-offering and make atonement for thyself and for the people. Thy sacrifices will serve as*

213

atonement not only for thee but also for the people that caused thee to sin."

—*Meshekh Hakhmah*

* * * *

"And Aaron lifted up his hands toward the people and blessed them . . ." (Leviticus 9:22)

The traditional reading is *yadav* ("his hands"), but the spelling is *yodo* ("his hand")

This tells us that Aaron raised both his hands to bestow the Priestly Blessing upon the people, but he placed them together in such a manner that the two hands seemed like one hand. Hence the spelling in the singular.

—*Shaar Bet Rabbim*

* * * *

This is the reason for the Cabbalist view that the Priests, when bestowing the Priestly Blessing, must raise both their hands but must keep the right hand slightly above the left, even as Aaron did, making his two hands appear like one hand.

—*Bet Joseph*

* * * *

At the time when he became eligible for the Priestly gifts, he also became eligible to bestow the blessing — he and his descendants until the time of the resurrection of the dead.

—*Midrash*

* * * *

Concerning the Priestly Blessing, Scripture (*Num.* 7:28) says: "In this way shall you bless the Children of Israel." But there is no explicit commandment in the Torah to the effect that it is the duty of the Priests to bless the people at all. Why was this commandment not explicitly set down?

Because the Priests were endowed with loving-kindness so that they were eager to bless the Children of Israel of their own accord. For this reason Scripture did not find it necessary

214

to command them to do it and confined itself to giving directions
as to *how* the Priests were to give the Blessing.

—Attributed to the Rabbi of Ger

*   *   *   *

"And Moses and Aaron went into the tent of meeting . . ." (Lev.
9:23)

> Why did Moses enter together with Aaron? To instruct
> him concerning the incense.

—Rashi

Why did Moses not instruct Aaron concerning the incense
ceremony before, when he had taught him the other sacrificial
procedures?

Moses did not go with Aaron to instruct him in the incense
procedure, but to prepare him for a tragic occurrence in which
incense was to be involved, namely, the death of his sons Nadab
and Abihu who were devoured by fire when they brought their
incense with "strange fire before the Lord" (*Lev. 10:2*).

Scripture relates that when this tragedy struck, Aaron took
it with exceptional self-control for, like all exceedingly righteous
men, he was willing to accept even sorrow with serenity and
gratitude. It was this ability to praise the Lord even for tragedy
and to accept suffering with serenity that Moses went to teach
Aaron in the Tent of Meeting. The solemn moment when Moses
and Aaron entered the Tabernacle for the first time was the
most fitting occasion for Moses to teach Aaron "concerning the
incense", to be calm, and to praise the Lord even for the crush-
ing sorrow that was to befall him because of an offering of incense; namely, the death of his two sons.

—Imrei Shofar

*   *   *   *

*"And Nadab and Abihu . . . offered strange fire before the Lord,
which He had not commanded them."* (Leviticus 10:1)

Nadab and Abihu both were great and holy men who performed the ritual with sincerity and devotion. Yet they erred

when they offered incense "which the Lord had not commanded them," for even the course of action that seems most logical must yield place to the will and command of the Lord.

It stands to reason, therefore, that if a Jew performs a Divine commandment for no other reason than that it is the will of the Lord, and despite the fact that he does not know its purpose and is unable to comprehend its meaning, then the strength inherent in the commandment will sustain and hallow him.

It is in view of the foregoing that every blessing we recite before performing a Divine commandment includes the phrase "Who hast sanctified us by Thy commandments and commanded us to . . .". The Divine commandment is the fundamental force that hallows man.

—Hiddushei HaRIM

* * * *

(Nadab and Abihu) died because they entered the Sanctuary in a state of intoxication from wine.

—Rashi

How can one say that men like Nadab and Abihu could have been guilty of profaning their priestly office by allowing themselves to become intoxicated?

This statement is not to be taken literally. It simply means that the two men approached their sacred task with perception and rapture not of Divine origin. The allegory of wine is used to describe their conduct because wine is the symbol of wisdom, adding, as it does, to wisdom and opening the heart to understanding, as it is written: "Wine causes the close-mouthed to speak" and the Sages say that "wine makes wise."

Nadab and Abihu went to the Sanctuary with thoughts and emotions that originated from within their hearts. Therein lay their error, because priests, as representatives of the Merciful One, were expected to perform their functions inspired only by the spiritual implications of the mission entrusted to them

216

by God, without any thoughts and feelings of their own.
                                                —*Sefat Emet*

                    *   *   *   *

*"And there came forth fire from before the Lord and devoured them
and they died . . ."* (Leviticus 10:2)

>   Nadab and Abihu died only because they had not taken
>   wives.   —*Midrash*
>   (Nadab and Abihu) would go after Moses and Aaron and
>   ask: "When will these two old men die so that you and I
>   can lead the generation?"
>   —*Midrash*

The two reasons given in the Midrash for the death of
Nadab and Abihu are closely interrelated, with each serving to
explain the other. Their failure to marry would not in itself have
made them liable to death by the hand of Heaven. Even as the
Sages say that Ben Azai chose to remain unmarried because "his
soul yearned for the Torah", so it could have been assumed that
Nadab and Abihu also had been so utterly devoted to the study
of the Law that they did not want to assume the added responsibility of starting a family.

But the second statement clearly indicates that their failure
to marry was not motivated by such noble ideals. For the
position of leadership which Nadab and Abihu coveted would
have left them little time for the study of the Law. Centuries
later the Tannaim would fast and pray so that they might be
spared the responsibilities of communal leadership which would
have taken them away from their sacred studies.

Therefore, if we know that Nadab and Abihu aspired to
become leaders of the Children of Israel, we know, too, that their
devotion to study could not have been so all-absorbing that it
would have explained their unwillingness to marry, which, unless motivated by a passion for the study of Torah, is considered
a grave sin.

217

It was for this transgression that Nadab and Abihu were punished by death by the hand of Heaven.

—*Divrei Geonim, attributed to*
MaHaRaM of Vilna

* * * *

"*And Moses made diligent inquiry concerning the goat of the sin-offering . . .*" (Leviticus 10:16)

This is half of the Torah.   —*Masorah*

* * * *

One of the principal causes of sin and violation of the Torah is rashness, the failure to "make diligent inquiry" before acting as to whether the action contemplated is permissible.

To "make diligent inquiry" is half of the Torah — half the observance of the Law depends upon careful deliberation before embarking on a course of action.

—*Hadrash VeHaEyun*

* * * *

A similar thought is conveyed by the words of the Psalmist (*Ps. 10:13*): "Wherefore does the wicked man spurn God and say in his heart: 'Thou wilt not inquire,' " which may also be rendered as "How does the wicked man anger God? He says in his heart: 'Do not inquire.' "

"Do not inquire so much, O man," the sinner says, in effect. "Do not deliberate too carefully. Whatever you desire to do, act quickly and do not ask too many questions."

Such rashness causes God to become angry, while "diligent inquiry" is conducive to the proper observance of the Law.

—*Ibid*

* * * *

"*And Aaron spoke to Moses: 'Behold, this day they have offered their sin-offering and their burnt-offering before the Lord, and there have befallen me such things as these; and if I had eaten the sin-offering today, would it have been pleasing in the eyes of the Lord?' "*
(Leviticus 10:19)

218

Aaron told Moses that he had not partaken of the he-goat that had been sacrificed as a sin-offering because he had been *onen** and mourners at that stage are not permitted to partake of "occasional offerings." Moses agreed that Aaron had done the right thing (*Verse 20*).

This is the most impressive proof in Scripture itself that all the laws of the Oral Tradition were already known when the Written Law was given to the Children of Israel on Mount Sinai. Scripture itself does not cite a law that a mourner awaiting the burial of a member of his family is not permitted to partake of "offerings". This ruling was subsequently deduced by the Sages from a Scriptural law pertinent to tithing, according to which the individual giving the tithe must declare, among other things, that "I have not eaten thereof in my mourning . . ." (*Deut. 26:14*). Since the laws concerning "offerings" are more stringent than those of tithing, it stands to reason that no one in the first stage of mourning may partake of "offerings."

It is clear, then, that this law, which the Sages deduced from a Scriptural passage, was already known to Moses and Aaron at the time when the Written Law had been given to the people of Israel in the wilderness. The above would be a most effective argument against those who refuse to accept the authority of the Oral Tradition on the grounds that it had its origins in a period long after the giving of the Written Law.

—*Maoz HaDat*

* * * *

"*. . . would it have been pleasing in the sight of the Lord?*" (Leviticus 10:19)

> (Aaron said to Moses) If you had heard in the case of occasional offerings, to which category the meal offering

---

* A mourner on the day of death and burial of members of his immediate family — in this instance, his two sons, Nadab and Abihu.

... belonged, you have no right to take a lenient view and to permit this also in the case of sacrifices that are binding on all generations.

—*Rashi*

How did Aaron know how to differentiate between "occasional" offerings and offerings binding on all generations?

He arrived at the distinction as the result of the death of his two sons.

The Sages relate that actually, Nadab and Abihu had already incurred the death penalty at the time of the Giving of the Law because they had looked too closely at the splendor of the *Shekhina* but that God had deferred their death in order not to mar the festivity and rejoicing attendant on that occasion.

But, we may reason, was not the dedication of the Tabernacle also an occasion for great rejoicing? Why did the Lord choose to mar the joy of that day?

The answer is that the rejoicing on the occasion of the Giving of the Law was greater than that set off by the dedication of the Tabernacle. The Tabernacle was only a thing of "occasional" or "timely" holiness, for it was subsequently destroyed. The Law, on the other hand, is binding on all generations forever, so that it will never be forgotten.

Applying the same reasoning to the question of sacrifices, Aaron inferred that, by the same token, sacrifices binding on all generations were more important than "occasional" or "timely" offerings. He therefore said to Moses: ". . . *and there have befallen me such things as these.* Such things have already happened to me before. Nadab and Abihu already sinned once before, at the time of the Giving of the Law, and yet they were not punished at that time. Only this later rejoicing was marred by their death. Therefore there must be a difference between the significance of the 'timely' offering and of that of the offerings

220

that are binding on all generations."

—Agudat Ezov

*   *   *   *

"And Moses heard that, and it was pleasing in his sight." (Leviticus 10:20)

Moses was pleased with Aaron's reaction to the tragedy that had befallen him.

When Aaron "held his peace" (*Lev. 10:3*) at the time of the death of his two sons, one could have attributed his silence not to resignation to the will of God but to grief and bitterness too great to be put into words. But when Moses saw that Aaron's mind was clear enough to be able to discuss laws, make distinctions between them and render decisions superior to his own, he was satisfied that Aaron's silence was not due to the numbness of shock and grief, and was pleased that his brother had so calmly and willingly accepted the decree from Heaven.

—Torat Moshe

*   *   *   *

"...you shall not eat of...the swine, because he has a cloven hoof and is cloven-footed, but does not chew the cud; he is unclean to you."

There is a Midrash to the effect that in days to come it will be permitted to eat the flesh of swine.

This does not mean that the Law — Heaven forbid — will be altered, "for this is the Torah and it shall never be changed." It is the character of the swine that will change in that he will become a ruminant, and animals which have cloven hooves and also chew the cud may be eaten.

This is the implication of the statement "because he has a cloven hoof and is cloven-footed, *but does not chew the cud.*" The swine is forbidden only as long as it is his nature not to chew the cud. Once his character will change and he will become a ruminant, he will no longer be unclean.

—*Or HaHayyim*

* * * *

"And these you shall have in detestation among the fowls . . . and the stork . . ." (Leviticus 11:13-19)

> Why is the stork called *hassidah* (kindly one)? Because it deals kindly with its fellow-creatures with regard to food.

—*Rashi*

According to Nachmanides, birds labeled as unclean have been so classed because of their cruelty. But why should the stork, which deals kindly with its fellow-creatures, be classed as unclean?

Said Rabbi Isaac Meir Alter, the author of *Hiddushei HaRIM*:

"It is because it is kind only to others of its species but will never give food to a creature not of its own kind."

This teaches us that when giving food to the needy, we must make no distinction between friend and stranger.

* * * *

"And every earthen vessel, into which any of them falls, whatever is in it shall be unclean, and you shall break it . . . Whatever goes on the belly . . . them you shall not eat . . ." (Leviticus 11:33, 42)

An earthenware vessel can become unclean only on the inside, never on the outside, for it has no value in itself. Its sole worth lies in the fact that it can serve as a receptacle for an object of value. Metal utensils, on the other hand, have value in themselves and can therefore become unclean on the outside also.

Man, being made of dust, is like an earthenware vessel. His worth lies not in the outer shell but in the human qualities within.

—*Rabbi Menahem Mendel of Kotzk*

* * * *

Haphtarah Shemini (II Samuel 6:1-7:17)

"And David danced before the Lord with all his might ... and Michal, the daughter of Saul, came out to meet David, and said:'How did the King of Israel get honor for himself ... who uncovered himself today in the eyes of the handmaids of his servants ...' And David said to Michal: 'Before the Lord, Who chose me above thy father and above all his house, to appoint me prince over the people of the Lord ...'" (II Samuel 6:21)

Why did David stress to Michal that the Lord had chosen him "above thy father and above all his house"?

In order to give her to understand that unlike Saul, her father, he, David, refused to think of what "people might say" and that this was the reason why Saul had been rejected and David chosen above him.

It is stated in Tractate Yoma 22 that Saul had been guilty of only one sin; namely, that, despite an explicit Divine prohibition, he had permitted the cattle of the Amalekites to remain alive (*I Sam. Chap. 15*). But that one sin had been considered so serious that it cost him his throne.

The reason why Saul spared the cattle was his over-eagerness to please the people. He allowed himself to be led by the opinions of the masses. When the Prophet Samuel reproved him for his sin, the King replied: ". . . *the people spared the best of the sheep and of the oxen to sacrifice to the Lord thy God* (*I Sam. 15:15*) ... *I have transgressed ... because I feared the people and hearkened to their voice."* (15:24)

This shortcoming, which Saul was honest enough to admit, showed that he was not fit to be a leader in Israel, for where the worship of God is involved, a leader must not permit himself to be swayed by the masses. Instead of allowing himself to be led, he must stand firm and guide the people.

Accordingly, Samuel replied to him: *"Though thou be so little in thy own sight, art thou not head of the tribes of Israel?* (15:17) Thou are a leader in Israel. Why, then, shouldst thou hearken to the voice of the people and do their bidding?"

And Samuel further said: *"The Lord has rent the kingdom of Israel from thee this day . . .* (15:38) for a leader who, instead of leading, allows himself to be led, cannot continue in his position of leadership."

Now, when Michal reproved him for dancing before the Ark in a manner she considered unbecoming a King, saying: "How did the king of Israel get honor for himself today in the eyes of the handmaids of his servants, as one of the vain fellows who shamelessly uncovers himself?" meaning that the people would laugh to see their king dancing through the streets in this manner, David, recalling that audience of Samuel with Saul, wisely replied:

"Before the Lord, Who chose me above thy father and above all his house. Thy father was afraid of the people and of what they might think of him. It was for this reason that the Lord found him unfit to be king. Therefore, seeing that God has chosen me to be king in thy father's place, I must not make the same mistake, to wonder whether the people will laugh at me when I dance through the streets to express my rejoicing in the Lord. For was I not chosen king to lead the people rather than to let myself be led by them?"

* * * *

Weekly Portion of Thazria (Lev. 12:1-13:59)

"If a woman is delivered, and bears a man-child, then she shall be unclean seven days . . ." (Leviticus 12:2)

> If a man is worthy of it, they shall say of him: 'You come before all the works of creation; but if he is not worthy, they shall say of him: 'Even the gnat comes before you.'
> —*Midrash*

(Why do the laws pertaining to unclean animals precede those pertinent to uncleanness in humans?)

As a matter of fact, man is weaker in body than any other living thing. Moreover, while other animals can obtain their food from field and forest without preparation or toil and are not in need of clothing, man must work for his food and clothing. Nevertheless, man is higher and more important than all the other living things on earth because he has been entrusted by God with the task and purpose of serving Him and studying His Law. However, he retains his position of importance only as long as he will be "worthy," as long as he fulfills his task and works to fulfill his Divinely-ordained purpose. Once he becomes "unworthy" by not performing the task set him as a human being, he is lower than all the other creatures because none of them is saddled with the toil and cares with which he must cope.

—*Ketav Sofer*

*   *   *   *

A similar thought is conveyed by Rabbi Jose: "Whoever honors the Torah will himself be honored by his fellow-creatures; whoever dishonors the Torah will himself be dishonored by his fellow creatures." (*Ethics of the Fathers 4:8*).

Since *gufo*, the Hebrew term for "himself," is literally rendered as "his body," Rabbi Jose literally means that if a man honors the Torah and fulfills his duty as a human being, even his body will be on a higher plane than the bodies of other living things. But if he should dishonor the Torah and become remiss in the performance of his task, he will lose the respect of his fellow-creatures because his body alone, without the distinctive qualities that make him human, is weaker and frailer than that of all the other creatures on earth.

*   *   *   *

"*. . . she shall touch no hallowed thing, nor come into the Sanctuary, until the days of her purification shall be fulfilled.*" (Leviticus 12:4)

This is to teach you that you, too, must not touch hallowed things, much less be in a place where the *Shekhina* dwells as

225

long as you have not completed your own "days of purification" by cleansing yourself of sin and baseness. Without purity there can be no holiness.

—*Noam Elimelekh*

* * * *

"But if she bears a girl-child, then she shall be unclean two weeks . . ." (Leviticus 12:5)

Why must the mother bring a sin-offering after childbirth, and why must she keep more "days of purification" for a girl-child than for a boy-child?

According to the Sages, she must bring a sin-offering after childbirth because many women in the agony of their labor vow never again to have relations with their husbands, but then, in their rejoicing over the new-born infant, they regret their resolution. The sacrifice serves to atone for the rashly-made vow.

The above explains also why she must wait longer to make the offering in the case of a female infant than in the case of a male (thirty-three days for a male, but sixty-six for a female). When a girl-child is born, the rejoicing is not so great as it would be over a boy-child, so that the mother will take longer to regret her rash vow than if the baby had been a boy.

—*K'lei Yakar*

* * * *

"When a man shall have in the skin of his flesh a rising, or a scab, or a bright spot . . ." (Leviticus 13:2)

The *tzara'at* lesions which Scripture lists as rendering the victim unclean have nothing in common with the leprous diseases known to medicine. *Tzara'at* is a supernaturally caused affliction imposed by God on man to punish him for a sin or to atone for a wicked deed.

—*Sforno*

* * * *

226

Why does *tzara'at* no longer occur in man today?

Because it was set off by the spark of holiness within the Jew which could not tolerate sin and hence reacted against all impurity by pushing it to the surface where it then manifested itself in the form of lesions which rendered the individual unclean.

But this would occur only in the generations of the past in whom the element of holiness was strong enough to be able to expel any and all impurity. In our own day, this powerful force of sanctity is no longer present and therefore the violent reaction which manifested itself in *tzara'at* no longer occurs.

—*Alshekh HaKodosh*

* * * *

When Israel heard the portion of the Law dealing with the plague of *tzara'at,* they became afraid. But Moses said to them: "Do not be afraid. The other nations of the world may be afraid, but you should eat and drink and rejoice, for it is written: 'Many harm the wicked man but he who puts his trust in the Lord will be surrounded by loving-kindness.'"

—*Midrash Rabba*

There are two ways in which man can be made to realize that there is a God in this world and that he should turn his thoughts to repentance and to the higher things of the spirit. The one way is through plagues and suffering, which remind man that there is a Supreme Being Who will demand a strict accounting for all his deeds and to Whom he must therefore return in repentance. The other way is through Divine grace which enlightens the eye of man so that he will be able to perceive the deeper meaning of his purpose. Such enlightenment from above most frequently comes during the hallowed seasons, on Sabbaths and on the Holidays, the *mikroei kodesh,* "holy convocations," as Scripture calls them, which summon man to commune with himself and to draw nearer to sanctity.

The wicked and the heathen nations do not have the benefit of the joy and holiness of Sabbaths and Holidays. Therefore, if God has compassion upon them and desires to stir them to repentance, their awakening can be brought about only through plagues and suffering like *tzara'at*. Hence they have reason to be afraid. But those who are willing to observe the Law of the Torah and hence rejoice in the Sabbaths and Holidays will receive the same summons not through suffering but through loving-kindness, through the "eating, drinking and rejoicing" with which they will celebrate their holy seasons.

—*Avnei Ezel*

* * * *

"*. . . and the priest shall look at the plague . . .*" (Leviticus 13:3)
Man sees any plague except that on himself and even except the one on his relatives.

—*Mishna Negaim 2:45*

A man can immediately see the faults of others, but not his own, and he finds the fault of strangers more readily than those of his own kin. —*Anon.*

* * * *

"*. . . (his flesh) is all turned white; he is clean.*" (Leviticus 13:13)
The Son of David will not come until all of the kingdom will have turned to heresy. Said Rabba: "How do we know this? From the Biblical verse stating that he whose flesh has turned entirely white is clean."

—*Sanhedrin, 96*

When all the heathen kingdoms will have turned to wickedness, it is a sign that the Messiah is surely about to appear, for it is obvious that God will have allowed a "king as cruel as Haman" to arise solely in order that oppression and evil decrees might cause the Jews to repent of their transgressions. When all men will be so utterly depraved that all shame and fear of God will vanish, and the Jews will be tortured without mercy, oppression will purify the hearts of the Jews. And when

228

the "evil kingdom" will have accomplished this task, it will be destroyed, yielding place to Messiah, the Son of David.

—*After the Hatham Sofer*

* * * *

Endowed with vision as they were, the Sages foresaw the coming of an era of utter spiritual decadence, when heresy and unbelief — the *tzara'at* of the spirit — will gain control of the body of the Jewish people. Afraid that the Jews might despair, they left a message of comfort, pointing out that when all our merits would have vanished, that would be the time of our cleansing, when the Lord will have mercy on His people and send Messiah, the scion of the House of David, to deliver us.

—*HaDrash VeHaEyun*

* * * *

Haphtarah Thazria (II Kings 4:42-5:19)
"(Elisha) *sent to the king, saying:* . . . '*Let* (Naaman) *now come to me and he shall know that there is a prophet in Israel.*' " (II Kings 5:8).

According to the Sages, *tzara'at* is caused by arrogance. Hence the cure is that the person so afflicted must humble himself.

Accordingly, the Prophet Elisha said to the king: "*Let Naaman now come to me.* It is true that I would be able to heal him even from a distance. But his trouble was caused by his arrogance, in that he imagined himself a great man, *a mighty man of valor* (5:1) and did not consider it befitting his high position that he should come to me. Now since the only cure for his affliction is humility, he must humble himself and come to me."

When Naaman finally did come, Elisha did not receive him personally but sent a messenger (5:10) to give him his instructions, all in order to rid him of his arrogance and to

229

humble him so that he might be healed of his affliction.

—*Maskil LeAithon*

* * * *

"And Elisha sent a messenger to (Naaman), saying: 'Go and wash in the Jordan seven times and thy flesh shall come back to thee, and thou shalt be clean.' " (II Kings 5:10)

Naaman shared the view of those unbelievers who, while acknowledging the existence of a Divine Creator, claim that nature, once created, functions without Divine supervision and therefore regard only supernatural phenomena as manifestations of Divine Providence. He therefore expected that the Prophet would perform some supernatural act to heal him.

Elisha, however, wanted to teach him that the ordinary day-to-day happenings in nature are guided by God no less than supernatural events. This is the reason why he told Naaman to immerse himself in the River Jordan. When the captain would see that while the waters of the mighty Damascus, the Amanah and Pharpar, had been of no avail, the waters of the Jordan, a river like all other rivers, would cure him, he would realize that even the common elements of nature are guided by Divine Providence and can act only in accordance with God's will.

—*Shir Meon*

* * * *

Weekly Portion of Metzorah (Leviticus 14:1-15:33)
"This shall be the law (lit. "the Torah") *of the leper on the day of his cleaning . . ."* (Leviticus 14:2)

HaMetzorah (the leper) = HaMotzi Ra (he who spreads evil reports about others).

—*Talmud*

According to the Sages, the plague of *tzara'at* is a punishment for evil gossip.

Our Midrashic literature and ethical treatises are replete with warnings of the serious consequences of evil gossip. Quite

aside from the fact that this sin is regarded as one with idol
worship, immorality and murder, he who indulges in evil gossip
renders his mouth unclean so that even such words of Torah
study and prayer as may subsequently issue from his mouth will
also be defiled and annulled by the forces of corruption.

When David said: "Keep thy tongue from evil and thy
lips from speaking guile. Depart from evil and do good . . ."
(*Ps. 34:14*), he meant that "doing good" has value only if one
guards one's lips from evil gossip. For without this precaution,
the good a man does cannot be credited to him because it is
barred from fulfilling its purpose.

This, too, is the thought conveyed by the statement concerning the leper. *"This shall be the Torah of the leper.* The
sacred studies in which the leper engages will be accepted only
on the day of his cleansing. Only if the leper will repent and
cleanse himself from his sin will his studies be accepted and
credited to him as good deeds. As long as he has not done so,
all his studies will be to no avail."

—*Kametz HaMinha*

*   *   *   *

> The law pertaining to him who spreads an evil report is
> that the *tzara'at* lesions come as the result of evil gossip.
> —*Midrash and Gemarah*

Since evil gossip is considered a very serious transgression,
it is not only forbidden to speak ill of a person, but the Sages
even warn us against spreading the praise of another, for fear
that while extolling his virtues we may come to reveal his shortcomings.

The Sages warn us against making any statement that may
even verge on evil gossip. Thus one should not say that a fire
is always burning in the hearth of Such-and-Such, because that
could be construed by others to mean that he is living on too
lavish a scale.

231

In view of the fact that even such talk is regarded as verging on evil gossip, the Sages admit that it is very difficult to guard against it and that almost every human being becomes guilty of this sin every day (Cf. "There are three things which a person can never avoid: [one of them is] . . . association with evil gossip . . .") . . .

> (This) is told of a peddler who used to go around the towns in the vicinity of Sepphoris, crying out: "Who wants to buy the elixir of life?" and drawing huge crowds around him. Rabbi Jannai was sitting and expounding (the Law) in his room, and heard him calling out: "Who wants to buy the elixir of life?" And he said to him: "Come here and sell it to me." Said the peddler: "Neither you nor people like you require what I have to sell." The Rabbi pressed him and the peddler went up to him and brought out a Book of Psalms and showed him the verse which reads, "Who is the man that desires life" and what is written immediately after: "Keep thy tongue from evil . . ." (Psalm 34). Said Rabbi Jannai: "All the days of my life I have read this verse and did not know how this was to be explained, until this peddler came and made it clear to me."
>
> —*Midrash Rabba*

The peddler who went about peddling cures and remedies demonstrated to the people that keeping one's tongue from evil gossip is in itself a remedy which insures health and a happy life. Men tend to avoid quarrels, hatreds, worry and intrigue — in short, all those things that endanger health, irritate the nerves and shorten life.

Before the coming of the peddler, Rabbi Jannai had interpreted the verse "Who is the man that desires life . . ." as referring to life in the world to come, meaning that he who would keep from evil gossip on earth would receive his reward in heaven. It had never occurred to him that it might refer to a reward to come during life on earth until he met this peddler

232

who explained to him that guarding one's tongue from speaking evil was not only a good deed, deserving of reward in the world to come, but also an aid to health, prolonging man's life on earth by helping him avoid those worries and excitements which undermine health and hasten death.

—*Kokhav MiYaakov*

* * * *

"... *he shall be brought to the priest* ..." (Leviticus 14:3)

A man who spreads evil gossip usually is one who underestimates the power of the spoken word. He reasons: "All I did was talk; I have done my neighbor no harm." But if he were to become aware of the great power inherent in human speech, and to realize that the gossip he has spread about his neighbor will bring Divine condemnation upon himself as well as upon his victim, he would surely be careful to refrain from evil gossip.

The Sages say: "Say not: 'Behold, I am spreading gossip, but not a soul knows about it.' For the Holy One, blessed be He, says: 'Know that I am sending out an angel who stands near you and records every word you are saying about your neighbor.' " (*Midrash Tetzei*).

We know, therefore, that any word uttered by a human being endures and will reach up even into the highest places in Heaven.

It follows that anyone who spreads gossip must be given an impressive demonstration of the importance of speech. For this reason he is stricken with *tzara'at*, and must then be brought to the priest. At that time he will find out that his fate is entirely dependent on one single word to be uttered by the priest. Until the priest pronounces over him the word "unclean," the leper is not unclean, even if all can see that he has been stricken. Conversely, even if all who see him think he has been cured, he remains unclean until such time as the priest will utter the word "clean." This should teach him who would talk ill of his neighbor

233

how great is the power of each word uttered by men, and he will no longer allow his tongue to wag . . .

—*Ohel Yaakov*

* * * *

"For lo, He that forms the mountains and creates the wind and declares to man what is his conversation . . ." (Amos 5:13). The Sages comment: "Even trifling talk passing between a man and his wife will be recalled to the man at the hour of judgment." (*Haggigah* 4)

What connection is there between the verse from the Book of Amos and the comment of the Sages?

A man may think: "Of what importance are my words? A word has no substance, neither can it be seen or touched."

To him the Prophet says: *"For lo, He that forms the mountains* — the Lord, Who has created the great and towering mountains, surely the mightiest mass on earth — *and creates the wind* — is also He Who has made the wind which, though it has no substance at all and can neither be seen with the eye nor perceived with the sense of touch, is capable of eroding even the mightiest of mountains. *And declares to man*: This fact alone should impress upon man most forcefully — *what is his conversation* — the great importance of every word that passes his lips. It is true that words have no substance and cannot be seen but, like the wind, they can cause entire worlds to crash."

—*Anon.*

* * * *

". . . he shall be brought to the priest. And the priest shall go forth out of the camp . . ." (Leviticus 14:2-3)

If it is the priest who must go forth to examine the leper, why is it stated in the verse immediately preceding that he "shall be brought to the priest"?

The Sages teach us that any credit the gossipper may have received in the past for the amount of Torah he has studied and for the good deeds he has performed is subtracted from his account and "added" to the account of the one about whom he has spread the gossip.

According to the Sages, the Hebrew verb *ve-huvah* may be rendered not as *"he* shall be brought" but as *"it* shall be brought," thus referring not to the leper but to the study of the Torah.

It is to this explanation that the first part of Verse 2 alludes: "This shall be the Torah of the leper . . ." The study in which the leper engaged in the past must be brought forth and credited to the account of the priest, with "the priest" symbolizing any righteous man about whom the leper may have spread evil gossip, for it is the righteous, the leaders who are described as the "priests" of the Lord that have always been the most likely targets for gossip and calumny.

—*Ketav Sofer*

*   *   *   *

Also implicit in this verse is the thought that the leper, even while he is still outside the camp, should be impelled by his own free will to repent and to come to the priest in order to be cleansed. It is only in response to his personal resolve to become pure that he should be taken to the priest and thus brought closer to the state of purity.

Only after the leper has decided to bestir himself, to take positive action leading to repentance and purity, shall "the priest go forth out of the camp" to cleanse him.

Man must rise to action himself before he can expect action from Above.

—*Shem MiShmuel*

*   *   *   *

In Verses 7 and 11 the text uses the reflexive rather than the passive inflection to refer to the leper's process of purification. In both instances the leper is referred to as "he who is *to cleanse himself"* and not as "he who *is to be cleansed·*" This

235

is to indicate that the leper must do his share to become pure. He himself must seek to attain purity by way of repentance and appropriate conduct.

—*Meshekh Hakhmah*

* * * *

"And the priest shall go forth out of the camp and the priest shall look and, behold, if the plague of tzara'at is healed from the leper . . ." (Leviticus 14:3)

Why does the text not read: ". . . and, behold, if he *has been healed* from the plague of *tzara'at"?*

A leprous condition due to natural causes is aggravated by gloom, melancholia and loneliness. Logically, then, an improvement in the condition could be brought about by making the victim go among people and letting him be in good company in order to dispel his depression. In the case of the *tzara'at* described in the Book of Leviticus, however, Scripture explicitly stipulates that the leper must be left alone outside the camp. This is to teach us that the affliction in this case is not due to natural causes but was supernaturally ordained as his punishment for sin. Therefore, if only he will repent of his transgression, he will be cured, even if he sits in seclusion.

This is the thought conveyed by the text: *"And the priest shall go forth out of the camp,* and behold, if he will see that *the plague of* tzara'at *is healed from the leper* despite the fact that he was isolated and normally isolation might be expected to aggravate the condition, the priest will understand that the cure did not come about by natural process but came *from the leper,* from within the leper himself. In this condition, the cure depends entirely on the victim. Since his own evil deeds have brought the plague upon him, he could only have been cured by his repentance."

—*HaAri HaKodosh*

* * * *

"Then shall the priest command to take for the person to be cleansed two living clean birds, and cedarwood and scarlet hyssop." (Lev. 14:4)

> The plague came as a punishment for arrogance. What is the remedy he shall use in order to be healed? Let him, abandoning arrogance, regard himself as lowly as a worm and as hyssop.
>
> —*Rashi*

If the purpose of this ceremony of purification is to have the leper abandon arrogance, what is the function of the cedarwood, which symbolizes pride?

To teach the leper the proper attitude. Humility and submission do not mean that the body must be bowed. They imply that inner spiritual humility or contriteness which can be present even while the body stands erect and unbowed.

As Rabbi Israel ben Eliezer Baal Shem Tov explains it: *"And all that stands before thee shall bow* — one can bow even while one appears to be standing erect."

The cedarwood is used to teach the sinner that he need not think he is required to go about bent over and cringing in abject humility. He can stand erect as a cedar and still be as "bent" and humble in spirit as hyssop.

> —*Avnei Ezel*

*   *   *   *

"And the priest shall command to kill one of the birds in an earthen vessel over running water." (Leviticus 14:5)

Of all immersions, why does Scripture explicitly specify in this case that running water is required?

The literal meaning of the Hebrew expression *mayim hayyim* ("running water") is "living water."

Since the leper was lowly in his own eyes, there was reason to fear that he might become despondent. For this reason, "living water" was required to refresh and revive him. He could only be revived and strengthened by the water of knowledge

from the wellsprings of the Torah which is called "living water."
—*Sihot Tzaddikim*

* * * *

"*. . . he shall shave all his hair off his head and his beard and his eyebrows . . .*" (Leviticus 14:9)

The three principal transgressions punished with *tzara'at* are haughtiness, evil gossip and an envious eye. Hence, in order to become clean again, the leper must symbolically cleanse himself of these three sins. He must shave all the hair off his head because he was haughty and wanted to be "at the head" of everything. Next, he must shave off his beard because it failed to guard the mouth, which it surrounds, from uttering evil gossip. Finally, he must shave his eyebrows which failed to keep his eye from envy.
—*K'lei Yakar*

* * * *

"*And the priest who cleanses him shall set the man who is to be cleansed . . . at the door of the Tent of Meeting.*" (Leviticus 14:11)
Not in the court of the Temple, but in the Gate of Nicanor.
—*Rashi*

Scripture allowed the leper a privilege extended to no other unclean person: namely, to stand at the Gate of Nicanor which led to the Temple Court, and from there to extend his hand and foot into the Court in order to smear his fingers with the blood of the guilt-offering.

This was permitted him because he was repentant and had cleansed himself of his trangressions. Symbolically, a door was opened to him through which to "return," as the Sages have said concerning repentant sinners: "The Holy One, blessed be He, opened for them a new entrance beneath the Throne of Glory" so that they might return to Him.

* * * *

Weekly Portion of Aharei Moth (Leviticus 16:1-18:30)
"*And he shall put the incense upon the fire before the Lord . . .*"
(Leviticus 16:13)

238

Let him not prepare it outside (The Holy of Holies) and then bring it in. This is to refute the view of the Sadducees who say that he must prepare it outside and then bring it in.

—*Yoma 53*

It has been the way of the "Sadducees" of every generation to seek to make changes and reforms in religious observance according to patterns prevailing in the world outside. They take "ordinances from the world outside" and "bring them into" the Sanctuary of Judaism. The Sages have always bitterly fought these reformers who seek to graft alien ways onto Judaism. By contrast, the ordinances set forth by our Sages come from within, from the sacred roots of the Law.

—*HaDrash VeHaEyun*

*   *   *   *

"And he shall make atonement for the Holy Place . . . and so he shall do for the Tent of Meeting that dwells with them in the midst of their uncleanness." (Leviticus 16:16)

This verse implies that arrogance is a much more serious sin than any other transgression. For we are told here concerning sinners that the Tent of Meeting "dwells with them in the midst of their uncleanness," meaning that even when Jews have been defiled by sin, the Lord is still in their midst. There is, however, one exception to this rule; namely, when the sin is arrogance. For we are explicitly told elsewhere (*Psalm 101:5*) that "whoso is haughty of eye and proud of heart, him I will not suffer" and the Sages say: "I (the Lord) and he (the haughty man) cannot dwell together in this world."

—*Baal Shem Tov*

*   *   *   *

The Rabbi of Lublin used to say: "I prefer the wicked man who knows he is wicked to the righteous man who knows that he is righteous."

When the Rabbi of Przysucha asked him to explain this statement, he replied:

"The wicked man who knows he is wicked still has some truth in his heart and hence has retained a link with God. But the righteous man who considers himself righteous is not truthful because he is guilty of a sin — the sin of pride, for 'there is no righteous man in the world who always does good and never sins.' And since he is guilty of arrogance, he has cut himself off from God because the Lord and a haughty man cannot dwell together in this world."

* * * *

". . . and have made atonement for himself and for his household and for all the assembly of Israel." (Leviticus 16:17)

How foolish are those communal leaders who want to reform their community but fail to effect the same improvement in themselves and their own families! Their leadership cannot be fruitful of good results. Before a leader can make atonement "for all the assembly of Israel," he must first make atonement "for himself and for his household." If he does not do so, his home will be a blemish in the community and whatever measures he may take in an effort to improve his community will be of no avail.

—*Musarist Writings*

* * * *

"And Aaron shall come into the Tent of Meeting . . ." (Lev. 16:23)
Only then did he come into the Tent of Meeting in order to bring out the spoon and the censer in which he had burned the incense in the Holy of Holies.

—*Rashi*

Even such seemingly menial functions as removing the spoon and the censer had to be performed by no less a person than the High Priest.

From this, said Rabbi Israel ben Eliezer Baal Shem Tov, we learn that in ministering to a scholar, the clearing away of the utensils with which he ate his meal is as important a function

as the removal of the spoon and the censer after the burning
of the incense in the Holy of Holies.

*   *   *   *

*"For on this day shall atonement be made for you to cleanse you
from all your sins. You shall be clean before the Lord."* (Lev. 16:30)

The Lord will make atonement for all your sins, but only
if you will be clean before the Lord — if you will first repent
and cleanse yourselves of your transgressions.

—*Binah LeIttim*

*   *   *   *

Rabbi Akiba said: "Happy are you, O Israel; before Whom
you are cleansed, and Who is it that cleanses you? Your
Father in Heaven; for it is written: 'You shall be clean
before the Lord.' "

—*Mishna* (end of *Tractate Yoma*)

When a physician heals a sick man he will not stop to think
whether his cure will cause the patient pain, but will do whatever
is necessary to cure him of his illness. However, if the patient
is his own child, he will make every effort to find a way to cure
him with as little pain as possible.

Being our Father, the Lord, seeking a way of making
atonement for our sins without causing us undue pain and suffering, gave us the Holy Day of Atonement. "And who is it
that cleanses you? Your *Father* in Heaven."

—*Ohel Yaakov*

*   *   *   *

*"And thou shalt say to them: 'Whatsoever man there is in the House
of Israel or among the strangers who sojourn in their midst, who
offers a burnt-offering or a sacrifice and does not bring it to the door
of the Tent of Meeting to sacrifice it to the Lord, that man shall
be cut off from his people.' "* (Leviticus 17:8-9)

Said the Lord to Moses: "To you I have revealed the reason
for the prohibition against slaughtering sacrifices outside the
Sanctuary (*'And they shall no more sacrifice their sacrifices to*

241

the satyrs after whom they go astray' — Verse 7). But you must not tell it to the Children of Israel. For if they were to know the reason, there would be some who would persuade themselves that their offering would be no less sincere if it were made outside the Sanctuary. But for every commandment there are other, hidden reasons and purposes beyond those explicitly stated in Scripture. Therefore, it is just as well that you do not give them any reason at all for My command."

—*Bikkurei Aviv, Mekor Barukh*

* * * *

The Mishna (*Sabbath 11*) states that it is forbidden to read by a light on the Sabbath. The Baraitha (*Sabbath 12*) gives a reason for this prohibition: "Because he might then adjust the light, which is one of the activities forbidden on the Sabbath."

In this connection, the Gemarah relates: "Rabbi Ishmael ben Elisha said: 'I will read and I will not adjust the light.' But it came to pass one Sabbath that he read and wanted to adjust the light, and he said: 'How great are the words of the Sages in that they said: *It is forbidden to read by a light on the Sabbath.*' "

Are we to understand that Rabbi Ishmael really did not become aware of the greatness of the words of the Sages until that time?

Said the Gaon of Vilna: "When Rabbi Ishmael read the reason for this prohibition in the Baraitha, he said to himself: 'I will read and I will not adjust the light.' But when he saw that he escaped being trapped into sin by a hair's breadth, he cried out: 'How great are the words of the Sages in the Mishna in that *they simply stated the law without giving any reason for it.*' Where reasons are given, men are led to seek dispensations and then to fall into sin. The greatness of the Sages lies in the fact that they understood this and therefore refrained from stating the reasons for the law."

242

*   *   *   *

(If anyone takes in hunting any beast or fowl that may be eaten)
"he shall pour out its blood and cover (the blood) *with dust."*
(Leviticus 17:13)

When Cain slew his brother Abel and left the body lying
on the ground unburied, the birds and animals came, dug a hole
in the ground and buried Abel in it. For this reason they were
deemed deserving of having their blood covered with earth if
they should meet a violent death.

—*Midrash*

*   *   *   *

*"My ordinances shall you do, and My statutes shall you keep, to
walk in them; I am the Lord, your God."* (Leviticus 18:4)

You shall keep My commandments not for the sake of
receiving a reward but only because you will thereby grow and
advance in holiness *"to walk in them."* Your reward for observing one commandment shall be the commandment which
it brings in its wake. On the other hand, you must not be under
the impression, as were Zadok and Boethus, the disciples of
Antigonus of Sokho, that there is no reward at all for observing
My commandments. For *"I am the Lord your God,"* faithful to
keep My promise to reward those who fulfill My commandments. All I ask of you is that when you perform them, you will
not do it solely for the sake of that reward.

—*Ketav Sofer*

*   *   *   *

The statement "I am the Lord, your God" is placed at the
opening of the list of practices which are immoral and therefore
forbidden in order to tell us that we should not regard these
prohibitions as running counter to human nature and therefore
difficult to observe.

The Lord tells us: "I am the Lord, your God. I created
you, and I know your nature, and therefore I am in a position

to assure you that you can refrain from these practices without harm to your bodies. As a matter of fact, if you will keep these statutes and ordinances, you shall live by them." (18:5)

—*Meshekh Hakhmah*

* * * *

"You shall therefore keep My statutes and My ordinances, which, if a man shall do them, he shall live by them; I am the Lord." (Leviticus 18:5)

"He shall live by them": Man is expected to dedicate all the strength of his life into the observance of the commandments as he fulfills them.

This is the explanation for the law according to which "one who is engaged in the performance of one commandment is exempt from the other." If he has already immersed his entire being into the observance of one commandment, it is physically impossible for him to bring the same devotion to the performance of another commandment at the same time.

—*Hiddushei HaRIM*

* * * *

"None of you shall come near to anyone closely related to him, to uncover their nakedness; I am the Lord." (Leviticus 18:6)

This portion is read during the Afternoon Service of the Day of Atonement. This is to teach you that even during the holiest hour of the year one must guard against the basest of abominations.

—*Musarist Writings*

* * * *

Haphtarah Ahare Moth (Amos 9)

" 'Are you not as the children of the Ethiopians to Me, O Children of Israel?' says the Lord. 'Have I not brought up Israel out of the land of Egypt, and the Philistines from Caphtor and Aram from Kir?' " (Amos 9:7)

Alternative rendering: *". . . but what of the Philistines of Caphtor and Aram of Kir?' "*

244

Even as the Ethiopians, whose skin is dark, stand out from amidst the white peoples and hence cannot merge with them, so you, O Children of Israel, will remain apart from the other nations and will never merge with them.

Have I not brought up Israel out of the land of Egypt? All through the difficult period of their exile in Egypt, the Children of Israel preserved their identity, so that I brought them forth as "Israel," a nation in its own right. *But what of the Philistines* who were driven into exile in Caphtor and the people of Aram whom the King of Assyria drove into exile in Kir? Could I say that I would take them out of their exile as "Philistines" and "Aramites," as nations in their own right? I could not, for when they went into exile they merged with the nations in whose midst they had to dwell and disappeared from the scene of history. Only the Children of Israel had the strength to preserve their own tradition even in the worst exile ever to befall a people.

—*Malbim*

*   *   *   *

Weekly Portion of Kedoshim (Leviticus 19:1-20:27)
"You shall be holy, for I, the Lord, your God, am holy." (Lev. 19:2)
The word *kedoshim* ("for you shall be holy") is spelled without the *vav,* but *kadosh* (in "I, the Lord, your God, am holy") is complete with the *vav.* According to the Midrash, this shows that "My holiness is greater than yours." Complete holiness belongs to the Lord alone.

—*Anon.*

*   *   *   *

"You shall be holy . . ." (Leviticus 19:2)
This section was proclaimed in full assembly.

—*Rashi*

Rashi points out that we can be worthy of attaining such holiness only if we merge our own personalities into the larger community and identify completely with the people of Israel.

Only "in full assembly" can we be holy.

—*Sefat Emet*

* * * *

Be not holy merely in the privacy of your home and ashamed of your faith in public. Be not, as the assimilationists put it, "A Jew at home and a man outside." Be holy "in full assembly," in public, out in the open, in society. Among your own people or in the midst of strangers, wherever you may find yourself, never be ashamed of your character and sanctity as a Jew.

—*Divrei Shaarei Hayyim*

* * * *

"You shall be holy ... You shall fear, every man, his mother and his father ..." (Leviticus 19:2-3)

Wherever the Jews preserved the sanctity of their family lives, their children would honor and obey them. But ever since that sanctity began to decline among the Jews the honor Jewish children pay their parents has declined also.

—*Rabbinic Literature*

* * * *

"You shall fear, every man, his mother and his father, and you shall keep My Sabbaths ..." (Leviticus 19:3)

You must honor your parents not only while you still look to them for your food, clothing and support but even when you are a "man" and no longer dependent upon them.

—*Ketav Sofer*

* * * *

"And thou shalt not glean thy vineyard ..." (Leviticus 19:10)

Thou shalt not take the tender grapes of it.

—*Rashi*

Take great care that the children, the tender grapes of the vineyard of Israel, should not be plucked from the stem of

246

Judaism and estranged from their people.

—*HaDrash VaHaEyun*

*   *   *   *

"*. . . in righteousness shalt thou judge thy neighbor.*" (Lev. 19:15)
Judge thy fellow-man with an inclination in his favor.

—*Rashi*

When Nathan the Prophet came before King David to re-buke him, he told to the King the story of a poor man who was robbed of the only lamb he had. Deeply affected by the report, David ordered the thief put to death. Only then did Nathan tell him that the story had only been a parable illustrating what David himself had done and that, in condemning the alleged thief to death, he, the King, had pronounced his own sentence. (*II Samuel, Chap. 12*)

God proceeds in a similar manner with any person due to be condemned to punishment for a transgression. He is told the story of his own sin in slightly disguised form, as if it had been committed by another person. When, outraged by the report, he harshly condemns the alleged sinner, he actually pronounces his own sentence.

Therefore the Sages tell us: "Judge thy fellow-man with an inclination in his favor. Do not be quick to pass sentence on another, for it is said: 'Do not judge thy neighbor until thou hast been in his place.' Know that if thou art placed in a posi-tion to pass sentence on another, it is only because thou hast already been in his place. Thou hast committed the same wrong he has done, and therefore when thou condemnest him, thou art actually condemning thyself. Hence, if thou wilt judge him with an inclination in his favor, thou art only being kind to thy own self."

A similar thought is conveyed by Verse 9 of Psalm 39: "*Deliver me from my transgressions; make me not the reproach of the base.*" David says to the Lord: "Save me from my transgressions so that I should not be punished for them. Let me not be one of those who reproves my fellow-man for base conduct. For if I refrain from condemning him, I will be delivered from punishment for my own sins which are equal to his."

—*Baal Shem Tov*

* * * *

"Thou shalt not go up and down as a talebearer among thy people; neither shalt thou stand idly by the blood of thy neighbor . . ." (Leviticus 19:16)

According to the Sages he who speaks ill of another is regarded as if he had killed three persons — him who speaks ill, him of whom ill was spoken, and him who heard it.

By transgressing the prohibition against talebearing, you also transgress the commandment not to "stand idly by the blood of thy neighbor," for your talebearing has endangered the very life of him whom you regard as your neighbor.

—*Anon.*

* * * *

". . . thou shalt surely rebuke thy neighbor and not bear sin because of him." (Leviticus 19:17)
Alternative rendering: *". . . thou shalt surely rebuke thy neighbor and do not place sin upon him."*

In rebuking another, do not treat him as a wicked man but put stress on his dignity, making him understand that the wrong he committed was beneath his dignity. Only thus will your rebuke have the desired effect.

This, then, is the thought Scripture seeks to convey:

"Thou shalt surely rebuke: if thou rebukest a man, regard him as *thy neighbor,* as thy friend and thy equal, and *do not place sin upon him,* do not treat him like a sinner, lest he turn aside from thee entirely and thou wilt have accomplished nothing."

—*Havot Yair*

* * * *

Alternative rendering: *". . . thou shalt surely rebuke* (thyself) with *thy neighbor"*

When you rebuke your neighbor, rebuke yourself at the same time. Know that you, too, have a share in his transgression. Do not cast the entire burden of sin upon him. Only if you will feel guilty and repent together with him will your rebuke persuade him to repent also.

—*Sefat Emet*

* * * *

In rebuking another, address him in keeping with his qualities, his intellectual abilities and his character. Do not rebuke another person in terms of your own qualities. *"Thou shalt surely rebuke thy neighbor*: rebuke him as thy neighbor — as he is and not as thou art."

—*Divrei Torah*

* * * *

Thou shalt surely rebuke him: Even one hundred times.

—*Gemarah*

When you rebuke him the first time, you may not be able to say to him what you should, or the man whom you are rebuking may not be listening as he should. But if you repeat your reproof one hundred times, it may occur just once that you will succeed in saying to him what should be said and that he will be able to listen to you as he should.

—*Rabbi David Blacher of Mezhirich,
in the name of a great Sage*

* * * *

A scholar who does not avenge and guard after the manner of the serpent is not a scholar.

—*Talmud, Yoma 22*

It is written in the Midrash: "If you ask a serpent: 'What pleasure do you get from biting a human? Does not all the food you eat taste like soil to you?' he will reply: 'I do not bite for the sake of pleasure but only when God commands me to bite

249

a person because he must be punished for some transgression."

Thus the Sages say that when a scholar wishes to rebuke a person who insulted him, he must do it "after the manner of the serpent" — not in order to satisfy his personal honor but only for the purpose of preserving the honor of the Law, of fulfilling the command of God.

He who is unable to rebuke the wicked "after the manner of the serpent" but is solely out for vengeance, is not a true scholar.

—Sifthe Tzaddik, attributed to the Baal Shem Tov

* * * *

"... and thou shalt love thy neighbor as thyself; I am the Lord." (Leviticus 19:18)

It is not easy to carry out the commandment "and thou shalt love thy neighbor as thyself" in the fullest sense of its meaning. Therefore, immediately after this command, the Lord declares: *"I am the Lord"*, i.e., I, the Lord, stand ready to help you to fulfill My commandment, provided that you sincerely wish to keep it.

—Sefat Emet

* * * *

Rabbi Akiba said: "This is the fundamental principle of the Torah."

—Rashi

If a man, making his accounts, wants to see whether the totals agree, he makes a trial balance.

In the same manner, a man who wants to establish whether the study of the Law in which he has engaged was truly performed in the spirit of devotion and sincerity should make a "trial balance" by determining the amount of love he bears for his fellow-Jews. His observance of the commandment "thou shalt love thy neighbor as thyself" is the test which will show him whether his study was of value, for "this is the fundamental principle of the Law."

—Devash HaSadeh

*   *   *   *

"Thou shalt rise up before old age ..." (Leviticus 19:32)

Before old age befalls thee, rise up and act to improve thy soul.

—Sefarim

*   *   *   *

"...and honor the face of the old man and thou shalt fear thy God ..." (Leviticus 19:32)

Alternative rendering: *". . . and honor the face of the scholar and thou shalt fear God."*

> If thou wilt fulfill the commandment to "honor the face of the old man" thy reward will be that thou wilt be endowed with the fear of the Lord.

—Midrash

When Rabbi Zeira would rest from his studies he would make it a practice to sit by the gate of the house of study so that he might be able to rise to greet passing scholars and be rewarded (*Berakhot 28*).

Even though he was aware that it is not permitted to fulfill a commandment in the expectation of a reward, Rabbi Zeira felt that it would not be wrong to covet the reward of being endowed with the fear of the Lord.

—From the Writings of a Sage

*   *   *   *

Haphtarah Kedoshim (Ezekiel 22:1-19)

"Her priests have done violence to My Law ... and have hid their eyes from My Sabbaths ..." (Ezekiel 22:26)

This clearly explains the statement of the Sages that "Jerusalem was only destroyed because they desecrated the Sabbaths there, as it is written 'and they have hid their eyes from My Sabbaths.' " (*Sabbath 119*)

Why does the Talmudic text specify "because they desecrated the Sabbaths *there*"? Would it not have been sufficient to say "because they desecrated the Sabbaths"?

Because the verse from Ezekiel "they have hid their eyes from My Sabbaths" refers to the priests. The priests themselves did not desecrate the Sabbath; their sin lay in the fact that they looked away when others desecrated the Sabbath. The statement "because they desecrated the Sabbath *there*" conveys the thought that the Sabbath was being desecrated right *there* in Jerusalem, where the priests resided, and yet the priests did nothing to put a stop to this conduct.

This saying of the Sages fits in well with the saying immediately before; i.e., that Jerusalem was destroyed because the people did not rebuke one another (*ibid.*); this would imply that they also failed to rebuke Sabbath violators.

—Avnei Ezel

* * * *

Weekly Portion of Emor (Leviticus 21:1-24:23)
"And the Lord said to Moses: 'Speak to the priests, the sons of Aaron . . .' " (Leviticus 21:1)

> The utterances of the Lord are pure, because the Holy One, blessed be He, enlightened Israel in order to hallow and to purify it.
>
> *—Midrash Tanhumah*

This weekly portion deals with the laws of priestly purity. Since Israel is a pure and holy nation, he must keep away from impurity and corruption much more carefully than the people of the heathen nations. A peasant may eat all manner of food without ill effects, but if a prince partakes of coarse food, he will become ill. The Children of Israel are like the prince in that they are so holy and noble that contact with even the smallest impurity may cause them great harm. For this reason they must be sternly admonished to keep away from it.

—Divrei Shaarei Hayyim

* * * *

"Thou shalt sanctify (the priest) *therefore, for he offers the bread of thy God; he shall be holy to thee, for I, the Lord, Who sanctify you, am holy."* (Leviticus 21:8)

Although the priest depends for his living on the "Priestly Gifts" which thou givest him, thou art not permitted to treat him with disrespect or contempt. Instead, thou are required to sanctify him, because *he offers the bread of thy God.* The meal of a righteous man or of a scholar has the same hallowed character as a sacrifice. Accordingly, the gifts which thou givest to the priest are equal in value to the offerings which serve to atone for thy sins. Moreover, the priest in his turn hallows the people of Israel with his study and worship. For all these reasons, the priest *shall be holy to thee, for I, the Lord, Who sanctify you, am holy.* I, the Lord, have sanctified you through the priest who hallows you with his study and worship. Hence you must honor and hallow him even though he is dependent on your gifts for his living.

—*Ketav Sofer*

* * * *

"And the daughter of any priest if she should profane herself by acting the harlot, she profanes her father . . ." (Leviticus 21:9)

There are men who regard themselves as "priests," as men of so great distinction and sanctity that they consider it beneath them to concern themselves with the training of their daughters. They are too busy with their own studies. But while they are rapt in the mysteries of the Zohar, their daughters have their noses in cheap books. In the end, such girls will adopt un-Jewish ways and thus reduce the holiness of their fathers. This is to teach us that the kind of holiness which leads men to care only for their own training, leaving them no time to concern themselves with the education of their children, is not holiness at all, but the opposite.

—*Avnei Ezel*

* * * *

253

"And when the sun is down, he shall be clean, and afterwards he may eat of the holy things . . ." (Leviticus 22:7)

At the outset of Tractate Berakhot, the Mishna specifies that the time limit for the reading of the *Shema* is identical with the time when priests who had become defiled might partake of their offering. Cf. "When is the *Shema* to be read in the evening service? When the priests go in to eat of their offering."

Why should these two time limits be related to one another?

At nightfall, it becomes permissible for the priests to eat of their offering, even if they had been unclean all day. They were not permitted to partake of it even after their immersion, but had to wait until the evening. This teaches us that the appearance of the first stars in the evening sky ushers in an entirely new period which has no connection with the day just ended. From this we infer that when evening comes the *Shema* we recited that morning no longer has any effect and we must renew our acceptance of the sovereignty of the kingdom of heaven with a new reading of the *Shema*.

> —*Attributed to the father of Abraham Bornstein,*
> author of *Eglei Tal*

*　*　*　*

". . . but I will be hallowed among the Children of Israel; I am the Lord who hallow you." (Leviticus 22:32)

This statement is followed by the commandments pertaining to the observance of the holidays which hallow the people of Israel and "which you shall proclaim to be holy convocations." (23:2)

It is because Israel is holy by nature that God endowed it with holiness, which in turn enables Israel to proclaim as holy the days which the Court of Law sanctifies as festivals.

> —*Hiddushei HaRIM*

*　*　*　*

"The appointed seasons of the Lord . . . even these are My appointed seasons. Six days shall work be done, but on the Seventh Day is a Sabbath of solemn rest (lit.: 'A Sabbath of Sabbaths . . .')" (Leviticus 23:2-3)

This weekly portion discusses the holidays. Why, then, does it interrupt the discussion with a statement about the six days of the week and the Sabbath?

The Gaon of Vilna explains that the "six days" may be construed to mean not the six days of the week but the six Festivals of the Jewish year on which, according to the Law, work connected with the preparation of food is permitted; namely, the first and last days of Passover, Shavuot, Rosh Ha-Shana and the first and last days of Succoth (according to Biblical law, only one day each).

Accordingly, Verse 3: "Six days shall work be done . . ." fits into the portion as a general statement concerning the holidays which are treated in greater detail in the verses that follow. *"Six days shall work be done*: there are six holidays on which all work connected with the preparation of food may be done, *but on the Seventh Day is a Sabbath of Sabbaths;* the seventh holiday is Yom Kippur, the Day of Atonement, the 'Sabbath of Sabbaths' on which work connected with the preparation of food is forbidden."

—*Shem MiShimon, attributed to the Gaon of Vilna*

* * * *

"And you shall make proclamation on the selfsame day; there shall be a holy convocation for you . . . And when you reap the harvest of your land, thou shalt not wholly reap the corner of thy field . . ." (Leviticus 23:21-22)

You are to observe Shavuot, the festival commemorating the Giving of the Law not only for the sake of the statutes for which we would never have felt a need if they had not been set down in the Torah, but also in thanksgiving for the laws which

255

readily make sense even to the human mind, such as the laws pertaining to compassion on the unfortunate and charity to the poor. For experience has shown that, without faith in God, man is liable to become like a wild beast which has not a spark of compassion and is therefore capable of committing the basest crimes in order to satisfy his selfish desires.

Only if you will observe the commandments concerning the leaving of parts of your harvest for the poor and the stranger are you permitted to proclaim the festival of Shavout as "a holy convocation" to give thanks even for such readily understandable commandments of charity and compassion as these, for had the Torah not been given, you might never have come to observe them.

—*Meshekh Hakhmah*

* * * *

"*... and you shall afflict your souls; in the ninth day of the month in the evening ...*" (Leviticus 23:32)

> He who eats and drinks on the ninth day of Tishrei is regarded by Scripture as if he had afflicted his soul on both the ninth day and the tenth.

—*Gemara*

Why should eating on the eve of the Day of Atonement be regarded as "afflicting one's soul"?

Said Rabbi Elimelekh of Lizensk: "If, on the eve of Yom Kippur, we contemplate the holy and awesome Day about to begin, how could we possibly wish to eat? Indeed, observing the commandment to eat on the ninth day of Tishrei then turns out to be a real hardship."

* * * *

According to the Sages, the Confession of Sins must already be recited in the Afternoon Service of the Eve of Yom Kippur. Why so?

Said the Rabbi of Ger: "If eating on the Eve of Yom

Kippur is regarded as a hardship no less than the fast enjoined upon us for Yom Kippur itself, it is only proper that we should recite the Confession of Sins then just as we will during the great Fast of the next day."

*   *   *   *

"... and you shall rejoice before the Lord your God seven days ..." (Leviticus 23:40)

> Said Rabbi Joshua Ben Halaphtah: When we rejoiced on the Rejoicing of the Drawing of Waters, we did not see sleep with our eyes."
>
> —Sukkoth 13

How could they have been expected to "see sleep with their own eyes"?

Rabbi Joshua meant that they did not have time to indulge in the kind of sleep during which the eyes are not closed; (i.e., in idleness which has been likened to sleeping with one's eyes open) because they were continually busy with the performance of the rites of worship and had not even a moment left to waste.

—Hatham Sofer

*   *   *   *

"That your generations may know that I caused the Children of Israel to dwell in booths ..." (Leviticus 23:43)

> This does not mean "booths" in the literal sense but is symbolic of the clouds of glory.
>
> —Rashi

*   *   *   *

In view of Rashi's statement, Rabbi Jacob ben Asher asked why Sukkoth is not observed in Nissan, the month when the Children of Israel left Egypt, protected from the blazing desert sun by the "clouds of glory."

Rabbi Isaac Meir Alter replied:

"In connection with Sukkoth, Scripture tells us 'that your generations may know.' This implies that one of the requirements for the observance of this festival is knowledge. All year long, man is full of transgressions and since it is said that man sins only when the spirit of folly has entered him, it must be assumed that he is then lacking in knowledge and hence cannot properly fulfill the commandment to observe the Festival of Sukkoth. Only in the month of Tishrei, after he has cleansed himself and obtained atonement on Rosh HaShana and Yom Kippur, does the Jew have that knowledge which qualifies him to observe Sukkoth. Hence that season, rather than the month of the Exodus, is the proper time for the celebration of the feast of Sukkoth."

*   *   *   *

"For this same reason," Rabbi Alter used to say, "the Law also specifies that 'the one who is ill or pained is exempt from the commandment to dwell in booths,' for one who is laden with sorrow lacks wise counsel and hence is not qualified to fulfill the commandment concerning which Scripture has specified 'that your generations may *know*.'"

*   *   *   *

Also in connection with the question raised by Rabbi Jacob ben Asher, the Gaon of Vilna said:

It is a well-known fact that after the Children of Israel had sinned with the Golden Calf, the clouds of glory were removed from them, for we read (in *Exodus 32:25*) "And when Moses saw that the people were broken loose" (lit. "And when Moses saw that the people were *uncovered*"). This means that the clouds of glory had departed, leaving the Israelites *exposed* in their disgrace. Only after the tenth day of the month of Tishrei, after the Lord had forgiven them, having said to Moses: "I have forgiven as thou hast spoken" and the Israelites had been commanded to build the Tabernacle, did the clouds of glory return to protect them.

It was on the eleventh day of Tishrei, the day after the Day of Atonement, that Moses first requested the Children of Israel to bring offerings for the construction of the Tabernacle. For two days, the Israelites brought him their offerings, as it is written: "And they brought yet to him free-will offerings every morning (lit. "in the morning, in the morning"), (*Exodus 3:63*) which means for two days; i.e., the twelfth and the thirteenth days of Tishrei." On the third day — the fourteenth day of Tishrei, all the "wise-hearted men" (*Exodus 36:8*) took the offerings from Moses, and on the fifteenth day they began work on the construction of the Tabernacle. It was on that day that the sheltering clouds of glory reappeared. Clearly, then, the fifteenth day of Tishrei is a most appropriate time to observe Sukkoth, the feast of Tabernacles.

*　*　*　*

"And thou shalt set them . . . upon the pure table before the Lord." (Leviticus 24:6)

> It teaches, therefore, that they used to lift it and show the show-bread thereon to the Festival pilgrims and say to them: "Behold the love in which you are held by the Omnipresent; it is taken away as fresh as it is set down."
>
> —*Haggigah 26*

Why were the pilgrims shown just this particular miracle; i.e., that the show-bread would remain fresh for eight whole days?

The Sages begin their answer with a question. "Why," they asked, "did the *manna* fall down from heaven every day and not just once a year?"

"There are two reasons," they continue. "One was that they might meet with their Father in Heaven each day, just as a king gives his son each day whatever he needs, so that he may visit with him at least once a day. The other reason was so that the Children of Israel might have fresh bread to eat each day." (*Yoma 77*)

The miracle of the show-bread is proof that the first reason is the correct explanation. For if the show-bread could still be as fresh and warm a whole week after baking as it had been when it had come out of the oven, the *manna*, too, could have remained fresh all year long. Hence it would have been enough for God to have the *manna* come down from heaven once a year only. But the Lord chose to send down the *manna* each day, because like the king who loved his son, He loved the Children of Israel so much that He wanted them to come out each day to meet with Him. Hence the show-bread was shown to the festival pilgrims as a symbol of the Lord's abiding love for His people.

—*Imrei Tzvi*

* * * *

Haphtarah Emor (Ezekiel 44:15-31)

"And in the day that he goes into the Sanctuary, into the Inner Court, to minister in the Sanctuary, he shall offer his sin-offering ..." (Ezekiel 44:27)

According to the Commentators, this means that when an ordinary priest entered the Sanctuary to minister there for the first time he had to bring a tenth of an *ephah* as his tribute of consecration.

But this was already specified in the Scriptural text. Why should Ezekiel have reiterated the law?

He did so in order to teach his people that when the Second Temple would be built and the priests would enter it to minister there, they all, even those who had still served in the First Temple, would have to bring a tribute of consecration just as if they had been newly installed into office, for the destruction of the First Temple had marked the end of an old order and the dedication of the Second would be the beginning of a new era.

Likewise, in days to come, when the Priests of the Temple will be resurrected from the dead to serve in the Third Temple, they will have to offer a sacrifice of consecration just as if they had been newly installed, for Israel's long exile marked the end of one era and the dedication of the Temple in the days of the Messiah will be the beginning of a new epoch in the history of our people.   —*Malbim*

*   *   *   *

Weekly Portion of Be-Har (Leviticus 25:1-26:2)
"And the Lord spoke unto Moses on Mount Sinai . . . Speak to the Children of Israel and say to them: When you come into the land . . . then the land shall keep a Sabbath to the Lord." (Lev. 25:1-2)
        What does the subject of the Sabbatical year have to do with Mount Sinai?

                                                      —*Rashi*

The commandment pertaining to the observance of the Sabbatical year is in itself a convincing proof that the Torah was certainly not a mere figment of the mind of Moses, but of Divine origin. What human being could have said of himself: "Then I will command my blessing upon you . . . and it shall bring forth produce for the three years" (*Lev. 25:21*)? Only God could have made such a statement.

This makes it clear that none other but God Himself could have given Israel the Law on Mount Sinai.

                                                —*Hatham Sofer*

*   *   *   *

But the Sabbatical year itself also has fifty-two Sabbaths which the soil still desecrates in part by producing after-growth. For this reason Scripture ordered that after seven Sabbatical years — three hundred sixty-five Sabbaths not properly observed — have passed, there should be a Jubilee Year when the soil rests for another whole year to compensate for the Sabbaths which it did not observe during the seven Sabbatical years that have gone before.

                                                        —*Ibid*

*   *   *   *

261

"And you shall not wrong one another ..." (Leviticus 25:17)

The Sages tell the story of a man named Samuel who bought a golden pitcher from a Gentile for the value of an iron pitcher; namely, four florins, and then paid him one florin less than the four he demanded. *(Baba Kama 17)*

Why should Samuel have taken advantage of the Gentile and cheated him of a florin in the bargain? And why did the Sages find it necessary to tell us this story?

The Sages wanted to point out Samuel's great righteousness. Samuel saw that the pitcher which the Gentile wanted to sell him was not made of iron but of gold and hence worth a great deal of money. Yet the Gentile asked only four florins for it. Samuel did not know how to proceed. If the Gentile sold the pitcher so cheaply because he did not know that the pitcher was made not of iron but of gold, he would have to be told the truth. But if he had done so because he had stolen the pitcher from its rightful owner and was anxious to dispose of it, it would actually be a good deed to buy it for as little money as possible in order to redeem it and to restore it to its rightful owner.

Actually, Samuel did not withold one florin from the Gentile, but paid him five florins, one more than the four the Gentile had asked. We know this because the Hebrew word *mablia* may also imply giving *more than is due*. Cf. "When paying for the Lulab, one should include also *(mablia)* the money for the Ethrog." *(Mishna, Succoth 39)*. He did this in order to test the Gentile. If the Gentile would return the extra florin to him, it would be proof that the Gentile was an honest man and really thought that the pitcher was of iron. But if the Gentile would not return the money, Samuel would know that the man was aware of the true value of the pitcher and hence must have stolen it. In that case it would be a good deed to buy the article for the smallest possible price and restore it to its rightful owner, and then Samuel would pay him no more than the four florins.

We see, then, that the purpose of the Sages in telling us this story was to point out the detail in which our *Tannaim* and *Amoraim* observed the laws of redress in case of overreaching even in their dealings with heathens, and the wisdom with which they conducted their daily affairs.

—Nathan ben Simeon HaKohen Adler

*   *   *   *

Rabbi Simcha Bunim of Przysucha used to say: The Torah forbids us to fool another man. Now a Hassid has to do more than the law requires. He must not fool himself either. by deluding himself into considering his virtues greater than they actually are.

*   *   *   *

"And you shall not wrong one another; but thou shalt fear thy God, for I am the Lord your God." (Leviticus 25:17)

Every Rosh HaShana it is decreed in Heaven how much each man will earn during the next year. And when a man acquires riches through deceit and swindling, against the will of God, he will be punished by illness or some other calamity to deprive him of his ill-gotten gains.

Therefore Scripture says: *"You shall not wrong one another*: You must not seek to gain riches by overreaching, because *thou shalt fear thy God* Who, in His quality of justice will impose punishments upon you to deprive you of the riches you obtain by unfair means."

—Melo HaOmer

*   *   *   *

"And if you will say: 'What shall we eat in the Seventh Year? Behold, we must not sow, nor gather in our increase,' then I will command My blessing upon you in the sixth year and it shall bring forth produce for the three years." (Leviticus 25:20-21)

If they will find it necessary to doubt Him and ask "What

shall we have to eat in the Seventh Year?" the Lord will have to "command" His blessing. If they had had perfect faith and not questioned Him, the blessing would have come of itself.

—Attributed to Zusia, brother of Rabbi Elimelekh
of Lizensk

* * * *

A similar explanation, though with a slightly different approach, was advanced by Rabbi Leibush Harif.

If a Jew has complete faith in the Lord and asks no questions, he has no need for a rich harvest which would only entail more work in reaping, threshing and grinding. As we read in Verse 19, "and you shall eat until you have enough." This means that he will be satisfied if he does not have much to eat. But if he asks "What shall we eat?", he shows that his faith is not perfect, and in that case God "commands" His blessing so that he should harvest a large crop which will entail much toil but will bring him no benefit when he eats it.

* * * *

"*. . . for you are strangers and settlers with Me.*" (Leviticus 25:23)
Said the Lord to Israel:

"The relationship between yourselves and Me is always that of 'strangers and settlers.' If you will live in the world like strangers, remembering that you are here but temporarily, then I will be a settler in your midst in that My Presence will dwell with you permanently. But if you will regard yourselves as settlers, as permanent owners of the land on which you live, when the land is actually not yours but Mine, My Presence will be a stranger in that it will not dwell in your midst.

"In any case, you, O Israel, and I cannot be strangers and settlers at the same time. If you act the stranger, then I will be the settler, and if you act the settler, I must be the stranger."

—Ohel Yaakov

* * * *

264

"And if a man sells a dwelling-house in a walled city, then he may redeem it within a whole year after it is sold . . ." (Lev. 25:29)

Why is the law with regard to dwellings in a walled city different from that pertaining to the sale of a field, in that the dwelling cannot be repurchased by its owner any later than one year from the sale, and that it does not revert to its original owner in the Jubilee Year?

Because of the special conditions obtaining in a walled city. The "walled cities" were fortresses, designed to protect the inhabitants in case of enemy attack. For this reason it was imperative that all the inhabitants be familiar with every secret passageway, cave or shelter in the city. Moreover, it was vitally necessary that they all be well acquainted with one another in order to be able to act together for purposes of mutual defense and protection.

If all the dwelling houses in the walled city would have reverted to their original owners during the Jubilee Year, the result would have been a wholesale change of owners, with strangers with no knowledge of the city and its people taking possession. This situation would have greatly reduced the effectiveness of the fortress as a defense against enemy invaders.

It was to avoid this possibility, too, that Scripture imposed the time limit of one year for the repurchase of a dwelling. After that period, the house would be deeded to the purchaser. This was meant to discourage quick sales, and to avoid frequent turnovers in population.

—Meshekh Hakhmah

*   *   *   *

"And if thy brother grows poor and his means fail with thee, then thou shalt uphold him . . ." (Leviticus 25:35)

> Of this it is written: "Blessed be he who gives understanding care to the poor; the Lord will deliver him in the day of evil." (*Psalm 41:2*)

—Midrash

At the beginning of each year, it is decreed for every man how much financial loss he will suffer in the year to come. If he is wise, he will give away to the poor the money he is destined to lose. In that case it will not be a loss at all but a gain in that he will receive credit for having done a good deed. But if he will not give it away to the poor, the money he is destined to lose will be taken from him under less pleasant circumstances.

The thought conveyed by the Midrashic text is as follows: If one is sufficiently wise to support the poor, *the Lord will deliver him on the day of evil;* that is, on the day when it was intended, Heaven forbid, that evil should befall him, the Lord will deliver him because he has already given away what he was destined to lose. But if he was not wise enough to give some of his money to the poor, he will have to give it away *in the day of evil* and nothing will be able to save him from that fate.

—*Ohel Yaakov*

* * * *

A Musarist was asked whether one may take a loan of money when one knows that, in the normal course of events, he would not be able to repay the loan, but has faith that God will help him clear the debt.

"You may," the sage replied, "provided that you yourself would be willing to lend money to a person who lacks the means to repay the loan, because you are confident that his faith in God's eventual help will be rewarded. But if you are not willing to lend money to a person with only his faith as his collateral, you, too, must not borrow money under such conditions."

—*Rabbi Abraham Zelmans of Warsaw*

* * * *

"Thou shalt not give him thy money upon interest, nor give him thy victuals for increase, I am the Lord your God, Who brought you forth out of the land of Egypt . . ." (Leviticus 25:37-38)

All those who believe in the prohibition against charging

interest on loans are believers in the Exodus from Egypt; and all those who reject the prohibition against charging interest thereby reject the Exodus as well.

—Yalkut

The early Sages ask: "Why were the Egyptians punished for having enslaved the Hebrews? Was it not decreed by Heaven that the Egyptians were to make the Children of Israel work and to oppress them?"

Replied Rabbi Abraham ben David of Posquieres (RA-vaD) (Chapter 6, *Hilkhot Teshuva*) that they were punished for adding to the Divine decree and enslaving the Children of Israel "with rigor" (*Exod. 1:13*) when the decree commanded them merely to enslave the Israelites.

The Egyptians took interest from the Children of Israel, as it were, exacting from them more toil than the Israelites owed them according to the Divine decree. Therefore they were punished.

Obviously, then, anyone who disregards the prohibition against charging interest thereby demonstrates that he does not believe that God had a hand in the Exodus from Egypt, for by taking interest from his debtor, he proclaims his view that similar conduct on the part of the Egyptians had been no sin and that the Egyptians therefore had not been deserving of punishment.

—HaDrash VeHaEyun

*   *   *   *

Haphtarah BeHar (Jeremiah 32:6-27)
"Great in counsel and mighty in action, Whose eyes are open upon all the ways of the sons of men, to give every one according to his ways and according to the fruit of his doings." (Jeremiah 32:19)

If a man commits a transgression that makes him liable to the death penalty by the hand of Heaven, the Lord, before passing sentence, takes into account also the man's parents, his wife, his children and his other relatives who are innocent and would be caused great suffering if the punishment were to be carried out. Hence, the Lord does not mete out punishment before making certain that none of the kin of the accused should suffer more anguish than he deserves.

"Great in counsel and mighty in action; Thou alone, O Lord, art so great in wisdom and in the ability to determine when Thou art about to punish — *to give every one according to his ways and according to the fruit of his doings* — that none of the individuals concerned should be given more suffering than he deserves.

—*MaHaRa Yitzhaki*

* * * *

Rabbi Bunim of Przysucha had the following interpretation for Psalm 19, Verse 10, *"the judgments of the Lord are true and righteous altogether"*:

"The judgments of the Lord are true in that they are righteous for all those concerned together, even for the family and kin of the condemned. God's judgment takes their sorrow into account and is righteous to them all."

* * * *

Weekly Portion of BeHukkothai (Leviticus 26:3-27:34)
"If you walk in My statutes and keep My commandments . . ."
(Leviticus 26:3)

If you are occupied with the study of the Law.

—*Rashi*

It is written in the Psalms: "I considered my ways and turned my feet to Thy testimonies." (*Psalm 119:59*) David said: "Every day when I would plan to go to a certain place or to a certain dwelling, I would walk, and my feet would lead me to houses of worship and houses of study."

—*Midrash*

The Hebrew word *"im"* can be rendered either as "if" or as "whether." This implies that even if one is about to perform a good deed or to observe a commandment he must first carefully consider *whether* it is fitting that he do it and whether the time is appropriate. There are some commandments which are meant only for scholars, and there are others — such as bearing the Holy Ark and taking apart the Tabernacle — which scholars are not meant to perform. Likewise, if a man dons his prayer shawl and phylacteries to pray in the morning immediately after rising from bed without first performing the proper preparatory rites, he has not observed the commandment properly. Hence one must always consider whether, and how, the commandment should be performed. "I considered my ways," David said. "And only thereafter did I *turn my feet to Thy testimonies.*"

—*Attributed to Rabbi Isaac of Warka*

* * * *

"... *and you shall eat your bread until you have enough, and dwell in your land safely.*" (Leviticus 26:5)

> The Sages say: "Eat one-third, drink one-third, and leave one-third over, for if you should grow angry, you will have had your fill." —*Gittin 70*

A man should not eat his fill, for if he should be seized by anger, he may become bloated, to the detriment of his health. Therefore he should leave over one-third of his food and drink.

Now anger and worry are curses of the Exile. Scripture says: "But the Lord shall give you a trembling heart . . ." (*Deut. 28:65*), and to this the Sages comment: "This refers to (the exile in) Babylonia" (*Nedarim 22*)

The verse from the Book of Leviticus, on the other hand, holds a promise of a brighter future, for it conveys the following thought:

"*And you shall eat your bread until you have enough*: you will be able to eat your fill, for you will have no cause to fear the consequence of anger on a full stomach. *You will dwell in your own land safely* so that you will have no occasion for anger or worry." —*Tifereth Yonathan*

* * * *

A similar thought is conveyed in the interpretation of the saying in the Book of Proverbs that "the righteous eats to the satisfying of his desire, but the belly of the wicked shall want." (*Prov. 13:25*) The righteous man, being slow to anger, can safely eat as much as he wants, but the wicked man, who is angry all the time, can never eat as much as he needs in order to satisfy his hunger, because he has reason to fear the consequences of anger on a full stomach.

—*Ibid*

* * * *

"And I will give peace in the land, and you shall lie down and none shall make you afraid . . ." (Leviticus 26:6)

Ba-aretz may be rendered either as "in the land" or as "in the world." Hence this verse may be interpreted to mean that "when there will be peace in the world, you, too, O Israel, will be able to sleep in peace and none shall make you afraid." Whenever war comes to the world, the Jews suffer the most.

— After *Or HaHayyim*

". . . and I have . . . made you go upright." (Leviticus 26:13)
Erect in stature.

—*Rashi*

Cattle walk with head bent to the ground. When a man acts like a beast, his head, too, is bent down, toward the lower, baser things of life. But if he does not behave like a beast, he is said to walk upright, with head erect and turned heavenward.

"If you walk in My statutes," says the Lord (*Verse 3*), "I will indeed cause you to go upright."

—*The Maggid of Mezhirich*

* * * *

270

"And if you will reject My statutes and if your soul abhors My ordinances so that you will not do all My commandments but break My covenant." (Leviticus 26:15)

Those who seek to cast off the yoke of the Law and the commandments begin by rejecting the "statutes" of the Torah on the grounds that they have no logical reason or purpose. Man, they claim, cannot be forced to do things for which he can find no good reason. But this is only an excuse, for from the "statutes" he proceeds to reject also those commandments for which there are logical reasons. For their aim is nothing less than to break the yoke of the Torah.

The Lord says to the Children of Israel: *"And if you will reject My statutes*: You will begin by rejecting My statutes, the laws for which you can find no obvious reason. Next, *your soul will abhor My ordinances,* you will not want to observe even those commandments which have logical reasons, because it is your intention *not to do all My commandments but to break My covenant."* —*HaDrash VeHaEyun*

* * * *

". . . and you shall flee when none pursues you." (Leviticus 26:17) Alternative rendering: *". . . and you shall flee and none pursues you."*

What is the curse implicit in this prediction?

It is written in the Book of Ecclesiastes: "And God seeks that which is pursued." *(3:15)* To this the Sages comment: "Even the righteous man pursues the wicked." Accordingly, the victim of pursuit should have reason to expect speedy rescue. Hence "and none pursues you" is a curse, meaning that you will not even enjoy the advantage of being a victim of persecution.

* * * *

"And I will bring a sword upon you that shall execute the vengeance of the covenant . . ." (Leviticus 26:25)

When a king conquers a foreign country he does not punish its inhabitants for having waged war on him, for they had not been his subjects then and fighting against the king of another country is not considered a crime.

But if the people of a conquered province, after having been incorporated into the king's empire, revolt against the king in a bid for independence, he will punish them severely after he has reconquered the territory because their rebellion is a violation of their oath of allegiance to him and therefore treason.

The people of Israel, too, took an oath of allegiance to their King, for when He made His covenant with them on Mount Sinai, they vowed to be His people and to serve Him. Hence, if they break the covenant, they are guilty of treason, and God will "execute the vengeance of the covenant."

—*Naphtali Tzvi Yehuda Berlin*

* * * *

"Then shall the land be paid her Sabbaths . . ." (Leviticus 26:34)

Of all the laws of the Torah, what makes the law of the Sabbatical Year so important that its violation is named as a cause of Israel's exile?

The observance of the Sabbatical Year is meant to give us to understand that the whole world belongs to the Lord, Who is the sole true Owner of all the land in it. If man conducts himself in accordance with God's will, God gives him a lease on the land, renewable every seventh year. But if man defies God by not observing the Sabbatical Year, he thereby indicates that he regards himself as the sole proprietor of the land on which he dwells, and then God, the true Owner, has no other choice but to drive him from the land to teach him that it is not his at all. —*Hashava LeTorah*

* * * *

"And they shall confess their iniquity and the iniquity of their fathers in their treachery which they committed against Me . . . I also will walk contrary to them . . ." (Leviticus 26:40-41)

272

If they will confess their sins, why should they still be considered deserving of punishment?

The Sages explain that a confession not accompanied by repentance is of no avail.

The thought conveyed by the verse is as follows:

"If *they confess their iniquity . . . in the treachery which they committed against Me;* i.e., if they make their confession in *the midst of* their treachery, without ceasing to sin, their confession will be of no avail and this in itself is a transgression deserving of punishment."

—Binah LeIttim

* * * *

The Holy Books interpret the Yom Kippur confession: ". . . and for the sin which we committed before Thee with the confession of the mouth" to mean the transgression committed by confession without repentance. Confession without repentance is a sin in itself.

* * * *

"Then I will remember My covenant with Jacob, and My covenant with Isaac, and also My covenant with Abraham will I remember, and I will remember the Land." (Leviticus 26:42)

What relationship does this promise have to the predictions of punishment directly preceding it?

It is placed into this context to show us that our illustrious ancestry, our descent from Abraham, Isaac and Jacob, makes our sinful conduct even more reprehensible.

It is like the case of a child of noble family, who has been reared in the Royal palace and then becomes guilty of a transgression against the king's law. His transgression is considered much more serious than would be the same act committed by a peasant who was reared in a village hovel.

—Rabbi Isaiah Horowitz

* * * *

It is related in the First Book of Kings concerning Adonijah the son of Haggith that "his father had not grieved him all his life in saying: 'Why hast thou done so?'" (*I Kings 1:6*)

The Gaon of Vilna interprets this to mean that the fact that his father was no less a man than King David never caused Adonijah grief or remorse so that he might have said to himself: "Why hast thou done this evil?" This was the reason why Adonijah was found unworthy of assuming the kingship of Israel.

* * * *

Haphtarah BeHukkothai (Jeremiah 16:19-17:14)
"Blessed is the man who trusts in the Lord, and whose trust the Lord is." (Jeremiah 17:7)

If a man will put his trust in the Lord even though he might find it difficult to do so, the Lord will help him attain perfect faith in Him. Man must first do his part by trusting in the Lord; once he has done that, he will be deemed worthy of having the Lord as his "trust."

—*Shir Meon*

* * * *

The mere fact that one trusts in the Lord is already the greatest blessing, for trust brings him nearer to the Lord, and even if he should not receive what he hoped for, he has still attained faith. But he who puts his trust in men is cursed even if he should get his wish, because he is one "whose heart departs from the Lord." (*Jeremiah 17:5*)

—*Rabbi Joseph Josel Hurwitz*

* * * *

WELLSPRINGS OF TORAH

NUMBERS

THE BOOK OF NUMBERS

במדבר

Weekly Portion of Bamidebar (Num. 1:1-4:20)

"And the Lord spoke to Moses in the wilderness of Sinai..."
(Numbers 1:1)

> With three things was the Torah given — with fire, with
> water, and in the wilderness.
>
> *—Midrash Rabba*

The character trait that has distinguished the Jewish people
from its very beginning is the spirit of self-sacrifice it has always
shown in the observance of its law and adherence to its faith.
Throughout the ages, Jews have mounted scaffolds, have
stretched out their necks to slaughter, hurled themselves into
the seas and sacrificed their lives rather than give up the Torah.

We can find the most eloquent demonstrations of this great
strength in the history of the Jewish people. Abraham, the
first of our Patriarchs, allowed himself to be thrown into the
burning lime kiln for the sake of the pure faith which he spread.
By this act, he imparted to his descendants the will and the
strength to submit to martyrdom, if need be, for their Judaism.
Now some may argue that this was only one isolated act of
heroism by a great and distinguished individual. But let them
consider the second instance which involved the entire Jewish
people. When the Red Sea was divided, the people of Israel
marched as one into the midst of the raging waters at the command of God. Now some may argue that this test extended only
over a relatively short period of time. But let them consider
the third instance, the fact that the Jews willingly entered a
wilderness full of wild beasts, without food or drink, not know-

ing how long they would have to stay there, for no other cause but love and loyalty to God and to His Prophet, as is written in the Book of Jeremiah: *"I remember for thee the affection of thy youth, the love of thy espousals, how thou didst go after Me in the wilderness in a land that was not sown"* (Jer. 2:1).

It was by virtue of these three tests of fire, water and wilderness, when the Jews were called upon to demonstrate the spirit of self-sacrifice in obeying the Word of God, that the Torah was given to them as their eternal possession. These three tests have been the surest guarantee for the eternal survival of the Jewish people.

—Rabbi Meir Shapiro of Lublin

*　　*　　*　　*

"Take the sum of all the congregation of the Children of Israel." (Numbers 1:2)

> When Israel received the Torah, the nations of the world were envious of them, and wondered why the Jewish people should be deemed worthy of coming closer to God than all the other nations. But the Holy One, blessed be He, closed their mouths, saying to them: "Bring Me your book of genealogy as My children bring it to Me." There at the beginning of the book, it is written: "These are the commandments which the Lord commanded to Moses for the Children of Israel on Mount Sinai." (Lev. 27:34) Next, it is written: "And the Lord spoke to Moses in the wilderness of Sinai. (Num. 1:1) ... Take the sum of all the congregation of the Children of Israel ..." (Num. 1:2), and they were deemed worthy of receiving the Torah only because of their pedigree.

—Yalkut

*　　*　　*　　*

The Sages say that on the day when the Lord will reward the Jewish people for their observance of the Torah the nations of the world will protest: "Why didst Thou not force us to accept the Torah as Thou didst force the Jews to accept it by threatening to lower the mountain upon them if they would refuse?" But then the Lord, may His Name be blessed, will ask them in His turn: "And did you observe those seven commandments which you did accept from Me?" (*Avoda Zara, 2*) This may be compared to the case of a man's son and stepson who are both taken ill, and the physician prescribes a bitter medicine which neither of them wants to take. The father forces his own son to take the medicine, but does not seek to force his stepson to do likewise. As a result, the son recovers, but the stepson remains ill. Later on, the stepson asks the father: "Why did you not force me to take the medicine too?" And the father replies: "Long ago, I forced you to take a medicine that tasted better than this one, but you rejected even that. Therefore I made no attempt now to force you to take this medicine, for it is bitter."

In the same manner, when the nations of the world will protest: "We knew that the Torah was difficult to keep. But Thou, O Lord, didst know that it would be good for us. Why, then, didst Thou not force us to accept it?", the Lord will answer: "Long ago, I gave you seven commandments. You tried them and found that they were good, and yet you did not want to keep them. Why, then, should I have given you these commandments, which are much more burdensome than the others?"

This, too, is the sense of the *Yalkut*. The nations of the world want to know why the Jews were found worthy of receiving the Torah, when the Jews, too, had not wanted it at first but had to be forced to accept it. To this, the Lord, may His Name be blessed, will reply: "Bring Me your book of genealogy and see what your ancestors long ago did with the seven commandments I gave them. Then compare their conduct with that of the ancestors of the Jewish people who observed the commandments of the entire Torah long before the Torah had been given to them. Now do you understand why I forced the Jews to accept the Torah but did not see fit to force you to do so?"

—*Shaar Bet Rabim*

*   *   *   *

"...by their families, by their fathers' houses, according to the number of names..." (Numbers 1:2)

The circumstance that the Jews succeeded in preserving the purity of their families and their pedigrees through such a long and oppressive exile as their sojourn in Egypt, where they were enslaved and outlawed, was due to the fact that they zealously clung to those characteristics which set them apart from the other nations and that they refrained from any conduct that would have led to assimilation. They made no concession whatever to the alien environment in which they lived, refusing even to change their names. This way of living kept them from losing their identity and merging with the people in whose midst they dwelt.

The fact that they kept their own names ("according to the number of names") enabled them to be counted "by their families, by their fathers' houses."   —*Melo HaOmer*

*   *   *   *

"...every one head of his fathers' house..." (Numbers 1:4)

Two men were quarrelling, and in the course of the quarrel one accused the other of not being of good family. To this, the other man retorted: "You may be of good family, but your lineage ends with you, while mine begins with me."

This is the implication of the phrase "every one head of his father's house." Each one of them was the "head of his fathers' house." His lineage did not end with him; instead, it was he who began a new family of noble lineage. The families which these men founded were able to declare their pedigrees after them.

—*Rabbi M. Chafetz*

*   *   *   *

". . . and they declared their pedigrees after their families, by their fathers' houses . . ." (Numbers 1:18)

The fact that every one of the Children of Israel passed before (Moses) the Father of all Prophets and his brother (Aaron), the man who was sanctified to the Lord, and that the Jews also had to make their names known to them in writing enabled the Israelites to be worthy of remaining alive, for as the Jews passed before Moses and Aaron, the two leaders would look upon them with kindness and ask the Lord to be merciful to them, to cause them to multiply and to let their numbers increase.

—Nachmanides

*   *   *   *

From the above explanation by Nachmanides was derived the custom that when we come to a *tzaddik* with the request that the holy man pray for some one person, we give to the *tzaddik* a piece of paper on which the name of that person is written.

*   *   *   *

"These are those who were numbered, which Moses and Aaron numbered. . . . And all those who were numbered of the Children of Israel . . . all that were able to go forth to war in Israel, even all those who were numbered were six hundred thousand and three thousand and five hundred and fifty." (Numbers 1:44, 45, 46)

The word "numbered" is mentioned in each of these three verses in order to stress that the census was commanded for three distinct purposes as follows: (1) In order that the people might receive added merit by passing before Moses and Aaron and being mentioned by name (Nachmanides). Hence the statement in the first verse: "These are those who were numbered, *whom Moses and Aaron numbered."* (2) In order to determine who was fit to go forth to battle and how many there were fit to do such service. Hence the statement in the second verse: "And all those who are numbered of the Children of Israel . . . from twenty years old and upward, *all that were able to go forth to war* in Israel." (3) In order to make known the greatness of God's mercies, since the seventy souls who had originally come to Egypt grew into a host of over six hundred thousand, counting only the men above the age of twenty. Hence the third verse: "Even all those who were numbered were *six hundred thousand and three thousand and five hundred and fifty.*"

—*Rabbi Abraham Samuel Benjamin Schreiber (Ketav Sofer)*

* * * *

"...by their fathers' houses; every man with his own standard, according to the ensigns..." (Numbers 2:2)

> Why is it written "with his own standard, according to the ensigns"? It is so written because when our father Jacob was about to depart from this world, he said to (those around him): "Take up my body with reverence and respect. You (alone shall) bear my body and let no other man lay his hand on my bier."
>
> —*Midrash*

Our father Jacob showed his children the way to take up his body reverently. Symbolically interpreted, this request means that the descendants of Jacob should hold aloft the name of their departed ancestor by displaying the awe and reverence properly due God. Now there are some who are reverent to God but evil to their fellow men. Such individuals will cause the name of their ancestor to be mentioned not with respect but with disdain. People will criticize their evil conduct and put them to shame. For this reason Jacob commanded his children to take him up not only with "reverence" but also with "respect", or, symbolically interpreted, to maintain such good relations with their fellow-men that they will increase the respect in which the world holds God and the people of Israel. Only if the descendants of Jacob will conduct themselves in this manner will "no other man lay his hand on my bier"; only then will no human being dare speak evil of them or put them to shame.

That we lift up the bier of Jacob with reverence and respect, with reverence for God and love for one's fellow-men — this was the last will and testament of our father Jacob and this is the device, the standard by which his descendants should abide — "every man with his own standard . . ."

—*Divrei Shaarei Hayyim*

* * * *

"*. . . the tribe of Zebulun . . .*" (Numbers 2:7)

All the other tribes counted with their standards are accompanied by the conjunction "*and*" ("*and* the tribe of Gad . . . *and* the tribe of Benjamin . . . *and* the tribe of Naphtali"). Why is the conjunction omitted in the case of the tribe of Zebulun?

The tribe of Zebulun engaged in commerce, supporting the tribe of Issachar to enable the latter to engage in study. (See Rashi's commentary to Gen. 49:13-14.) The Torah writes "the tribe of Zebulun" without the conjunction in order not to create the impression that the tribe of Zebulun was inferior or in any way secondary to the tribe of Issachar. The tribe of Zebulun is regarded as an independent unit in itself and as equal in merit to the tribe of Issachar. This is to teach us that he who supports those who study the Law is just as great as he who studies himself.

—*Rabbi Jacob ben Asher (Baal Ha-Turim)*

* * * *

"*Now these are the names of the sons of Aaron, Nadab, the firstborn . . . These are the names of the sons of Aaron, the priests that were anointed . . .*" (Numbers 3:2-3)

Why does the statement "these are the names of the sons of Aaron" occur twice in two consecutive verses?

It is well-known that in some other religions, priests are regarded as superhuman beings who are immune to error. For this reason when a member of these religions is ordained to the priesthood he is given a new name to signify that he is no longer the same as he was prior to his ordination but has become a new person. Not so the Jews. Even the greatest Jew is regarded as a human being who is by no means immune to error. "There is no righteous man on earth who always does good and never sins," and it is written: "He shall not believe in his own holiness." We are indeed duty-bound to give due honor to scholars. However, we do so not because of their persons but only in order to honor the Law which they study and observe, just as we pay honor to a Scroll of the Law not because of its physical character — after all, it is only plain parchment — but because the sheets of parchment from which it is made bear the sacred words of the Law. We do not believe that the clay of which a scholar of the Law is made is any different from the substance from which ordinary men are formed.

The statement "these are the names of the sons of Aaron" occurs twice, first in the naming of the sons, and then in the characterization of the sons as priests, in order to show that even after their anointment to the priesthood, the sons of Aaron did not receive new names but were still considered the same human beings as before.

—*Eglei Tal*

*　*　*　*

"And the Lord spoke to Moses, saying: 'Bring near the tribe of Levi . . .'" (Numbers 3:6)

> Of them it is written: "The righteous will flourish like a palm tree; he will grow like a cedar in Lebanon."

—*Midrash Rabba*

There are two kinds of righteous men. One is constantly busy with his devotions and with the performance of the divine service, but does all this only for himself and not for others. He makes no effort to influence others to be righteous also. Such a man who studies and worships for himself but does nothing

284

to help increase the number of righteous men in the world is like a cedar, which is a great and mighty tree but bears no fruit. The other is not only pious himself but also causes others to flourish in spirit, to repent of their sins and to come closer to God. He is like a palm tree which not only grows but flourishes and yields fine fruit. The "cedar of Lebanon" only "grows" by itself, but the "palm tree flourishes"; it yields fruit, increasing the good there is in the world.

The tribe of Levi was constantly engaged in the study of the Law and in the performance of the divine service. Nevertheless, the Levites were like the palm tree in that they also took the time to study the Law of God with others (*"They taught Thy judgments to Jacob and Thy Law to Israel"*), and brought others closer to the ways of Judaism (*"Loving all of God's creatures and bringing them closer to the Torah"*).

—*Testament of Israel ben Eliezer Baal Shem Tov*

*   *   *   *

"For all the first-born are Mine . . . Mine they shall be: I am the Lord." (Numbers 3:13)

Said the Lord: "Originally I took the first-born unto Myself to perform My service, under the condition that they should belong to Me and believe in My Divinity (*"Mine they shall be: I am the Lord"*). But since they worshipped the Golden Calf, thus denying My Divinity, they are no longer Mine and I have taken unto Myself instead the tribe of Levi which refused to pay homage to the Golden Calf.

—*Meshekh Hakhmah*

*   *   *   *

"All that were numbered of the Levites . . . were twenty and two thousand." (Numbers 3:39)

Why was the tribe of Levi smaller in number than the other tribes of the Children of Israel?

The Sages explain that when the Children of Israel were in

285

Egypt, the tribe of Levi was not compelled to perform hard labor like the rest of the Israelites. We read in the Book of Exodus: *"The more they afflicted them, the more they multiplied and the more they spread abroad"* (Exod. 1:12). The Sages take this to mean that God caused all the other tribes, which were under the whip of the Egyptian taskmasters, to increase and multiply in a supernatural manner. Since the Levites, unlike the other tribes, were not so afflicted, this statement was not applicable to them, and they increased and multiplied only by natural means.   *—Nachmanides*

* * * *

"And the Lord spoke to Moses and Aaron: . . . 'Do not cut off the tribe of the families of the Kohathites from among the Levites . . .'" (Numbers 4:17-18)

Moses and Aaron were commanded to establish a definite order for the assignment of the care of the holy vessels to the Kohathites, rather than permit them to choose their tasks for themselves. For if the Kohathites would have been allowed their way, each one of them would have wanted first choice, to bear holier vessels than the others, and the ensuing arguments would have resulted in disaster.

The Sages relate that the drawing of lots was instituted for the purpose of determining who was to perform the various duties in the Temple. For in the olden days each man would rush to receive a part in the service, and it happened one day that one man pushed another in the rush, causing him to fall and break his leg (*Yoma 22*). To prevent such trouble in the future, it was commanded that "Aaron and his sons shall go in, and appoint them, every one, to his service and to his burden" (Num. 4:19), so that the Kohathites would not be "cut off" by death as the result of bickering for first place.

—Sforno

* * * *

Haphtarah Bamidebar (Hosea 2)

". . . the number of the Children of Israel shall be as the sand of the sea which cannot be measured nor numbered." (Hosea 2:1)

> It is written: "And the number of the Children of Israel shall be as the sand of the sea" and, immediately following, "which cannot be measured nor numbered." Is this not a contradiction? One (prophecy) will come true when Israel will do the will of the Omnipresent and the other will come true when Israel will not do the will of the Omnipresent.
>
> *—Yoma 22*

How are we to understand the implication in Tractate Yoma that, supposing the Jewish people were to repent and mend their ways from one moment to the next, they would suddenly become so great in number that while it was possible to count them before it would no longer be possible to do so after their change of heart?

We know that there are individuals who, though they are only one single unit in quantity, are equal to many thousands in quality. Thus the Sages say of our Master Moses that he "outweighed all of Israel" and of Yair ben Menasseh that he "was equal to the greater part of the Sanhedrin" (*Baba Bathra 121*). This is what the Sages mean by their statement: If the Jews will do the will of the Omnipresent, every single Jew will become so great and important that his quality will be beyond measure.

Thus the interpretation of the verse in the Book of Hosea is as follows: *And the number of the Children of Israel shall be —* Once the Children of Israel will do the will of the Omnipresent, the Children of Israel who are finite in number now (when they do not do the will of the Omnipresent) will become great beyond measurement in terms of quality (*"they cannot be measured nor numbered.*) For "it will come to pass that, instead of that which was said to them: 'You are not My people,' it will be said to them: 'You are the children of the Living God'" (Hosea 2:1), and as a child of the Living God, every single member of the Jewish people will be endowed with the worth of hundreds of thousands, so that it will be impossible to define the greatness of the people of Israel in terms of numbers.

—Musarist Writings

* * * *

Men tread upon the sand with their feet, but regard the stars above as obejcts to which no human being can attain. Even if the Jews will be "as the sand of the sea" and trodden upon by all, they still will be regarded as the "stars of heaven," as the highest among men, to whose virtues and talents no other humans can attain.

—Anon.

* * * *

"And it shall come to pass that, instead of that which was said to them: 'You are not My people', it will be said to them: 'You are the children of the Living God.'" (Hosea 2:1)

The Hebrew word for "instead" (*ba-makom*) may be translated also as "in the place." Hence the above text may also be construed to read: "And it shall come to pass that *in the place* in which it was said to them 'You are not My people,' it shall be said to them: 'You are the children of the Living God.'"

History has shown that it was precisely in those countries where the Jews suffered oppression and persecution, that the spirit of Judaism has thrived and Jewish identity was strengthened, while in countries where the Jews fared well, where they were emancipated and accorded all the rights of citizenship, the strength of Judaism was sapped by assimilation and by conversion movements which snatched away large segments of our people.

We hear the Prophet say: *"And it shall come to pass that*

in the place in which it was said to them: 'You are not My people,' in that place where the others will humiliate you and say that you are a base people, *it shall be said to them: 'You are the children of the Living God.'* The humiliations to which you will be subjected will impel you to guard your identity zealously and to adhere more closely to the Torah, so that you will be regarded as true children of the Living God."

—Bikkurei Aviv

*   *   *   *

Weekly Portion of Nasso (Num. 4:21-7:89)

"And the Children of Israel did so, and put them (the lepers and individuals afflicted by specified types of uncleanness) *out of the camp, as the Lord had said to Moses, so the Children of Israel did."* (Numbers 5:4)

We read at the beginning of the verse that "the Children of Israel did so." Why, then, does the Torah say again at the end of the verse "so the Children of Israel did"?

The commandment to remove these defiled individuals from the camp of the Children of Israel was given with the hope that if the Israelites were to see a leper, his body disfigured by disease, removed from the camp, they would guard zealously against those sins — pride, vicious gossip and envy — which bring on leprosy. It was felt that if they were to see one suffering from a discharge put out from the camp, they would remember *"from where thou camest — a malodorous drop"*; that if they were to behold a person rendered unclean by the dead taken out of their midst, they would remember *"whither thou goest — to a place of dust, worms and ashes,"* and that, remembering all these things, they would be exceedingly careful to keep away from sin.

For this reason the Torah desired to stress that the Children of Israel fulfilled both aspects of the commandment. Not only did they fulfill the letter of the law *"and put them out of the camp,"* but they also acted in accordance with the spirit of the law, keeping away from the sins that cause leprosy, foul discharge and death. *As the Lord had said to Moses, so the Children of Israel did;* that is, they acted in keeping with the purpose for which God had given them this commandment.

—*Binah Le-Ittim*

* * * *

"When a man or woman shall commit any sin that men commit, to commit a trespass against the Lord . . ." (Numbers 5:6)

Rashi notes that this "trespass against the Lord" refers to the sin of robbing a proselyte. This crime is considered a trespass against the Lord because he who robs a proselyte who has come to seek shelter beneath the wing of Judaism causes a grave desecration of the Name of the Lord and therefore is guilty of a trespass against the Holy One.

—*Sforno*

* * * *

"And every man's hallowed things shall be his; whatsoever any man gives to the priest shall be his." (Numbers 5:10)

What bearing does this statement have on the portion dealing with robbery?

Fools believe that the money which they have lying in their coffers is theirs, while the money which they give away to charity is theirs no longer. They therefore commit robbery, filling up their coffers with the money of others.

Actually, quite the reverse is true. Only those possessions which are given away for sacred purposes (*every man's hallowed things*) such as those which we give to priests and scholars of the Law (*whatsoever any man gives to the priest*) remain the property of the original owner (*shall be his*) forever. But those possessions which a man greedily amasses for himself, not to speak of the money of others, are not his at all. Such gains will not remain with him for longer than a fleeting moment.

—*Binah Le-Ittim*

* * * *

"And the Lord spoke to Moses saying: ... If any man's wife should go aside ..." (Numbers 5:11-12)

Saying: to the generations to come.

—*Midrash*

Why should the explanation "to the generations to come" be attached specifically to the passage dealing with the procedure to be followed in the case of a wife suspected of faithlessness?

The Sages relate that while the Israelites were in the wilderness, the *manna* which was sent down from heaven to nourish them served also to clear up any suspicion of unfaithfulness on the part of a wife. If she had not sinned, her measure of *manna* would appear at the dwelling of her husband. If she had sinned, so that her husband was no longer permitted to live with her, her portion of *manna* would be found near the tent of her father (*Yoma 75*).

This means that as long as the Children of Israel were in the wilderness receiving their rations of *manna* from heaven, it was not necessary to give the "water of bitterness" to the suspect woman to determine whether the accusation made against her was based on fact. It was only later, in the generations that were yet to come, that this device had to be employed to confirm or disprove charges of unfaithfulness made against a married woman in Israel.

—*Tifereth Yonathan*

* * * *

"If any man's wife should go aside ..." (Numbers 5:12)

No man sins unless the spirit of folly has possessed him.

—*Saying of the Sages*

In the olden days people would sin only if the spirit of folly possessed them. Today people do good only if the spirit of wisdom happens to move them.

—Rabbi Josel Horowitz

* * * *

If thou retainest the gifts due the priest, upon thy life, thou wilt have to come to him in order to bring him thy faithless wife for the ordeal of the waters.

—Rashi

According to the Sages two things bring wealth; namely, tithing (*"tithe so that thou mayest become rich"*) and giving honor and fine clothes to one's wife (*"respect thy wife because thus thou wilt become rich"* — Baba Mezia 49).

Now a man may think that he can become rich without tithing because he has many beautiful and costly garments made for his wife. Therefore we are told that "the result will be that he will have to bring her to the priest." If a man makes too many fine clothes for his wife, he exposes her to temptation so that she may forget herself and he may have to bring her to the priest to have her guilt or innocence established. Therefore, the best course to follow under any circumstances is to tithe.

—Torat Moshe

* * * *

"When either a man or a woman shall clearly utter a vow, the vow of a Nazirite . . ." (Numbers 6:2)

Why is the portion dealing with the Nazirite put in juxtaposition with the portion dealing with the faithless wife? To teach you that a person who beholds a faithless wife in her disgrace should abstain from drinking wine.

—Rashi's Commentary to Tractate Sotah 2

The sin of the faithless wife runs counter to all reason and human nature but so does the abstinence practiced by the Nazirite. It was Rashi's intention to point out that as long as there are in the world individuals whose immoral conduct is contrary to reason and custom, there must be others who will exceed the bounds of reason in saintly conduct and keep away as far as possible from immorality by imposing all manner of legal safeguards on their own behavior.

—*Musarist Writings*

*   *   *   *

"And the priest shall . . . make atonement for him, for that he sinned by reason of the dead . . ." (Numbers 6:11)
Alternative rendering: *"for he sinned* against his soul."

Because he denied himself wine.

—*Rashi*

All Nazirites must abstain from wine, and the Torah characterizes them as saintly men. Why, then, should Rashi imply that the defiled Nazirite is a sinner because he abstains from wine?

Abstinence from wine in order to be a Nazirite and to keep away from physical pleasure is not a sin. In fact, it is considered saintly conduct. But if the Nazirite became defiled due to his own carelessness, so that the law "but the former days (of his Naziriteship) shall be void" applies, then all his previous abstinence from wine had served no purpose and constituted a sin (since he vainly denied himself what God had made for the use of mankind).

—*K'lei Yakar*

*   *   *   *

The Sages say that he who "sits and fasts"; i.e., one who fasts longer than the Law requires, is regarded as a sinner.

If he "sits still" while he fasts, if he fasts but makes no spiritual progress, if the fast had no deeper effect on him, then he afflicted himself without purpose and therefore is considered a sinner.

—*Abraham Samuel Benjamin Schreiber (Ketav Sofer)*

*   *   *   *

"When the days of his consecration are fulfilled, he shall bring it to the door of the tent of meeting." (Numbers 6:13)

> He shall bring himself (to the door of the tent of meeting).
>
> —*Rashi*

If it is intended that the Nazirite should come alone, why should the wording of the Hebrew text be such that it can be interpreted to read "he shall bring *him*" (as if another person had to bring him).

The Nazirite's vow is primarily a kind of cure which man undergoes so that he may be able to set bounds to his baser lusts and appetites and to fight against the selfishness in him. Now if the fulfillment of this vow has taught the individual to view his own concerns with the same objectivity as he would look upon those of another person, and to be able to resist his selfish lusts, then the Nazirite's vow has served its purpose and he can cease afflicting himself.

For this reason the Biblical verse implies that once the Nazirite is able to "bring *himself*" to the door of the tent of meeting just as if he were bringing another person, when he can be entirely objective about his own purpose, it is a sign that "the days of his consecration are fulfilled" and that his Naziriteship has truly served the purpose for which it was intended.

—*Meshekh Hakhmah*

* * * *

"Speak to Aaron and to his sons as follows: In this manner shall you bless the Children of Israel. You shall say to them ..." (Numbers 6:23)

> You shall say to them — In this manner shall you speak to them. —*Onkelos*

If the Jewish people receives blessings, the priests benefit also, for they will then receive more priestly gifts. As a result it may happen that when the priests bless the Children of Israel they will think also of their own advantage as they recite the blessing. To forestall this possibility, Scripture says: "You shall say *to them"*; implying, in the words of Rashi: "Bless them not hurriedly and hastily but devoutly and with a whole heart." As you bless the people your thoughts should be only of them and not of yourselves.

This thought is stressed by the translation of Onkelos: "In this manner shall you speak *to them,*" implying that "your blessing will be accepted and fulfilled only if you will bless the people for their sake, without thought of selfish gain."

Aaron is mentioned in this verse by name because in the days when he officiated as High Priest, Israel was still in the wilderness and the law concerning the priestly gifts was not in operation. Hence when he blessed the Children of Israel his thoughts must have been solely of the welfare of his people, unmotivated by prospects of selfish gain. The Scripture, by recalling Aaron, implies that once the Israelites will be in the Promised Land and obligated to observe the commandment concerning the priestly gifts, the sons of Aaron must continue to bless the Israelites "in this manner", in the same selfless spirit in which Aaron had blessed them in the wilderness.

—*Abraham Samuel Benjamin Schreiber* (*Ketav Sofer*)

*   *   *   *

"May the Lord lift up His countenance toward thee . . ." (Num. 6:26)
        The ministering angels asked the Holy One, blessed be He: "Why dost Thou lift up Thy countenance toward Israel? Is it not written in Thy Torah: He will not lift up His countenance?" Replied the Holy One, blessed be He: "Why should I not lift up My countenance toward them, when I wrote in My Torah: 'And thou shalt eat and be satisfied and bless the Lord thy God,' and they are particular to fulfill My commandment regardless of whether the amount of nourishment they have taken was the size of an olive or whether it was the size of an egg."

        —*Tractate Berakhot* 20 and *Midrash*

Can this great zeal in performing the commandment to

bless the Lord after partaking even of small amounts of nourishment be regarded as a "lifting up of the countenance toward the Lord" on the part of Israel, so that the people of Israel are truly deserving of having the Lord, in His turn, lift up His countenance toward them?

A gift from a person of importance, even if it is only trifling in itself, assumes added significance by virtue of the importance of the giver. The people of Israel "lift up their countenance toward the Lord" by their act of gratitude, in that even if the Lord should only give them little nourishment, they consider His gift an occasion for reciting blessings, because the Giver is very dear to them and they enjoy even the little He has given them, knowing that it is from Him.

For this reason the Lord, in His turn, lifts up His countenance toward them and attaches great importance even to this act of worship. For although the blessings the people of Israel recite are not of great significance in themselves, He cherishes them since His people, who recite them, are acting to the best of their limited possibilities of showing gratitude. It is "measure for measure."

—*Kol Simcha*

* * * *

They are particular, *for themselves,* to be satisfied with little nourishment, but when they give food to a poor man they let him eat until he is satisfied. This is their way of "lifting up their countenances toward the Lord."

—*Rabbi Hayyim of Volozhin*

* * * *

"... *And grant thee peace."* (Numbers 6:26)

If a group of Jews, zealous in their desire to "lift up their countenance toward the Lord," divide even a small amount of food into many small portions so that as many individuals as possible should have an amount of food the size of an olive (in order to be able to recite the Grace after Meals), contention may ensue, because wherever there is only little to eat, with many mouths to feed, there is likely to be quarrelling. For this reason the Priestly Blessing includes the blessing of peace.

—*Kehilat Yitzhak*

*   *   *   *

"On the second day Nethanel the son of Zuar, prince of Issachar, made an offering . . ." (Numbers 7:18)

Seeing that the offerings of the princes were all identical and in the same amount, why should the Scripture mention the offerings of each prince separately?

Because each of them brought his offering of his own accord, not in order to ape the others, but solely of his own free will.

—*The Rabbi of Przysucha*

*   *   *   *

"This was the dedication offering of the altar on the day when it was anointed . . . This was the dedication offering of the altar after it was anointed." (Numbers 7:84, 88)

We must make sure the renewal that takes place on the day of the dedication remains with us and never loses its power. The spirit of dedication which marked the "day on which the altar was anointed" must remain with us even "after it was anointed."

—*The Rabbi of Ger*

*   *   *   *

Haphtarah Nasso (Judges 13:2-25)

"(The Lord said to the wife of Manoah) Now therefore beware . . . and drink no wine nor strong drink, and do not eat any unclean thing . . . for thou shalt conceive and bear a son, and no razor shall come upon his head, for the child shall be a Nazirite to God from the womb." (Judges 13:3-5)

This means that the destiny of the child to be a Nazirite

was determined by the conduct of his mother while he was still in her womb.

It is written "They shall bless the Lord in assembly"; the children of the Jewish people are to praise the Lord together. But whether they can do this depends on their family background. Only if their background is truly Jewish can they bless the Lord; if their antecedents are not pure, the result — Heaven forbid — will be blasphemy. *—Attributed to a Sage*

* * * *

"(The woman told her husband) *But* (the man of God) *said to me; behold, thou shalt conceive and bear a son, and now drink no wine nor strong drink, and do not eat any unclean thing, for the child shall be a Nazirite to God from the womb to the day of his death."* (Judges 13:7)

Why did the woman not also tell her husband of the angel's directive that no razor was to touch the child's head?

Because she had added the qualification "to the day of his death." Now her words were inspired by the holy spirit of prophecy, and she knew that, before his death, her son's locks would be cut off. Thus she could not tell her husband about the angel's prohibition against shaving Samson.

Meshekh Hakhmah

* * * *

"*And the angel of the Lord said to (Manoah): 'Why dost thou ask after my name, seeing that it is hidden?' "* (Judges 13:18)

The more one seeks to find out the name of an angel of holiness, the more one realizes that it remains hidden. But if one seeks to learn the name of the angel of Esau, he will find out that this angel (of evil) has no name at all. The evil impulse seems of consequence only as long as one does not attempt to inquire into its true nature. Once we have learned its true character, we will find that, actually, there is nothing worth knowing about the impulse of evil. *—Musarist Writings*

* * * *

Weekly Portion of Be'ha'alothekha (Num. 8:1-12:16)

"And the Lord spoke unto Moses saying: Speak to Aaron, and say to him: When thou lightest the lamps . . ." (Numbers 8-1-2)

> Why is the section dealing with the candelabrum put in juxtaposition with the section describing the offerings of the princes? Because Aaron, seeing the dedication of the princes, became uneasy, because he was not with them at the dedication. But the Holy One, blessed be He, said to him: "Upon thy life, thy part is more important than theirs, because thou wilt kindle the lamps and set them in order."
>
> —*Rashi*

Why was the lighting of the lamps in the Sanctuary more important than the offerings made by the tribal princes?

The Midrash Rabba explains: "The offerings could be made only as long as the Holy Temple was standing, but the lamps must be kindled forever."

This explanation is difficult to understand. Once the Temple is destroyed and the offering of sacrifices has ceased, where should the lamps be kindled?

According to Nachmanides, God's promise refers not only to the lamps of the Temple but also to the lamps of the festival of Hanukkah. God gave Aaron the promise that one day his descendants, the Hasmoneans, would have a part in miracles that would bring about a second dedication at which a candelabrum would be lit, and that the duty to kindle those lights of rededication would be binding on the Jewish people even when there would be no Temple.

These are the lights of which the Midrash Rabba states that they must be kindled forever.

*   *   *   *

"(The seven lamps) *shall give light in front of the candelabrum.*"
(Numbers 8:2)

> In this connection it is written: The beginning of Thy
> words shed light, and it is according to the view of the one
> who says that the height of the candelabrum was seventeen
> hands' breadths.

—Midrash Pliya

The candelabrum had seven stems, nine flowers, eleven
pomegranates, and twenty-two cups. There is some controversy
as to the height of the candelabrum; the authorities cannot
agree whether it was seventeen hands' breadths or eighteen.

The number of parts of the candelabrum correspond to the
number of words in the opening verses of each of the Five Books
of Moses. Thus the seven stems correspond to the seven words
in the first verse of the Book of Genesis, the eleven pomegranates to the eleven words in the first verse of the Book of Exodus, the nine flowers to the nine words in the first verse of the
Book of Leviticus, and the twenty-two cups to the twenty-two
words in the first verse of the Book of Deuteronomy. Similarly,
the seventeen words in the opening verse of the Book of Numbers would account for the height of the candelabrum — seventeen hands' breadths.

This is the sense of the Midrash starting with "the beginning of Thy words shed light . . ." All the figures pertaining
to the candelabrum correspond to the opening verses of the
Books of the Pentateuch. However, this is only true if one accepts the premise of the one who says that the height of the
candelabrum was seventeen hands' breadths.

—Divrei Noam, by the Rabbi of Shepitovka

*   *   *   *

"And thus did Aaron: he lighted the lamps . . ." (Num. 8:3)

> "This is to say in praise of Aaron that he did not change."

—Sifri

Although he had been privileged to attain such great honors, Aaron never changed. He did not become conceited or arrogant, but remained as humble and meek as he had been before.

—*Attributed to the Rabbi of Przysucha*

*   *   *   *

It is human nature to become conceited as one rises in the world. Not so Aaron. *Thus did Aaron*: he did as the lamp does. Even as the light of a lamp remains the same irrespective of whether the lamp is raised or lowered, so Aaron, too, was in no way changed by the honors he received.

—*Sifthei Kodesh*

*   *   *   *

In this connection, Rabbi Shmelke of Nikolsburg interpreted the Biblical verse *"And the minstrel became like the instrument and the spirit of the Lord was upon him"* (II Kings 3:15) as follows: Once man will be as the minstrel who became like the instrument; when, like the instrument which is not changed by the beautiful tune it plays, he, too, will not be affected by the awareness of his own virtues, then the spirit of the Lord will be upon him and he will be found worthy of being endowed with prophetic vision.

—*Havot Yair*

*   *   *   *

"And I have given the Levites to do the service of the Children of Israel in the Tent of Meeting ..." (Num. 8:19)

> Five times are the Children of Israel mentioned by name in this verse, in order to show in what affection they are held by the Lord, in that the mention of them is repeated five times in one verse, corresponding to the Five Books of the Torah.
>
> —*Rashi*

Why the special emphasis on the Children of Israel in this particular section?

Since only the Levites were chosen for the service in the Sanctuary, the other Israelites might have been disturbed, wondering why they had not been deemed fit to perform these functions. Therefore the Scripture chose this particular place to recall the affection in which they are held by God. Even as the Torah is composed of five separate books, which are independent units but all combine to form one Torah, so the Jewish people is divided into Priests, Levites and Israelites who represent separate units, each with its own function, but who all combine to form one nation which is very precious and important to its God.

—Hiddushei HaRIM

* * * *

"And the man Moses was very meek, above all the men that were on the face of the earth." (Numbers 12:3)

And the man Moses: Moses was found worthy of being a true man, a master among men and a "father" of all the prophets that were to come after him, because *he was very meek, above all the men that were on the face of the earth*: He regarded all the others as being above him, and therefore he, in fact, was superior to them all.

—Binah Leïttim

* * * *

". . . and he (Moses) *beholds the similitude of the Lord . . ."* (Numbers 12:8)

Does not the Hebrew verb *"Habata"* implay a looking down from somewhere above? (*See Rashi's Commentary on the Book of Genesis*)

"The similitude of the Lord" which Moses beheld refers not to a likeness of God but to His Divine qualities of graciousness and mercy, qualities which Moses brought down with him from above, down to earth and into the hearts of the Children of Israel. *—The Rabbi of Ger*

* * * *

302

"Lay not, I pray thee, sin upon us, for that we have done foolishly and for that we have sinned." (Numbers 12:11).

> If we did it unintentionally, then forgive us as if we had done it on purpose.
>
> *—Yalkut*

What is the meaning of this statement?

It may be that Aaron and Miriam were not really aware of the greatness of their brother Moses. But even if that was so, they sinned gravely against the Lord, for they should have known that if the Lord loved him so greatly He did not love him without reason. (*"You should have said: 'The King does not love him without reason.' But if you argue: 'I am not cognizant of his works [i.e., I love him even though he might not deserve it], then this statement is even worse than your previous one —* Rashi's Commentary to Verse 8).

But if they did believe in the greatness of Moses their sin against him was even greater, an intentional sin, though that would be less of a sin against the Lord, blessed be His Name.

Aaron and Miriam therefore said to Moses: "If we sinned against you unintentionally because we were not aware of your greatness, then we would be guilty of a grave sin against God. Therefore, if this is the case, forgive us as you would if we had done it on purpose. Consider it as if we had known of your greatness and wilfully insulted you, for if that were the case, our sin against God would be less grave than our sin against you." They knew that Moses would have forgiven an insult to his own honor much more readily than an insult to the honor of the Most High.

—Shev Shmattso, Preface

*   *   *   *

Haphtarah Be'haalothekha (Zechariah 2:14-4:7)

"And the Lord said to Satan: The Lord rebuke thee, O Satan, yea, he who chose Jerusalem . . ." (Zech. 3:2)

"He who chose Jerusalem" refers not to the Lord but to Satan. The verse means that the Lord will rebuke Satan who pretends to single out Zion and Jerusalem, feigning love for these holy places, in order to lure the Jewish people away from their faith.

—*The Great Sage of Minsk*

* * * *

Weekly Portion of Shelach (Num. 13:1-15:41)

"And Moses called Hoshea the son of Nun Joshua." (Num. 13:16)
> (He called him Joshua) because he prayed: "May the Lord save you from the counsel of the spies!"

—*Rashi*

A humble person will not stubbornly persist in his own views but will be ready at any time to defer to another opinion. Seeing that the spies were princes of their respective tribes and enjoyed great public esteem, and knowing that Joshua was a humble man, Moses feared that Joshua might be led to defer to their opinion. It is for this reason that he prayed in behalf of Joshua: "May the Lord save you from the counsel of the spies."

Of course, when it comes to the observance of our religion, it is not always proper to act the part of the humble man. Indeed, persistence may be imperative there. But to know when to persist in one's own opinion and when to defer to the views of others — ah, this truly requires Divine support.

—*The Rabbi of Ger*

* * * *

"(And Moses sent the spies to spy out the land of Canaan to see) *what the land is that they dwell in, whether it is good or bad . . ."* (Numbers 13:19)

(Said Moses to the spies): Even if the land should seem bad to you, it is good. Though it may be hidden, the sanctity of the land is always there. Hidden beneath its superficial disadvantages is all the good that is in it, and once you have entered the Land, all this sanctity that was hitherto concealed will lie revealed before you.

—*Sefer HaZehut*

Rabbi Joseph Hayyim Sonnenfeld* used to say: It is written: "And seek the good of Jerusalem" — This means that we must always endeavor to see only the good in Jerusalem.

* * * *

"And (the spies) *cut down from there a branch with one cluster of grapes . . . they took also of the pomegranates and of the figs . . ."* (Numbers 13:23)

The saintly Rabbi Isaac ben Solomon Luria** comments with regard to the verse: *"And the time was the time of the first fruits of the grape vine"* (13:20) that the commandment to offer up the first fruits of the harvest was given in order to compensate for the sin of the spies. The spies had spoiled the Promised Land for the people. The commandment to offer up the first fruits was given to emphasize the pleasantness of the Promised Land. It is therefore applicable only to the seven species of fruit for which the Land is famous.

Interestingly enough, we read in the Mishnah, Tractate Bikkurim: "If a man goes down into his field and sees a first-ripe fig, a first-ripe bunch of grapes, and a first-ripe pomegranate, he shall tie them up in a basket and say: 'Behold, these are the first fruits'" (Bikkurim 3:41). Significantly, of all the fruits in the Land, this passage makes mention only of those three species — the grape, the pomegranate and the fig — which the spies brought back with them.

—Rabbi Menahem Zemba

* * * *

"And (the spies) *went and came to Moses and Aaron . . ."* (Numbers 13:26)

---

* Chief Rabbi of the old Orthodox Community of Jerusalem; 1849-1932.

** Known as *Ari;* 1534-72.

The intention here is to compare their 'going' with their 'coming' to Moses. How was their coming to Moses? With an evil plan. So too, their going out on the journey was with an evil plan.

—Rashi

In view of the fact that, in his commentary on Verse 3, Rashi himself states that "they sinned later, but at that time (i.e., when Moses sent them out) they were still worthy men," this comment seems difficult to understand.

However, these two statements, contradictory though they seem, can be reconciled most readily.

The Sages say that an evil thought or plan in itself is not counted as an evil deed. But once that plan is translated into action, it is retroactively counted as a separate sin (*Kiddushin 40*). Thus, at the time when the spies went forth on their mission with an evil plan, that evil plan was not counted against them, and they "were still worthy men." But when, by "coming" to Moses and Aaron with an unfavorable report, they translated their evil plan into evil action, their sinister plan became a sin in itself, and therefore Rashi now finds a basis for comparing their "going" forth on their mission with their "coming" back to Moses.

—Attributed to the Rabbi of Ger

* * * *

"And Caleb stilled the people toward Moses, and said: 'We should go up at once and possess (the land), *for we are well able to overcome it' "* (Numbers 13:30).

Why did Caleb, rather than Joshua, speak up then?

The main cause for the panic that had taken hold of the Children of Israel was the prophecy of Eldad and Medad to the effect that Moses would die, to be succeeded by Joshua. Hearing this prediction, they could not imagine how, without the

leadership of Moses, they would be able to conquer the giants
and the great fortified cities of which the spies had told them.

It was for this reason that Caleb "stilled" the frightened
people by telling them that it would be an error to think that
only Moses was able to perform miracles. On the contrary, he
told them, they themselves, the Jewish people, possessed those
qualities which made them worthy of miracles, so that actually,
Moses himself derived his greatness only from their sanctity.

This, then, is the interpretation of the verse in the Scriptural text: *And Caleb stilled the people toward Moses* — Caleb
dissuaded the people from their belief that everything depended
on Moses; *And said: We should go up at once and possess it,
for we are well able to overcome it.* Even without Moses, we
should be able to go up at once and conquer the Promised Land.

Caleb, and not Joshua, had to be the one to tell them that.
For had Joshua said it, the people, knowing the prophecy of
Eldad and Medad, would have thought he was saying this only
because he knew he would take the place of Moses and because
he was eager for personal honor and glory.

—Meshekh Hakhmah

*   *   *   *

> We can indeed go up. Even if the land were in heaven
> and if he (Moses) were to say: "Make ladders and go
> up there", we should listen to him because we would be
> successful in whatever he wishes us to do.
>
> —Rashi

Who would think of making ladders to reach the sky in
order to go up to the Promised Land?

The thought derives from the account in the Book of
Deuteronomy, where we read of the report of the spies that the
cities of the Promised Land were *"great and fortified up to
leaven"* (Deut. 1:28). This thought, according to Rashi, inspired Caleb to declare that "even if Moses should command

307

us to make immense ladders on which to scale the sky-high fortifications of these cities, we would succeed in climbing to the very top and conquering them all."   —*Attributed to a Sage*

*   *   *   *

The spies argued that *"the Land is a land that eats up its inhabitants"* (lit., "those that *sit* in it") (14:32), that the Promised Land is a land in which one cannot "sit" still in one place but must move onward and upward all the time, climbing up to ever greater heights of sanctity, for if one ever stops climbing, one must fall. This, of course, would be most difficult. Who, the spies wondered, would be equal to it?

To this, Caleb replied: *"We can indeed go up.* Let us make ladders. We need not climb up to heaven all at once; it is enough if we do it by degrees. Let us, therefore, endeavor to go up, step by step, as on the rungs of a ladder, until we arrive at the highest level of holiness."   —*The Rabbi of Ostrowicze*

*   *   *   *

"And we were in our own sight as grasshoppers, and so were we in their sight." (Numbers 13:33)
> We heard them say to one another: "There are ants in our vineyards that look like human beings."
> —*Rashi*

Note that Rashi writes of ants instead of grasshoppers. Why did he not abide by the Scriptural text?

We are told in the Book of Proverbs: *"Go to the ant, thou sluggard; consider her ways and be wise"* (6:6). From this we gather that the lowly ant can teach man how to accept the yoke of the Kingdom of Heaven. By making an evil report about the Promised Land, the spies cast off that Divine yoke. It is for this reason that Rashi here reminds us of the ant, from whom the spies, and anyone else for that matter, could learn much about obedience to God.   —*Kedushat Levi*

*   *   *   *

308

If we are lowly in our own eyes and regard ourselves as
nonentities, our adversaries will think the same of us and tread
on us with their feet. If "we are in our own sight as grasshoppers" then "so shall we be in their sight."

—Anon.

* * * *

*"Then Moses and Aaron fell upon their faces ... and Joshua the
son of Nun and Caleb the son of Jephunneh, who were among those
that spied out the land, rent their garments ..."* (Num. 14:5, 6)

We already know from earlier verses that Joshua and
Caleb were among the spies who had been sent out to explore
the Promised Land. Why, then, is this fact stated again here?

We read that Moses and Aaron fell upon their faces. They
could have done so only for the purpose of praying, for, as the
Sages put it; *"A person should not prostrate himself unless
he is sure that his prayer will be answered as that of Joshua had
been"* (Taanith 14).

If, at this critical point, they prayed, it must have been
an attempt on their part to prevail on God to set aside the
evil decree He had ordained for His people. But we are told
that while Moses and Aaron were praying, Joshua and Caleb
rent their garments — a sign of mourning. Joshua and Caleb
were grief-stricken because they already knew that the decree
had become final and that prayer would be of no avail.

This is difficult to understand. How was it possible that
Moses and Aaron, who surely were greater than Joshua and
Caleb, should have had no knowledge of what Joshua and Caleb
already knew? It is in order to answer this question that the
Scriptural text reiterates that Joshua and Caleb were "among
those that spied out the land." By virtue of the fact that they

309

had actually trod upon the soil of the Promised Land they had grown so greatly in wisdom and holiness that they really knew more than Moses and Aaron, who had never set foot on the Land.

—*Imrei Shofar*

*　*　*　*

"Their defense is removed from over (the people of the land)". (Numbers 14:9)

Their defense is removed — Their worthy shield and defense had died. Their defender had been Job.

—*Sotah* 38

We gather from this statement by our Sages that Job was a righteous man. There is a similar statement to this effect in Baba Bathra: "What is said of Job is greater than what is said of Abraham" (B.B. 15). But in the very next section (B.B.16) we read "Rabba said: Job sought to turn the dish upside down," which would mean that Job always wanted to deny the existence of G-d. Would this not imply that Job was not a worthy man after all?

The answer given by the Gaon of Vilna to this question is based on the assumption that the metaphor "to turn the dish upside down" as used in connection with Job alludes to a story which was popular in those days and which was written down in a book entitled "The King's Son and the Nazirite" (Chapter 14).

Once there was a wicked, cruel king to whom forgiveness and pardon were unknown. The least misdemeanor on the part of subjects would be liable to the death penalty, with no chance of reprieve.

It came to pass one day that the king's servant inadvertently omitted some food from the platter which he served his master. The king was furious. Knowing from past experience what his fate would now inevitably be, the servant took the dish and deliberately turned it upside down so that all the food that was on it was spilled upon the royal table. Of course the king immediately commanded that he be beheaded. Just as the sentence was about to be carried out, the king asked his servant: "Why did you do this thing? Did it not occur to you that you might have fared better if you had been guilty only of an unintentional misdemeanor and not of a wilful crime?"

Replied the servant: "My lord King, I knew that whatever I would do would not change my death sentence. Now I did not want your honor impaired by having people say that the king had his servant executed for so trifling a misdemeanor as forgetting to serve him some of his food. So, in order to make my death sentence seem well deserved, I deliberately turned the dish upside down and emptied all the food onto your table."

This answer pleased the king so greatly that he pardoned the servant and freed him at once.

The metaphor "Job sought to turn the dish upside down" alludes to this story. The Sages meant to imply that when Job, who was so widely known as a man of great righteousness, was stricken by the misfortunes which Heaven had sent him, he feared that the honor of the Lord might be impaired in the eyes of men who would not understand the deeper meaning of the inscrutable ways of the Most High. Job therefore railed against Divine providence, so that the people would come to believe that he was indeed a sinner and that the evil which God had sent to him was well deserved.

The Sages give a similar explanation (*Sanhedrin 107*) in connection with King David, pointing out that David wanted to sin purposely so that the Lord and the sentence He had passed against him should appear righteous in the eyes of the people. They deduce this from David's own statement: *"Against Thee, and Thee only, have I sinned, and done that which is evil in Thy sight, that Thou mayest be justified when Thou speakest, and be in the right when Thou judgest"* (Psalm 51:6).

* * * *

"The Lord is slow to anger and abundant in loving-kindness" (Numbers 14:18)

Why does the text here not read "abundant in loving-kindness *and truth,"* as in Exodus 34:6?

The word "truth" had its proper place in the thirty-fourth Chapter of the Book of Exodus, in which Moses recalls the promise which the Lord gave to our fathers, to give the land to their descendants: *"Remember Abraham, Isaac and Israel, Thy servants, to whom Thou didst swear by Thy own self . . . and all this land of which I have spoken will I give to your seed"* (Exodus 32:13). There Moses recalled God's attribute of truth, so that God might fulfill His promise. But in the episode described in this part of the Book of Numbers, the Jews were not willing to accept the Promised Land. Now if someone is offered a gift by another and says: "I do not want it," he does not deserve that gift. Accordingly, the Lord was now freed from His promise and a mention of His attribute of truth would have been out of place.

—*Meshekh Hakhmah*

* * * *

"Visiting the iniquity of the fathers upon the children" (Num. 14:18)

The Hebrew word *poke'd,* used here for "visiting," may also be translated in the sense of "lessening" (as in *v'ilo nefkad mimenu ish*) (Numbers 31-49). The verse then could be construed to read: "Lessening the inquiry of the fathers for the sake of the children"; i.e., if the fathers have good children, their iniquity will be forgiven them for the sake of the merits of their children.

—*HaKetav VeHakabala*

* * * *

Why should children be blamed for the sins of their parents so that they, the children, should be made to suffer for the wrong done by their fathers and mothers? Even if the children, following in the footsteps of their parents, should also sin, would it not be proper that they need suffer only for their own sin but not for the iniquities of their parents?

In a book entitled "Parables of Wolves," there is a tale as follows:

A wolf was very hungry and wanted to devour a fox. Said the fox to the wolf: "Why eat my scrawny flesh, when you could have that large, fat human over there? Why not eat the human and really have a good meal?"

Said the wolf: "It's forbidden to eat humans, you know. Wouldn't I be punished?"

"Do not worry," replied the fox. "You will not be punished. The punishment will come only to your young."

The wolf, persuading himself that the fox was right, trotted toward the man, but a trap had been set and he fell into a deep pit. Hearing the wolf's howls, the fox rushed to the pit.

"Liar," the wolf growled. "Did you not say that only my young would be punished?"

"Fool," replied the fox. "You didn't fall into the trap because of your deed. This is the punishment for the deed of your father. He once ate a human."

"Do you mean to say," the wolf shouted, "that I have to suffer for the wrong my father did?"

"You insisted on getting ready to eat that human even though you knew that your young would suffer on your account," the fox answered. "Therefore you must now suffer on account of your father."

The above parable makes it easier to understand why children should be punished for the sins of their parents. When people sin although they are aware that their children will have to suffer as a result, it is only right that they themselves should be made to suffer for the sins of their parents. If they follow in the evil footsteps of their parents the Lord will visit the iniquity of the fathers upon the children, measure for measure.

—*Pardes Yosef*

* * * *

"And when you shall err and not observe all these commandments. . . ." (Numbers 15:22)

> Why is the section dealing with the commandment of taking *hallah* linked with that on idol worship? This is to teach you that anyone who observes the commandment of *hallah* is as if he had repudiated idol worship.

—*Midrash*

The observance of the commandment to take *hallah* because one believes that all which man has is derived from the Lord, and that therefore the first portion of whatever man possesses must be given to the Lord as an offering of gratitude, constitutes the most effective repudiation of paganism. It gives the lie to the erroneous notion that "my own strength and the skill of my own hands have done all this for me," which is the most heathen idea of all. As the Psalm has it: *"Their idols are silver and gold, the work of man's hands"* (Ps. 115:3). Their idolatry is that they regard the silver and gold they possess as having been obtained by their own might, by "the work of man's hands." These are the "idols" which are destroyed by the observance of the commandment to take *hallah* from every mass of dough that is prepared.

—*Avnei Ezel*

* * * *

"They found a man gathering sticks on the Sabbath Day." (Numbers 15:32)

> The expression "found" is used here to imply that Moses appointed watchmen and that the watchmen found the

man who was gathering up the sticks on the Sabbath."

—*Yalkut*

This implies that Moses organized a Society for Sabbath Observance, as it were, a group of men who went about seeking to prevent violations of the Sabbath.

The foregoing proves that it is the duty of the Jewish community to organize Societies for Sabbath Observance in every city to investigate whether — Heaven forbid — the Sabbath is being violated, and to prevent such violations from occurring.

—*Anon.*

*   *   *   *

Haphtarah Shelach Lecha (Joshua 2:1-24)

"And Joshua the son of Nun sent out of Shittim two spies secretly, saying: 'Go view the land, and Jericho'" (Joshua 2:1)
    They disguised themselves as potters and they called out aloud, "Here are pots, here are pots."

—*Midrash*

According to the Law, an earthenware vessel can become impure on the inside through its contents, but not on the outside.

Any other material, by virtue of its intrinsic value, can contract impurity in any one of its parts. Earthenware, however, has no worth of its own and has value only to the extent that it serves as a container for some other substance. For this reason the only valuable thing about an earthenware vessel is its contents.

Now the spies whom Joshua sent out to view the land remembered the fate of the spies whom Moses had dispatched and who, instead of deferring to the one who had sent them, went after their own minds and their own will.

Therefore Joshua's men made themselves be like earthenware pots which have no intrinsic value and have significance only according to the contents which others put into them. They

315

set aside all their own personalities, subordinating themselves entirely to the mind and the will of him who sent them on their mission. They did only what Joshua told them to do and for this reason their mission was crowned with success.

—*Rabbi Isaac Meir Alter of Gur*

* * * *

Weekly Portion of Korah (Numbers 16:1-18:32)

"And Korah . . . took . . ." (Numbers 16:1)

Korah failed because he wanted to seize greatness and strength for himself with his own hands. Greatness is good only if it is bestowed on a man by Heaven. You cannot go out and take it for yourself.

—*The Rabbi of Przysucha*

* * * *

> Which controversy was in the name of Heaven? The controversy between Hillel and Shammai. And which one was not in the name of Heaven? The controversy of Korah and all his company.
>
> —*Ethics of the Fathers*, 5:20

Why does the verse not read "the controversy between Korah and Moses," parallelling "the controversy between Hillel and Shammai"?

Because Moses was guided solely by honorable motivations. Only the intentions of Korah and his company definitely were not "in the name of Heaven."

—*Midrash Shmuel*

* * * *

How do we know that the controversy of Korah was not in the name of Heaven?

Because Korah's controversy was directed against his teacher (Moses) and it is written that "he who initiates a controversy against his teacher is regarded as if he had initiated a controversy against the Holy Presence Itself." Obviously, then,

Korah's controversy could not have been "in the name of Heaven."

—Attributed to a Sage

*　*　*　*

"Wherefore, then, do you lift yourselves up above the assembly of the Lord?" (Numbers 16:3)

It is interesting to note that those who engage in a controversy with righteous men will attribute to these men traits which are the very opposite of their true character.

It was thus also in the case of Moses, of whom the Torah states that he was "very meek, above all the men that were on the face of the earth." His detractors, seeking to find fault with him, settled on arrogance, of all things, as the failing for which to attack their leader.

—The Rabbi of Kotzk (Menahem Mendel Morgenstern)

*　*　*　*

Rabbi Naphtali of Rapshitz interpreted the sixteenth verse of Psalm 106 as follows:

"They were jealous also of Moses in the camp, and of Aaron, the holy one of the Lord." This is the way of all those who initiate controversies and incite rebellion. Whatever the righteous man may do, they will find fault with him. If he withdraws from the world and devotes all his time to study and good works, they claim that the world derives no benefit from him. If he does take an active part in communal life and speaks his mind on issues affecting the community, they attack him for meddling in politics instead of sticking to his *Gemarah.*

"They were jealous also of Moses in the camp" — Moses spent all his time studying within his tent, which had been pitched outside the camp. As a result, Korah and his company criticized him for not being within the camp and taking an interest in issues of public concern.

"And of Aaron, the holy one of the Lord" — As opposed
to Moses, Aaron mingled with the others, made peace among
his fellow-men and took an active interest in everyone around
him. But Korah and his company protested that Aaron, who
was "sanctified to the Lord," had no business meddling in communal affairs but should remain secluded in the house of study.

It has been thus throughout our history. When pious Jews
refrain from active participation in communal affairs, they are
criticized for keeping aloof from the rest of the community.
But as soon as they begin to assume an active role in the community, the others shout: "What business do you have in
politics? Go back to your *shtibel.*"

Such is the way of Dathan and Abiram and their ilk.

*   *   *   *

"And when Moses heard it, he fell upon his face." (Numbers 16:4)

On none of the other occasions when the Children of Israel
rebelled had Moses ever fallen on his face. Why did he do so
at this time?

Hearing the statement of Korah and his company that the
entire congregation of Israel was holy and that every single
Israelite was therefore holy in his own right, Moses immediately
fell upon his face in awe, for no one knew better than he how
difficult it is to achieve holiness.   *—Musarist Writings*

*   *   *   *

(And Moses said to Korah and his company) *"You take too much
upon yourselves, O sons of Levi."* (Numbers 16:7)

> But Korah, who certainly had open eyes — what reason
> did he have to commit this folly? His mind's eye misled
> him. He saw by prophetic vision a long line of great men
> descending from him, among them several prophets —
> including Samuel — who were equal in importance to
> Moses and Aaron together . . . and he said to himself:
> "On his (Samuel's) account I shall escape punishment."
> But he had not seen correctly, for his sons repented of
> their rebellious attitude . . . but Moses foresaw this.
>
> *—Rashi*

According to the Sages (*Sanhedrin 118*), the reference in the Scriptural text to *sar hamishim* "the leader of fifty" implies that no one below the age of fifty should be given a position of leadership in the community. This requirement alone would have made Korah ineligible for a position of leadership among the Children of Israel in the wilderness, because he was not yet fifty years old at the time. We know this, because, according to Rashi, Korah was one of the bearers of the Ark of the Covenant and the Levites who performed this function were all below the age of fifty, for after the age of fifty they were no longer considered capable of bearing that burden.

Another interpretation construes the term *sar hamishim* to imply familiarity with the *Hamisha Humshei Torah,* the Five Books of the Torah, and deduces from this that only a man who is well-versed in all the Five Books of Moses is fit to become a leader in the community (*Sanhedrin ibid.*).

Korah saw by prophetic vision that one of his descendants would be Samuel of Ramathaim who would only reach the age of fifty-two, but would be Judge over the people of Israel for eleven years. He regarded this as proof that it was possible to hold a position of leadership in Israel even if one was below the age of fifty, as long as one was familiar with the Five Books of Moses.

It was for this reason that Korah aspired to become a leader of his people though he was not yet fifty years old.

—*P'ninim Yekarim*

*   *   *   *

How is it that the sons of Korah repented of their rebellious attitude?

Because Moses said to Korah and his company: *"Hear now, O sons of Levi . . ."* (Num. 16:8) and remonstrated with them, seeking to make them repent.

Now we know that the words spoken by a righteous man remain forever. Even if they should have no effect on the person to whom they were originally addressed, they will leave their mark on the descendants of those to whom they were spoken. Thus, too, while the words which Moses addressed to Korah had no influence on Korah himself, they had a profound effect on his children, so that they repented of their rebellious attitude.

But since Korah did not believe in the power of Moses and in the Divine force inherent in his words, he could not possibly have foreseen that his children would repent.

—Attributed to a Sage

* * * *

A similar view was taken by Rabbi Zaddok Ha-Cohen of Lublin, in his interpretation of the statement in Tractate Berakhot: *"The words of any person who fears the Lord will be heard, for it is written: 'In the final analysis everything will be heard, G-d shalt thou fear' "* (Berakhot 6).

At first glance, this statement seems difficult to accept, because we often see that men of great righteousness reprove a person and the person still does not mend his ways.

What Rabbi Zaddok Ha-Cohen of Lublin means is that, in the end, the words of the righteous man will be heard. Even if they make no impression when they are first uttered, they are sure to take effect eventually. Either the person to whom they were originally addressed will remember them and repent, or he may tell them to another person who will then repent of his own sins. At any rate, the words of a righteous man will leave their mark, somehow, somewhere.

For this reason the Sages deduce from the words "In the final analysis, everything will be heard" that "in the end, the word of a God-fearing man will be heard."

—Rabbi Mordechai Joseph Silberberg of Warsaw

* * * *

(And Moses said) *"By this you shall know that the Lord has sent me to do all these works, and that I have not done them of my own mind."* (Numbers 16:28)

"My own mind" — of my own free will.

—*Onkelos*

Why does Onkelos translate "of my own mind" as "of my own free will"?

The Sages relate that when Moses performed all the functions of the Divine service during the seven days of the inauguration of the first priests, he thought that he would remain High Priest permanently, and continued to be under that impression until the Lord, blessed be His Name, informed him that the office would go to his brother Aaron.

Thus Moses now meant to tell Korah and his company: "Certainly, I did not make my brother Aaron High Priest out of my own free will. I wanted to have that office for myself. Why, then, should you believe that I had raised my brother to the priesthood of my own accord? Had the choice been mine, I would have taken the priesthood for myself. If I conferred that office on Aaron it was only because I was commanded to do so by none other than the Lord Himself."

—*Mishna de-Rabbi Abba*

* * * *

Weekly Portion of Hukkath (Numbers 19:1-22:1)
"Speak to the Children of Israel that they bring thee a red heifer." (Numbers 19:2)

To be sure, there are reasons also for the commandment concerning the red heifer. But the true and basic reason for this Divine enactment was disclosed to no human being save Moses.

At one time King Solomon, having divined the reasons for all the commandments, believed that he had succeeded in discovering their true and deeper purpose. But when he came to the Scriptural portion dealing with the red heifer, he realized that while he knew of many superficial reasons for this law, he was still unable to fathom its basic purpose, which had not been revealed to any man. And then he said to himself:

"If this is so, could it not be that the other commandments, whose reasons I thought I had discovered, may have other more profound and mysterious purposes which have eluded my grasp?"

Therefore he said:

"*I said I had acquired wisdom* — I thought I had become wise enough to understand the reason for all the commandments of the Torah, but now, studying the Scriptural portion dealing with the red heifer, I see — *but it is far from me* — that, indeed, the entire Torah is still very far from my understanding, and even as I do not know the reason for the commandment concerning the red heifer, so, too, I still do not know all the reasons for the other commandments."

—*Hanukkat HaTorah*

* * * *

"*A red heifer, faultless . . .*" (Numbers 19:2)

It should be perfect as regards its redness, so that even if there are only two black hairs on it, it is unfit.

—*Rashi*

The Sages relate the story of one Dama ben Nethina who incurred great financial loss as the result of having fulfilled the commandment to honor his father. The Lord rewarded him by causing a red heifer to be born in his household, for which he received a great deal of money so that his loss was more than offset (*Kiddushin 31*).

Why should this man have received his reward through a red heifer, of all things?

Rabbi Isaac Meir Alter of Ger pointed out that when a heathen sustained such great financial loss as the result of having fulfilled the commandment to honor his father, a grave accusation was raised in Heaven against the Jewish people. To refute this charge, God sought to prove that while heathens might spend much money on a commandment which is completely in keeping with the dictates of common sense, the Jews were still better because they were willing to spend immense amounts even for the performance of a commandment which is as completely contrary to ordinary reason and the purpose of which is unknown, such as the statute pertaining to the red heifer.

* * * *

"Where there is no blemish; upon which a yoke has never come." (Numbers 19:2)

A person who considers himself faultless obviously still has not accepted the yoke of the Kingdom of Heaven. For if he had accepted the yoke of the Kingdom of Heaven to any extent at all, he would know that he still has many faults.

—*Rabbi Yaakov Yizhek HaLevi Hurwitz, "The Seer of Lublin"*

* * * *

"Then the priest shall wash his clothes." (Numbers 19:7)

While the red heifer served to cleanse the unclean, it rendered unclean the clean individuals who had contact with it.

The reason for this is that the red heifer served to atone for the sin the Children of Israel committed when they worshipped the Golden Calf. The Sages point out that it certainly did not behoove the Israelites of that generation to sin. But in order that it might show to future generations a way in which they might be able to repent of their sins (*Avoda Zara 4*), that generation alone was punished and it was through that unclean generation that a means was given to the generations of the future to cleanse themselves by repentance.

So, too, is the red heifer, which atones for the worship of the Golden Calf. It serves as a means to cleanse the unclean, but it is unclean in itself so that the priest must wash his garments after contact with it.

—*Rabbi Moses Schreiber (Hatham Sofer)*

* * * *

"But the man who shall be unclean and shall not cleanse himself, that soul shall be cut off from the midst of the assembly." (Numbers 19:20)

Actually, only that unclean individual who enters the Sanctuary or who eats consecrated food in his unclean state is subject to the punishment of *kareth* (lit. "being cut off"). Why is this not specified in the present verse?

Because this specification was not deemed necessary. The Sages relate that the burning of the first red heifer in accordance with the Law took place on the first day of the month of Nisan to enable the Israelites to cleanse themselves before bringing the Passover sacrifice. Since it was forbidden to enter the Sanctuary when one was in an unclean state, any unclean Israelite who failed to avail himself of this opportunity to be cleansed would not be permitted to participate in the Passover sacrifice. If he were to participate in the sacrificial rites, he would be liable to *kareth* for entering the Sanctuary in his unclean state. On the other hand, if he were not to make the offering because he was unclean, he would likewise be subject to *kareth* because of his wilful neglect to observe the commandment of the Passover offering. Thus, since he would be liable to *kareth* in either case, the Scripture omits further specifications here.

—*Melo HaOmer*

*   *   *   *

(The Lord said to Moses and Aaron): *"Because you did not believe in Me, to sanctify Me in the eyes of the Children of Israel."* (Numbers 20:12)

There are two views concerning the character of the sin which Moses committed at the waters of Meribah.

Maimonides holds that Moses sinned in that he became angry and insulted the Children of Israel, saying to them: *"Hear now, you rebels"* (Verse 10). Nachmanides, on the other hand, claims that his sin lay in the fact that he struck the rock instead of speaking to it as he had been commanded to do.

Actually, both views are valid, *for the end result was the same.* There are two kinds of righteous individuals. The one rebukes others with harsh words until, stricken by remorse, they repent of their sins. The other achieves the same end by positive means; by his kind words, he makes the people feel so greatly uplifted that they become ashamed to sin.

The difference between the results of these two opposite approaches may be summed up as follows: He who succeeds in persuading the Jews with kind words to repent will find that nature, too, will do his bidding gladly for the benefit of the Jewish people, for was not all of Creation made only for the sake of the people of Israel? But that righteous man who forces the Jews with harsh words to repent will find that he must also use force to have nature do his bidding for the Jews, for it will not do so of its own accord.

Because Moses became angry and spoke harshly to the Jews: "Hear now, you rebels," the rock refused to do his bidding, and Moses was forced to strike it to make it obey.

—*Kedushat Levi*

*   *   *   *

"And the Lord spoke to Moses and Aaron . . . by the border of the land of Edom, saying: 'Aaron shall be gathered unto his people.'" (Numbers 20:23, 24)

> This tells us that because at this point they wanted to unite in close friendship with wicked Edom, a breach was made in their work and they had to lose (Aaron) this righteous man.   —*Rashi*

The Bible explicitly states in Verse 24 the reason why Aaron had to die; i.e., *"because you rebelled against My word at the waters of Meribah."* Why, then, should Rashi give another reason; i.e., *"because at this point they wanted to unite in close friendship with wicked Edom"*?

325

Rabbi Bunim of Przysucha used to say:

"It is written that 'the judgments of the Lord are righteous altogether.' When a king of flesh and blood punishes a subject, he is doing justice with regard to the criminal, but he is doing an injustice to the friends and relatives of the condemned, for he is causing them to suffer through no fault of their own. But when the Lord, blessed be His Name, punishes a sinner, even the sorrow felt by the family of the condemned is only just punishment for some misdeed of which the family has been guilty.

"The same holds true also in the punishment God meted out to Aaron. The Torah gives only the reason for Aaron's death; i.e., *"because you rebelled against My Word . . ."* Rashi, however, means to tell us the reason not for Aaron's death as such, but for the sorrow that came to the Children of Irael as a result of this great loss. Why, he asks, did the Jewish people have to be punished by losing this righteous man whom they loved so dearly? *'Because at this point they wanted to unite in close friendship with wicked Edom.' "*

—Attributed to the author of "Sefat Emet"

* * * *

"And they wept for Aaron thirty days, even all the house of Israel . . ." (Numbers 20:29)

This verse proves that during all those years that the "House of Israel" had spent in the wilderness there had not been even so much as one case of manslaughter among the Jewish people.

How do we know this? Because we are explicitly told that "all the House of Israel" mourned for Aaron. Had there been a manslayer among the people of Israel, the mourning for the High Priest would not have been universal. For according to law, anyone guilty of manslaughter had to leave his tent and the Levite camp and to dwell outside the Camp of the

Children of Israel. He would have been permitted to return to his family only after the death of the High Priest, so that a manslayer and his family would have had more cause for rejoicing than for mourning when the High Priest died.

Therefore, by stressing that "all the House of Israel" mourned the loss of Aaron, that every Jewish family wept for the departed High Priest, the Torah means to call to our attention that in all "the House of Israel" there was not one family to whom the death of Aaron brought joy in the form of the return of a dear one, for there was not even one manslayer among the Children of Israel at the time.

—*Meshekh Hakhmah*

* * * *

"The well which the princes dug, which the nobles of the people delved with the scepter and with their staves, and from the wilderness to Mattanah, and from Mattanah to Nahaliel . . ." (Numbers 21:18, 19)

The well: This is the Torah, which is likened to a well of living waters. *Which the princes dug*: Into which our princes, the scholars, have searched. *Which the nobles of the people delved* (the Hebrew word *karuah*, used here for "delved" can also be translated as "acquired"): The nobles of the people, who are not great scholars themselves, have an opportunity to acquire the Torah with their money by supporting scholars, as the Torah puts it: *"It is a tree of life to those who cleave to it."* In other words, both the scholars and the noble, generous supporters of scholarship can have a share in the Torah; the scholars through the lawgiver (the Hebrew word *mehokek*, used in the verse for "scepter", can also be translated as "lawgiver"); i.e., by studying themselves, and the "nobles" by acting as "staves" to support the students of the Torah.

In keeping with the above, the Gemarah relates the passage "from the wilderness to Mattanah, and from Mattanah to

Nahaliel" to the giving of the Torah, pointing out that *mattanah* is also the Hebrew word for "gift" and that the literal meaning of *nahaliel* is "the inheritance of God."

—*The Gaon of Vilna*

* * * *

Weekly Portion of Balak (Numbers 22:2-25:9)
"And Balak the son of Zippor saw all that Israel had done to the Amorites." (Numbers 22:2)

Why should this weekly portion be named after a man who was a heathen and an enemy of the Jewish people at that?

It is true that all the heathens hate the Jews; as it is written: "It is a known rule that Esau hates Jacob," but they usually cloak their hatred in honeyed words so that the Jews will not be aware of the need to protect themselves. Balak, however, was quite outspoken in his hostility, and there certainly can be no objection to naming a weekly portion of the Torah after a heathen who is actually honest.

—*Rabbi Meir of Przemysl*

* * * *

"And (Balak) *sent messengers to Balaam the son of Beor . . ."* (Numbers 22:5)

> And if you ask: Why did the Holy One, blessed be He, cause His glory to rest upon so wicked a heathen? I reply: In order that the heathens should have no excuse to say: If we would have had prophets, we would have changed for the better. He therefore raised up prophets for them but they broke down the (moral) fence of the world.
>
> —*Rashi*

The great men among any people are not individual exceptions, but are produced as a result of the concentration of the spiritual strength of that people in one person who then becomes their leader and prophet.

The spiritual might inherent in the holy nation of Israel gave rise to a Moses, while the spirit of the nations of the world

could produce nothing better than a Balaam. The peoples of
the world had no more excuses to offer. They had a prophet
of their own, but he had to be evil, as Balaam was, because they
were not capable of producing a better man.

—Anon.

*　*　*　*

(God said to Balaam) *"Thou shalt not curse the people for they are
blessed."* (Numbers 22:12)

> (Balaam) said to (God): "If so, I will bless them." (God)
> replied to him: "They do not need thy blessing, for they
> are already blessed." A parable: People say to the hornet:
> "I want neither thy honey nor thy sting."

—Rashi

There are two ways in which the nations of the world seek
to bring about the destruction of the Jewish people. While
some want to do it by humiliating and oppressing them, there
are others who want to achieve the same end by showing them
too much friendship, thereby leading them into assimilation
and conversion.

The evil Balaam first tried to curse the Children of Israel.
When he saw that it was to no avail, because the Lord always
saves the Jews from their oppressors (*"in every generation
there are those who rise up against us to annihilate us, but the
Holy One, blessed be He, always saves us from their hands"*),
he wanted to employ the other method, to lavish blessings and
kind words on them so that they might want to cease being
Jews. For this reason, the Lord, blessed be His Name, said to
him: "Keep your favors and your blessings; as I do not want
your sting, so, too, I do not want your honey."

—Divrei Shaarei Hayyim

*　*　*　*

*"And God came to Balaam at night, and said to him, "If the men
have come to call thee, rise up, go with them." And Balaam rose
up in the morning . . . and went with the princes of Moab. And God's*

329

anger was kindled because he went . . ." (Numbers 22:20, 21, 22)

If God really gave Balaam permission to go with them, why should He have become angry with Balaam when he actually went?

When the Lord told him to go "with them," He used the Hebrew word *itam,* for "with them." Now *itam* implies going with a person on one path, but not with the same intent or to the same destination. In other words, what God really wanted Balaam to do was to go with them on their way but *not* to "go along" with their intentions. He was explicitly commanded: "Thou shalt not curse the people." But in Verse 21, where we are told that Balaam went with the princes of Moab, the term used for "with" is *im,* which, as opposed to *itam,* implies a going together toward one and the same destination with one and the same intention. In other words, we are told that Balaam's intentions corresponded to those of the Moabite princes; namely, that he and they both intended to curse the Children of Israel. It was for this reason that God was angry with him.

Subsequently, of course (in Verse 35), we find even the angel using the expression *im* in telling Balaam to go with the men. To this, Rashi comments: "God will lead a man in whatever path he wants to go."

—*Kol Eliahu*

* * * *

"And (Balaam) *saddled his donkey . . ."* (Numbers 22:21)
> Said the Holy One, blessed be He: "Thou wicked man, their ancestor Abraham has already anticipated thee in this, as it is written (Gen. 22:3): And Abraham rose early in the morning and saddled his donkey (to sacrifice Isaac)"

—*Rashi*

What is the meaning of this parallel between Balaam and Abraham?

The Lord said to Balaam: "Abraham also arose early in

330

the morning and saddled his donkey, and unlike yourself, he did it in preparation for a journey to give Me pleasure and to do My will. Yet nothing came of it. I did not allow him to sacrifice his son Isaac to Me because Isaac was to be the ancestor of the Jewish people. Now when you, O wicked Balaam, rise up early in the morning and saddle your donkey, and do it for the purpose of doing evil to the Jewish people against My will, do you not see that I will surely keep you from carrying out your plan?"

—*Attributed to Rabbi Menahem Mendel Morgenstern,*
the Rabbi of Kotzk

*   *   *   *

"*And the Lord opened the mouth of the donkey.*" (Numbers 22:28)

This was to bring it home forcibly to Balaam that he had no cause to consider himself great because he had been endowed with prophetic vision. Why, even the donkey, which certainly would not be considered fit to look upon an angel, or to speak, was enabled to do both because it was for the good of the Children of Israel. Balaam was no more fit to be a prophet than the donkey, and was given the gift of prophecy only in order that the Children of Israel might benefit thereby.

—*K'lei Yakar*

*   *   *   *

(And Balaam said to the donkey): "*Because thou hast mocked me . . .*" (Numbers 22:29)

The Lord wanted Balaam to go out to bless the Children of Israel instead of cursing them, for He knew that if the nations of the world were to hear Balaam, their own prophet, praise the greatness and the virtues of the Jewish people, they would be overcome with fear and would keep away from the Jews. However, the nations of the world knew that Balaam loved money, and hence they might have believed that he was only blessing and praising the Jews because they, the Jews, had

331

bribed him to do so. It was in order to show to the nations that this was indeed a Divine plan and that Balaam spoke as he did not because he was bribed to do so, but because he had been commanded by Heaven to say it, that the Lord performed a miracle and "opened the mouth of the donkey."

—*Meshekh Hakhmah*

* * * *

(And Balaam said): *"Behold a people that rises up as a lioness, and as a lion does he lift himself up . . ."* (Numbers 23:24)

The lion is stronger than the lioness. When a Jew first rises in order to serve the Most High he is only like a lioness, but then the Lord will help him ("the Lord will help him who comes to be cleansed") and he will rise up strong as a lion.

—*Attributed to the Maggid Dov Ber of Mezhirich*

* * * *

". . . and the saying of the man whose eye is opened . . ." (Numbers 24:3)

The Sages explain that Balaam was blind in one eye.

They point out that every human being needs two eyes; one to perceive the greatness of the Creator, and the other to behold his own humbleness and insignificance.

Balaam knew of the greatness of God (*"and he knows the knowledge of the Most High"* — Num. 24:16), but he could not see his own insignificance and therefore was arrogant.

It was therefore clear to the Sages that Balaam must have been blind in one eye.   —*Rishfei Esh*

* * * *

"And when Phinehas, the son of Eleazar . . . saw it . . ." (Numbers 25:7)

> He saw what was happening and was thereby reminded of the law on this subject (i.e., illicit relations with heathen women): "Zealous people may attack him." (*Sanhedrin 82a*)

—*Rashi*

Beholding the reprehensible conduct of the sinners, one is reminded of the law pertaining to righteous zeal. If their conduct is so brazen, how could one possibly remain silent and not take action in behalf of the honor of God?

—Attributed to a Sage

*   *   *   *

Haphtarah Balak (Micah 5:6-6:8)
"And I will cut off thy graven images and thy pillars out of the midst of thee." (Micah 5:12)

There is such a thing as idolatry deep within the spirit of a man. The Sages say that "a person who is angry is as if he were worshipping idols," and it is written in the Holy Books that a person who performs a commandment for the sake of financial gain is as if he were worshipping money as an idol (*"Their idols are silver and gold . . ."*).

The prophet promises that the time will come when the Lord will destroy *"thy* graven images and *thy* pillars", i.e., the unseen idols which are *"in the midst of thee,"* which are concealed deep within the spirit of men.

—Ahavat Yonathan

*   *   *   *

". . . and to walk humbly with thy God." (Micah 6:8)
>This refers to the dowering of brides and to the escorting of the dead.

—Makkot 24

In order to know a man's true inner character, one must see how he behaves at those times of great joy or great grief when he is thrown off balance and unable to disguise his real nature. Baseness and vulgarity readily come to light at the time of great rejoicing, when drink loosens tongues. Spiritual stamina and inner strength are best revealed at the hour of grief when the faith and integrity of lesser men may crumble.

Whether a man truly "walks humbly with his God" can be judged only when he "dowers the bride" or when he "escorts the dead" — at moments of great joy or at the time of deep sorrow.

By remaining pure and honest in joy, and strong and steadfast in sorrow, he proves that he "walks humbly with his God" at all times.

—*Kokhav MiYaakov*

* * * *

Weekly Portion of Phinehas (Numbers 25:10-30:1)
"Phinehas, the son of Eleazar, the son of Aaron the priest . . ." (Numbers 25:11)

> Because the tribes spoke disparagingly of him, saying: "Have you seen this grandson of Puti, the father of whose mother used to fatten calves for idolatrous sacrifices, and he has dared to slay a prince in Israel's tribes?" Therefore Scripture comes and links his genealogy with Aaron.

—*Rashi*

The tribes of Israel suspected that Phinehas had slain Zimri because he, Phinehas, descendant of idol-worshippers that he was on his mother's side, was cruel by nature and did not find it distasteful to shed blood. Therefore Scripture traces his genealogy to Aaron the priest, who loved peace and pursued it, to show that Phinehas was a quiet and peace-loving man by nature and had slain Zimri solely out of zeal on behalf of the Lord.

—*Sefarim*

* * * *

"In that he was very zealous for My sake in the midst of them." (Numbers 25:11)

By killing Zimri out of his own zeal for the sake of the Lord, Phinehas brought "into the midst" of the Jewish people the ideals of righteous zeal which would make them utterly unable to tolerate idol worship.

Attributed to Rabbi Menahem Mendel Morgenstern,
(the Rabbi of Kotzk) and Sefath Emeth

* * * *

Even though Phinehas was so zealous in the cause of the Lord, he remained "in the midst of them"; he remained "in the midst" of the people of Israel, refusing to set himself apart from them in any manner.

—Rabbi Isaac of Warka

*   *   *   *

"Wherefore say: 'Behold I give to him My covenant of peace ...'" (Numbers 25:12)

Even though zeal is the opposite of peace and may indeed be equated with open controversy, the Torah states that honest zeal on behalf of a sacred ideal leads to peace.

—Kosnot Or

*   *   *   *

"... because (Phinehas)*was zealous on behalf of his God ..."* (Numbers 25:13)

Sinners are in the habit of justifying their conduct by pointing to others and saying: "This one did likewise."

It is for this reason that the Lord, blessed be His Name, addressed the Ten Commandments to the Children of Israel in the second person singular. Every Jew was to feel that the Torah had been given to him alone and that it was none of his concern how the others behaved.

Surely, when he beheld the immoral conduct of the Israelite and the Midianite woman, Phinehas could have pointed to Moses, Aaron and the seventy elders and said: "If they take no action, why should I be more zealous than they?" However, he did not wait to see what they would do, but proceeded to do on his own what he felt had to be done on behalf of the honor of the Lord. Therefore it is written "Because he was zealous for *his* God." He acted as if God had been his alone, believing that it was his duty to defend the honor of God even if no one else would do it."

—Homat Esh

*   *   *   *

335

"And Moses brought their case before the Lord." (Numbers 27:5)

When the daughters of Zelophehad brought their case before Moses, they told him that their late father had not been "among the company of those who gathered themselves together against the Lord in the company of Korah" (27:3), thus informing him that their father had not been among his adversaries. Moses therefore conceived a personal interest in their welfare and so felt disqualified to decide the case. This is the reason why Moses brought the case of the daughters of Zelophehad before the Lord.

—Sefarim

* * * *

(The Lord told Moses) *"Thou shalt surely give them a possession of an inheritance among their father's brethren . . ."* (Num. 27:7)

In referring to the daughters of Zelophehad in this verse, the Scriptural text uses *lahem*, the masculine, rather than *lahen*, the feminine form of "them."

Why so? Because, according to the Tosefta (*Baba Bathra 115*), when a woman assumes an inheritance she is like a man for all legal purposes. Therefore, since the Lord commanded that the daughters of Zelophehad were to be given an inheritance as if they had been men, this verse refers to them in the masculine rather than in the feminine gender.

—Tifereth HaGershuni and *Hanukkat HaTorah*

* * * *

(And Moses said to the Lord) *"Let the Lord . . . set a man over the congregation who may go out before them and who may come in before them, and who may lead them out, and who may bring them in . . ."* (Numbers 27:16, 17)

A true leader must "go out before" his people and not trail behind them. He must raise them to his level and not allow himself to descend to theirs. He must "go out before them" and "come in before them," always at the head of his people. He must have them follow him, and not keep looking back to see what they want and then follow their wishes.

A leader who truly leads his people will raise them to his own level. He has a chance to "lead them out" from corruption and "to bring them in" to holiness (as Rabbi Isaac Meir Alter of Ger explains it). A leader who trails behind his people will finally be dragged down by them to their own low level.

—*Avnei Ezel*

*   *   *   *

A similar thought was expressed by Rabbi Israel Salanter to explain the statement in Tractate Sotah that the face of the generation of the era immediately preceding the coming of the Messiah "will be as the face of a dog." A strange analogy, indeed.

Said Rabbi Salanter: "The dog is in the habit of racing ahead of his master, but he keeps looking back to see what direction his master is about to take and then continues to trot ahead in the direction indicated by his master."

In the era immediately preceding the coming of the Messiah the "faces of the generation," i.e., those who will be regarded as the leaders and the spokesmen of that generation, will be like those of dogs. They will always be in the lead of their people, always racing ahead of them. But the path they will follow will not be of their own choosing and they will not seek to persuade the people to follow them. Instead, they will keep turning back to see what the "man in the street" thinks, what the press has to say and will parrot the views of the mob and the press in order to gain the favor of the people. Instead of being the leaders, they will be led by the masses, whom they will regard as their masters. They will therefore be no better than dogs.

In short, the trouble with that generation will be that they will have no true leaders, for a true leader in Israel is one who

337

goes before the people and teaches them the ways of the Lord, even if this should make him unpopular and the target of criticism from the man in the street.

*   *   *   *

"Take . . . Joshua the son of Nun, a man in whom there is spirit . . ." (Numbers 27:18)

Moses appealed to the Lord, *"the God of the spirits of all flesh"* (Verse 15) to appoint a leader who would have knowledge of the spirit of each individual among the people and who would be able to treat each person with forbearance in keeping with what he knows (Rashi ibid.).

Said the Lord to Moses: "Take for thyself Joshua the son of Nun, *a man in whom there is spirit"* because only he who knows his own spirit can have knowledge also of the spirit of others.

—Rabbi Y. Hurwitz

*   *   *   *

"And thou shalt put some of thy honor upon him . . ." (Num. 27:20)
> (The text reads) *Some of thy honor,* not *all of thy honor.* The elders of that generation said: "The countenance of Moses is as the face of the sun, and the countenance of Joshua is as the face of the moon. Oh, the disgrace of it! Oh, the shame of it!"

—Baba Bathra 75

What is the shame which the elders so deplore?

According to the Midrash, the reason why Joshua was deemed worthy of becoming the leader of the Children of Israel after Moses was that, while Moses was alive, Joshua always acted as his servant (*"and Joshua the son of Nun, the servant of Moses . . ."*) arranging the seats in the house of study and sweeping the floor there, so that it could be said of him: "He who cares for the fig tree will eat of its fruit."

The elders had been ashamed to perform these menial tasks. But now, when they saw that Joshua had become the

leader of the people precisely because he had not been unwilling to do this work, and that his "countenance shone as the
moon," they all cried out: "Alas for that foolish pride of ours
which kept us from cleaning the house of study, for now we
must endure the shame and the disgrace of having to be the
disciples of this young Joshua in our old age."

*—Rabbi Hayyim Joseph Azulai, Commentary
on the Ethics of the Fathers*

*   *   *   *

Weekly Portion of Mattoth (Numbers 30:2-32:42)
*"And Moses spoke to the heads of the tribes of the Children of Is-
rael, saying: "This is the thing which the Lord has commanded.' "*
(Numbers 30:2)

> All the (other) prophets prophesied with: "Thus says
> the Lord." Moses, however, had an additional superiority
> in that he also prophesied with the expression: "This is
> the actual word that God has spoken."   *—Rashi*

There are righteous men of whom we may believe that
their words are uttered in accordance with the will of the Lord,
that the Lord had spoken "thus"; i.e., as they had said it.

But there are others where there is no need to "believe."
Once one hears their words, one can instinctively feel that this
is the "actual word that God has spoken," that the words they
utter are truly Divine.

This is the difference between the utterances of the other
prophets and those of Moses. In the case of the other prophets
in our history, there was cause to "believe" that their words
could be justly prefaced with "Thus says the Lord"; that they
had spoken in accordance with the will of God. But in the case
of Moses, the Divine Presence actually "spoke from out of his
throat." All who heard that voice knew that this could be the
word of none other than the Lord Himself.

—Noam Elimelekh

*   *   *   *

(When a man makes a vow to the Lord) *"he shall not break his word, he shall do according to all that proceeds from his mouth."* (Numbers 30:3)

Of him who is careful in his utterances so that no word of his should lose its binding force or should have been spoken in vain, it is said: "According to all that proceeds from his mouth, he shall do," with the pronoun "he" construed as referring not to that righteous man but to none other than God Himself. This is to teach us that the Lord will cause all that proceeds from the mouth of the righteous man to come true. The blessings he utters will be fulfilled; indeed, all his words will be considered as enactments to be enforced by the Lord, as it is written: "And He will pronounce the enactment and will fulfill it for thee — this means that the righteous man will pronounce the enactment and the Holy One, blessed be He, will fulfill it."

—Avodat Yisrael

*　　*　　*　　*

(After the Lord had told Moses to avenge the Children of Israel of the Midianites, and informed him that after that war, he, Moses, would die), *"Moses spoke to the people, saying: 'Arm men ...'"* (Numbers 31:3)

> Although he (Moses) had heard that his death was associated with the matter, he did it gladly and did not delay.
>
> *—Rashi*

The Lord said to Moses: "Avenge *the Children of Israel* of the Midianites" (Verse 2). Why, then, did Moses, relaying the message to the Children of Israel, say: ". . . to execute the vengeance *of the Lord* on Midian"?

It was quite true that the Midianites had sinned against the Lord, for they had caused His people, the Children of Israel, to fall into immorality. But they had sinned against the Children of Israel, too, because they had caused the death of twenty-four thousand Jews from the plague (*Num. 25:9*).

340

Therefore the Lord said to Moses: "I will forgive them the affront to My own honor, but what they did to the people of Israel I cannot forgive. Therefore avenge the Children of Israel of the Midianites."

But when Moses heard the rest of God's command, the news that "afterwards thou shalt be gathered to thy people" (*Verse 2*) so that he knew that the time of his death would coincide with the end of the battle against the Midianites, he feared that the Children of Israel would protest that there was no need to avenge their honor, because they would naturally want to prolong the life of their leader.

It was for this reason that Moses told the people that they would have to go to battle "to execute the vengeance of the Lord," thus stressing that what was at stake was not their personal honor but the honor of the Lord Himself, and that it was not in their power to forgive an affront to the honor of God.

Thus it is written:*"So there were delivered . . . twelve thousand armed for war"* (Verse 5), and Rashi comments: *"So there were delivered*: this means that they were drafted against their own will, and that they heeded the call only because Moses had told them that they had to execute the vengeance of the Lord."

All the foregoing shows, too, that Moses "did it gladly," for he could easily have delayed the execution of the vengeance by relaying to the Children of Israel the exact words which the Lord had said to him; namely: "Avenge the Children of Israel;" and the result would have been that the Jewish people would have been content to ignore the affront to their honor and to take no action, so that Moses might not die.

Moses wanted to make sure that the will of the Lord would be done and went about making plans to this end, even though he was aware that "his death was associated with the matter."

—*K'lei Yakar*

* * * *

"Arm men from among you for the war . . . to execute the vengeance of the Lord on Midian." (Numbers 31:3)

The Hebrew term *hehaltzu,* used here for "arm" may also be used in the sense of "to remove"; as in removing a garment (*ve-haltzah . . .* — "and she shall *loose* his shoe from off his foot" — Deut. 25:9).

Moses used this expression to imply that in going forth to battle, these men should remove from themselves all thoughts of personal honor or glory and think only of the honor of the Lord, of "executing the vengeance of the Lord" on Midian.

—*Sefat Emet*

* * * *

Any battle waged in the cause of Judaism must be entirely "in the name of heaven," devoid of thoughts of personal gain or honor. There is some evil inherent in any fight, but when that fight is motivated by pure and honest intentions, for the sake of the honor of heaven, there is no harm in that. However, if the motives behind the fight are not sincere, it can do no good but only harm.

For this reason the Torah commanded that only righteous men were to be chosen to fight in the battle against the Midianites.

It is written in Deut. 20:8: *"What man is there that is fearful and faint-hearted? Let him go and return to his house."* To this the Sages comment: *"This refers to him who is afraid because of the transgression he has committed. He who speaks between donning one phylactery and the other has committed a transgression and returns home under the regulations pertaining to war"* (Sotah 44).

Why should the Sages, from among all the transgressions, choose the transgression involved in having speech come between the donning of the arm phylactery and the head phylactery?

Because the head phylactery symbolizes the intentions of the mind and the arm phylactery represents the actions performed by the body. The thoughts of a man going forth to battle must be in complete harmony with his actions. Nothing may intervene to disrupt this harmony between thought and action. His intentions and motivations must be entirely pure and honest, and all his actions must be in keeping with his ideals. Now an interruption between the act of donning the arm phylactery and that of putting on the head phylactery would symbolize a lack of harmony between thought and action, and if this symbolic defect were to be carried over into the plans and activities of the warrior, the battle which he wages would no longer be a war fought for the sake of fulfilling a Divine commandment but only a fight carried on for selfish gain.

Therefore anyone guilty of the transgression of speaking between donning one phylactery and the other thereby disqualified himself from active front-line service.

—*Avnei Ezel*

"And Moses was angry with the officers of the host ... and ... said to them: 'Have you saved all the women alive?' " (Num. 31:14,15)

Actually, Moses had given them no explicit command to kill the women of Midian. Why, then, was he now angry with the officers for having allowed them to remain alive?

This incident proves that when it stands to reason that a thing should be done, one must do it without first waiting for an explicit command to that effect.

In a similar vein, Balaam, too, said: "I have sinned, for I did not know that Thou stoodest in the way against me" (22:34). Ignorance or failure to understand what should be readily understood constitute sins in themselves.

—*SheLaH HaKodosh*

*   *   *   *

343

"And Eleazar the priest said to the men of war who went to the battle . . . the gold, and the silver . . . ye shall cause to go through the fire, and it shall be clean . . ." (Numbers 31:21, 22, 23)

The men had already returned from the battle in triumph. Why, then, does the Scriptural text not read "to the men of war who *came from* the battle"?

It is told in Bahya ben Joseph ibn Pakuda's *"Duties of the Heart"* that a pious man said to a group of soldiers who were returning proudly and happily from a victorious battle: *"You* have won a battle, but that battle was small compared to the struggle which you must wage now, the battle against the evil inclination, which man must fight at all times and which grows stronger with the pride that comes with victory."

This warning was given also by Eleazar to the soldiers. He made them aware even as they were now returning as victors from the battle against Midian, that their true fight, namely, their battle against the evil inclination, was only beginning.

It was to symbolize this warning that Eleazar at this point commanded the Israelites to cleanse the vessels they had captured from the enemy. Even as they were bidden to remove from these vessels the uncleanness absorbed from the food of the heathens, so they were commanded to purify also their hearts from every remnant of arrogance, in order to arm themselves spiritually for the new and great struggle that lay before them.

—*Shaar Beth Rabbim,* attributed to *Yetev Lev*

* * * *

It was written that "Moses was angry with the officers of the host . . . who came from the service of the war" (*Verse 14*). Moses was angry to see that the officers had become arrogant, regarding themselves as victors returning from the wars, when, actually, they should have girded themselves for an even more important struggle, the struggle against the evil inclination.

—*Ibid.*

* * * *

"*And* (the Children of Gad and the Children of Reuben) *came near to* (Moses) *and said: 'We will build sheepfolds for our cattle here ... but we ourselves will be ready armed to go out before the Children of Israel ...'* " (Numbers 32:16, 17)

Why did the Children of Gad and the Children of Reuben allow Moses to rebuke them bitterly for cowardice before telling him the true motives behind their request for the land east of the River Jordan?

There is in the writings of the Hassidim a story from the boyhood of the Old Rabbi of Ger, the author of the treatise *Sefath Emeth*. It happened that the boy slept late one morning after having sat up all night long studying with a friend.

His grandfather, Rabbi Isaac Meir Alter of Ger, in whose home he was raised, came into his room and reprimanded him sternly and at considerable length for having slept so late instead of rising early in the morning to study.

Throughout the scolding, the lad stood quietly, listening attentively to the words of his grandfather without even attempting to utter so much as one word in his defense.

Later, the other young man, who had been witness to the scene, turned to him in surprise, and asked him: "Why did you not tell your grandfather that we had been up all night studying?"

Said the lad, who was to become the author of the treatise *Sefath Emeth*:

"I didn't want to stop Grandfather because I wanted to hear more of his words of reproof."

As he spoke these words, the boy opened his Bible and pointed out to his friend this very verse from the Book of Numbers, saying: "If the tribes of Gad and Reuben had the intention to cross the River Jordan armed for battle to help their brethren conquer the land, should they not have told Moses so at once, when he began to reprimand them, saying:

'Shall your brethren go to the war and shall you sit here? . . . Thus did your fathers act when I sent them from Kadesh-Barnea to see the land . . .' Why should they have allowed him to heap upon them so much rebuke and chastisement (see Verses 6-17), to call them a 'brood of sinful men' and to threaten them that if they would turn away from the Lord again He would leave them in the wilderness 'and so you will destroy all this people'?

"My answer is that they allowed him to continue because they would have considered it their loss if Moses would have stopped. They were eager to hear more words of moral instruction from him."

* * * *

"And the Children of Gad and the Children of Reuben spoke to Moses, saying: 'Thy servants will do as my lord commands.'" (Numbers 32:25)

At first glance, we do not see any essential difference between what Moses told the Children of Gad and of Reuben and what the members of these tribes had said to Moses before. Why, then, did they not say: "Thy servants will do as we have spoken", but "Thy servants will do as my lord commands"?

Originally, they had said to Moses: *". . . but we ourselves will be ready armed to go before the Children of Israel"* (Verse 17). At that time they had been concerned only with going out to aid their brethren in the conquest of the Promised Land. They did not say then that they would do so for the sake of heaven, in order to do the will of the Lord.

But in his answer to them (Verses 20-24) Moses consistently stressed that their preparation for battle was to be "before the Lord." "If you will do this thing; if you will arm yourselves to go *before the Lord* to war" (Verse 20); "and every armed man of you will pass over the Jordan *before the Lord* . . ." (Verse 21); "and the land will be subdued *before the Lord* . . ." (Verse 22); ". . . and do that which has proceeded out of your mouth" (Verse 24). Rashi comments that after Moses had impressed this important fact on them, the Children of Gad and Reuben corrected themselves and said: "And your servants will pass over, every man that is armed for war, *before the Lord* to battle . . ." (Verse 27).

"My Lord" in the statement "as my lord commands" refers to God, implying that the Children of Gad and Reuben intended to arm themselves for the sake of heaven, not out of considerations of patriotism and self-interest, but solely for the sake of the honor of heaven and in order to do the will of the Lord.

—Attributed to the Rabbi of Amshinov

* * * *

"We will pass over armed before the Lord into the land of Canaan and the possession of our inheritance shall remain with us beyond the Jordan." (Numbers 32:32)

The Children of Israel were to enter the Promised Land "before the Lord"; namely, their main purpose in entering the Land was to be to lead a holy life there and to preserve the sanctity of the Land of Israel by keeping the Torah and its commandments. Without the Torah, the Land of Israel is no better and no more important than any other country.

Therefore the Sages say: "He who makes no mention of the covenant and of the Torah in the 'Blessing over the Land' (after meals) has not fulfilled his obligation" (*Berakhot 49*). He who recites the Blessing over the Land of Israel but omits to give thanks "for the Torah which Thou hast taught us and for the statutes which Thou hast made known to us", thus failing to stress that the Land of Israel has value only as long as the people who live there observe the Torah and the Divine statutes, has not fulfilled his obligation with regard to his work for the Holy Land.

In a similar vein, the Children of Gad and the Children

347

of Reuben said to Moses: *"We will pass over armed* (the Hebrew expression used here for "armed" is *halutzim* which is the word also for "pioneers") *before the Lord*: the purpose of *our halutziut,* of our pioneering, will be to do the will of the Lord, in order to preserve the holiness of the Promised Land, for were it not for this high purpose *the possession of our inheritance shall remain with us beyond Jordan;* we could have other countries in plenty beyond the Jordan. What would be the distinction of the Land of Israel if not the fact that it was given to the Jewish people "in order that they may keep His statutes and observe His teachings" and that they may be pioneers "before the Lord"?

—*Avnei Ezel*

* * * *

This is also the intent of the statement by the Sages that "the countenance of Moses was as the face of the sun, and the countenance of Joshua was as the face of the moon" (*Baba Bathra 75*).

It is a known fact that the moon has no light of its own but only reflects the light of the sun. Thus, if it were not for the sun, the moon would be nothing but a huge dark sphere. Indeed, we know that whenever the earth comes between the sun and the moon the moon is eclipsed.

Moses stands as the symbol of the Torah because he accepted the Torah in person on Mount Sinai and taught it to the Jewish people. Joshua stands for the Land of Israel because it was he who led the Children of Israel into the Promised Land. Even as the countenance of Moses is likened to the face of the sun, and as the countenance of Joshua is likened to the face of the moon, so the relationship between the Torah and the Land of Israel corresponds to that existing between the sun and the moon. As long as the light of the Torah will irradiate the Land of Israel, as long as the way of life there will "reflect" Torah, the Land will be bright and light the path of the Jewish people in turn. But if a barrier should ever come between the light of the Torah and the Land of Israel so that the light of the Torah will be cut off from the Holy Land, Palestine will be just another expanse of land, with no light of its own and without special significance to the Jewish people.

As long as the countenance of Moses (The Torah) will be as the face of the sun, which spreads warmth and light over the land, the countenance of Joshua (the Land of Israel) will be like the face of the moon, gathering brightness from the light of the Torah and in turn bringing new light and warmth into the gloom which now surrounds the Jewish people.

—*Anon.*

*   *   *   *

Haphtarah Mattoth (Jeremiah 1-2:3)
"Thus says the Lord: 'I remember for thee the affection of thy youth, the love of thy espousals, how thou wentest after Me in the wilderness, in a land that was not sown. Israel is the Lord's hallowed portion; His first fruits of the increase; all those that devour him shall be held guilty.' " (Jeremiah 2:1-3)

Why is Israel compared to sand? What is sand? If a man takes a handful of it and turns it into a paste or cooks it, he will not be able to eat it because the grains will injure his teeth. So, too, is Israel. Any one who will humiliate him or rob him in this world will have his teeth set on edge (lit. "have his teeth knocked out") in the world to come. Why? *Because Israel is holy, as it is written: 'Israel is the Lord's hallowed portion; His first fruits of the increase; all those that devour him shall be held guilty.'*

—*Midrash Rabba, Book of Numbers*

Some day the Lord will call the nations of the world to account not only for their own sins, but also for the sins which the Jews committed. For whatever transgressions the Jews may have committed in exile were directly attributable to the humiliation and oppression which they had to suffer at the hands of the Gentiles who did not leave them in peace to worship the Most High as would have been fitting. When the Jews wandered through the wilderness, untroubled by other nations and blessed with peace and prosperity, they subordinated themselves entirely to the Lord and did His will properly. This is proof that the Jews are good by nature and that it was only due to the tortures to which they were subejcted by their wicked neighbors that they, too, became evil. For this reason it is only proper that the evil nations of the world should be held accountable for the sins of the Jewish people.

The above has been likened to the case of a rabbi who took his good and clever son and had him marry into an uncultured family in an isolated village. In the course of time the young man acquired the habits of the people of that village and became as common as they.

Eventually, his father came to the village and took him home. Soon the enraged father-in-law arrived in the city and demanded the reason why the rabbi had made him suffer by taking away his daughter's husband.

"Is it my fault," he shouted angrily, "that your son became wicked?"

"My son is a good and fine young man by nature," the rabbi replied, "for as you know, all the time he was in my home, he was pious and constantly engaged in his studies. After all, he comes of good stock. It is only since he went to live with you in the village and was exposed to the bad habits of your people that he has changed. Hence, if he is evil now, it is not his fault but yours."

This is what God, too, will say to the peoples of the world when they will demand why they should be made to suffer for the sins of the Jews:

"I remember for thee the affection of thy youth, the love of thy espousals, how thou wentest after Me in the wilderness.

in a land that was not sown: I remember how well the Children
of Israel behaved when they were still with Me, before they
were thrust into your midst. This is proof that *Israel is the
Lord's hallowed portion; His first fruits of the increase*: the Jews
are good and holy by nature, due to the good stock from which
they come, and if they became evil, it is not their fault but yours.
*Therefore all those that devour him shall be held guilty; evil
shall come upon them*: It was you who by your mistreatment of
them and by your own evil ways led the Jewish people into sin.
Therefore it is only proper that you must suffer for their transgressions."

—*Kokhav MiYaakov*

*   *   *   *

Weekly Portion of Masseh — Numbers 33:1-36:13
*"These are the stages of the Children of Israel, by which they
went forth out of the land of Egypt by their hosts under the hand
of Moses and Aaron."* (Numbers 33:1)

A Parable: It may be compared to the case of a king
whose son was ill and whom he took to a distant place to
cure him. When they returned home, the father began to
enumerate all the stages of the journey, saying: "Here we
slept, here you caught cold; here you had a headache (and
so forth)."

—*Rashi*

How can this parable be applied to the journey of the
Children of Israel through the wilderness? Was it so unusual
for the tribes to sleep or to catch cold during their wanderings?

"Here we slept" may be interpreted as referring to the fact
that the Children of Israel slept late on the day the Torah was
given and Moses had to awaken them (see Midrash: *"He came
and found them asleep . . ."*).

"Here you caught cold" may be taken to refer to the chill
(Heb. *kerirut*) whereby the Amalekites cooled the ardor with
which Israel had served the Lord, as it is written (Deut. 25:18):

"How (Amalek) met thee by the way" (the Hebrew term *karcha,* used in this verse for "met" may also be translated as "chilled").

"Here you had a headache" may be construed as recalling the worship of the Golden Calf. The Hebrew phrase used for "here you had a headache" is *hashashta et rosh'cha. Hashash* may also be translated into the sense of "doubting" and *rosh'cha* may be interpreted as denoting an "appointed head" or a "leader." Hence this recollection may be translated as "here you doubted your leader"; here you came to doubt the principles of your faith and backslid into idolatry.

—*The Rabbi of Ger*

* * * *

"And Moses wrote their goings forth, stage by stage by the commandments of the Lord, and these are their stages at their goings forth." (Numbers 33:2)

When the Children of Israel were in Egypt they had sufficient faith to follow Moses into the wilderness and it was for the sake of this great merit that they were redeemed, as is written in the Book of Jeremiah: *"I remember for thee the affection of thy youth . . . how thou wentest after Me in the wilderness in a land that was not sown"* (Jer. 2:1). Thus the "goings forth" of the Children of Israel had been granted them because of the merits they had gained by assuming the burdens of wandering through the wilderness.

Later, however, when the Jews sinned and complained to the Lord, they were threatened with annihilation, and they were saved only because Moses prayed for them: "O Lord, why does Thy wrath wax hot against Thy people which *Thou hast brought forth from Egypt?"* (Exod. 32:11) "Why should the Egyptians speak, saying: 'For evil *did He bring them forth'?"* (Exod. 32:12). It is clear, then, that they were able to go on and enter the Promised Land solely because of their having

gone forth from Egypt. *And these are their stages;* the stages
that followed — *their goings forth* — came to pass only because they had gone out of Egypt.

—Torat Moshe

*   *   *   *

"*. . . they shall be the six cities of refuge, which you shall give for
the manslayer to flee thither, and beside them you shall give forty
and two cities.*" (Numbers 35:6)

The six cities of refuge correspond to the six words *Shema
Yisrael Adonai Elohenu Adonai Ehad,* "Hear, O Israel, the
Lord is our God, the Lord is One." Add the names of the forty-
two other cities, and you have forty-eight words, corresponding
to the total of forty-eight Hebrew words in the passage beginning with "*Hear, O Israel . . .*" (Deut. 6:4) and ending with
"*. . . and upon thy gates*" (Deut 6:9).

The foregoing implies that the words of the declaration of
faith beginning with "*Hear, O Israel*" (Deut. 6:4-9) constitute
those "cities of refuge" where any Jews, no matter what his sin,
can find shelter and protection. If he accepts the yoke of the
Kingdom of Heaven and loves the Lord, he will be saved from
the accusers who pursue him.

—Oheb Yisrael

*   *   *   *

"*. . . cities to be cities of refuge for you . . .*" (Numbers 35:11)

To any Jew who has had the misfortune of having slain a
man by accident and is therefore so abjectly crushed that he
can no longer find his place in this world, the Lord says: "I shall
appoint a place for you," a city of refuge where he will be safe
from the avenger and find peace.

But as for him who is not so greatly stricken by what he
has done and who can still "find his place", there actually is
no safe place and the cities of refuge will not offer him asylum.

Thus the Sages say that the prince of Edom is destined to

make three errors, as it is written: "Who is it that comes from Edom with dyed garments from Bozrah?" He will err, first, as only Bezer affords asylum, but he will go to Bozrah; he will err again because asylum is offered only to slayers in error, but he slays with intent; and he will err again, since asylum is offered only to men, but he is an angel."

The fact that this evil angel is capable of finding a place for himself where to hide as in a fortress proves that he is not so crushed as to be unable to "find his place," and therefore the cities of refuge cannot afford him asylum.

—*Rabbi Isaac Meir Alter*

* * * *

This is the reason why *Sukkoth* comes after *Yom Kippur*. If a Jew truly repents of his sins on the Day of Atonement and as a result he feels so humble and dejected that he cannot "find his place", the Lord will make a place for him beneath His own shadow — the shade of the *Sukkah* — and protect him from all evil.

—*Sefat Emet*

* * * *

"... *and he shall dwell therein until the death of the High Priest, who was anointed with the holy oil.*" (Numbers 35:25)

When a High Priest died, the entire nation trembled and repented of its sins. It could therefore be assumed that the blood-avenger would also reconsider, calm himself, and no longer seek to execute vengeance for the accidental killing of his kinsman. For when he would consider that even the High Priest, "who was anointed with the holy oil," could not live forever, he would be comforted for the death of his own kinsman. It would therefore be considered safe then for the manslayer to leave the city of refuge and return to his home.

—*Isaac Abarbanel*

* * * *

The Gemarah (*Makkot 11*) inquires what the second High Priest (the one who succeeded to the High Priesthood only after the act of manslaughter) could have done that the exiled manslayer could regain freedom only through his death. The Gemarah answers: "Because he should have prayed that the manslayer should be declared innocent, but had failed to do so."

But how could one pray that the Sanhedrin should declare innocent a man who might actually has been guilty? Would that not have been a prayer uttered in vain?

The law states that, "if all the members of a Sanhedrin declare the defendant guilty, he would be dismissed." If the members of a Sanhedrin were unanimous in declaring the defendant guilty, that defendant had to be released. Hence the High Priest could have prayed that no member of the Sanhedrin should make a mistake in judgment, and that all the members should state the truth as it really was; i.e., that the defendant is liable to exile, for if the Sanhedrin would be unanimous in its verdict of "guilty," the defendant would have to be declared innocent and allowed to go free.

—*Teshuva MeAhavo*

* * * *

Haphtarah Masseh (Jeremiah 2:4-28; 3:4; 4:1-2)
"Has a nation changed its gods, which yet are no gods? But My people has changed its glory for that which is of no profit." (Jeremiah 2:11)

The Maggid of Dubno would give the following parable in connection with this verse:

At the end of the period of *kest* (arrangement agreed upon prior to the wedding, whereby the father-in-law would support his new son-in-law so that the young man could devote himself entirely to study), a father-in-law handed a dowry to his son-in-law and sent him off to Leipzig to the fair. The son-in-law, who had no business sense whatever, used up all the money to buy several wagonloads of toothpicks. When the young man returned home with his purchase, his father-in-law was angry and shouted at him: "What have you done? I'll not be able to sell that stuff in seventy years!" But since it was too late to do anything about it, the merchant had no other choice but to send his son-in-law back to the houe of study and to dump the merchandise into his warehouse.

A few years passed. Then the merchant bethought himself and said: "What will become of my son-in-law? Will I have to support him for the rest of his life?"

So he gave him money again and sent him to Leipzig a second time to buy merchandise. This time he warned him not to buy any more toothpicks because he had not yet been able to dispose of the first shipment.

Seeing that the High Holidays were approaching, the young man decided to buy several wagonloads of ram's horns, because he thought that ram's horns would be much in demand. But when he returned home, he again received a scolding from his father-in-law.

"Fool!" the old man shouted. "A synagogue needs only one ram's horn and that can last them for decades, but here you went and brought back enough of them to last me until the Messiah will blow his horn!"

And so he sent his son-in-law back again to the house of study and dumped the ram's horns into his warehouse where the toothpicks still lay.

After a while, the old man sat down to ponder what to do with all this useless merchandise. He summoned a broker, asking him to take the toothpicks and to see whether he would not be able to exchange them for some other merchandise that would sell better. Then he gave orders to another broker to do likewise with the ram's horns.

But as things turned out, the two brokers met on their errand and made an exchange with one another, so that the toothpicks were exchanged for the ram's horns, and the ram's horns for the toothpicks.

When the two brokers returned and the merchant found that he had been taken in again, he was speechless with rage and frustration and decided to write the matter off as a loss. But then his son-in-law said to him:

"You see, you are experienced in the ways of business, but it didn't keep you from being taken in, even as I was."

"Fool!" the old man replied. "I had two shipments of dead stock. I could hardly have expected anything else than that the one would be exchanged for the other. But you had good and ready money and yet you went and spent it all on white elephants."

Jeremiah speaks to the people of Israel in a similar vein. *"Has a nation changed its gods which yet are no gods?"* When two heathen nations exchange one god for another between themselves, neither nation really suffers a loss, because neither of the gods is really a god. But *"My people has changed its glory for that which is of no profit";* my people, the people of Israel, had the Living God, and then it went and exchanged that true God, its pride and glory, for wooden idols which are good for nothing except to have toothpicks made from them, and one cannot even have profit from them when they are broken up into toothpicks because Jewish law forbids us to derive gain or benefit from material originally intended for idolatrous purposes.

WELLSPRINGS OF TORAH

DEUTERONOMY

THE BOOK OF DEUTERONOMY

דברים

Weekly Portion of Devarim (Deut. 1:1-3:22)

"These are the words which Moses spoke . . . and it came to pass in the fortieth year, in the eleventh month, on the first day of the month, that Moses spoke to the Children of Israel . . . beyond the Jordan, in the land of Moab, Moses took it upon himself to explain this Law." (Deuteronomy 1:1, 3, 5)

The fact that Moses addressed himself to the Children of Israel is mentioned three times in the first five verses of the first Chapter of the Book of Deuteronomy; cf., "which Moses spoke"; ". . . that Moses spoke to the Children of Israel . . ." and "Moses took it upon himself to explain . . ."

This was done because these first five verses are an introduction, as it were, to the entire Book of Deuteronomy. The Book of Deuteronomy is divided into three distinct parts, corresponding to the three other Books — Exodus, Leviticus and Numbers. It is therefore referred to as *Mishne Tora* — a repetition (recapitulation) of the Torah.

The first part consists of the first four chapters and contains words of reproof and rebuke. The second part extends from Chapter Five, where the Ten Commandments are repeated, to the ninth verse of Chapter Twenty-seven, and contains a summary of all the commandments of the Torah. The third part, which contains the Blessings and the Curses, continues from there until the end of Deuteronomy.

Hence, *"These are the words which Moses spoke . . ."* (Verse 1) refers to the first part, the section of reproof, in which reference is made to all the past sins of the Children of Israel in the wilderness; ". . . *that Moses spoke to the Children of Israel*

361

according to all that the Lord had given him in commandment to them," to the middle part in which the Divine commandments are listed; and *"Moses took it upon himself to explain this law",* to the final part containing the Blessings and Curses. Indeed, it is written concerning the Blessings and Curses (Deut. 27:8) "and thou shalt write upon the stones all the words of this Law *explaining them well,"* implying a general explanation of how the commandments are to be observed.

—The Gaon of Vilna

* * * *

". . . in the wilderness . . . between Paran and Tophel, and Laban, and Hatzeroth and Di-Zahab." (Deuteronomy 1:1)

> *Hatzeroth* refers to the controversy of Korah, and *Di-Zahab* — literally "gold" — alludes to the worship of the Golden Calf.

—Rashi

Why should the reference to the controversy of Korah precede the allusion to the worship of the Golden Calf, when the latter preceded the former by far in the chronological order?

We often encounter individuals who do not believe in any higher ideal, but cling fanatically and stubbornly to their own superstitious beliefs. They laugh at those who are truly religious, but persist in their own irrational faith in palmists, sooth-sayers, fortune-tellers and other frauds.

Such individuals are guilty of much graver sin than those of average religious steadfastness who hold the right beliefs and only occasionally dabble in superstition. He who dismisses the great truths but clings to folly is much worse than one who is rooted in religion and only makes periodic excursions into superstition.

These thoughts provide the answer to the question why the allusions to the two historic events mentioned above are given in reverse order.

The controversy of Korah, in which Korah and his followers refused to believe in Moses, forcibly recalled the incident of the Golden Calf.

Scripture asks, as it were: "How is it that you could not believe that Moses was your true leader, but were most ready to believe in the Divine powers of a calf? How is it that you could find fault with Moses but dance around a calf and shout: 'These are thy gods, O Israel'?"

—*Rabbi Yitzhak Katz*

*   *   *   *

"And it came to pass in the fortieth year, in the eleventh month, on the first day of the month, that Moses spoke to the Children of Israel . . ." (Deuteronomy 1:3)

> From the fact that Jacob waited to reprove his sons until just shortly before his death we learn there are four things on account of which one should not reprove a person except shortly before one's death, so that one should not reprove him and then (have to) reprove him again.
>
> —*Rashi*

When a person is reproved, he usually attempts to answer the charges to justify himself. In reply, the one delivering the reproof must remonstrate with him again and show him that all his excuses are worthless. This is usually the start of a quarrel. If, on the other hand, the reprover makes no reply, the person may think that his excuses were justified and he will do wrong again.

Therefore the best course to follow is not to reprove a person except shortly before one's death so that the person reproved should not have time to answer, but that the words of reproof should penetrate into his heart and remain there forever. This is the thought conveyed by Rashi's statement ". . . so that one should not reprove him and then have to reprove him again."

—*Torat Moshe*

363

*   *   *   *

". . . Moses took it upon himself to explain this Law." (Deut. 1:5)

The summation of the laws of the Torah does not begin until Chapter Five, with the restatement of the Ten Commandments. The First Chapter is primarily a recapitulation of Israel's sins. Why, then, does this verse, which refers to the expounding of the Law by Moses, occur here rather than in Chapter Five? Would it not be much more appropriate there?

According to Rabbinical literature, it is one of the fundamental principles in the worship of God in Judaism that one must repent of one's past transgressions before beginning to study. The Rabbi of Lublin said that Verse 16 of Psalm 50, "But to the wicked, God said: 'What hast thou to do to declare My statutes?' " refers to him who does not repent before he sits down to study.

It was in keeping with this basic tenet of Judaism that Moses reproved his people before he proceeded to expound to them the commandments of the Torah. The verse under discussion was placed immediately preceding these admonitions in order to indicate the reason why Moses wanted to recall the sins of the Children of Israel. It was because Moses "took it upon himself to explain this Law" that he had to reprove his people in order to make them repent of their sins.

—*Mo'or VoShomesh*

*   *   *   *

"Moses took it upon himself to explain this Law, saying: 'The Lord our God spoke to us in Horeb saying: You have dwelt long enough in this mountain; now turn and take your journey, and go to the hill country of the Amorites.' " (Deuteronomy 1:5, 6, 7)

> In the seventy languages of the world did he explain it to them.
>
> —*Rashi*

Why did Moses deem it necessary to explain the Law in all the seventy languages of the Ancient World?

In every nation there are forces which oppose the Torah. Knowing that the Children of Israel would have to dwell among the nations, Moses wanted to enable them to defend and to observe the Torah wherever they might be. Wherever they would dwell, the Jews would have to be able to overcome any resistance which their environment might offer to the Torah. It was to equip the Jewish people to assert the views of Judaism wherever they might be scattered that he explained the Torah to them in the languages of the seventy nations of the Ancient World.

—Rabbi Isaac Meir Alter

*   *   *   *

There are those unbelievers who claim that the Torah was meant to be observed only in the wilderness far away from the settlements of other groups and nations or in the Holy Land, where the Jews dwelt among their own, and where no one would interfere with their customs. They insist that when the Jews dwell among other nations, when they live in the midst of another culture and civilization, they must not keep aloof from their neighbors by clinging to the observance of the Torah and its commandments.

It was to refute this argument that Moses explained the Law to the Children of Israel in all the seventy languages of the world before they entered the Promised Land. He wanted to impress upon his people that they were duty-bound to observe the Torah regardless of what lands they might dwell in, because the Torah was valid for all time and for all countries and was not subject to change.

—Ketav Sofer

*   *   *   *

"The Lord our God spoke to us in Horeb, saying: 'You have dwelt long enough in this mountain.'" (Deuteronomy 1:6)

(Said Moses to the Children of Israel): When you were

on the mountain of Horeb, the Lord told you that you are not to look upon every obstacle and hindrance as an unconquerable *mountain,* but that you must surmount any obstacles that might stand in the way of your worship of the Lord.

—*Mo'or VoShomesh*

* * * *

(Moses said) *"I am not able to bear you myself alone; the Lord, your God, has multiplied you and behold, you are this day as the stars of heaven for multitude."* (Deuteronomy 1:9, 10)

The people of Israel have been likened to sand as well as to the stars. It is typical of sand that its grains tend to cling together. The stars, on the other hand, must be separated from one another by vast areas of space so that each star is a separate world to itself.

As long as the Jews are like the sand, united, clinging together, they do not place an undue burden on those who guide them. But once they are scattered and far distant from one another as the stars in the sky, worlds apart from one another, their leaders find themselves faced with a well-nigh impossible task. Accordingly, Moses says here:

"I am not able to bear you myself alone — I can no longer lead you by myself because *the Lord, your God, has multiplied you;* besides, *you are this day as the stars of heaven,* scattered, and worlds apart from one another, so that no one person will be equal to the task of leading you. *How,* then, *can I bear your cumbrance, and your burden and your strife, all by myself?* (1:12)

—*Afikei Yehuda*

* * * *

"May the Lord, the God of your fathers, make you a thousand times as many more as you are (now) *..."* (Deut. 1:11)

Why has this blessing not come true?

Because it was intended not for the present but for that

future day of which the Prophet Isaiah says: "The smallest shall
become a thousand, and the least a mighty nation" (Isaiah
60:22). In that day the Jewish people which is now "small"
and insignificant will grow a thousandfold in stature and importance, just as Moses foretold it in the blessing he gave the
Children of Israel.

—*Binyan Ariel*

*   *   *   *

*"How can I bear your cumbrance, and your burden, and your strife,
all by myself?"* (Deuteronomy 1:12)

These terms — "cumbrance," "burden," and "strife" —
refer to the three tasks of leadership which Moses had to fulfill.

"Your cumbrance" alludes to the responsibility given to
Moses to study the Law with the Children of Israel, as he himself described it to his father-in-law Jethro: *"And I make known
to them the statutes of God and His laws"* (Exodus 18:16).

"Your burden" is a reference to the duty devolving on
Moses to pray for any Israelite who might be in trouble; as he
put it to Jethro: *". . . the people come to me to inquire of
God"* (Exodus 18:15).

"Your strife" refers to the role of Moses as arbitrator and
judge in disputes arising among the people *". . . and I judge
between a man and his neighbor"* (Exodus 8:16).

These three functions are the principal responsibilities of
the leader in Israel.

—*Nachmanides*

*   *   *   *

(Moses said to the people) *"Get you . . . wise men . . ."* (Deuteronomy 1:13)

If we wish to be facetious, we could say that this verse is
aimed specifically at those rabbis and communal leaders whose
wives meddle in their husbands' affairs, telling them how to
carry out their functions, and poking their noses into their

367

husbands' communal work, so that actually the community is led not by the rabbi but by his wife.

The verse specifies "wise *men*" to teach us that the functions of leadership belong to men, and not to their wives.

—*Ketav Sofer*

* * * *

"*. . . And the cause which is too hard for you you shall bring to me and I will hear it.*" (Deuteronomy 1:17)

Nachmanides said that if a man is in a quandary concerning a problem, he must try to dissociate his emotions from it, as if it were of no personal concern to him at all. Only once he has done this will he be able to arrive at the truth and know how to proceed in accordance with the will of the Lord.

This is the explanation of the present Scriptural verse:

"*And the cause which is too hard for you*" — the problem in connection with which you have difficulty in deciding what to do — *you shall bring to me,* so that you may be able to consider it with detachment, to see it from a distance and regard it solely from the viewpoint of God's will. If you proceed in this manner, you will be able to arrive at the truth.

—*Sefat Emet*

* * * *

"*. . . And you came near to me, every one of you . . .* (and requested me to) *send out spies to explore the land.*" (Deut. 1:22)

> But further on, it is stated: "And you approached me, even all the heads of your tribes, and your elders." That approach to me was a proper one, young people showing respect for their elders, letting these precede them, and the elders showing respect to the heads of the tribes, that these should precede them. Here, however, (when you showed your lack of faith, asking me to have the land explored before you entered it) you approached me, all of you, in a crowd, the young pushing aside their elders and the elders pushing aside the heads of the tribes.

—*Rashi*

If that other approaching — when the Children of Israel gathered about Mount Sinai to receive the Law — was indeed a "proper" one, why should Moses think of it now, when he enumerates the sins of the Children of Israel?

Said Rabbi Isaac Meir of Ger: At this time Moses found even this a cause for remonstrating with the people, for when there is an opportunity to hear the Law expounded, it would be entirely proper to want to crowd around the master, pushing others aside in order to be able to hear every word.

"But you, O Childen of Israel, did not do so," said Moses to the people as they were about to enter the land of Canaan. "At Mount Sinai, where it would have been only proper for you to push ahead eagerly, you held back, politely yielding first place to others. But when you requested me to send out spies to explore the land, you did not come to me in an orderly fashion but in an unruly mob, jostling for first place and shoving your elders aside. When you had the privilege to hear the Law proclaimed, you went forward slowly and in ordered ranks, but when you were driven on by sinful lack of faith, you rushed to me pell-mell, with no regard for the rules of propriety."

—*Torat Moshe*

*   *   *   *

"*. . . And the thing pleased me well, and I took twelve men of you . . .*" (Deuteronomy 1:23)

If it indeed "pleased Moses well" to send out the spies, why did he count that request among the sins of the Children of Israel?

Moses reproved them, saying:"Behold how great was your sin. Your wickedness brought things to a point where even I was willing to accede to your request, which was entirely unjustified and proved your lack of faith. Your blemish was so great that it infected even me, for any blemish attaching to the

369

Jews will infect their leaders as well."

—*Sefat Emet*

* * * *

Haphtarah Devarim (Isaiah 1:1-27)
"Righteousness lodged in her, but now murderers." (Isaiah 1:21)
Righteousness lodged in her — Acts of righteousness were compelled to "stay the night"; the people "slept on them," putting them off from one day to the next.

But now murderers — But when there was an opportunity to do evil, such as to commit a murder, they did not wait until the next day, but did the deed *"now,"* immediately, losing no time at all. —*Rabbi Jonathan Eibeschuetz*

* * * *

Weekly Portion of Va-Ethchannan (Deut. 3:23-7:11)
"And I besought the Lord at that time . . ." (Deut. 3:23)
> Although the righteous might properly make a claim to reward on the basis of their good deeds, they solicit it from the Omnipresent only as an *ex gratia* gift.
> —*Rashi*

It never even occurs to the truly righteous man that he has done anything good. How, then, could he support his claim to reward by citing a record of his past good deeds?

Actually, the righteous may base their claims on the good deeds which they may perform at some future date, if they are preserved in life. Nevertheless, they do not approach the Lord with that plea but solicit their reward only as an *ex gratia* gift.

Moses, too, could have based his claim for reward on the good deed which he expected to perform in the event he would live to enter the Promised Land, fulfilling the commandment to "cleave to the Land." Nevertheless, he did not request anything of the Lord. He only "besought Him," praying for an *ex gratia* gift.

—*Menahem Mendel Morgenstern, Rabbi of Kotzk*

* * * *

"Let me go over, I pray Thee, and see the good land ..." (Deuteronomy 3:25)

Is it not obvious that if he will go over into the land, he will be able to see it?

But a man must pray at all times that God may cause him to see the good in everything.

Therefore Moses prayed: "Let me go over . . . and see the *good land* . . . cause me to see only the *good* side of the Promised Land."

—Ohel Torah

*   *   *   *

". . . And the Lord said to me: 'Let it suffice thee; speak no more to Me of the matter.' " (Deuteronomy 3:26)

It is related in the Yalkut that when Moses prayed to be allowed to live to enter the Promised Land, he told the Lord:

"Thou hast written in Thy Law: *'And if the slave should say: I have come to love my master . . . I will not go out free'* (Exodus 21:5-6) he may remain with his master forever. Now when I, Thy servant, make the same request, why should my request be refused and I should be made to leave this world?"

But the Lord replied: "Let it suffice thee, speak no more to Me of the matter."

What is the meaning of this reply from the Lord, blessed be His Name?

The Gemarah (Tractate Kiddushin) explains: *"And if the slave should plainly say:* this means that he must say it twice. The servant must say twice: *I have come to love my master. . . . I will not go out free."*

Now, according to this interpretation, if Moses would have had an opportunity to repeat his request, God would have been duty-bound to grant it, but that would have been impossible because God had decreed that Moses could not live to enter

the Promised Land, and a Divine decree, once given, is irre-
versible. Therefore the Lord, in order to keep Moses from re-
peating his plea, said to him: "Speak no more to me of the
matter."

—Sifthei Kohen

* * * *

"You shall not add to the word which I command you, neither shall
you diminish from it . . . Your eyes have seen what the Lord did in
Baal-Peor, for all the men that followed the Baal of Peor, the Lord
thy God has destroyed them from the midst of thee." (Deuteronomy
4:2, 3)

There are those who sin not with the intention to transgress
the commandments of God, but because they allow their reason
to persuade them that actually they are not violating a Divine
law at all.

Therefore the Torah admonishes the Israelites: *"You shall*
not add to the word . . . neither shall you diminish from it —
You shall not add or detract from the commandments of the
Torah according to the dictates of your reason, *because* your
eyes have seen what the Lord did in Baal-Peor. There, too, the
Children of Israel did not intend to worship the Baal of Peor;
on the contrary, they only wanted to disgrace him, for Baal-
Peor was worshipped by obscene acts. Yet *the Lord thy God*
has destroyed them. This should teach you that you cannot
alter the commandments of the Torah, not by even a fraction
of an inch, according to the dictates of your own reason, for the
logic of the Torah is quite different from your own, and much
loftier, and cannot be gauged by the human mind."

—Moses ben Hayyim Alshekh

* * * *

"But you who did cleave to the Lord your God are alive, every one
of you, this day." (Deuteronomy 4:4)

The philosophers hold various views concerning whether
man can achieve communion with God. Some hold that, at best,

man can commune with Him indirectly, through an angel. Others believe that communion with God cannot be achieved in life but only after death. Still others, though conceding that exceptional individuals can achieve it even in life, insist that it is impossible for an entire people to attain this lofty moral level, and some say that communion with God can be attained only after long years of struggle and toil.

None of the above views is in agreement with the Torah. It is written: *"After the Lord your God shall you walk . . . and to Him shall you cleave"* (Deut. 13:5). This means that any Jew can achieve communion with God. The Sages (Tanna Rabbi Eliyahu) say that even a slave, male or female, can reach the spirit of God and that he or she needs no more than one brief moment of sincerity to do so. It is written that "one can acquire his world within one hour."

It is in order to refute all the false notions mentioned above that the Scripture states: *"But you who did cleave to the Lord your God —* This means that you can commune with the Lord directly, without need for an angel — *are alive —* you can commune with God in your lifetime; there is no need to wait until after death — *every one of you —* every one of you, and not just exceptional individuals, can attain to it — *this day —* and it can happen this very day — even today if only you will listen to His voice.

—*Kanfei Nesharim*

*   *   *   *

"For what great nation is there that has God so near to them . . ."
(Deuteronomy 4:7)

> "The Lord will answer you in the day of trouble." A parable: It is like a woman who sits upon the travailing stool. They say to her: "May He who answered your mother answer you."
>
> —*Midrash*

373

The Midrash asks: "Why should it be written 'in the *day* of trouble'? Day implies light, which is the very opposite of trouble. Would it not have been more fitting, then, to say 'in the *night* of trouble'?"

And the Midrash proceeds to provide the answer:

This is to teach us that any trouble that may come to the Jewish people bears the seed of happiness in it. Even as the pains of a woman in labor are only a prelude to the birth of a child, so, too, the pains and sufferings of the people of Israel are simply precursors of the deliverance which is to come.

We say to the woman in labor: "May he who answered your mother answer you." It is in the order of things that child-birth entails suffering. Your mother also suffered before giving birth to you. And even as her suffering ended in the birth of a child, so the pain you are feeling now will serve to bring a new life into this world.

Likewise, the Jews, too, may be certain that their sufferings must carry salvation and deliverance in their wake.

This is the meaning of the verse: "For what great nation is there that has God so near to them?" Even the sterner aspects of Divine judgment are not intended to show that God has cast off the people of Israel but are meant only to bring Israel closer to its Creator. For any deliverance must be preceded by sufferings, by the "birth pangs" of the Messiah, as it were.

"This is a time of trouble for Jacob and he will be saved from it." It is "from it," this very trouble, that salvation will spring forth.

—*Sefat Emet*

* * * *

"'Only take heed to thyself, and keep thy soul diligently lest thou forget the things which thine eyes saw . . ." (Deut. 4:9)

"Only" implies a qualification, a limitation. With regard to "thyself," your body, your physical well-being, you are told to

374

take "only" ordinary precautions. The important thing is "thy soul" which you must "keep diligently."

—Attributed to the Rabbi of Lublin

* * * *

"Therefore take good heed to your souls . . ." (Deuteronomy 4:15)

The Hebrew expression for "take good heed" is in the passive mood, and "your souls" is preceded by the particle *le* (literary "for") instead of *eth,* which would ordinarily precede the object of the verb. What is the reason for this?

This Biblical verse is taken as a basis for the commandment to care for one's body and to protect one's health. We are told: "See that your body should *be protected"* (hence the passive) *"for* your souls" (for the sake of your souls). For any illness of your body will also injure your soul.

—Or Tzaddikim

* * * *

"And there you shall serve gods, the work of men's hands . . . which neither see, nor hear, nor eat, nor smell. But from thence you will seek the Lord thy God and thou shalt find Him if thou wilt search after Him with all thy heart . . ." (Deuteronomy 4:28, 29)

Why are only four of the five senses mentioned, omitting the sense of speech?

Because the Scripture was referring to a specific event which was to take place centuries later, while the people of Israel was in exile in Babylonia. The Midrash pertaining to the Song of Songs relates that when Nebuchadnezzar, the King of Babylonia, made his great idol, he removed the Ineffable Name of God from the priestly frontlet and placed it into the idol's mouth so that the idol was able to speak. When Daniel learned of this, he asked the king for permission to kiss the idol. As he kissed it, Daniel managed to remove the Ineffable Name of God from the idol's mouth, depriving the idol of its power to speak and thus exposing it to all the people as the work of human folly.

All this was forecast here in the Book of Deuteronomy; as follows:

And there you shall serve: There, in Babylonia, you will be forced to serve a man-made idol. *Which neither see, nor smell*: Although he will not be able to see, hear, eat or smell, he will be able to speak, and therefore the people will be duped into believing that he has real power. *But from thence you will seek*: But from the place whence his speech will emanate, *the Lord thy God*: the Name of the Lord on the Tetragrammaton in his mouth which will make it possible for him to speak, *and thou shalt find Him if thou wilt search after Him with all thy heart and with all thy soul*: if you will search for it even at the risk of your life, you will find the Name inside the idol and thus remove error from the world.

It was this Biblical verse, then, that led Daniel to seek the Tetragrammaton, the Ineffable Name of the Lord, in the mouth of the idol and to remove It from there.

—*Gaon of Vilna*

* * * *

"But from thence you will seek the Lord thy God . . ." (*Deuteronomy* 4:29)

From thence — you will be able to search for the Lord your God from the depths of your heart and find Him there, if only you will seek Him diligently.

—*Attributed to Rabbi Yaakov Yitzhak of Przysucha*

* * * *

"Know this day, and lay it to thy heart that the Lord, He is God . . ." (Deuteronomy 4:39)

It is not sufficient merely to "know" it; this sublime knowledge must be taken into your very heart, so that your will and your virtues both should function in conformity with what you know. This task constitutes the entire "worship" incumbent on the Jew.

The space that separates "knowing" from "laying it to thy heart" is as great as that which stands between knowledge and ignorance.

—*Rabbi Israel Salanter*

* * * *

If the main thing is to "lay it to thy heart," it follows that the heart must be cleansed before in order to make room for all this knowledge so that it may take root there.

—*Rabbi Isaac Meir Alter of Ger*

* * * *

"And know this day . . . that the Lord, He is God in heaven above and on the earth below; there is none else." (Deuteronomy 4:39)

En od — "there is none else" or "there is nothing else."

"The Lord, He is God in heaven above and on the earth below" — there is nothing else we need to know, for this one knowledge is the foundation and the root of all knowledge in the world.

—*Sefarim*

* * * *

". . . that the manslayer might flee there . . . Bezer in the wilderness . . . and this is the law which Moses set before the Children of Israel . . ." (Deuteronomy 4:42, 43, 44)

Moses set aside three Cities of Refuge even though they could not be used by manslayers for this purpose until the other three cities would be set up in Canaan across the river Jordan and he, Moses, knew, that he would not be permitted to enter the land and complete the task. For, as Rashi comments to Verse 41, Moses said to himself: "Any duty that is possible for me to perform, I will perform."

This should teach us with regard to the performance of each and every command in the Torah that we must set about the task of fulfilling it even if we know that we will not be able to complete the work. King David, too, made all the preparations for the construction of the Holy Temple, even though he knew that the actual work was to be done not by him but only by his son Solomon.

And this is the law: This is the teaching derived from the fact that Moses "separated" the three Cities of Refuge, even though he knew he would not be able to complete the task — *which Moses set before the Children of Israel*: which Moses taught the Jews to follow in connection with the performance of each and every commandment.

—*K'lei Yakar*

* * * *

"I stood. between the Lord and you at that time . . ." (Deut. 5:5)

It is the "I," egotism, selfishness, that stands between God and man. As long as man is the slave of his ego, he cannot come near to His God.

—*The Rabbi of Kobrin*

* * * *

"Honor thy father and thy mother, as the Lord thy God commanded thee . . ." (Deuteronomy 5:16)

The Sages say that if a child is commanded by his father to transgress a commandment of the Torah, he must not obey because the Lord said that "you and your father are both duty-bound to honor Me."

This verse is to be understood as follows:

Honor thy father and thy mother, but only *as the Lord thy God commanded thee*, only in the manner commanded by God, in keeping with all the other things God has commanded.

It is only fitting that the modification "as the Lord thy God commanded thee" should be given at this point rather than in the original enumeration of the Ten Commandments in the twentieth chapter of the Book of Exodus. When the Ten Commandments were first given on Mount Sinai, the other precepts of the Torah had not yet been made known. But by the time Moses reiterated the Ten Commandments before his death, all the precepts were already known to the Children of Israel. It was therefore appropriate to add at this point that honor paid one's parents must not be permitted to conflict with the other commandments of the Torah.

—*Kedushat Levi*

* * * *

(The Lord said to Moses) *"Go say to them: 'Return to your tents.'"* (Deuteronomy 5:27)

Said the Lord, through Moses, to the Children of Israel: "Here, at Mount Sinai, I beheld your reverence and devotion. Now let Me see how you will conduct yourselves in your tents, in the privacy of your homes."

—*The Rabbi of Kotzk*

* * * *

"That thou mightest fear the Lord thy God, to keep all His statutes and His commandments ... thou, and thy son, and thy son's son, all the days of thy life." (Deuteronomy 6:2)

Should the wording not have been "All the days of thy life, thou, and thy son, and thy son's son?"

The order was reversed deliberately. As our Sages put it: "Do not be sure of thyself till the day of thy death" (*Ethics of the Fathers 2:5*).

The Scriptural verse is to be understood as follows:

That thou mightest fear the Lord thy God, to keep all His statutes: You shall fear the Lord, and devise legal safeguards for the commandments of the Torah to keep yourself from transgressing its precepts. *Thou, and thy son, and thy son's son:* Even if you already have children and grandchildren, even though you may be at an age when the evil impulse has already grown faint within you, you still must not be sure of your immunity to temptation, but must continue to keep these legal safeguards *"all the days of thy life."* As long as there is life within you, you can never be so sure of yourself that you could afford to do without them.

—*Meshekh Hakhmah*

* * * *

"Hear, therefore, O Israel, and observe to do it . . . as the Lord, the God of thy fathers, has promised to thee, a land flowing with milk and honey." (Deuteronomy 6:3)

Should the text not read *"in* a land flowing with milk and honey"?

It is the intention of the text to stress that the prosperity of the Promised Land — whether or not the Land of Canaan will indeed be a "land of milk and honey" — is dependent entirely on the conduct of the Jewish people. Only if they will live in accordance with the Laws of the Torah will their land be blessed and fertile.

Therefore Scripture says: *"Hear, therefore, O Israel, and observe to do it ... . as the Lord, the God of thy fathers has promised to thee.* If thou wilt do it, the land will be *a land flowing with milk and honey,* but if thou wilt not keep the commandments of the Lord, it will not be so."

—*Meshekh Hakhmah*

* * * *

"And these words which I command thee this day shall be upon thy heart . . ." (Deuteronomy 6:6)

Twice each day, every Jew recites the verse *"And thou shalt love the Lord thy God with all thy heart* and *with all thy soul and with all thy might."* This verse is phrased entirely in the second person singular. Hence, when he recites it, it is as if he were saying it not to himself but to some other person. This explains the command in the verse immediately following; i.e., "And these words which I command thee this day shall be upon thy heart." They should not be only on your lips but also in "thy heart . . ." For as a rule the span that separates lip-service from the service of the heart is as great as the distance that parts heaven from earth."

—Attributed to Rabbi Yaakov Yitzhak of Przysucha

*   *   *   *

In a similar vein, Rabbi Israel Salanter said: "When a Jew recites the verse *'Hear, O Israel, the Lord, our God, is One,'* with the purpose of proclaiming God's rule over the four ends of the earth, he must not forget to allow God to reign also over his own person."

*   *   *   *

May these words always lie ready upon your heart so that, if perchance your heart should open, they may enter it immediately.

—The Rabbi of Kotzk

*   *   *   *

"And these words which I command thee this day shall be upon thy heart, and thou shalt impress them sharply upon thy children..." (Deuteronomy 6:6, 7)

If you would impart the laws and the moral teachings of the Torah to others, you yourself must be imbued with the words you want to teach. Only then will your words leave an impression on your listeners, for "only those words that proceed from the heart can enter the heart of another."

Only if the words will "be upon thy heart," only if they are engraved upon your own heart, will you be able to "impress them sharply" also upon your children. Then your own words of instruction will act like sharp, penetrating arrows when you direct them at your children or your disciples. But if the words of God are not firmly impressed upon your own heart, your words of instruction will have no effect on others.

It is in order to stress this fact that the Scripture uses the term *ve-shinantam* ("and thou shalt impress them sharply")

381

ιather than the more common *ve-limadtam* ("and thou shalt teach them").

—*Moses ben Hayyim Alshekh*

* * * *

This word (*ve-shinantam*) expresses the idea of being sharply impressed, the meaning being that they should be impressed in your mouth, so that if a person should ask you anything about them, you will not need to hesitate about it but will be able to tell him forthwith.

—*Rashi*

In matters of faith and religion everything must be set forth sharply and clearly, without any hesitation or ambiguity, for any hesitation would verge on atheism.

—*Attributed to one of the Musarists*

* * * *

Haphtarah of Va-Ethchannan (Isaiah 40:1-26)

"Comfort ye, comfort ye, My people, says your God." (Isaiah 40:1)

Comfort yourselves with the thought that you are My people, says the Lord. Let the thought that you are My people be your greatest comfort in times of trouble.

—*Zvi Elimelekh, Rabbi of Dinov*

* * * *

Weekly Portion of Ekev (Deut. 7:12-11:25)

"And it shall come to pass because you hearken to these ordinances . . . ." (Deuteronomy 7:12)

For the conjunction "because" the Scripture uses the expression *ekev* which, when employed as a noun, means "heel"; i.e., a part of the foot used in walking. This is to teach us that whenever a person takes a step, literally or figuratively, he must first reflect whether it would be in accordance with the will of the Lord, and if he should find that it is not, he must desist from it.

The Scriptural verse should be understood as follows:

Ve-haya ekev — And it shall be that at every step *you hearken* to learn whether it is the will of the Lord that you should take that step.

—*Or Tzaddikim, attributed to the Rabbi of Sassov*

*   *   *   *

If you will hearken even to the lighter commands which a person usually treads upon with his heels, then the Lord will keep His promise to you.

—*Rashi*

Actually, according to the Sages, "the reward for performing a commandment comes only in the Life of the World To Come"; in other words, the reward for the proper observance of the commandments is not given us in this life. True, the Scripture makes frequent reference to rewards that are given in this world; e.g., "and I will give you your rain in due season," "and I will give rain to your land" and other such material blessings. Maimonides, however, explains that these promises should be taken not to imply a reward but only an assurance that the Lord will provide favorable conditions on earth in order to make it possible for us to observe the laws of the Torah, for poverty and suffering would impede the observance of the commandments (cf., "Poverty causes a man to sin against his knowledge and against the knowledge of his Creator," *Erubin 41*).

The Sages comment as follows on the verse *"Therefore shall you keep My charge"* (Lev. 18:30): "This means 'Make a hedge about My charge,'; i.e., that a man should keep God's charge inviolate by means of legal safeguards and 'hedges' of his own making so that he should never have the chance to transgress one of the commandments of the Torah. If a man makes every effort to devise such legal safeguards in order to guard against violating the commandments, the Lord in His turn will guard him from suffering, poverty, or any other

383

obstacle or impediment that might interfere with his observance of the Law.

Therefore we are told:

"*And it shall come to pass because you hearken* — if you will keep the 'light' commandments, the 'legal safeguards' which man finds easy to observe, *and keep and do them* — and keep them inviolate within hedges and legal safeguards of your devising in order that you may be able to observe the commandments, *then the Lord thy God shall keep with thee the covenant and the loving-kindness* — He will reciprocate by sending you only goodness and mercy so that nothing may disturb or hinder you in the observance of the commandments which you are so anxious to keep."

—*Imrei Shofar*

* * * *

"*. . . And He will put none of the evil diseases of Egypt . . . upon thee, but will lay them upon all those who hate thee.*" (Deut. 7:15)

We read in the Passover Haggadah how the Tannaim Rabbi Jose of Galilee, Rabbi Eliezer and Rabbi Akiba sought to demonstrate that the number of plagues with which the Egyptians were stricken was much in excess of ten. R. Jose said that there were, in fact, fifty plagues; R. Eliezer held that there were two hundred, and R. Akiba declared that the Egyptians had been stricken by a full two hundred and fifty plagues.

What difference does it make whether the Egyptians suffered ten plagues, fifty, two hundred or two hundred and fifty?

"These Rabbis," the Gaon of Vilna explained, "sought to derive the greatest possible number of plagues from the Biblical account in order to add to the number of ills which the Jews would be spared, for it is written that *He will put none of the evil diseases of Egypt upon thee.*

384

*   *   *   *

"Thou shalt not be frightened of them; for the Lord thy God is in the midst of thee, a God great and awesome." (Deut. 7:21)

The author of "Duties of the Heart"* records that a pious man of long ago has said: "I would be ashamed to fear anyone in the world other than God."

If one loves another mortal man, honors him or feels beholden to him, this constitutes no infringement on the love or honor due to God. But it is different with fear. If one is afraid of another mortal, it is a sign that he does not truly fear the Lord, for one who truly fears the Lord cannot possibly be afraid of a mere creature of His.

Therefore Scripture says: *"Thou shalt not be frightened of them:* thou shalt not be afraid of the other nations, *for the Lord thy God is in the midst of thee, a God great and awesome*: The Lord alone is to be feared, and fear of other mortals constitutes an infringement on the fear of the Lord."

—*HaKetav VeHaKabbalah, attributed to MaHaRal Margolith*

*   *   *   *

". . . thou shalt not covet the silver or the gold that is on them nor take it for thyself, lest thou be ensnared by it . . ." (Deut. 7:25)

It may come to pass that silver and gold which you have taken from an idol will bring you great profit in commerce. This may lead you to wonder whether your good fortune is not due to the power of the idol from whom you have taken them. And thus the gold and silver which you took from the idol may lead you into idol-worship.

—*Sforno*

*   *   *   *

". . . to test thee, to know what was in thy heart . . . and He afflicted thee, and allowed thee to hunger and fed thee with manna . . ." (Deuteronomy 8:2, 3)

---

* Bahya ben Joseph Ibn Pakuda

From this we learn that we are to kindle lights on the Sabbath.

—*Yalkut*

When they ate the *manna* from Heaven, the Children of Israel could taste in it the flavor of any number of delicacies. Yet they were hungry and said: "But now our soul is dried away; there is nothing at all; we have nothing except this *manna* to look to" (Numbers 11:6).

According to the Sages, the reason for the complaint by the Children of Israel was that while they could taste a great variety of flavors when they partook of the food from Heaven, all they could see with their eyes was the same *manna* each day.

Similarly, the blind will not be satisfied, regardless of how much they eat, because they are unable to see what it is they are tasting.

From this we may deduce that we must kindle lights on the Sabbath in order to increase our enjoyment of the Day of Rest, for if we do not have enough light to see our Sabbath dinner, our tables may be piled high with fine foods but we will remain hungry.

Scripture speaks of the *manna* in terms of affliction and hunger because the Children of Israel could not see the delicacies of which the flavor of the *manna* reminded them. It stands to reason, therefore, that we should kindle lights in order to make the Sabbath a delight, as it should be, instead of a hardship.

—*Attributed to Rabbi Hayyim Joseph David Azulai*

* * * *

"...that He might make thee know that man does not live by bread only but by every thing that proceeds out of the mouth of the Lord does man live." (Deuteronomy 8:3)

How could the soul, which is purely spiritual, partake of physical food?

Every creature exists only by reason of the command which

the Lord gave at the time of Creation (Cf. "the heavens were made by the word of the Lord" and "by ten Divine utterances was the world created"). It is the strength of the Divine command which is inherent in our physical food that provides no ˙shment for the soul.

When a Jew takes a fruit and recites the blessing over it, he releases that inner, spiritual essence with which that fruit was endowed by the word of the Lord at the time of its creation, and it is that inner essence which provides the spiritual food the soul requires.

This is the meaning of the Scriptural verse:

"Man does not live by bread only: man does not live from the physical bread we can see, *but by every thing that proceeds out of the mouth of the Lord does man live*: man lives only by the word that went forth from the Lord at the time of Creation which caused the bread to come into existence. It is from this spiritual essence that man lives, because that is the food which provides nourishment for his soul."

—*Likutei Torah* from *Ari HaKadosh*

* * * *

". . . a land whose stones are iron . . . and thou shalt eat and be satisfied and bless the Lord thy God . . ." (Deuteronomy 8:9, 10)

This means that you shall be satisfied by virtue of the blessing which you will recite after you have partaken of the food.

—*Rabbi Shelomo of Karlin*

* * * *

"And it shall be, if thou shalt forget the Lord thy God . . ." (Deuteronomy 8:19)

The words "and it shall be" imply joy.

—*Sages*

"And it shall be if thou shalt forget the Lord thy God" — when you will have sunk so low as to be happy and gratified

387

at the thought that you have forgotten the Lord, then *"I fore-warn you that you shall surely perish,"* then you will no longer be able to withstand destruction.

—*Rabbi Meir ben Gedaliah of Lublin*

* * * *

"And I took hold of the two tablets, and cast them out of my two hands, and broke them before your eyes." (Deuteronomy 9:17)

Only the stone tablets which were "before your eyes" were broken. The letters which had been engraved upon them flew away and remained whole. Cf. Rashi: *"And (Joseph) bound (Simeon) before their eyes* (Gen. 42:24): This means that he bound Simeon while his brothers were watching, but later freed him and gave him food and drink."

—*Attributed to Rabbi Israel of Ruzhin*

* * * *

"And now, Israel, what does the Lord thy God require of thee, but to fear the Lord thy God . . ." (Deuteronomy 10:12)

> Our Rabbis derive from this that everything is in the hands of of God except the fear of God.
>
> —*Rashi*

When man prays to God to fulfill a request of his, he cannot be certain that his prayer will be answered. The decision is entirely "in the hands of God." God is free to choose whether or not to fulfill the request.

But such doubts do not obtain when a man prays to God to inspire him with the fear of God. In that case he may be sure that his prayer will be answered.   —*Ohel Torah*

* * * *

Rabbi Israel Meir HaKohen (the *Haphetz Hayyim*) used to say: "He who believes will not be troubled by doubts and as for him who does not believe, explanations will be of no avail."

* * * *

". . . . who regards not persons nor takes a bribe. He executes justice for the fatherless and the widow, and loves the stranger, in giving him food and clothing. Therefore love the stranger, for you were strangers in the land of Egypt." (Deuteronomy 10:17, 18,19)

Nor will He take a bribe, that one should appease Him with money.

—*Rashi*

How could one possibly associate God with monetary bribes?

The implication of this comment by Rashi is that one cannot buy Divine forgiveness for wicked deeds by giving large donations to charity.

In view of the fact that providing support for widows and orphans or for a stranger who has no kin represents the highest form of charity, Scripture says:

"Nor takes a bribe: God does not accept bribes in the form of charity performed by a person motivated by the desire to buy forgiveness for his sins. *He executes justice for the fatherless and the widow, and loves the stranger, in giving him food and clothing:* Even if the man's good works should take the form of caring for widows, orphans and strangers, giving them food and clothing, God will not accept his charity as atonement for past sin, for it is written *love the stranger, for you were strangers in the land of Egypt* — you are to love the stranger because you were once strangers yourselves, and not in order to bribe God into forgiving your wicked deeds."

—*Ketav Sofer*

* * * *

Haphtarah Ekev (Isaiah 49:14-51:3)

"Thus says the Lord: 'Where is the bill of your mother's divorcement with which I have put her away?'" (Isaiah 50:1)

We read in the Book of Jeremiah (3:8): "I had put her

(Israel) away and given her a bill of divorcement."

However, according to Jewish law, divorce can be valid only if the wife "is sent away and does not return." A foolish woman cannot be divorced because she will return to her husband after he has sent her away.

Judah is like that foolish woman as regards her relationship to God. Even if God were to send Judah away a thousand times, she will always return to Him because she has no one else to whom to turn. After all, the Most High is her life's sole purpose. Therefore, according to the law, the divorce is invalid, and the prophet cries out in the name of the Lord: "Where is the bill of your mother's divorcement? I have handed it to her, but it is not valid."

—*Attributed to Rabbi Isaac Meir Alter of Ger*

* * * *

Weekly Portion of Re'eh (Deut. 11:26-16:17)

"Behold (thou), *I set before you this day a blessing and a curse."* (Deuteronomy 11:26)

Take care that you do not go after "middle roads" and compromises. Behold: I have put before you two extreme opposites — a blessing and a curse. There is no other alternative. If you do not choose the path that leads to the blessing, you have thereby taken the path that leads to the curse. There is no "middle road." —*Sforno*

* * * *

Why does the verse begin with the second person singular — ""Behold *thou*" — and then shift to the plural — "before *you*"?

"Because," said the Rabbi of Kotzk, "the portion that is set before 'you', the many, is the same for all. But when it comes to beholding it, each individual sees it after his own fashion. What he beholds depends on what he is."

* * * *

390

If you want to make a child study, you show him a penny
and a whip and say to him: "If you will study, you will get the
penny, but if you will not study, you will feel the whip." You
do this because the child is too young to understand that being
able to study is a joy in itself and that not being able to study
is a misfortune. Only when he is older and more mature will
you no longer need to let him choose between the penny and
the whip. For then he will understand that one should want to
study of one's own accord, because the possibility to study is
a blessing and ignorance is the greatest misfortune.

Therefore Moses said to the Children of Israel:

"*Behold*: look at yourself, O Israel, and be ashamed. Look
where you are after forty long years of toil and trials. *I set before you a blessing and a curse*: After all this I still must confront you with the choice between a blessing and a curse, a
penny and a whip. *The blessing, if you shall hearken*: By this
time you should have been able to understand that 'hearken-
ing' is its own blessing, *and the curse if you shall not hearken*:
and that failure to 'hearken' is its own curse. But behold, after
all these years you still are no better than a small child who
must be goaded by promises of reward and threats of punishment."

—*Rabbi David of Lelov*

*   *   *   *

"*And the curse if you shall not hearken . . . but turn aside out of
the way . . .*" (Deuteronomy 11:28)

Why is the threat of the curse given with an added qualification "*. . . but turn aside out of the way*" while the promise
of the blessing carries no other prerequisite than "*if you shall
hearken*"?

Because the Holy One, blessed be He, regards even the
good intention as equal to the deed. Accordingly, even "hearken

391

ing" in itself, without the actual performance of the good deed, is rewarded by a blessing. Evil intentions, on the other hand, are not judged as evil deeds in themselves. Therefore the curse does not come as soon as you *"do not hearken"* but only after you have actually *"turned aside, out of the way which I command you this day."*

—*Be'er Mayim Hayyim,* also
quoted by *Meir Leibush Malbim*

* * * *

". . . even unto His habitation shall you seek, and there thou shalt come." (Deuteronomy 12:5)

Why does Scripture say "shall *you* seek" and then, in the same verse, *"thou* shalt come."

The Hebrew term for "seek" also denotes "inquiring after" a person or thing.

The Sages say with regard to Zion, the habitation of the Lord: "She is Zion; there is none that inquires after her. From this we learn that she ought to be inquired after" (*Rosh Ha-Shana* 30).

What is the "search" or "inquiry" implied in this verse? It is an "inquiry" or "investigation" into the conditions that caused the destruction of the Temple, followed by an effort to correct them so that the Temple may be rebuilt.

The cause of the destruction of the Second Temple was the hatred without just cause which disrupted the unity of the Jewish people. The one remedy for this evil is the restoration of mutual love and unity in Israel.

Hence, the message inherent in this Scriptural verse is as follows:

"Unto His habitation shall you seek: You shall all search for the causes of the destruction of His habitation. Do that, and you will discover that it was due to the circumstance that you were divided into countless opposing factions. The way to re-

medy this evil is to unite, to become as one again, and then "*thou* shalt come" to Zion as one person, a people welded together by the force of unity.

—*The Rabbi of Ger*

* * * *

"*After the Lord your God shall you walk, and Him shall you fear, and His commandments shall you keep, and to His voice shall you hearken, and Him shall you serve, and to Him shall you cleave.*" (Deuteronomy 13:5)

Much the same has already been said in the preceding weekly portion (10:20): "Thou shalt fear the Lord thy God, Him shalt thou serve, and to Him shalt thou cleave." Why, then, it the commandment repeated at this point, and in the plural?

It is because Scripture is dealing with a critical situation at this point. Under normal circumstances it is enough if the individual fears God and serves Him, each person for himself. But in days when instigators and seducers are abroad in the world, the individual alone can accomplish nothing but must join with all other like-minded persons to form a group to resist these evil men.

Since Scripture here is dealing with the trouble caused by false prophets (see Verses 1-4), the Torah repeats the commandment in the plural form, to imply that in such situations all individuals must become part of a group to carry out the command "*Him shall you fear, and His commandments shall you keep, and to His voice shall you hearken, and Him shall you serve, and to Him shall you cleave.*"

—*The Rabbi of Ger*

* * * *

"*And thou shalt gather all the spoil* (of the forsaken city) *into the midst of the broad place thereof and shalt burn with fire the city and all its spoil . . .*" (Deuteronomy 13:17)

If an entire city could be led to worship idols, it is obvious

393

that its people cared only for amassing riches and had no interest in the higher things of life. This is why they sank so low that they could be induced to become pagans. Certainly, then, it is only fitting that all the wealth which caused them to descend to this state should be destroyed.

—*Avnei Ezel*

* * * *

(But these are the birds of which you shall not eat) *"... and the stork and the heron after its kinds ..."* (Deuteronomy 14:18)

Why is the stork called *hassidah* (lit. "the kind one")? Because it deals kindly with its fellow-creatures.

—*Rashi, to Lev. 11:19*

The Sages say: "Mice are evil because they call all the other mice to eat after they themselves have eaten their fill of the food they have found" (Jerusalem Talmud, *Baba Metzia,* 3).

When the stork shares its food with its fellow-creatures it is regarded as an act of kindness and the stork is called *hassidah.* Why, then, should mice be judged as evil when they do the same thing?

The mice call their fellow-creatures to eat of the wealth of others, and that only after they themselves have already eaten their fill of it. This is evil. The stork, on the other hand, gives to its comrades only of that portion of food which has been given it as its own share.

The stork's kindness lies in that it does good with its own portion, and not with the wealth of others.

—*Anon.*

* * * *

"If there be among you a needy man, one of thy brethren ... thou shalt not harden thy heart nor shut thy hand from thy needy brother." (Deuteronomy 15:7)

Scripture already speaks of "a needy man, one of thy brethren" at the outset of the verse. Why, then, does it repeat "thy needy brother" at the end?

In order to show us what our attitude should be toward the needy, regardless of the suppliant's background.

As a rule, when the suppliant is a refined person of distinguished background, one will be much more readily inclined to help him than one would an ordinary beggar with no particular distinction.

Therefore Scripture states:

If there be among you a needy man, one of thy brethren: When there will come to you a needy man who is an honorable person and of good family — "one" of his kind among thy brethren, I, the Lord, am sure that *thou wilt not harden thy heart,* but wilt gladly give him what he needs, because thou wilt be impelled by thy own heart to do so. But I require of thee that *thou shalt not shut thy hand from thy needy brother*: that if an ordinary beggar from among thy brethren should come to thee and thy heart does not impel thee to help him because he has no particular distinction, thou art not to shut thy hand but shalt assist him even if thy heart should be quite indifferent to him.

—*Imrei Shofar*

*　*　*　*

"Beware . . . that thy eye be evil against thy needy brother and thou wouldst give him nothing . . ." (Deuteronomy 15:9)

Some people, when approached for a donation, will turn down the request, saying: "I have a needy brother (or some other relation) and therefore cannot afford to give charity to strangers." One should know that such an excuse shows that the man is close-fisted by nature and does not even help the brother or relative whose need he has pleaded as a reason for not giving to others.

The interpretation of this Scriptural verse is as follows:

If *thy eye be evil,* if thou lookest askance at the poor and refusest to give charity, pleading the excuse that thou hast a *needy brother,* it is an indication that *thou wouldst give him nothing,* that thou wouldst not even assist him, thy brother, if he were to approach thee for help in his need.

He who is willing and able to support his own kin should be able to help strangers also.

—Anon.

* * * *

Haphtarah Re'eh (Isaiah 54:11-55:5)

"And all thy children shall be taught about the Lord, and great shall be the peace of thy children." (Isaiah 54:13)

According to our Sages, Jerusalem was destroyed because "they neglected the education of school children" (*Sabbath 119*). The people did not take the time to study the Law with their children. Another reason for the fall of Jerusalem was that its inhabitants harbored feelings of hatred for one another without just cause (*Yoma 9*).

Therefore, when God wishes to comfort His people and to assure them of redemption, He promises that the evils which brought about the destruction of Jerusalem will be eliminated.

"All thy children shall be taught about the Lord," we are promised. "All the children in Israel will study the law, *and great shall be the peace of thy children,* and peace and harmony shall prevail in your midst."

—Rabbi Hayyim Joseph David Azulai

* * * *

Weekly Portion of Shofetim (Deut. 16:18-21:9)

"Judges and officers shalt thou make for thyself in all thy gates . . . which the Lord thy God gives thee . . ." (Deuteronomy 16:18)

This command is intended for the officials and communal leaders who are entrusted with the task of engaging rabbis. They must not believe that because they have appointed the rabbi they are exempt from giving him the respect and obedience due him. For the rabbi is appointed not only for the congregation or the community but "for thyself," for every individual, and you must heed his instructions, because only if you will give him the respect due him will he be able to *judge the people with righteous judgment,* only then will the people obey the rabbi and abide by his judgment.

—*K'lei Hemda*

*   *   *   *

"... *for a gift blinds the eyes of the wise, and perverts the words of the righteous.*" (Deuteronomy 16:19)

One can make an inference from minor to major that personal involvement tends to "blind the eyes" to wisdom and justice. We know that the words dispensed by God are greater than His punishments. How much more, then, is it true that when a person divests himself of all personal involvement and selfish motivations and endeavors to pursue justice only, his eyes will be opened and enlightened so that he will be able to see and understand the truth.

—*Sefat Emet*

*   *   *   *

"*Justice, justice shalt thou pursue* ..." (Deuteronomy 16:20)

This means that you must pursue justice with justice. The means by which you seek to attain justice must be righteous also. You must not allow yourself to be guided by the Godless principle that the end justifies the means.

—*Rabbi Yaakov Yitzhak of Przysucha*

*   *   *   *

"*Thou shalt not plant for thyself an Asherah of any kind of tree beside the altar of the Lord thy God* ..." (Deuteronomy 16:21)

This prohibition is addressed to one who would plant a tree or build a house on the Temple Mount.

—*Rashi*

You are to see the beauty of a holy place in its sacred

character, and not look for external trappings such as beautiful landscaping or impressive edifices. If you find it necessary to beautify a holy place by such superficial decorations, it is an indication that you lack appreciation for the true beauty of holiness.

Similarly, the Sages say that "anyone who engages a judge who is not worthy is considered as if he had planted an Asherah beside the altar" (*Sanhedrin* 7). If, guided only by superficial considerations such as secular education and power of oratory, one engages a judge who lacks the qualities of scholarship in the Law, piety and morality required for that office, it is truly as if one had "planted an Asherah beside the altar," for then one has cast aside the inner beauty of Torah and the fear of the Lord for superficial, alien trifles.

—*Avnei Ezel*

*　*　*　*

"Neither shalt thou set up for thyself a pillar, which the Lord thy God hates." (Deuteronomy 16:22)

> Although it was pleasing to Him in the days of our ancestors, He hates it now because the Canaanites made it a pagan ordinance. —*Rashi*

From this we derive the maxim that, in Judaism, once a custom or thing that is good and fine in itself is taken over by the irreligious as a weapon in their fight against religion and it has become identified with their ideology we must keep away from it as from something that has become hateful in the eyes of the Lord. —*Anon.*

*　*　*　*

"If there arises a matter too hard for thee in judgment, between blood and blood, between plea and plea, and between stroke and stroke, matters of controversy within thy gates . . ." (Deut. 17:8)

If you cannot understand why so many cruel judgments and sufferings have come upon the Jewish people, *between blood and blood,* why Jewish blood is spilled like water; *between plea and plea,* why new evil laws and decrees pour forth against the Jews each day; *between stroke and stroke,* why persecution and oppression grow with each passing day, if you will not understand why the Jewish people should have to suffer so cruelly, then, know that it is all due to *matters of controversy within thy gates.* It is the constant strife among the Jews in the cities and towns and the hatred for no just cause that have brought those sufferings upon us.

—Attributed to the Maggid of Khelm

*   *   *   *

In one of his debates with Gentile scholars of his day, Rabbi Jonathan was asked by a priest:

"Why do the Sages say that he who transgresses the sentence of the Sages is subject to the death penalty? Not even every violation of the Torah itself is punishable by death. Why, then, should the procedure be so harsh against disobedience to the words of the Sages?"

"It is the same as in any kingdom," Rabbi Jonathan replied. "If someone comes into the presence of the king and commits an act of disrespect or disobedience, the king will not execute him but will turn him over to a court of justice for sentencing. But if a man disobeys the command of one of the soldiers standing guard at the gate of the royal palace, the soldier has the right and even the duty to shoot him down on the spot.

"Now in Judaism, the Sages are the soldiers who stand on guard for the Torah of our Heavenly King. Therefore any transgression of their command has more serious immediate consequences than a violation of a commandment of the Torah itself."

*   *   *   *

"Only he shall not multiply horses for himself, and he shall not cause the people to return to Egypt in order that he might multiply

399

horses ... Neither shall he multiply wives to himself, that his heart should not turn away ..." (Deuteronomy 17:16, 17)

Why, in the case of these two commandments, should Scripture list a reason not given in connection with other commandments?

Because these reasons are each commandments in their own right. The reason "and he shall not cause the people to return to Egypt" refers to the fact that Jews are forbidden to dwell in Egypt and the warning that "his heart should not turn away" represents the commandments that the Children of Israel must not allow themselves to be led astray from the path of the Law.

—Hiddushei Aggadot

*   *   *   *

"*... he shall write for himself a copy of this Law in a book ...*" (Deuteronomy 17:18)

This means that the king must write two scrolls of the Law.

—Rashi

Why did the King need two scrolls of the Law?

Because the greater the person, the more stringently must he take upon himself the yoke of the Law in order to remain humble. A King in Israel must take upon himself a double yoke of the Law of God.

It was for the same reason that the King had to remain in a bowed position throughout the prayer service. It was to symbolize that, as the King, he had to work harder than others to attain humility.

—Yalkut David

*   *   *   *

"*And* (the scroll) *shall be with him, and he shall read therein all the days of his life ...*" (Deuteronomy 17:19)

The King in Israel was to use the Law to guide him along his life's path. He was to consult the Torah on every issue brought to him, and the views set forth in the Law had to be regarded as decisive in all matters of state.

According to the Sages, King David would consult the Sanhedrin before declaring a war (*Berakhot* 3).

—*Hatam Sofer*

* * * *

"That his heart may not be lifted up above his brethren . . ." (Deuteronomy 17:20)

A king must always act sternly in order to preserve discipline and to inspire awe (*"so that his fear may be upon you"*). But this must be to the outside only. In his own heart the King must not regard himself as superior to his brethren. He must never permit the regal dignity he must preserve to the outside to penetrate into his own heart.

—*Commentators*

* * * *

(The Lord said to Moses) *"I will raise them up a prophet from among their brethren like thee . . . and it shall come to pass that whoever will not hearken to My words which he shall speak in My Name, I will require it of him."* (Deuteronomy 18:18, 19)

Said the Lord to Moses:

"That prophet will be 'like thee,' but not in every respect. When the congregation of a Korah refused to listen to thy words, thou wert permitted to decree their punishment by thyself, saying: *'But if the Lord make a new thing, and the ground will open her mouth and swallow them up . . .'* (Num. 16:30). The prophets who will come after thee will not be able to do this. I will have to take up their cause. I, the Lord, will personally deal with him who will not hearken. I, the Lord, *will require it of him."*

—*Meshekh Hakhmah*

* * * *

"(If the witness had been false) *then shall you do to him as he had intended to do to his brother . . ."* (Deuteronomy 19:19)

(We are told) "as he had intended to do" but not "as he

had done". Hence they stated that if the false witnesses have already killed (the defendant by their false evidence) they (the witnesses) are not put to death. —*Rashi*

Why does the law rule that once the defendant has been put to death for the crime with which he was charged, the witnesses who gave false evidence against him are no longer subject to the death penalty? If they are liable to execution for the mere wish to kill, would it not stand to reason that if they had actually caused the death of another by their evidence, they would be punishable by death?

Nachmanides replies:

"It is written that *'God stands in the assembly of God.'* This means that God is present at every session of the Court of Justice, to make sure that no perversion of justice will occur. Hence, the fact that the defendant has been put to death is regarded as proof that there was truth, after all, in the testimony of the accusing witnesses and the defendant was indeed guilty, for, with God Himself present during its deliberations, the Court of Justice could not have put a man to death in vain."

* *

"...*What man is there that has built a new house and has not dedicated it as yet? Let him go and return to his house, lest he die in the battle and another man dedicate it.*" (Deuteronomy 20:5)
Which is a matter that causes grief of mind. —*Rashi*

Why should the fact that another man should dedicate the fallen soldier's new home be greater cause for grief than the mere fact of his death in battle?

The pity and grief is that a Jew should die with that regret uppermost in his mind. For then his last thoughts will not be of repentance but solely of chagrin that someone else should dedicate the home he built for his own use.

—*Attributed to the Rabbi of Ger*

* * * *

"When thou shalt besiege a city for a long time . . . thou shalt not destroy its trees . . . for thou mayest eat of them . . ." (Deut. 20:19)

As a rule, when an army realizes that it will not win the victory and may have to retreat, it destroys whatever it finds in the enemy territory before retreating, in order to inflict as much loss as possible on the enemy. But if the army is sure that it will win and conquer the territory, it would not want to destroy any of the property there, because it may make use of it at a later time.

Intending to assure the Children of Israel of their ultimate victory, Scripture tells them:

"Thou shalt not destroy its trees, for thou mayest eat of them; thou art certain to conquer this land, because the Lord Himself has promised it to thee and thou wilt be able to eat the fruit of these trees once thou hast settled in the land. Why, then, shouldst thou inflict loss on thy own people by destroying the vegetation of the country?"

—*Sforno*

*   *   *   *

Haphtarah Shofetim (Isaiah 51:12-52:12)

"I, even I, am He Who comforts you . . ." (Isaiah 51:12)

The Yalkut mentions a statement by the Sages that in the end of days the Lord will ask the nations of the world to comfort the people of Israel. But then the Jews will protest, saying: "After all our years of pain and exile we have suffered at their hands, wouldst Thou really want the nations of the world to comfort us? We want the consolation from Thee, not from the nations who have caused our sufferings."

And the Lord will reply:

"If you will truly refuse to be comforted by the nations of the world but will turn to Me instead, I will comfort you Myself."

This saying of the Sages is based on the sequence of the first four "Haphtaroth of Comfort" from the Book of Isaiah, by the text of the opening words of each.

The Haphtarah (Isaiah 40:1-26) for the weekly portion of *Ve-Ethhannan* (Deut. 3:23-7:11) begins with the words: *"Comfort ye, comfort ye, My people."* The Haphtarah (Isaiah 49:14-51:3) for the weekly portion of *Ekev* (Deut. 7:12-11:25) starts with the words: *"But Zion says: 'The Lord has forsaken me, and the Lord has forgotten me.'"* The Haphtarah (Isaiah 54:11-55:5) for the weekly portion of *Re'eh* (Deut. 11:26-16:17) opens with: *"O thou afflicted, tossed with tempest and not comforted."* Finally, the Haphtarah (Isaiah 51:12-52:12) for the weekly portion of *Shofetim* (Deut. 16:18-21:9) opens with the words: *"I, even I, am He Who comforts you."*

This is a logical arrangement: The Lord first turns to the nations of the world, saying: "Comfort ye, comfort ye My people." But then Zion will say: "The Lord has forsaken me and the Lord has forgotten me. *Why, O Lord, hast Thou forsaken and forgotten me,* and allowed the Gentiles to comfort us?" Then the Lord will reply: *"O thou afflicted, tossed with tempest and not comforted,* if thou wilt refuse to be comforted by the Gentiles but wouldst have comfort only from Me, then let it be so. *I, even I, am He Who comforts you."*

—*Rabbi Meir Shapiro of Lublin*

*   *   *   *

Weekly portion of Ki Thetze (Deut. 21:10-25:19)

"When thou goest forth to battle against thine enemies and the Lord, thy God, delivers them into thy hands and thou carriest them away captive..." (Deuteronomy 21:10)

The verse may be taken to refer to the constant fight which man must wage against his eternal foe — the evil inclination.

The Sages say: "Man's evil inclination gathers strength

against him each day . . . and were not Holy One, blessed be He, there to help him, he would not be able to prevail against it."

It is very difficult to conquer the evil inclination, and this thought might deter the human being from persisting in the battle. Therefore Scripture tells him:

"When thou goest forth to battle against thy enemies, just begin the battle, and thou canst be sure that *the Lord thy God will deliver them into thy hands.* The Lord will help thee conquer the evil inclination because it is said that 'the Lord will help him who comes to purify himself.' "

—*Torat Moshe (Rabbi Moses Schreiber)*

* * * *

"If a man has a refractory and rebellious son . . ." (Deut. 21:18)

It is only fitting that the section dealing with the "refractory and rebellious son" should come immediately after the section dealing with the prerogatives of the first-born son. The first-born son enjoys special status over and above those born after him because he is the first son to be born to his parents. In the same manner, the first years of a child are considered of special importance because of the bearing they have on his future life. If he conducts himself badly in the first three months after his coming of age, when he is legally responsible for his actions (this is the age at which a bad child may be classified as a "refractory and rebellious son") it is a sign that he is a potential criminal and that eventually he will become subject to the death penalty. Biblical law deals so harshly with the "refractory and, rebellious son" (*"Let him die innocent of such crimes and let him not die guilty of them."*) because, as Rashi puts it, it is better that he should die before he actually commits "adult" crimes than after he has become guilty of them.

From this we learn that we must be careful of our conduct particularly during the period immediately following *Bar Mitzvah,* during the first days of every New Year, and indeed during the first hours of each new day, because a bad beginning can have an adverse influnce on all the future.

—*Shem MiShmuel*

* * * *

According to the Sages a man who marries a "woman of goodly form", one who has no other merit than physical beauty, will have a refractory and rebellious son by her (see Rashi's comment to Deut. 21:11).

The only way in which to raise a child successfully is not to attach importance to outer beauty but only to inner quality. The important thing is not the *appearance* of the place where one studies but the *kind* of learning one acquires. No matter how nice the classrooms, how elegant the teachers, and how fine the uniforms the students wear, if the content of what is taught is alien to the spirit and the law of Judaism, the product will not be a good Jew but a "refractory and rebellious son."

Likewise, a man who is so taken by a woman's physical beauty that he marries her despite her heathen origin is obviously one who attaches more importance to superficial glamor than to inner virtue, and it is only natural that a man with such an attitude should beget a son who is "refractory and rebellious."

—*Avnei Ezel*

* * * *

"... *So shalt thou put away the evil from the midst of thee, and all Israel shall hear, and fear.*" (Deuteronomy 21:21)

If you will eliminate all evil from your own character, others will listen to your words of reproof. But if any evil should still be left in your own conduct, they will not listen to you.

It is written: "First they adorn themselves, and only then do they adorn the others."

—*Perot Levanon*

* * * *

"Thou shalt surely let the mother bird go, but the young thou mayest take for thyself . . ." (Deuteronomy 22:7)

> And what will be your reward? If you have no children, I (the Lord) will give you children. By keeping this commandment you hasten the coming of the Messiah . . . and the coming of the Prophet Elijah.
>
> —*Midrash Rabba*

Why should the reward for the observance of this one commandment be so great; namely, that he who observes it is promised progeny and is regarded as hastening the coming of the Messiah and of the Prophet Elijah?

Because the observance of this commandment symbolizes the repudiation of selfishness.

The root of all evil and sin in this world, be it in the rearing of children, in the worship of God or in the relations between man and man is egotism, the failure on the part of the individual to set aside his own concerns and personal interests for the sake of the common welfare, of an ideal, or of spiritual perfection. Financial considerations on the part of parents may deprive children of an education in the spirit of the Law, and lust for honor or gain make for strife, jealousy, hate and many other evils. But once men will be able to set aside their personal interests for the sake of an ideal, of a great cause, there will be a thoroughgoing change for the better in all aspects of life — in the education of children, as well as in social living and in religious observance, and then the final, complete redemption will be at hand.

This is the moral lesson taught us by the observance of the commandment to send away the mother bird before taking the young from their nest. You may have captive in your hands the large mother bird and could use her for food or other personal gain. But the law of the Torah commands you to consider the welfare of others and send her away so that she should be

407

able to produce more young and the species should not become extinct.

Thus, the observance of this commandment teaches man to fight his egotism for the sake of the common good, and it is for this reason that the reward for its fulfillment is so great.

—Avnei Ezel

* * * *

"An Ammonite or a Moabite shall not enter into the assembly of the Lord ... because they did not meet you with bread and with water on the way." (Deuteronomy 23:4-5)

Why this gesture of retaliation?

We read in Tractate Sabbath 17 that the Sages prohibited the eating of the bread of the Gentiles because that might lead Jews to drink wine together with them and that, in turn, might result in marriages between Jewish men and Gentile maidens.

In view of the above, could it not be said, then, that, actually, the peoples of Ammon and Moab did well not to welcome the Children of Israel with food?

However, the Ammonites and the Moabites were not motivated by the same consideration as our Law; i.e., to preserve the integrity of the Jewish people. Their motivation in not welcoming the Children of Israel with their bread and water was to avoid closer relationships with the Jews because they knew that, in days to come, some of their daughters would indeed marry Jewish men — among them Ruth the Moabite and Naomi the Ammonite, who would become Jewesses and bring great gain to the Jewish people, a thought that was most distasteful for the Moabites and the Ammonites to contemplate.

Therefore it was only proper that they should be repaid measure for measure. Because these heathen peoples did not want their daughters to marry Jewish men, care was taken that it should be made impossible for Moabites and Ammonites to marry Jewish maidens. And because they did not want Ruth and Naomi to perform their assigned role in Jewish history, it was decreed that Jewish men should be permitted to marry Ammonite and Moabite women but that Ammonite and Moabite men should be forbidden to take wives from among the women of Israel. This was done in order that Ruth of Moab and Naomi of Ammon might be able to marry Jewish men and thus build up the royal house of David which was to wage war on these two nations and finally to destroy them.

—Yalkut HaLevi

*   *   *   *

"...and because they hired against thee Balaam the son of Beor." (Deuteronomy 23:5)

As regards their failure to meet the Children of Israel with bread and water, the Moabites and the Ammonites could have pleaded that they were poor nations and could not afford such elaborate gestures of hospitality. But apparently they did have enough money to hire Balaam to do evil to the Israelites. Therefore their refusal to extend hospitality to the Children of Israel was not due to their poverty but motivated solely by the desire to do evil to them. Hence it was sinful conduct, with no extenuating circumstances.

—Anon.

*   *   *   *

"Thou shalt not abhor an Edomite, for he is thy brother..." (Deuteronomy 23:8)

The expression Edomite (deriving as it does from *adom;* "red") may be taken as an allegory for sin, for it is written in the Book of Isaiah (1:18) "Though your sins be *red like crimson* ..."

Hence the Scriptural verse may be interpreted as follows: "Do not regard your sins as wasted threads of crimson, for you can turn them into your brothers by transforming them into merits through true repentance, and they will speak in your

409

favor, as the Sages say: 'Acts of insolence will become as merits for him.' "

—*Yesod HaTorah*

* * * *

Haphtarah Ki Tetzeh (Isaiah 54:1-10)

"Sing, O barren, thou that didst not bear . . ." (Isaiah 54:1)
Why is it written: "Sing, O thou that didst not bear?" It is "Sing O Assembly of Israel" because Israel is like a barren woman who did not bear children.
—*Berakhot* 11

Why does the Gemarah question the epithet "thou that didst not bear" but not the use of the allegoric term "O barren" for Israel?

The Sages say that the Matriarchs of Israel were barren because God wanted them to pray for offspring. "For the Holy One, blessed be He, takes delight in the prayers of the righteous" (*Yebamot 64*). We knew this because once they had prayed, these women were indeed blessed with offspring. Had they remained childless despite their prayers, this interpretation would not be valid.

This is the reason why we cannot question the use of the term "O barren" in connection with Israel. For the cause of her barrenness might well be that God considers her righteous and only yearns to hear her prayer for motherhood. If this is so, then she certainly has good reason for singing. But it is entirely justifiable to ask why, if she is one who "did not bear"; that is, one who remained childless even after uttering prayers, she should have cause to "break forth into song."

—*Mahari HaKohen*

* * * *

Weekly Portion of Ki Thabo (Deut. 26:1-29:8)

"And it shall be when thou art come in to the land . . ." (Deut. 26:1)
Fulfill this commandment (of the first fruits) because it

410

is as a reward for this that thou shalt enter the land.

—*Sifre*

Actually, the commandment to offer the first fruits was to come into force only after the Jews would have settled in the Promised Land, but the willingness of the Children of Israel, while they were still in the wilderness, to accept this obligation for that future day when they would be in their own country gave them sufficient merit to enable them to conquer the land of Canaan.

—*Malbim*

*   *   *   *

"'. . . that thou shalt take of the first of all the fruit of the ground . . . which the Lord, thy God, gives thee . . ." (Deuteronomy 26:2)

The Gemara tells us that if an important person accepts a gift, it is as if he had given a present to the giver, because of the pleasure he affords the giver by accepting his present (*Kiddushin* 7).

It is in this sense that the Scripture uses the verb "take" with reference to the offering of the first fruits. It implies that the individual making the offering thereby "takes" or accepts from God a gift in the form of the pleasure afforded him by being allowed to offer up the first fruits of his harvest. . . .

—*Nahal Kedumim*

*   *   *   *

"And now, behold, I have brought the first of the fruit of the land . . ." (Deuteronomy 26:10)

"And now" implies immediacy; "behold" implies rejoicing; and "I have brought" refers to "that which is mine."

—*Midrash*

These are the three prerequisites for the observance of any Divine commandment: Not to delay, but to perform it with speed and dispatch; to perform it with rejoicing, even as it is written: *"They rejoice and are glad to do the will of their Creator";* and not to wait until one has enough money put aside for that purpose, but to spend for the observance even those funds which he planned to use for his own needs.

—*Divrei Shaarei Hayyim*

* * * *

"And thou shalt rejoice in all the good which the Lord, thy God, has given to thee..." (Deuteronomy 26:10)

If a man receives a generous gift from a mighty king, he rejoices not so much at its actual value as in the fact that it has come from the King himself. The main reason for this joy at the gift is the thought of who its giver is.

Therefore Scripture says: *"And thou shalt rejoice in all the good* not only because it is good, but primarily in the thought that it is the Lord, thy God, who has given it to thee."

—*Tifereth Shlomo*

* * * *

(After tithing, thou shalt say before the Lord) *"I have not transgressed any of Thy commandments, neither have I forgotten them."* (Deuteronomy 26:13)

It is written in the Midrash that the mice will eat the harvest of those who have not tithed, and the Gemarah states that if one eats food from which mice have eaten, one loses his memory (*Horayot* 13).

Therefore Scripture bids him who tithed to say: *"I have not transgressed any of Thy commanments;* I have tithed in accordance with the Law, so that the mice did not eat of my harvest; *neither have I forgotten them*: and because the mice did not touch the fruit of my land, I have retained my memory and not forgotten the things I have learned."

—*Arvei Nahal*

* * * *

"Look forth from Thy holy habitation... and bless Thy people Israel..." (Deuteronomy 26:15)

And bless Thy people Israel with sons and daughters.

—*Sifri*

The commandment to offer the first of one's fruits to the
Lord applies not only to the fruits of the ground but also to
the fruit of one's own flesh — one's sons and daughters. The
very first years of their childhood must be consecrated to the
Lord, and this can be done only by rearing them in the spirit
of the Law.

The parent who does this will truly be "blessed" with sons
and daughters. His children will be a blessing to him and will
not become estranged from him when they grow up.

—*Avnei Ezel*

*   *   *   *

"Thou hast declared the Lord this day to be thy God." (Deut. 26:17)

The Hebrew term *he'emarta*, "thou hast declared", is in the
causative inflection of the verb "to say," implying that "by
reason of the good deeds thou hast performed, thou *causest the
Lord to say* that He will be thy God."

—*Abraham Ibn Ezra*

*   *   *   *

*"And the Lord has declared thee this day to be His own treasure . . .
and that thou shouldst keep all His commandments."* (Deut. 26:18)

The Lord has made you great and important by giving
you His commandments to keep. This is the distinction which
sets you apart from all the other nations. He did not give these
commandments to them, and, in fact, it is written that "any
Gentile who keeps the (Jewish) Sabbath is liable to the death
penalty."

—*HaKetav VeHaKabbalah*

*   *   *   *

(Moses and the priests said to the Children of Israel) *"This day thou
art become a people to the Lord thy God."* (Deuteronomy 27:9)

On this day, when thou takest the oath to observe the
Torah, wilt thou become a people. Israel became a nation not
by virtue of acquiring a land or language of its own, but only

413

by taking upon itself the yoke of the Torah even while it was still in the wilderness, without a land or the other tangible attributes of nationhood.

Therein lies the unique character of the Jewish people.

—Samson Raphael Hirsch

*   *   *   *

"Cursed be the man who makes a graven or molten image . . . and sets it up in secret . . ." (Deuteronomy 27:15)

The worst sin of all is to make a graven or molten image, an idol, an "abomination to the Lord" and set it up not for all to see but "in secret"; that is, to hide the idol beneath a cloak of pretty speeches and high-sounding ideals such as "national rebirth," "Jewish culture," "Jewish civilization" and so forth. When unbelief is proclaimed openly, the "graven and molten image" will stand exposed for all to see and will not constitute so great a danger as one that is concealed beneath a cover of pretty words and "sacred" concepts.

It is for this reason that Scripture deals so harshly with him who sets up his idol "in secret."

—Avnei Ezel

*   *   *   *

"Cursed be he who does not confirm the words of this Law to do them . . ." (Deuteronomy 27:26)

This curse applies to those who say that it is not necessary to observe the commandments of the Lord in practice, claiming that the important thing is that one should understand their meaning and that one should be good "in one's heart," and nothing more.

—Ketav Sofer

*   *   *   *

Nachmanides cites a Talmudic interpretation according to which "he who does not confirm the words of this Law" denotes one who "is in a position to promote the study of the

Law but does not do it." Said Rav Assi in the name of Rabbi Tanhum, the son of Rabbi Hiyya: "Even one who studies the Law, and teaches, observes and fulfills it, but fails to avail himself of an opportunity he has to strengthen it, is truly accursed."

—Jerusalem Talmud, Tractate Sotah

*   *   *   *

"Blessed shalt thou be in the city . . ." (Deuteronomy 28:3)
> In the city: by the reward for the commandments which you observe (publicly) in the city.

—Midrash

Some people observe their Judaism and perform its commandments within the walls of their own homes, but are ashamed of their religion when they go out among people, fearing that they might be called "fanatical," "old-fashioned" and such. Therefore Scripture says: "Only if you will not be ashamed to observe the commandments even in the city, when you are among others, will you receive the blessings."

In the same vein we read in the opening paragraph of the *Shulhan Arukh*: "And he shall not be ashamed in the presence of those who deride him."

—Divrei Shaarei Hayyim

*   *   *   *

He who is pious himself only without seeking to influence others to be pious is called *a tzaddik in peltz* (lit. "a pious man who envelops himself in his piety as in a cloak of fur"). What is the meaning of this expression?

Rabbi Bunim, of blessed memory, said:

"There are some who, when they are cold, wrap themselves up in fur and get warm, while the others in the room continue to freeze. But there are others who, when they feel chilly, will light a fire to make sure that the others in the room will be warm also. This is why one who is concerned only about his own piety, not caring whether or not those around him are 'warmed' by the spirit of Judaism, is described in Yiddish as *a tzaddik in peltz."*

* * * *

"And all the peoples of the earth shall see that the Name of the Lord is called upon thee, and they shall be afraid of thee." (Deuteronomy 28:10)

> "... that the Name of the Lord is called upon thee." Said the Tanna R. Eliezer HaGadol: This refers to the phylacteries on the head.
>
> —*Berakhot* 6

If this were true, would not the Gentiles have cause to be afraid of every Jew who puts on phylacteries? Why, then, is this not the case today?

Said the author of the work *Kedushat Levi*:

"The text reads not *she'al rosh,* 'the phylacteries (that are) *on* the head' but *she-be-rosh,* 'the phylacteries (that are) *in* the head.' Only if the phylacteries are not merely reposing on the head of the Jew, but are also deeply ingrained in his mind, only if the Jew will constantly recall and ponder on what the phylacteries are meant to teach us, will the Gentiles "be afraid of thee." Only a Jew of that sort is capable of inspiring such awe among the Gentiles that they will not find it in their hearts to harm him.

* * * *

"And the Lord will make thee the head, and not the tail ..." (Deuteronomy 28:13)

Why the double expression? Is it not obvious that if one is a "head" one is not a "tail"?

There are times when it is better to be a "tail" than a "head," as the Mishna puts it: "Rather the tail of a lion than the head of a fox."

—*Ethics of the Fathers 4:14*

416

Therefore Scripture says: *"And the Lord will make thee the head*: thou shalt be at the head of a 'head,' *and not the tail*: and not at the head of a 'tail,' the head of a lion and not the head of a fox."

—*Rabbi Abraham Joshua Heshel of Opatov,*
author of *Oheb Yisrael*

*   *   *   *

". . . and thou shalt be only above and thou shalt not be beneath . . ." (Deuteronomy 28:13)

It is a law of nature that stones drop quickly when thrown down, and rise only slowly when they are cast up into the air, because gravity tends to draw them down. Fire, by contrast, rises quickly and goes down slowly, because it is natural for flames to flare up. Both flames and stones move quickly in the direction in which their nature draws them and slowly when they are forced into the opposite direction.

In the same manner, the hallowed soul of the Jew is drawn up to heaven by its very nature, and any descent is out of keeping with its character. The impure soul, on the other hand, is pulled down to the ground by nature of its impurity and any ascent would be contrary to its character.

Th   the Scripture says: *"And thou shalt be only above*:   rapidly, because it is natural for thee to rise; *and thou sh...   be beneath*: and that rise shall not represent an increase in   o desirable trait which would act to drag thee down and make it   ficult for thee to rise."

However, at a later point, in connection with the curses, we read: *"The stranger that is in the midst of thee shall mount up above thee, higher and higher, and thou shalt come down lower and lower"* (Deut. 28:43). The stranger, whose soul by its nature tends to drag him down, will rise slowly and with difficulty, "higher and higher," only by degrees, like a stone which is cast up into the air. Likewise, your downfall. which is contrary to your nature, will be a gradual one. You will descend "lower and lower," and not plummet down all at once, because by nature you would tend to rise and it is difficult for you to fall.

—*Azriel Hildesheimer*

* * * *

Weekly Portion of Nitzavim (Deut. 29:9-30:20)

"You are standing this day, all of you, before the Lord your God, your heads, your tribes, your elders and your officers, indeed, even all the men of Israel." (Deuteronomy 29:9)

Whenever the need arises to take action in behalf of Judaism, to wage the good fight for the glory of God, the people all protest: "Why choose me, of all people? Leave it to the teachers, the rabbis, the leaders of the community. What can an ordinary citizen like myself do?"

But they are in grave error. When the need arises to act *before the Lord your God*, you must be *standing, all of you,* ready for action, from your "heads and tribes" down to "the hewer of thy wood and the drawer of thy water" (29:10). The entire people must unite and not be content to leave the responsibility to their leaders.

—*Butzina DiNehora*

> Because when Israel heard these ninety-eight curses (in addition to those contained in the Priestly Laws) their faces turned pale and they exclaimed: "Who could possibly stand up against these?" For this reason, Moses began to calm them, saying: "Behold, you are standing, this day, all of you, before the Lord, your God."
>
> —*Rashi*

The curses were clearly intended to make the Children of Israel afraid. Why, then, should Moses have sought to pacify the people and thus soften the impact of the curses?

Because the Children of Israel were dismayed at the idea of being thought in need of such blunt reproofs. A simple,

ignorant man must be reproved with warnings and curses. But
the man of breeding and education benefits more if one reasons
with him and gives him logical explanations why he must change
his ways.

Now the generation of the Children of Israel which stood
before Moses at that point in our history was one of breeding
and education. Hence, when they heard the crude, blunt curses,
their faces turned pale in chagrin that Moses and God should
consider them so low as to be in need of curses and threats
of physical chastisement. For this reason Moses thought it best
to calm them. He told them that the curses had not been intended for them but for future generations. *"You are standing
this day, all of you, before the Lord, your God,"* he said. "You
are standing today on a high moral level, very near to the Lord
your God, and therefore are not in need of such crude threats.
However, *not with you only do I make this covenant and this
oath . . . but with him who stands here with us . . . and also
with him who is not here with us this day"* (Deut. 29:13-14).
This covenant is made not only with you but also with the
generations yet to be born which may be less mature and hence
still in need of threats to make them obey."

—*Kehilat Yitzhak*

*   *   *   *

*"Lest there should be among you a root that bears gall and worm-
wood."* (Deuteronomy 29:17)

The initials of the Hebrew words *shoresh poreh rosh ve-
la'anah*, "a root that bears gall and wormwood" form the word
shofar. This is to teach us that the sounds of the *shofar* are
capable of uprooting from the heart the roots of evil that "bear
gall and wormwood."

—*Sefarim HaKedoshim*

*   *   *   *

419

"And it comes to pass, when he hears the words of this curse, that he blesses himself in his heart, saying: 'I shall have peace!' ... (then) all the curse that is written in this Book shall lie upon him..." (Deuteronomy 29:18, 19)

When he will hear the curses which include "every sickness and every plague which is *not* written in this Book of the Law; i.e., the death of the righteous," he may think: *"I shall have peace.* I can continue to do as I please, for as long as only the righteous will die for my sins, what reason have I to worry?"

Therefore Scripture warns him; saying: *"... all the curse that is written in this Book shall lie upon him.* He will be stricken with all those curses which are explicitly listed in this Book. For even without such calamities as the death of the righteous, which are not specified, there are still more than enough other curses which are explicitly enumerated in this Biblical portion, and therefore he must not believe that he 'shall have peace.'"

—*Artzot HaHayyim* (Commentary on the Psalms)

* * * *

"Even all the nations shall say: 'Wherefore has the Lord done thus to this land?...' then men shall say: Because they forsook the covenant of the Lord ...therefore the anger of the Lord was kindled against this land to bring upon it all the curse that is written in this book.'" (Deuteronomy 29:23, 24, 25, 26)

The Sages point out that it was an act of mercy on the part of the Lord to pour out His wrath upon the land, the stones and the wood, for if He had not destroyed the land, the Jewish people themselves, heaven forfend, might have been wiped out because of their great sins. But He chose to pour out His wrath upon the trees and the stones of the land, and the Jewish people survived.

This, then, is the meaning of the Scriptural verse:

"All the nations shall say: Wherefore has the Lord done thus to this land? They will stand and gaze in amazement at the terrible destruction and ruin which obviously were not due to

natural causes. And they will be told: 'It came to pass *because they forsook the covenant of the Lord.* The Jewish people had sinned so gravely that they themselves would have been deserving of annihilation. For this reason *the anger of the Lord was kindled against this land,* and rather than destroy the people, the Lord let out His anger upon the land, *to bring upon it all the curse.* The curse of utter ruin came only upon the land, and not upon the people, so that the Lord could *root them out of their land in anger . . . and cast them into another land* (29:27). But Israel survived and continued to exist as a people.' "

—*Likutei Ratzvo*

* * * *

"The secret things belong to the Lord our God, but the things that are revealed belong to us and to our children forever, that we may do all the words of this Law." (Deuteronomy 29:28)

Redemption will be ushered in by two distinct eras. The first is the "secret one," the time ordained for the actual coming of our deliverance, which is known only to God. But there is also another era which will be "revealed" and known before us; an era which will begin when the Jewish people will repent of their sins. The Sages say: "Even today, if only you will listen to My voice." The Messiah might come this very day, if only we would heed the voice of the Lord. When this day will come depends entirely on us and on our deeds, on whether we are willing to repent of our sins and mend our ways.

Thus, Scripture states:

The secret things belong to the Lord our God: the time appointed for the actual coming of deliverance is hidden from our view and known only to God, but *the things that are revealed,* the "revealed" era, *belongs to us and to our children forever, so that we may do all the words of this Law.* If we will faithfully observe the commandments of the Torah, we can

421

hasten the redemption so that it may even come this very day.

—*Ketav Sofer*

*　*　*　*

"And it shall come to pass when all these things will come upon thee, the blessing and the curse . . . and thou shalt bethink thyself . . ." (Deuteronomy 30:1)

It is during the time of the curse, when the Jewish people is in exile, beset with oppressors and foes, that the blessing becomes most apparent. That "blessing" is the special care and providence of the Lord which has permitted the people of Israel to survive in spite of all the persecution and oppression which it has suffered at the hands of so many great and mighty nations. As the Sages put it: "For but for the fear of Him, how could one single nation persist among the many nations?" (*Yoma 69*). If we but reflect on the great miracle that the blessing lies within the curse, that even in exile, we have with us the great Divine Providence which looks down from the windows and peers through the cracks (*Song of Songs, 2:9*), to protect us from the evil plans laid by our foes to destroy us, we must of necessity come to a point where we "bethink ourselves" and repent.

—*Ketav Sofer*

*　*　*　*

"And the Lord thy God will open thy heart . . . that thou mayest live." (Deuteronomy 30:6)

Once the Lord will remove the obstruction that is closing up your heart, you will be able to enjoy the Torah and its commandments and to delight in them even as you delight in pleasures of the body. Then you will love the Torah just as you love the other things that keep you alive, *"that thou mayest live."*

—*Ohel Yaakov*

*　*　*　*

In a similar vein, Rabbi Isaac Meir Alter, the author of the work *Hiddushei HaRIM*, explained Verse 93 of Psalm 119, *"I will never forget Thy precepts, for with them Thou hast revived me,"* as follows:

"I will never forget Thy precepts, because I know and I feel that they are life itself to me, and even as no human being ever forgets to eat, I cannot forget the precepts on which my very life depends."

* * * *

"And the Lord, thy God, will make thee overabundant in all the work of thy hand . . . for good . . . for the Lord will rejoice over thee again for good, as He rejoiced over thy fathers." (Deut. 30:9)

The Lord does good and takes great pleasure in doing good. Particularly does He take delight in being able to deal kindly with the people of Israel. Hence, if we repent of our sins and mend our ways, thereby enabling the Lord to do good to us, we afford Him pleasure by the mere fact that we have made ourselves worthy of receiving His favors. This pleasure we give to the Lord carries its own reward, quite apart from the reward due us for repentance.

Therefore, Scripture says:

"And the Lord will make thee overabundant . . . for good, the Lord will give you good things over and beyond the reward for your repentance. He will reward you also for the fact that *the Lord will rejoice over thee . . . for good;* this means that He will reward you for having made it possible, by your good deeds, for the Lord to rejoice and to take pleasure at the thought that He will be able to do good to you."

—*Yakar MiPoz*

* * * *

"It is not in heaven, that thou shouldst say: 'Who shall go up for us to heaven . . .' neither is it beyond the sea, that thou shouldst say: 'Who shall go across the sea for us and bring it to us . . . but

423

the word is very near to thee, in thy mouth and in thy heart, that thou mayest do it." (Deuteronomy 30:12, 13, 14)

It is told in *Tanna de-ve Eliyahu* that a hunter came to the Tanna Elijah and lamented that Heaven had not endowed him with the mental ability required to study the Law.

Said Elijah to the hunter:

"Has not Heaven given you sufficient intelligence to gather flax, set up snares and trap animals? Why, then, should you not have enough intelligence to understand the Law, of which it is written: 'But the Word is very near thee'?"

By this he meant to tell him: "You were not born with all the skills of hunting and trapping, were you? It was only the need to earn a living that caused you to go and learn to hunt. Do you not think that if you had felt the same inner drive to study the Law, if you had felt as great a need for the Law as you do for earning a livelihood so that you would have gone out after it and striven to acquire it even as you went out to acquire your other skills, you would be as skillful at study today as you are at hunting and trapping?"

—*Ohel Torah*

* * * *

"See, I have set before thee this day life and good, and death and evil." (Deuteronomy 30:15)

In Chapter 11, Verse 26, we are told only of a "blessing and a curse." There is no mention of "life and good," or "death and evil." The reason for their being mentioned in this chapter and verse is that this section deals with the commandments of repentance. This commandment imposes a great responsibility on man, much greater than the commandments not to sin, for it affords man a way to repent. Failure to avail oneself of this opportunity is a greater sin than even the transgression of which one has been guilty (*Shaarei Teshuva*). Hence, if the transgression alone carries a "curse" then failure to repent of it would mean death itself. Therefore, *"choose life"* (30:19).

—*Meshekh Hakhmah*

* * * *

Weekly Portion of Va-Yelekh (Deut. 31:1-30)

"And Moses went and spoke these words to all of Israel." (Deuteronomy 31:1-30)

Why are we not told *where* Moses went?

Because this verse implies that Moses "went into" or entered into the heart of every Jew. Every Jew, in every generation, bears within his heart a spark of the spirit of Moses, our Teacher. Thus the answer to our question may be found at the end of the verse. Moses, we are told, went forth *to all of Israel.*

—*Attributed to earlier Tzaddikim*

* * * *

This, too, is the reason why Scripture says of Moses that *"no man knows his burial place"* (Deut. 36:6). For Moses is enshrined not in an ordinary tomb but within the heart of every Jew.

—*Anon.*

* * * *

"And the Lord will deliver (the nations) *up before you, and you shall deal with them in accordance with all the commandment which I have commanded you."* (Deuteronomy 31:5)

When you execute vengeance on the seven nations of Canaan, you shall do it not for the sake of selfish gain and thirst for revenge but solely for the sake of Heaven, because I, the Lord, have commanded you to do it.

—*Tifereth Shlomo*

* * * *

"And Moses called to Joshua and said to him in the sight of all of Israel: 'Be strong and of good courage . . .'" (Deut. 31:7)

The melody to which this portion is chanted links the phrase "in the sight of all of Israel" with "Be strong and of good courage."

425

This is to teach us how a king or leader in Israel must conduct himself in public.

Two basic qualities are required of a King in Israel. He must be humble in his heart; he "must not lift up his heart above his brother." To the outside, on the other hand, he must present a stern front. He must be careful to guard his royal prerogatives and must not decline any of the honors due him, as it is written: "Thou shalt set a king over thee so that his fear shall be upon thee."

As we know, Joshua was an exceedingly humble man. He regarded himself as no more than a servant, making it a practice to sweep the floor of the house of study and to arrange the seats there in proper order (see *Targum Jonathan* to Num. 13:16 — "And Moses called Hoshea the son of Nun, Joshua" — "on account of Joshua's humility").

Now that Joshua was about to become a leader and ruler in Israel, Moses said to him:

"Be humble in thy own heart, but *in the sight of all of Israel be strong and of good courage.* In the sight of the people of Israel, show not humility but only strength and high resolve."

—*Meshekh Hakhmah*

* * * *

"*...thou shalt read this Law before all Israel in their hearing. Assemble the people...*" (Deuteronomy 31:11-12)

Should the command to "assemble the people" not have gone before the command to "read this Law"?

The commands were deliberately put in what seems to us reverse order, since the meaning of this Scriptural verse is as follows:

Thou shalt read this Law; thou shalt read to them the law which teaches us to *assemble the people.* When Jews dwell together in unity, that in itself is a manifestation of Torah.

—*Attributed to the Rabbi of Ger*

* * * *

"Assemble the people, the men and the women and the little ones . . ." (Deuteronomy 31:12)

> The men (came) in order to learn, and the women in order to listen, and the little ones — why did they come? For no other purpose but that a reward should be given to those who bring them.
>
> —*Rashi's Commentary on Hagiga* 3a

In this connection, the following question suggests itself:

If the men and women all had to come, it would stand to reason that they had to bring "the little ones" with them, for there would be no one with whom to leave them. Why, then, did Scripture have to state explicitly that the "little ones" were to come also?

Scripture made this specification "for no other purpose but that a reward should be given to those who bring them." Although the children would come in any case, the Torah made this a separate commandment so that it should represent a good deed in its own right and make those who bring the children eligible for a reward. "The Holy One, blessed be He, wanted to give merits to Israel; therefore He gave them a Law and many commandments."

> —*Yalkut HaUrim*

*   *   *   *

> . . . that a reward should be given to those who bring them.
>
> —*Ibid.*

By going through the trouble of bringing their little ones into the Temple, the parents demonstrate their sincere desire and firm resolve that their children should remain true to Judaism and heed the sacred words of the Law. This show of sincerity on their part will cause the Lord to reward their efforts with success, so that their children will become imbued with the spirit of the Law and grow up to become good Jews.

427

It is in direct proportion to the labor which the Jew is willing to put into the education of his children that the Lord will help him so that his efforts should bear fruit.

—*Sefat Emet*

* * * *

The work and effort a father devotes to the rearing of his child may be likened to the toil of a man who has found a pearl in a mud puddle and labors to clean and polish it. Just as this man cannot know, until he has completed his task, whether what he has found is really a pearl or whether it will turn out to be just a piece of glass, so, too, the father cannot know in advance what his child will turn out to be. It may be that all his work will be in vain and the child will remain no better than an ordinary piece of glass, as it were.

However, while the man who polishes the pearl receives no reward for his work unless what he has polished really turns out to be a pearl, the Law specifies that regardless of how his child will turn out, the father will be rewarded for the toil he puts into the education of his child, because he has then performed his duty.

This is the reason why Rabbi Joshua refers to the above saying of the Sages as a "precious jewel." For in it we are taught that the effort spent in educating a small child in the spirit of the Law is a precious jewel in its own right for which one receives a reward even if it should not yield perfect results.

—*Shaar Bet Rabbim*

* * * *

(The Lord said to Moses) *"Behold, thy days approach that thou must die; call Joshua, and present yourselves in the Tent of Meeting, that I may give him a charge . . ."* (Deuteronomy 31:14)

> When the pillar of cloud vanished, Moses went to Joshua and asked him: "What did the oracle say to thee?" And Joshua said to Moses: "When the oracle was revealed to thee, I used to know (without asking) what it had

told thee." At that moment Moses cried out: "Better one hundred deaths than one (moment of) jealousy."

—*Midrash Rabbah*

"Better one hundred deaths than one moment of jealousy." How could Moses possibly have felt jealous of Joshua, particularly since one is not jealous of one's disciples, as it is written: "One is jealous of any man except his son and his disciple."

In order to mitigate the grief of Moses at his impending death, the Lord deliberately implanted a little jealousy into his heart. When Moses realized this, he cried out in dismay: "All my life I labored to cultivate virtues. And now I find that I am afflicted with the vice of jealousy. I would rather die than go on living with that fault. *Better a hundred deaths than one* (moment of) *jealousy.*"

—*The Rabbi of Ostrowicze*

* * * *

"*. . . so that they will say in that day: 'Are not these evils come upon us because our God is not among us?' And I will surely hide My face in that day for the evil which they shall have done, in that they have turned to other gods.*" (Deuteronomy 31:17, 18)

Once they have admitted that these evils have come upon them "because our God is not among us" why should God still insist on punishing them by hiding His face from them?

Rabbi Bunim of Przysucha said that they are deserving of punishment because it is a sin to say that "God is not among us." We Jews must believe that God is with us and will not forsake us even when our troubles are at their worst; as it is written: "I am with him in the time of trouble." If they refuse to believe this, their punishment will be "in kind." Since they thought that God had forsaken them, He will really hide His face from them.

* * * *

When God hides His face from His people He does so primarily because they do not turn to God at once in times of

429

trouble with prayers and repentance. Instead, they attribute their trouble to natural, political or economic causes and as a consequence they look to natural or man-devised remedies for their deliverance. They "turn to other gods," to means of deliverance other than those which would bring them Divine assistance. "Had they turned to Me to begin with," says the Lord, "I would never have hidden My face from them."

—After Obadiah ben Jacob Sforno

* * * *

". . . that this song may be a witness for Me against the Children of Israel." (Deuteronomy 31:19)

Why does the Lord require a witness for Himself?

Actually, this song is intended to serve as a witness for the Children of Israel. God did not require the song as a "witness" to testify against the Children of Israel but only as a "witness" in their defense.

What is actually meant may be explained by the following parable:

A certain king freed his servant from prison and appointed him keeper of his treasures. Knowing that the servant had once been imprisoned for theft, the king feared that the man might be tempted to commit theft again. A second offense of this sort carried the death penalty. The king therefore entered into his record book the fact that the servant had once been guilty of theft. The members of the royal household thought that the king had made the entry to remind the servant that if he were to commit another theft, his punishment would be twice as severe as the one he had been given for his first offense. The fact, however, was that the king had made this entry not as a warning to his servant but as a personal reminder for himself not to deal too harshly with the servant in case he should repeat the offense. For, after all, he, the king, had given him the position of trust even though he knew that the servant was a habitual thief.

It is in a similar sense that the Lord took this song as *"a witness for Me."* It was to remind Him not to judge the people of Israel too harshly when they sinned. For, after all, He, the Lord, had chosen Israel to be His people even though He had known their nature (*"for I knew their imagination"* — Deut. 31:21) and their propensity to sin.

—*Malbim*

* * * *

Haphtarah Va-Yelekh (Hosea 14:2-10; Micah 7:18-20; Joel 2:15-27)*

"Return, O Israel, to the Lord thy God . . ." (Hosea 14:2)

If a man says that he will carry his case as far as the King's own throne chamber, it means that he has no chance of acquittal at the lower courts. Since he is guilty according to the law of the land, his only hope lies in obtaining a hearing from the King himself who has the right to pardon even those whose guilt has been established beyond a reasonable doubt.

The prophet Hosea says:

"Return, O Israel, to the Lord thy God: Thou canst come only to the Lord thy God with thy repentance, He alone has the power to accept thy repentance and to pardon thee now, *for thou hast stumbled in thine iniquity.* Thy sins were too great that thou shouldst have a chance for acquittal in the courts of earthly princes. Only the Lord in His mercy can forgive thy sins now and, being merciful, He will pardon them even though they were so numerous and grave."

—*Kokhav MiYaakov*

* * * *

---

* These selections from the Prophets are read on the Sabbath of Repentance (the Sabbath between Rosh HaShana and Yom Kippur.)

431

Weekly Portion of Haazinu (Deut., Chap. 32)
"My doctrine shall drop as the rain . . ." (Deuteronomy 32:2)

The hallowed words of the Torah may be likened to rain. While the rain falls we still cannot see the benefit it brings to the trees, the plants and the soil. It is only later, when the sun shines again, that we can see what the rain has wrought. We find the same to be true with regard to the words of the Law. While they are uttered we still cannot see what they will accomplish on earth, but in the end all will know what they have wrought.   —*Rabbi Simcha Bunim of Przysucha*

*   *   *   *

Rabbi Israel Salanter used to say:

"True, the mouth is said to be as far away from the heart as heaven is from earth, but we all know that when rain drops down from heaven it causes things to grow on earth."

In a similar vein, the Prophet Isaiah says:

"For as the rain comes down and the snow from heaven and does not return there, except in that it waters the earth, and makes it bring forth and bud . . . so shall My word be that goes forth out of My mouth; it shall not return to Me empty, except it accomplish that which I please and cause the thing to which I sent it to prosper" (Isaiah 55:10).

*   *   *   *

"Is corruption His? No; His children's is the blemish; a generation crooked and perverse." (Deuteronomy 32:5)

As regards the transgressions to which he is driven by lust, man can plead inability to conquer the strong evil impulse which God Himself has created and implanted into man — "for He knows our imagination, and remembers that we are dust," but he can offer no such excuse for sins he has committed out of lack of faith, because sins of that sort are not caused by physical appetites.

Which of these two motivations is the cause of a man's sins may be seen from the way in which he raises his children.

432

One whose sins are caused solely by his inability to control his physical appetites will still endeavor to train his children to become good and loyal Jews. But one whose transgressions stem from perverse views resulting from lack of faith will also corrupt his children by not raising them in the spirit of Judaism.

This, then, is the interpretation of the Scriptural verse: *Is corruption His* (God's)? *No.* The corruption of this generation cannot be blamed on the Lord Who created the evil inclination in the first place. *His children's is the blemish* ("his" here is taken to refer not to God but to the father). The sinful conduct of the children in this generation is proof that the sins of their fathers were motivated not simply by the evil inclination but by lack of faith.

—Ketav Sofer

*   *   *   *

"*. . . He set the borders of the peoples according to the number of the Children of Israel.*" (Deuteronomy 32:8)

Whatever happens among the nations of the world — their wars and disputes, the changes in their borders — all comes to pass for the sake of the Jewish people. Every political event affects the Jews. For the Lord guides the wheels of world history according to His plans for the present and the future destinies of the Jewish people.

—Rabbinic Literature

*   *   *   *

"*. . . gods that they knew not, new gods that came up of late, which your fathers did not dread.*" (Deuteronomy 32:17)

The younger generation is always a little weaker in religious conviction than the older. But in the past these differences were well within normal limits. They were differences between young and old such as could be expected and readily understood. But the gulf existing between the generations today is wide beyond belief. Indeed, the younger generation bears no resemblance at all to its parents. It is almost like a new people, with new ideals — and new idols — that were altogether unknown to the generation which went before.

New gods that came up of late — a new generation has arisen *which your fathers did not dread,* of which your fathers could not even have conceived.

—*Attributed to Rabbi Moses Schreiber (Hatam Safer)*

* * * *

"*Of the Rock that begat thee thou wast unmindful and didst forget God that bore thee.*" (Deuteronomy 32:18)

The Rock that begat thee — God created thee. *Thou wast unmindful;* He created thee with the ability to forget so that thou wouldst be able to put out of thy mind all the sufferings that may come to thee. But thou *didst forget God that bore thee.* Thou hast misused thy God-given ability to forget, promptly forgetting Him Who created you and Who gave you this skill.

What thou hast done may be likened to the conduct of a certain man who, continually in debt, was advised by a friend to feign insanity whenever he would meet one of his creditors. Unfortunately, the result was that the man eventually used these tactics also when he owed money to that same friend and the latter came to collect his debt. And his friend said to him in anger: "It was I who first gave you the advice to feign insanity when you meet a creditor of yours. Is it fair that you should now put my own counsel to use against me?"

—*Jacob ben Wolf Kranz,*
also attributed to the Rabbi of Kotzk

* * * *

"*They have roused Me to jealousy with a non-god; they have provoked Me with their vanities, and I will rouse them to jealousy with a non-people; I will provoke them with a vile nation.*" (Deut. 32:21)

When the Jews will give up their faith in the Torah for follies, when the most trifling un-Jewish fad, utterly ridiculous though it may be, becomes more important in their eyes than the eternal and hallowed commandments of the Torah, their punishment will be that they will be attacked and persecuted by a "non-people," by peoples devoid of the virtues that signify humanity, who will hate them without cause.

—*Avnei Ezel*

*   *   *   *

"See now that I, even I, am He, and there is no god with Me; I kill and I make alive; I have wounded and I heal . . ." (Deut. 32:39)

Wherever the statement "I am the Lord" appears in connection with the fulfillment of a precept, it implies that the Lord is "faithful to give reward." When the same statement appears with reference to a sin, it implies that He is "faithful to mete out punishment" (*Rashi's Commentary to Exodus 6*).

But does not the Tetragrammaton YHWH* imply the virtue of mercy? How, then, can it be used in connection with punishment? Should Scripture not have used the statement "I am God (*Elohim*)" whch would imply the Divine attribute of stern justice?

The reason why the statement "I am the Lord" is used in connection with both reward and punishment is that even punishment for sin is regarded as an act of Divine mercy and compassion. Like a father who chastises his child with the intention of making him mend his ways, so God, too, has only man's welfare in mind when He metes out punishment to the wicked.

This, then, is the meaning of the Scriptural verse:

See now that I, even I, am He: you can see that the statement 'I am the Lord (of mercy),' is used to apply not only to Divine reward but also to Divine punishment. *And there is no Elohim with Me*; even in connection with punishment I am

---

* Rendered in English by "the Lord".

described not as a "God" (of justice) but as the Lord (of mercy). *For I kill and I make alive;* whatever punishment I mete out serves solely to promote life and to further the good on earth. *I have wounded and I heal*: I smite only in order to bring about healing. Thus you can see that even the punishments I mete out are acts of mercy.

—Gan Raveh, attributed to Rabbi Solomon Kluger

* * * *

Haphtarah Haazinu (II Samuel, Chap. 22)

". . . and I kept myself from mine iniquity." (II Samuel 22:24)

Every man was created for the purpose of effecting some specific improvement in the world, and it is particularly in this regard that the evil inclination goes to work, attempting to cause him to sin.

Therefore King David prays:

"And I kept myself from mine iniquity. Let me continue to be able to protect myself from that sin which is regarded as my particular iniquity; i.e., from transgressions with regard to that which I was put into the world to improve."

—The Rabbi of Ger

* * * *

". . . and I kept myself from mine iniquity."

Another interpretation:

David prays:

"May I be guarded even from that sin which is regarded as an iniquity only in me (and not in others)." For "God judges His righteous ones by a hair's thread." He is particularly strict in His judgment of righteous men when they sin.

* * * *   *—Kodesh Yisrael*

Weekly Portion of Ve-Zot Ha Berakhah (Deut. 33:1-34:12)

"And this is the blessing with which Moses, the man of God, blessed the Children of Israel before his death." (Deuteronomy 33:1)

Why does Scripture call Moses a "man of God" in this verse?

To show his God-like virtues.

The preceding weekly portion ends with the words *"but thou shalt not go thither into the land which I give the Children of Israel"* (Deut. 32:52). Moses was not to be permitted to enter the Land of Israel. Now Moses himself stated that this tragedy had befallen him because of the behavior of the Children of Israel. (*"But the Lord was wroth with me for your sake"* — Deut. 3:26). Thus one might think that the Children of Israel were not worthy of being blessed by him. Therefore the Scriptural account goes on to tell that Moses, faithful leader that he was, did not permit himself to be influenced by such considerations but blessed his people. *"And this is the blessing with which Moses . . . blessed the Children of Israel."*

The reason why Moses is described at this point in the narrative as a "man of God" is that he acted "in the image of God," forgiving the inquity of his people and blessing them.

—*Tzror Hamor*

*   *   *   *

Why has Moses not been characterized as "the man of God" earlier in the Scriptural narrative?

Until that point Moses, who was "exceedingly humble," had not wanted to write these words about himself. But it was intended that future generations should know who Moses had been and that it was through him that the Jewish people had received the Torah. Hence, while Moses had not wanted to describe himself in such laudatory terms before, he had to do it now, *before his death.* In the words of Hillel, *"If not now — when?"*

—*Attributed to the Rabbi of Ger*

*   *   *   *

437

". . . at His right hand was a fiery law for them." (Deut. 33:2)

One day the author of the scholarly treatise *Torat Yekutiel* was asked by a Reformer to explain to him where the Oral Tradition is alluded to in the Written Law.

"The words *dat lomu,* 'a law for them,' contain the letters of the word *Talmud,*" the sage replied. "This is to teach us that, immediately after the Written Law had been given to the Children of Israel on Mount Sinai, the Talmud, the Oral Tradition, was waiting at the right hand of the Holy One, blessed be He, ready to be turned over to the Jewish people."

—*Mekor Barukh*

* * * *

"And there was a king in Jeshurun, when the heads of the people were gathered, all the tribes of Israel together." (Deut. 33:5)

There are three forms of government; namely, absolute monarchy, in which a king reigns supreme with unlimited authority, the parliamentary state ruled by a legislative body composed of the princes and "heads" of the people, and the republic where the government is in the hands of the broad masses.

It is self-evident that the laws of a nation will be fitted to its system of government. The laws of an absolute monarchy will differ from those of a parliamentary state, and the laws of a republic will resemble neither of the others.

The Jewish people, by contrast, has the Law of the Torah as its eternal heritage, no matter what system of government a future Jewish state may adopt. No matter who will reign over that state — be it a "king in Jeshurun" in an absolute monarchy, or the "heads of the people" in a parliamentary democracy, or "all the tribes of Israel together" in a republic — *"Moses commanded us a Law, an inheritance of the congregation of Jacob"* (Deut. 33:4) — the Torah will remain the law of the Jewish State forever.   —*Joseph Dov Halevi Soloveitchik*

* * * *

"Let Reuben live and not die in that his men become few." (Deuteronomy 33:6)

The men of the tribe of Reuben left their families on the other side of the River Jordan and went forth to the Land of Canaan as the advance guard of the Children of Israel. For this reason Moses blessed them as follows:

"Let Reuben live; let him remain alive and not fall in battle — *and not die* — le him not die of natural causes while the land is being conquered and distributed among the tribes, so that he may be able to return to his family. *In that his men become few* (alternative interpretation: *let the number of his men be maintained*): And when he returns, may he find all his family in the same numbers as he left them. May not one of them be missing when he comes home to stay."

—*HaKetav VeHaKabbalah*

*   *   *   *

"And of Joseph he said: 'Blessed of the Lord be his land ... and for the precious things of the earth and the fullness thereof and the good will of Him Who dwelt in the bush, let the blessing come upon the head of Joseph and upon the crown of the head of him who is prince among his brethren.' " (Deuteronomy 33:13-16)

As a rule the Law can be acquired only through moderation in pleasure (*Ethics of the Fathers 6:6*). Accordingly, the Lord first revealed Himself to Moses in a bush, an unlovely, thorny plant in the wilderness, in order to teach us that overindulgence in food and drink keeps man from truly serving the Lord.

The tribe of Joseph, however, was to be an exception to this rule. Moses promised to the tribe of Joseph that even though its land would be *blessed of the Lord, with the precious things of the earth and the fullness thereof,* he, Joseph, would still, be able to fulfill the *will of Him Who dwelt in the bush,* to do the will of the Lord Who revealed Himself in a thorny bush in the arid wilderness.

Why was the tribe of Joseph favored with this blessing? Because Joseph had had to suffer at the hands of his brethren. He had been "separated from his brethren" (alternative translation for "prince among his brethren"). This was the reason why he was deemed worthy of being able to serve the Lord even in the midst of wealth and plenty, without imposing restrictions or hardships upon himself.

—*Torat Moshe*

*   *   *   *

"And they are the tens of thousands of Ephraim, and they are the thousands of Menasseh." (Deuteronomy 33:17)

Why does Scripture speak of "tens of thousands" in connection with Ephraim but only of "thousands" in connection with Manasseh?

These numbers refer not to the size of the two tribes but to the number of enemies they will slay.

When Jacob blessed Ephraim and Manasseh, he placed his right hand on the head of Ephraim, the younger of Joseph's two sons, and his left hand on that of Manasseh, the elder (*Gen. 48:14*). It is written in the Book of Psalms: "A thousand may fall at thy side, and *ten thousand at thy right hand"* (Ps. 91:7). Therefore Moses prophecied that while the descendants of Ephraim, who had been blessed with the right hand of the patriarch, would slay "tens of thousands," the descendants of Manasseh, who had been blessed with his grandfather's left hand, would slay only "a thousand."

—*Attributed to the Gaon of Vilna*

*   *   *   *

"Iron and brass shall be thy bars, and as thy days, so shall thy strength be." (Deuteronomy 33:25)

And as the days that are thy best; namely, the days of thy youth, so shall be the days of thy old age.

—*Rashi*

440

If one locks the strength of one's youth behind iron and brass in order not to squander it on useless things, that strength will be preserved into his old age. "As thy days, so shall thy strength be."

—Hiddushei HaRIM

*   *   *   *

"*. . . Who is like unto thee? A people saved by the Lord, the shield of thy help, and that is the sword of thy excellency. And thy enemies shall dwindle away before thee, and thou shalt tread upon their high places.*" (Deuteronomy 33:29)

Remember always that thou art "a people saved by the Lord, the shield of thy help" and never boast of thy own strength. If ever thou shouldst become arrogant and believe that it was thy strength that defeated thy enemies, that excellency with which thou hast been blessed will be changed into a weapon turned against thee.

And that is the sword of thy excellency: Thy arrogance will turn into a sword which will cause the Lord to turn away from thee and to deliver thee up to thy enemies. For the Lord has said of the arrogant: "He and I cannot dwell in the same abode."

—Orakh LeHayyim

*   *   *   *

"*So Moses, the servant of the Lord, died there . . .*" (Deut. 34:5)*

If a teacher studies the Law with disciples and leads many to righteousness, the study and the worship conducted by the disciples are credited to the teacher as if he had performed these acts himself, even after he himself has died.

---

* The syntax of the Hebrew of this verse differs significantly from the English rendering. The literal translation of the Hebrew verse is: "So Moses died there, the servant of the Lord," and conveys a meaningful message concerning the personality of Moses.

The Mishna says of Moses that he "was righteous and led the people to righteousness; hence the merit of the people is attributed to him" (*Ethics of the Fathers 5:21*). Therefore whatever study and worship the Jewish people will perform until the end of time will be credited to Moses. Thus Moses will remain "the servant of the Lord" even *after* he "died there."

—*Mevasser Tzedek*

* * * *

"*. . . and no one knows his sepulchre until this day.*" (Deut. 34:6)

Why should Scripture have to tell us in so many words that no one knows where Moses was buried? Would the fact that the Scripture does not explicitly mention the place of his sepulchre not be sufficient indication that the place is unknown?

Scripture was so explicit on purpose, in order to show that every single word which Moses wrote in the Torah is true. In any other nation, a man who would have performed so many miracles as Moses and who would not have changed until the very end — ("*his eye was not dim nor his natural force abated*" — Deut. 34:7) would never have allowed it to be admitted that his burial place was unknown. If not he, then at least his people would have invented some legend to the effect that he was not buried at all but ascended straight into heaven, and they would have deified him.

Moses, however, did not resort to such fiction. He wrote out in so many words that he "died there" and that "no one knows his sepulchre," so that all the people should know the truth beyond the shadow of a doubt. We see, then, how true every single word of the Torah is, for had Moses wanted to falsify anything, this would have been his best chance to do it.

This was the reply of Rabbi Jonathan Eibeschuetz (1690-1764) to the question of an important nobleman about the fact that Moses had written of himself that he had spent forty days and forty nights on Mount Sinai without food or drink. How, the nobleman asked, could Moses have written down as facts alleged events of which no one knew except himself? Could not anyone have challenged the truth of these tales, insisting that this account had been a figment of Moses' imagination?

In reply, Rabbi Eibeschuetz cited this scriptural verse, pointing out that if Moses had ever wanted to give himself credit for things he actually had never done, this final section of the Pentateuch would have afforded him the best opportunity to do so. But Scripture points out deliberately that, instead, Moses merely wrote of himself that "no man knows of his sepulchre." The intention was to show us that every word of the Torah is true.

—Kehilat Yitzhak

* * * *

Haphtarah Ve-Zot HaBerakhah (Joshua, Chap. I)

". . . but thou shalt meditate therein day and night, that thou mayest observe to do according to all that is written in it." (Joshua 1:8)

If you will meditate in the Torah day and night and immerse yourself in it, you will find that everything you must "observe to do," including the laws of the Oral Tradition, the legal safeguards, and the customs and Rabbinical ordinances, is already implicit in the Written Torah. The entire Oral Tradition can be derived from the thirteen canons by means of which the Torah is interpreted, from homilies, grammatical rules, inferences and Biblical exegesis. Likewise, all the *novellae* that will ever be stated are directly implicit in the Written Law.

But if one is to understand this, he must study much and meditate in the Law most diligently.

—Malbim

THE END

WELLSPRINGS OF TORAH

PASSOVER

PASSOVER

"The Great Sabbath"

The Sabbath immediately preceding Passover is called "The Great Sabbath" because of the great miracle which came to pass on that day. In the year that the Jews went forth from Egypt, the tenth day of the month of Nissan fell on a Sabbath. It was on the tenth of Nissan that the Jews took lambs, which the Egyptians worshipped as idols, and consecrated them as the Paschal sacrifice. And the Egyptians gnashed their teeth and were powerless to put a stop to the slaughter of their idols.

—Rabbi Jacob ben Asher, Tur Orakh Hayyim

* * * *

The question has been asked whether this miracle would have been any less great if the tenth day of Nissan would have fallen on a weekday that year.

It is a known fact that the plagues were suspended on Sabbaths (*Baal HaTurim Vo-ere*). In that year the tenth of Nissan fell during the period when the land had been stricken with the plague of darkness. Now if the tenth of Nissan that year would have fallen on a weekday it would have been dark and the Egyptians would not have been able to see the Jews preparing to slaughter lambs. But since it was a Sabbath and the plague had been temporarily suspended, the Egyptians were able to see all that was going on, and the miracle lay in the fact that they could see it all, but were powerless to act to stop it.

—Devash L'Fee

* * * *

The preparation of the Paschal sacrifice was the first Divine commandment issued to the Jews. True, the Patriarchs and their

447

children had already observed the laws of the Torah before, but they had done so out of their own free will without having been explicitly commanded to do so.

The Sages say: "He who is given a commandment and fulfills it is greater than he who acts without having been given the commandment." The Sabbath directly preceding the Exodus was called "The Great Sabbath" because from that day on the performance of the commandment entailed more merit than it had before the commandment had been officially issued to the Jewish people.

—Olelot Ephraim

* * * *

Until the time of the Exodus the Sabbath had only one purpose; namely, to recall the creation of the world by the Divine Creator (*"for in six days the Lord made heaven and earth . . ."*). But with the Exodus, the Sabbath was given still another function: to commemorate the miracles wrought for us at the time of our departure from Egypt (*"And thou shalt remember that thou wert a slave in Egypt and that the Lord thy God redeemed thee from there"*). Thus the importance of the commandment to observe the Sabbath became even greater than it had been before; hence the designation "The Great Sabbath."

—Sefat Emet

* * * *

The Haftarah for the Sabbath Preceding Passover (Malachi 3)
"Bring the whole tithe into the storehouse and try Me now with this." (Malachi 3:14)

Why should the Lord have chosen the commandment of tithing as the precept by which to test Him?

When a merchant, coming into a large store to buy rolls of yard goods and reading on each roll a tag stating its yardage, wants to determine whether the yardage stated on the tags is correct, he will choose for testing one of the rolls which seems to have a yardage smaller than that stated on its tag. If, on measuring that one roll, he finds that, contrary to his expectations, the yardage is as stated on the tag, he will assume that the tags on the other rolls, too, are correct.

This same rule can be applied also to the question raised here. It is true that the Lord promised us a reward for the fulfillment of all His commandments; i.e., *"and if you will surely listen to My commandments . . . I will give you rain in due season . . . and you shall eat and you shall be satisfied . . ."* Now in the case of other commandments, one is more likely to believe in the validity of these promises, because the observance of these precepts entails no immediate, obvious loss. But in the case of the commandment to tithe, it is somewhat more difficult to believe that there is indeed a reward for its fulfillment, because its observance entails the sacrifice of part of the harvest, causing an obvious loss to the farmer.

Therefore the Lord says: "Choose tithing as the commandment with which to test Me, and you will see that even in the case of a commandment whose observance seems to you to entail a loss, the reward will be a blessing. Once you have found this out, you will be more inclined to believe that you will surely receive blessings also for fulfilling the other commandments, which do not involve such obvious losses as this one."

—*Maggid of Dubno*

* * * *

"Then they that feared the Lord spoke with one another, and the Lord hearkened and heard, and a book of remembrance was written before Him for those who feared the Lord and thought upon His Name." (Malachi 3:16)

Why is נדברו, the Hebrew for *"spoke with one another,"* in the passive and not in the active mood?

When God-fearing people gather, their conversation will deal with ways and means of strengthening the Law and religion of Judaism, and even if their deliberations should not bring concrete results immediately (as would be implied by the active mood) the Lord hearkens and hears, and a book of remembrance is written before Him. A record, as it were, is made in Heaven of their talks and deliberations, and of their thoughts on how the Jews may be led to be more punctilious in observing the commandments, and even if they should find themselves unable to carry out that which they planned to do (as implied by the passive mood), "the record is taken for the act . . ."

—Haphetz Hayyim

* * * *

"Then you shall again discern between the righteous and the wicked, between him who serves God and him who does not serve Him." (Malachi 3:18)

"The descriptions *'He who serves God'* and *'he who does not serve Him'* both refer to those who are perfectly righteous, but he who studied his chapter only one hundred times is not to be compared with him who read it one hundred and one times."

Come and see how important the study of the Torah is. Merely by reason of studying less than usual on just one day, a man may be considered as one who "does not serve God." He may have repeated his chapter one hundred times over, but by missing so much as only one period of study, he already ceases to be a servant of the Lord . . .

—Musarist Writings

* * * *

"Behold, I will send you Elijah the Prophet before the coming of the great and awesome day of the Lord" (Malachi 3:23)

Why does the text read ". . . *before the coming of the great and awesome day* . . ." instead of ". . . *before the coming of the great,* mighty *and awesome day* . . ."?

According to the Sages, God is described as "mighty" even in the days of our exile while His children are ground beneath

450

the heel of the heathen, because He is sufficiently "mighty" to restrain His anger and to look on in apparent silence while His children are being tortured by their foes (*Yoma 69*). However, when the great day of redemption will come, God will no longer remain silent and restrain His wrath but will exact vengeance for the Jewish blood that has been shed and for the sufferings of His people. For this reason the Hebrew term "mighty", which would connote the strength implied in self-restraint, is not used in this passage, which refers to the day of final judgment and deliverance.

—*Hatham Sofer*

* * * *

"*And he* (the Prophet Elijah) *shall turn the heart of the fathers to the children, and the heart of the children to their fathers.*" (Malachi 3:24)

If parents would concern themselves with the training of their children and not let them run wild but see to it that they receive a good education, the children would not become estranged from their parents. Today's tragic rift between parents and children is due to the fact that parents do not take an interest in the education of their offspring.

The Prophet Elijah will "turn the heart of the fathers to the children"; i.e. he will cause a change for the better in the hearts of the parents so that they will take a renewed interest in their children and attend to their education. Once this comes to pass, the hearts of the children will also be turned to their parents once again and they will no longer be estranged from one another as they are now.

—*Musarist Writings*

* * * *

Preparing for Passover

The observance of the Festival of Passover is surrounded by an abundance of legal safeguards against possible violations

451

of the pertinent laws. These legal safeguards occupy a most important position in Judaism. Even while they were slaves in Egypt and unable to observe some of the laws explicitly stated in the Torah—they were forced to do work connected with idol worship and to violate the precept of circumcision — the Jews continued to observe the legal safeguards; that is, they did not change their names or their language, and they kept away from immorality. And it was on the strength of their continued observance of these legal safeguards that they were redeemed from slavery. It is for this reason that the observance of the festival which commemorates their liberation entails the observance also of so many safeguards against violation of the actual Passover laws.

Indeed, the survival of the Jewish people in exile, the fact that they did not merge with the other nations, is due solely to their regard for the legal safeguards which stressed their isolation from the other nations and their unique character.

We need recall only what happened in the days of the Babylonian exile, when the Jews in Babylonia kept the laws explicitly stated in the Torah but ignored the safeguards, changing their language (*"there were among them people who spoke the language of Ashdod"*) and changing their names. When they adopted these alien ways, they fell victim to disastrous assimilation; they married non-Jewish women and mingled with the other nations.

The strength of the safeguards surrounding Jewish law lies in the fact that they have preserved the Jewish people and will eventually bring about Israel's redemption.

—*Meshekh Hakhmah*

*   *   *   *

It is a Jewish custom to collect money at Passover time and to distribute it among the poor, in order to enable them to prepare adequately for the holiday. (*ReMo 429*)

The custom of giving *tzedaka* or charity before Passover is based on the Biblical designation of the holiday as *Hag Ha-Matzot* (the Feast of Unleavened Bread), for the Hebrew letters which spell the word *matzot* (MaTZoT) form the initials also of the saying "*TZ*edakah *T*atzil *Mi*-mavet," or "charity delivers from death." In the word *matzot* the Hebrew *tz*, the initial letters of *"tzedaka,"* stand between the letters *m* and *t* which, if read consecutively, would spell *met*, "death". This implies that charity can nullify the decree of death.

—*Sefer Shimon VaLevi*

* * * *

The Sages relate the following incident: "Rabbi Mathnah preached to the people of the city of Paponia that their women should only use *mayim she-lanu* for the dough for the unleavened bread. Now the term *mayim she-lanu* (lit. "our water") refers to water which has been allowed to stand in a vessel overnight, and Rabbi Mathnah had meant that the people should use only water that they had taken from the lake and let stand in a container overnight. But all the people of the city brought their containers to him and said to him: "Give us water! Give us water!" They had misinterpreted the rabbi's directions, believing he had meant that *mayim she-lanu* referred to a special kind of water and he had to explain to them that he had meant nothing else but ordinary water which had been allowed to stand overnight (*Pesahim 42*).

Now why should the Sages want to tell us this story? What lesson is there to derive from the ignorance of the people of Paponia?

The intent of the Sages in relating this incident is to show how greatly even the ignorant masses of those olden days respected the Sages. If a rabbi in our own day were to announce

453

that his congregation could use only "our water" or "our flour"
for the baking of *matzot* for Passover, the entire community
would rise up in indignation and demand why the rabbi's water
and flour should be any holier than ordinary water and flour,
and suspect him of all sorts of impure, mercenary motives. Not
so the people of Paponia. When they heard their rabbi's directive that they use "our water," they asked no questions, but went
with great and simple faith and brought all their vessels to the
rabbi so that they might be able to get the prescribed water from
him.

This curious incident, then, is an illustration of the faith
which all the Jews in those days had in their sages and spiritual
leaders.

—Abraham Bornstein

*   *   *   *

The Search for Leaven
Only after having gathered the water for the fulfillment of
the commandment to bake the unleavened bread should one proceed with the observance of the commandment to search for
leaven.

—SheLaH Hakodosh

*   *   *   *

The search for leaven, which symbolically implies the search
of our own hearts for evil and the removal thereof, is a very difficult task. But if one proceeds to it after having already begun to
busy oneself with the baking of the unleavened bread, the fulfillment of that other positive commandment makes it easier to go
on with the labor of searching out the leaven.

The fulfillment of the command to "do good" helps one in
the observance of the more difficult precept to "keep away
from evil."

—Anon.

*   *   *   *

"All the leaven which I have in my possession." (Passover Haggadah)

According to the Sages, "leaven" denotes sin. All the leaven and bread existing in the world is "in *my* possession"; i.e. it exists because of me. I have a portion in it. The Sages say: "He who does one good deed causes the entire world to be judged on the scale of merit; he who commits one sin causes the entire world to be judged on the scale of sin." This would mean that I bear part of the guilt if there is any evil left in the world, for by my actions I could cause the entire world to be judged on the scale of merit, and then there would be no leaven left in the world.

—*Rabbi Barukh of Medzibozh*

* * * *

" . . . Pockets must be searched . . ." (ReMa #433)

Pockets and bags must be thoroughly inspected to make sure that they do not contain any money gained through theft, robbery or fraud. In view of the fact that the search for leaven symbolizes the uprooting of evil and the clearing away of all sin from our hearts, it behooves us to be exceedingly careful with regard to sins committed in our relations with our fellowmen, and to rid our pockets also of all money that is not rightfully ours, for otherwise our repentance will be of no avail.

—*SheLaH Hakodosh*

* * * *

The total numerical value of the Hebrew letters in *hametz* (leaven) is greater by three than the total numerical value of the Hebrew letters in *matzah* (unleavened bread). *Hametz* = 138; *Matzah* = 135. This difference of three alludes to the three vices — envy, greed and lust for honor, which are at the root of many evils symbolized by *hametz*. These three vices "remove man from this world," just as the eating of leaven on Passover is subject to the penalty of *karet* (being cut off). Even as people do not abstain from leaven all year long, so, too, do they not remove themselves from these three vices except on Passover.

—*Hatham Sofer*

* * * *

The Eve of Passover

"He who eats unleavened bread on the Eve of Passover is as if he had come to his betrothed in the house of his father-in-law." (Jerusalem Talmud)

Even as a man may come to his bride only after the Seven Blessings have been recited beneath the marriage canopy, unleavened bread may be eaten on Passover only after the following seven blessings have been recited at the *seder* table: (1) the blessing over the First Cup (of wine); (2) the *Kiddush*; (3) the blessing giving thanks for our redemption; (4) the blessing over the Second Cup; (5) the blessing over the washing of the hands; (6) the blessing over bread; and finally (7) the special blessing prior to eating unleavened bread.

The *she-heheyyanu* ("... who hast granted us life and sustenance and permitted us to reach this season") is not counted because that blessing can be recited in honor of the festival as soon as it grows dark, and even in the street, nor is the blessing over the greens included because we eat the greens only to bring to the attention of our children the fact that this is an unusual meal.

—*In the name of* מהר"א

* * * *

The Festival of Passover

Why do we refer to this festival as "Passover" when the Torah always refers to it as the "Feast of Unleavened Bread"?

It is a known fact that the Lord always take great pride in the virtues of the Jewish people, and that the Jewish people, in turn, extols the greatness of its God. The Sages say: "What is written upon the phylacteries of the Master of the Universe? (It is written) 'And who is like Thy people Israel, one nation on earth?' (*Berakhot* 6). As for the Jews, they always say: 'Hear O Israel, the Lord is One.' "

Thus, by referring to this festival as Passover, we recall the greatness of God Who redeemed the Jewish people by passing over the Children of Israel and sparing our homes. The term "Feast of Unleavened Bread" used in the Bible, in turn, signifies God's pride in the Jewish people, who had been willing and ready to follow Moses into the wilderness without even taking food with them for the journey.

Thus, God in the Torah refers to the festival as the "Feast of Unleavened Bread" in order to proclaim His pride in His people, while we call it Passover in order to declare the praise of our God.

—*Kedushat Levi*

WELLSPRINGS OF TORAH

SEFER HaMITZVOT

SEFER HaMITZVOT

1 *The Commandment To Procreate*

And God said to them: 'Be fruitful and multiply . . .' " (Gen. 1:28)

God wanted the world to be inhabited by men, because He did not want the world, which He created, to lie empty and barren, even as it is written, "He did not create it to be desolate but to be settled." This is a very important commandment because it is only through the fulfillment of this precept that all the other commandments can be observed. For the commandments were not given to the angels above, but to men on earth.

—*Sefer HaHinukh*

* * * *

Ben Azai said: "He who does not fulfill the commandment to procreate is as if he had shed blood" (*Yebamot* 63:72)

If a man has an opportunity to make a change for the better somewhere and fails to do so, it is as if he had destroyed the thing he had left unchanged. For instance, if someone sees an open pit and does not close it, it is as if he had dug it himself. (*Baba Kamma* 48)

Therefore it follows that if it is incumbent on man to increase the population of the world and he fails to do so, it is as if he had actually reduced the world's population by committing murder.

—*Rabbi Abraham Bornstein*

* * * *

The commandment to procreate is the first commandment of the Torah and the command that each man must write a

Scroll of the Law for himself comes last, because even as the commandment to write a Scroll of the Law is meant to insure the preservation of the Written Law, so the commandment to procreate is intended to assure the fulfillment of the laws of the Oral Tradition. For the Oral Tradition, which directly follows the Written Law, can be fulfilled only if parents beget children to whom they can transmit the tradition, and if these children in turn pass it on to their descendants in an unbroken chain.

—Paraphrased from Writings of
Rabbi Samson Raphael Hirsch

* * * *

As for those who are physically incapable of having children, or whose children — Heaven forbid — have all died, their study of the Law and their good deeds are credited to them to offset their failure to fulfill the commandment to procreate. Said Isaiah the Prophet: "Thus says the Lord concerning the eunuchs who keep My Sabbaths and choose the things that please Me, and hold fast by My covenant, even to them will I give in My House and within My walls a monument and a memorial better than sons and daughters." (Isaiah 56:4-5)

—Zohar (Va-Yeshev)

* * * *

2. Circumcision

"*. . . every male among you shall be circumcised . . .*" (Gen. 17:10)

It was the wish of the Most High that the people which He had set apart from all the other nations and to which He had given His Name bear a special permanent mark upon their bodies so that they may be set apart from all the other nations by a physical symbol even as they are distinct from them in mind and spirit.

462

It was the will of God that this physical mark, which is an improvement of the body, should be made by human hands in order to teach man that even as he can perform the act of circumcision with his own hands to improve his body, so, too, he is capable of acting on his own initiative to improve his mind and spirit by being righteous and performing good deeds.

—*Sefer HaHinukh*

* * * *

Our Sages say that the commandment of circumcision is so great that it reaches up to the Throne of Glory.

We know this from the text of the Torah itself, for the initials of the words in the verse *"Mi Ya'ale Lanu Hashamayima"* ("Who shall ascend to Heaven for us?") (Deut. 30:12) form the word *Milah* — Circumcision.

—*Sefer HaBohir*

* * * *

The first man with whom God made an everlasting covenant was our father Abraham, who had spread the belief in the One True God. For this reason the act of circumcision serves as the symbol of the covenant in Judaism.

Once a Jewish man has been circumcised, he remains a Jew even if he should transgress other laws of the Torah, important though they may be. But if he has not been circumcised, he cannot be considered a Jew under any circumstances because he then lacks the mark of the covenant that is symbolic of Judaism as proclaimed by our father Abraham.

—*Sho'el UMeshiv*

* * * *

3. *The Prohibition Against Eating the Sinew of the Thigh-Vein*

"Therefore the Children of Israel do not eat the sinew of the thigh-vein which is upon the hollow of the thigh to this day." (Gen. 32:33)

This prohibition is meant to teach the Jews that though

they may suffer exile and persecution at the hands of the nations and of the children of Esau, they must have faith that they will never perish. Their race and their name will endure forever, and one day a redeemer will come and deliver them from the enemy. Whenever they have occasion to observe this prohibition, they will remember this and hold fast to their faith and their righteousness at all times.

Even as the angel, the emissary of Esau, had wrestled with our father Jacob in order to kill him, so, throughout the ages, the descendants of Esau will fight the children of Jacob. But even as the angel was unable to do more than cause a slight injury to the leg of Jacob, so, too, the children of Esau may be able to hurt the children of Jacob, but they can never destroy them. Finally, even as the sun shone upon our father Jacob to heal him, so we, his descendants, will yet behold the sunlight of the Messiah who will redeem us and remove all our ills.

—Sefer HaHinukh

*   *   *   *

According to the author of the *Zohar,* the statement that "he (the angel) touched the hollow of his (Jacob's) thigh" carries the symbolic implication that the angel sought to inflict harm upon the "pillars of the Torah," meaning the men who act as supporter to those who are constantly engaged in the study of the Law.

This is to teach us that the agent of Esau makes war particularly on those who are engaged in the study of the Law because these are the men who insure the survival of Judaism. He fights them by keeping Jewish householders from supporting the students of the Law so that they will be unable to continue their sacred task.

The prohibition against eating the sinew of the thigh vein is a symbolic reminder to the Jews not to allow themselves to be led astray by the forces of evil which seek to inveigle them into using their wealth for their own enjoyment rather than for the support of the study of the Law. Jews must remember that, like the act of the angel to destroy the sinew of Jacob's thigh, such forbidden enjoyment of riches is a way of strengthening the evil symbolized by Esau.

—*HaDeah Ve-HaDibbur*

* * * *

4. *The Sanctification of the New Moon*

"This month shall be to you the beginning of months." (Exod. 12:2)

This is the commandment to "sanctify the months"; i.e., to establish the date of the New Moon every month and to observe it, and to institute leap years by intercalating an additional month — a "Second Adar" — in specified years. These arrangements must be made by a Court of Jewish Law which is great in wisdom and duly qualified to decide in matters of law and which has its seat in the Holy Land. This commandment includes also the establishment of the dates for the Festivals each year in accordance with the above procedure, as it is written in the Law: "This month shall be to you the beginning of months", (lit. "New Moons"), meaning that *Rosh Hodesh* is to be observed when you behold the New Moon. If you should be unable to see the moon, the date of Rosh *Hodesh* must be computed by the method devised for this purpose. Maimonides states that this commandment also includes the institution of leap years, as opposed to Nachmanides, who held that the "sanctification of the months" and the institution of leap years are two separate commandments. Maimonides bases his reasoning on the premise that the basic purpose of the leap year is the same as that of the commandment to "sanctify the months," namely, to enable the Jews to observe the Festivals of the Lord in their proper season. For example, we are commanded to celebrate Passover in the springtime when the harvest ripens, and Sukkot in the fall season when the harvest is gathered in from the fields. In order to make up for the difference between the solar year, which regulates the seasons, and the lunar year, by which the Jews count their months, an additional month must be intercalated in certain years so that the Festivals may always fall at the proper season of the year.

—*Sefer HaHinukh*

* * * *

The commandment to establish and to sanctify the New Moons, which includes also the Festivals, is incumbent only upon Jews and must be performed by the Court of Jewish Law. The Lord sanctified the Jewish people (". . . and ye shall be holy . . .) and since they are thus sanctified unto God, whatever they will sanctify will also be holy.

If you wish to understand this, study the laws pertaining to the holy vessels in the Temple. We are told that when Moses sanctified the Tabernacle he also sanctified the vessels in it, and that from that day forth, whatever the priest placed into these sacred vessel became holy also.

—*Midrash*

* * * *

The commandment to "sanctify the New Moon" can be observed only in the Holy Land. The Jerusalem Talmud takes the verse "From Zion shall go forth the Law and the Word of the Lord from Jerusalem" to refer specifically to the commandment to sanctify the New Moon.

Why should this verse which speaks of the "Torah" and the Word of the Lord" be construed to refer specifically to this one commandment?

The answer is that while the Law as such was given to

the Jewish people on Mount Sinai, and not in Zion or Jerusalem, the commandment to sanctify the New Moon was assigned explicitly to a Court of Jewish Law which sat in Jerusalem. We know that even if these scholars should be "wavering,
erring or proclaiming the New Moon when they had not really
seen it," any decision they may hand down is law. Hence the
"Law which goes forth from Jerusalem" can only be that law
which is implemented by the Court of Jewish Law in Jerusalem; namely, the sanctification of the New Moon.

—The Author of *Avnei Nezer*

* * * *

The Torah uses the term "Sabbath" also in reference to certain Festivals. Thus, "the morrow of the Sabbath" is the morning
after First Day of Passover. This is to teach us that the Festivals
whose dates must be established anew each year by the Sages
are no less sacred than the Sabbath which was fixed permanently
by the Lord Himself at the time of Creation.

However, the Sadducees, denying the validity of the Oral
Tradition, refused to recognize the authority of the Sages to
make enactments with binding force. They therefore rejected
the interpretation whereby the "morrow of the Sabbath" was
taken to refer to one of the Festivals, and insisted on the literal
construction of the term. As a result, they would always offer
up the *Omer* on a Sunday morning. However, this view was so
strongly opposed by the Sages, who could cite massive evidence
from the text of the Written Law itself in their support, that
eventually it became clear to all that "the morrow of the Sabbath" refers not to a Sunday morning but to the morning after
the First Day of Passover.   —*Rabbi M. Z. Margolies*

* * * *

5. *The Slaughtering of the Paschal Lamb*

"... *and the whole assembly of the Congregation of Israel shall kill*
(*the Paschal lamb*) *at dusk.*" (Exodus 12:6)

We are commanded to slaughter a yearling lamb without blemish in the Temple on the fourteenth day of the month of Nissan. This commandment is meant to have the Jews remember for all times to come the great mircles which the Lord wrought for them when they went forth from Egypt.

—*Sefer HaHinukh*

* * * *

In ancient Egypt the lamb was an object of worship. Thus the Jews, by publicly slaughtering a lamb as a sacrifice to the Lord, openly repudiated idol worship and proclaimed the Unity of God.

It is written in the Torah concerning the Paschal sacrifice: "Then Moses called all the elders of Israel and said to them: *Draw out and take for yourselves lambs. . . .*" The Sages interpret this verse as follows: *"Draw out* — withdraw your hands from idol worship; *and take for yourselves lambs* — for the observance of the commandment." It was by fulfilling this particular commandment that the Jewish people symbolically rejected idol worship.

—*Sefarim*

* * * *

The lamb is a very delicate creature so that even the slightest blow will cause hurt to its entire body. It is for this reason that the Jewish people is likened to a lamb ("Israel is a scattered lamb"). When any one Jew sins, the entire Jewish people feels it and bears full responsibility for the act, as it is written, "all Jews are responsible for one another." Since the first requirement for our redemption is that the Jewish people should be made aware of this responsibility, it was ordained that the Paschal offering, which is the offering of redemption, should be a lamb. . . . For this reason, too, allusion is made to the law

468

of "agency" in the Torah in connection with the law pertaining to the slaughter of the Paschal lamb.

—*Gevurot HaShem by Judah Loew ben Bezalel*

* * * *

" '*And the whole assembly of the Congregation of Israel shall kill it. . . .' "* Does then the whole congregation really slaughter? Surely, only one person does the slaughtering. It therefore follows that a man's agent is as himself." (*Kiddushin 14*)

The fact that in this rite one person functioned as an agent, as it were, for the entire Jewish community demonstrated the unity of the whole people of Israel and the responsibility of one for all and all for one. ("Just as you yourselves are members of the covenant, so must your agents be members of the covenant"). The unity of the "Congregation of Israel" is the basic requirement for the redemption of which the Paschal lamb is a symbol.

—*Sefarim*

* * * *

The Paschal lamb recalled the merits of the three Patriarchs, for we are told of Abraham that when he was about to sacrifice Isaac he said, *"God will provide Himself the lamb"* (Gen. 22:8); of Isaac, that he was bound upon the altar like a lamb; and of Jacob that he said, *"Remove from thence every lamb. . . "* (Gen. 30:32)

—*Rabbenu Ephraim*

* * * *

The three places on the door — the lintel and the two side-posts — upon which the blood of the Paschal lamb had to be sprinkled when it was first offered in Egypt at the time of the Exodus symbolically recalled the three Patriarchs by reason of whose merits the Jews had been granted redemption and the Passover.

—*Sefarim*

* * * *

6. *The Commandment to Eat the Paschal Lamb*

"And they shall eat the flesh in that night, roasted with fire and unleavened bread; with bitter herbs shall they eat it." (Exod. 12:8)

The commandment to eat the flesh of the Paschal lamb, roasted with fire, on the eve of the fifteenth day of Nissan, has the same purpose as the commandment to slaughter the Paschal offering; namely, to recall to us the great miracles which God wrought for us when He delivered us from slavery. The reason why we are explicitly commanded to eat it roasted is that roasted meat, which is particularly tasty, is the customary fare of kings and princes. The plain folk who cannot afford fancy meat must make do with any meat they can buy, and cook it to render it fit to eat. Since we eat the flesh of the Paschal lamb to remind us that we went forth from Egypt as free men to become a "kingdom of priests" and a holy nation, we are bidden to eat the lamb "roasted with fire" after the manner of kings and princes.

In addition, this procedure recalls the haste in which we had to depart from Egypt. There would not have been sufficient time in which to cook the meat.

—*Sefer HaHinukh*

* * * *

In the case of sacrifices other than the Paschal lamb, the eating of the flesh of the offering is not counted as a separate commandment but as part of the commandment of the sacrifice itself. Why, then, should the eating of the Paschal lamb be specified as a commandment apart from the slaughtering of the animal?

Said the author of the work *Avnei Nezer* of Sochatchov: "The reason is that the slaughtering and the eating of the Paschal lamb cannot take place at the same time of day. The lamb may

470

be slaughtered only at dusk, and if this is not done until the evening, the offering is invalid. On the other hand, it is not permissible to eat the flesh of the lamb at dusk. The feast can take place only after nightfall.

"In view of this difference in time, the partaking of the flesh of the Paschal lamb is specified as a commandment in its own right.

"Similarly, Nachmanides considers even the readings of the *Shema* in the morning and in the evening as two separate commandments because these acts must be performed at two different times of day." —*Hemdat Yisrael*

* * * *

The reason why we were bidden to roast the Paschal lamb with fire was that the offering of the Paschal lamb was meant to be an overt repudiation of idol worship, even as is written in the Torah: "The graven images of their gods shall ye burn with fire. . ." (Deut. 7:25) —*Zohar*

* * * *

According to the law, he who bolts down the bitter herbs without chewing them in order not to feel their bitterness has not fulfilled the commandment.

If, Heaven forbid, grief and trouble should come to a Jew, it is the will of God that he should feel their bitterness. For if he does so, the pain he suffers will serve to atone for his sins, and then God will have mercy and spare him from further ill. But if he should act as if he felt no pain and swallow it quickly without allowing himself time to feel it, he has not fulfilled the commandment properly and therefore prolongs his time of trouble because it may be the will of Heaven that he should feel the full force of the hurt and cry out in pain.

—*Attributed to a Hassid*

* * * *

According to Hillel, it was mandatory to wrap the un-leavened bread and the bitter herbs into the meat of the Paschal lamb and to eat it thus together. For this reason we still combine the unleavened bread with the bitter herbs at our Seder table today and recite the passage: "In memory of the Temple, as Hillel did. . . ." as we eat it.

The Paschal lamb and the unleavened bread are symbols of freedom, while the bitter herbs signify slavery and the bitter-ness of exile. In the midst of the bitterness of exile there is re-demption. The more bitter the sufferings of exile, the closer redemption is, even as in Egypt the hard labor of servitude served to hasten our deliverance.

The rite of combining the Paschal lamb, the unleavened bread and the bitter herbs — a symbolic combination of exile and redemption — recalls to us the memory of the Holy Temple and reminds us that the time will soon come when we will be delivered and the Temple will be rebuilt.

—Avnei Ezel

* * * *

7. *Forbidden Ways of Preparing the Paschal Lamb*

"Do not eat of it raw, or sodden with water . . ." (Exod. 12:9)

We are forbidden by the Torah to eat the Paschal lamb in-sufficiently roasted so that it is unfit for human consumption, or cooked in plain water or some other liquid. The reason for this prohibition is the same as that given for the commandment to eat the Paschal lamb roasted only; namely, to recall the miracle of the Exodus from Egypt.

—Sefer HaHinukh

* * * *

The rite of the Paschal sacrifice was meant to be a public act, performed in the open, without fear, to show that the

Jews dared slaughter and eat the very animal which the Egyptians worshipped as a deity. Now some might have said: "Let us not roast it too well, lest the Egyptians smell the odor of the roasted lamb." Others might have said: "Let us boil it in a covered pot so that no one should see it." Still others might have wanted to cut the carcass into small pieces so that the Egyptians should not know what it was. All this would have defeated the purpose of the act. Therefore the Torah explicitly commands: "Do not eat of it raw, nor sodden with water" and further specifies ". . . its head with its legs and with the inwards thereof." For the purpose of the entire ritual was to let the Egyptians know, see and feel that all this was done as a deliberate act to repudiate the paganism for which they stood.

—Tosafists, Da'at Zekenim

* * * *

8. *Prohibition Against Allowing Any Part of the Paschal Lamb to Remain Until the Next Day.*

"And you shall let nothing of it remain until the morning but whatever remains of it until the morning you shall burn with fire." (Exod. 12:10)

The Torah specifies that none of the meat of the Paschal lamb may be allowed to remain until the next morning (the fifteenth day of Nissan). The reason for this specification is the same as that given for the rite of the Paschal offering as such; namely, to recall the miracles of the Exodus. Just as kings and princes are not in the habit of saving cooked foods for "leftovers" but have fresh food every day, so we, "a kingdom of priests and a holy people," also must not leave any of the Paschal lamb to remain until the next day. The Torah explicitly states that whatever is left over must be burned like something no longer needed as is done at the courts of kings and princes who have food in plenty. All this, of course, is meant to impress

upon us that in those days the Lord delivered us from slavery
and brought us to freedom so that we became free men and could
attain to independence and greatness.

—*Sefer HaHinukh*

* * * *

The Sages say that he who has enough to eat today but
goes about worrying what he will have to eat tomorrow is lacking in faith, for he appears to doubt that the Most High will
supply him with the sustenance he needs. The time when the
Jews went forth from the impurity of Egypt was considered an
appropriate occasion to teach them to have faith. It was for this
reason that they were commanded not to worry about the morrow and to demonstrate this faith symbolically by not leaving
any of the Paschal lamb for the next day.

—*Torat Ha'Olah*

* * * *

The prohibition not to leave over any of the flesh of the
sacrificial animal for the next day is given also in connection with
the sacrifice of the Second or Lesser Passover,* concerning which
we are told in the Book of Numbers that "none of it shall remain
until the next morning."

However, the Hebrew term for "allowing to remain" in connection with the commandment pertaining to the Second Passover is not *'Toseyru'* (as it is in the commandment pertaining to
the Paschal offering) but *'Yasheyru.'* Why was not the same term
employed in both instances?

The Hebrew verb *'Sheor'* implies that something is saved
to remain for a specific purpose and not because it is considered
less important than the portion which has already been used.
'Yeser', by contrast, implies that an object has been left over

---

* Sacrifice offered on the fourteenth day of Iyyar by anyone who had
  been ritually impure or absent on a journey at the time of the
  Passover festival the previous month.

not for a specific purpose but because it is no longer needed or important.

The Paschal lamb sacrificed on Passover was preceded by a festival offering which was eaten before the Paschal lamb. Hence in the case of the Paschal lamb any "leaving oaer" would be expected to be in the nature of *Yeser;* that is, those partaking in the feast would have eaten their fill and no longer needed any more food. For this reason the Torah uses the term *Lo Toseyru* in connection with the prohibition pertaining to the Passover sacrifice.

The sacrifice for the Second or Lesser Passover, on the other hand, was not accompanied by an additional festival offering. Hence it would be expected that those partaking in the feast would eat the offering with great relish and that if anything would be left over, it would be in the nature of *Sheor;* that is, they would put it aside in order to have a good piece of meat also on the next day, Therefore the Torah employs the term *Lo Yasheyru* for this prohibition.

—*Haketav VehaKabbala*

* * * *

9. *The Commandment to Destroy All Leaven*

". . . but on the first day you shall destroy leaven out of your houses" (Exodus 12:15)

This is the commandment to clear all leaven from our dwellings on the fourteenth day of the month of Nissan. By "the first day," the Torah means the last day preceding Passover. The reason for this commandment is the same as that given for the Paschal sacrifice; namely, to recall all the miracles that were wrought for us at the time of the Exodus. He who does not fulfill this commandment and fails to clear the leaven from his dwelling not only acts counter to the purpose of this commandment but also violates an explicit prohibition; namely, that

"no leaven shall be found in your houses. . . ." (Exod. 12:19)
—*Sefer HaHinukh*

*   *   *   *

Leaven symbolizes the evil impulse, the evil forces and instincts in man. When the Jews went forth from Egypt, the Lord, desiring to make them a holy people fit to receive the Torah, taught them that man must keep away from evil not only in action but also in thought. The mind, too, must be kept pure of evil, which is symbolized by "leaven." For this reason the Torah specified that all leaven must be completely destroyed, not only literally but also figuratively in thought and spirit. The eye shall not behold the evil that is symbolized by leaven, nor shall the heart covet it.

—*Sefarim*

*   *   *   *

The search for leaven must be made by the light of a candle, because the Torah and its commandments are equated with light. This symbolic act is meant to impress upon us that the only way in which man can search himself for evil and destroy every trace of it is by studying the Torah and fulfilling its commandments. If one does not study, he will not be able to detect any faults in himself because he will have no way of knowing what is good and what is evil. Once he has brought to light the evil within him and has resolved to keep away from it, he must strive to be a "doer of good," to fulfill the commandments and to do good deeds. Even as the light of the candle is the best means for searching out leaven in our dwellings, so the "lamp of the commandments and the light of the Torah" are the most effective instruments for uncovering the evil in our hearts.

—*Shnei Lukhot HaBrit*

*   *   *   *

Before they were commanded at the time of the Exodus

476

to make the Paschal offering, the Children of Israel were bidden to destroy idolatry, as the Sages put it: "Take your hands away from idolatry and take for yourselves a lamb for the performance of the commandment." Today, every Passover must be preceded by a search for leaven which symbolizes the evil impulse, the tendency to idolatry within man. This is to teach us that, in fact, the performance of every commandment must be preceded by a "search for leaven." Before performing a commandment given by the Lord we must first remove every trace of "leaven", every mean thought, from our hearts.

—Tifereth Shlomo

* * * *

10. *The Commandment to Eat Unleavened Bread on the Night of Passover*

"*. . . On the fourteenth day of the month in the evening you shall eat unleavened bread . . .*" (Exodus 12:18)

We are commanded to eat unleavened bread on the evening of the fifteenth day of the month of Nissan, and this commandment is applicable regardless of whether or not we have a Temple in which to offer up the Paschal sacrifice. The reason for this commandment is the same as that given for the Paschal sacrifice; namely, to recall to us the wonders which the Lord wrought for us at the time of the Exodus, when the Jews departed from the land of Egypt in such great haste that they could not wait for their dough to rise and hence took it with them in the unleavened state.

—Sefer HaHinukh

* * * *

Why is the unleavened bread called the "food of faith"? In leavened bread, the dough begins to act independently after the baker has done his work. It rises by itself and cracks open in many places, all without any help from the master baker.

477

Unleavened bread, by contrast, never acts on its own; its life is dependent entirely on the work of the master baker who prepares it.

Accordingly, the unleavened bread becomes a symbol of conviction that we cannot do even the least thing without Divine Providence. Man cannot accomplish anything without the help of God, the true Master Creator. The commandment to eat unleavened bread on the night of Passover is meant to imbue us with the firm belief that all things in this world are like unleavened bread which can do nothing of its own accord but depends entirely on the will of the master baker. This is the reason why unleavened bread is called "the food of faith."

—B'nei Yissokhor

* * * *

The main teaching of the festival of Passover, which we observe in memory of the Exodus from Egypt, is that we should remember that it was God Who delivered us from Egypt by His own might and without human aid.

You are to "remember" that the Lord led you forth from there with a strong arm.

Do not deceive yourself that a new spirit took hold of your fathers after their centuries of slavery, that they rose up against the oppressors of their own free will, fought battles and wrested freedom from their tyrants by their own victory. Consider this carefully: it was only through the Word of God alone that Israel's prison burst open and they, who had been sunk in slavery and had been bereft of all physical and moral strength, went forth free, revived by the wonders and miracles of God. It was the Word of God that gave them freedom and raised them up to become God's nation, a particular creation which would survive all the changes of time. Testify to this, O son of Israel, for yourself and others, on the day of Israel's deliverance, by eating no leaven but only unleavened bread.

That bread of affliction, which the barbaric masters would give their slaves to eat, this very bread of affliction and slavery, should now serve the Jews as a symbol of the time of deliverance.

At that solemn moment of their redemption and deliverance they were supposed to know and to proclaim that they alone had done nothing in behalf of their liberation, because they regard themselves as servants even now. They still eat the bread of affliction and poverty, the bread of slavery, until the Word of God will come and create anew the freedom which had been wrested from them. And when the time of redemption comes, Israel does not go forth slowly like victorious heroes and freedom fighters, but in haste; their oppressors drive them out for fear of God's mighty hand, so that they do not even have time to prepare their bread but must carry away the dough in its unleavened state and continue to eat the bread of affliction.

All these commandments, then, are testimony for the Children of Israel for all times to come that the redemption from Egypt was brought about by God alone and not by human or natural forces, for truly the people of Israel did not attain their freedom by their own struggle; indeed, their exodus was so little dependent on their own strength and foresight that they could not even prepare themselves with bread, that staple food, for the journey but had to continue eating the bread of affliction. . . .

—*From 'Horeb', by Rabbi Samson Raphael Hirsch*

* * * *

Many of the Codifiers hold that the task to guard the unleavened dough from turning into leaven does not begin only when the dough is kneaded but immediately after the grain has been harvested.

For this reason pious Jews are careful on Passover, or at least on the Seder, to eat only *matzot* that have been under constant supervision from the harvesting of the grain until after the baking process. These *matzot* are known as *matzah shemurah* which means "guarded" or "supervised" *matzah*.

*   *   *   *

11. *Prohibition Against Keeping Leaven in the Home During Passover*

"Seven days shall no leaven be found in your houses." (Exod. 12:19)

We are forbidden to have leaven on our property during Passover. The term "houses" does not merely imply our dwellings, but all our property, and "leaven" includes not merely leavening agents which, when added to dough, will cause that dough to rise, but all *hametz*. The reason for this commandment is the same as that given for all the other commandments pertaining to Passover; namely, to recall the miracles which were wrought for us at the time of the Exodus, when we departed from Egypt in such great haste that we could not wait for our dough to rise and therefore took it with us in its unleavened state.

—*Sefer HaHinukh*

*   *   *   *

By its very nature, leaven symbolizes falsehood. For when the dough swells up in the leavening process it has not really grown in quantity, but its bloated appearance creates the false impression of greater volume.

The Torah has commanded us to "Keep far away from uttering falsehood." Falsehood is the only sin with regard to which the Written Law explicitly states that man must not merely refrain from committing it but even "keep far away" from it. In the case of other sins, the command to "keep far away" is not explicitly stated in the Written Law but only in the Oral Tradition as an added precautionary rule.

In the case of *hametz,* which by its very nature symbolizes falsehood, the Written Law itself explicitly commands that it must not be found in our homes so that we may "keep far away" from it, a symbolic act of avoidance to remind us of the commandment to "keep far away from uttering falsehood."

—*Shem MiShmuel*

* * * *

12. *Prohibition Against Eating Leaven Mixtures During Passover*

"You shall eat nothing leavened . . ." (Exodus 12:20)

The Torah warns us against partaking on Passover of foods which, although not *hametz* themselves, contain leaven. According to the Sages, this statement in the Book of Exodus implies a prohibition against contact with anything that may contain *hametz.* The reason for this prohibition is the same as that given for all the preceding commandments pertaining to Passover. It is in order to impress all this deeply on our minds that the Torah is so careful to have us keep far away from all leaven.

—*Sefer HaHinukh*

* * * *

The purpose of this commandment is a symbolic one; namely, to teach us how careful we must be to keep far away from the evil things which cause man to sin. Even only a little admixture of evil can do great harm and lead the human heart astray. For this reason we have been forbidden on Passover to partake even of foods that contain only a small amount of *hametz,* which is a symbol of the evil impulse.

—*RaMaH*

* * * *

Leaven is the symbol of arrogance; hence it is forbidden to eat even the least thereof on Passover. With regard to arrogance, the Sages say: "Employ it not at all, but let the spirit be exceedingly humble."

—*Yalkut David*

* * * *

The concept of nullity is utterly foreign to leaven. For leaven implies "rising" and arrogance, an exaltation of self, a refusal to be regarded as "null and void" by others. Thus the very concept of leaven is opposed to nullity, because once leaven becomes "null and void" to others, it is no longer leaven. . . .

—*Shem MiShmuel*

* * * *

13. *Prohibition Against Non-Jews Partaking of the Paschal Lamb*

"*. . . No alien shall eat thereof . . .*" (Exodus 12:43)

Not only non-Jews, but even renegade Jews who have abandoned Judaism for another faith are barred from partaking of the Paschal lamb. The reason for this prohibition is clear. In view of the fact that the Paschal sacrifice recalls the Exodus from Egypt, the time when we were first taken beneath the wing of the Divine Presence and accepted into the covenant of God, the covenant with His Torah and His faith, we surely cannot permit a non-Jew or anyone who has left the Jewish people and has denied his faith to partake of the Paschal lamb.

—*Sefer HaHinukh*

* * * *

Only one who is totally committed to the Jewish faith can be considered a Jew. He who has no faith and even denies the existence of the One God, Heaven forbid, ceases to be a Jew. There is no such thing as a mere "national Judaism" without religion. A Jewish unbeliever is considered a "son of a stranger," for his ways are alien to Judaism. On the other hand, a Gentile who embraces Judaism and accepts the Jewish faith is considered a true Jew just as if he had been a Jew by birth.

—*Ir Miklat*

* * * *

14. Prohibition Against "Sojourners" and "Strangers" Partaking of the Paschal Lamb

"A sojourner and a hired servant shall not eat of it." (Exod. 12:45)

According to the Sages, *toshav,* the Hebrew term for "so-journer" is used in this prohibition to denote a member of some other nation who has forsworn idolatry but has not agreed to observe the other commandments of Judaism. *S'khir,* the Hebrew term for "hired servants", is taken to refer to a non-Jew who is the process of converting to Judaism; e.g., an individual who may already have undergone circumcision but who has not yet performed the ritual immersion required of converts. According to the Torah, persons in these two categories must not partake of the Paschal lamb because they are not full Jews. In view of the fact that the Paschal sacrifice recalls our liberation and our convenant of faith with God, only those who have become steadfast in our faith and have become full Jews may be permitted to partake of it. Those who have not yet completely entered into our covenant have no right to partake of the Paschal sacrifice.

—*Sefer HaHinukh*

* * * *

15. Prohibition Against Carrying the Flesh of the Paschal Lamb away from the Place of the Feast

"Thou shalt not carry forth any of the flesh out of the house." (Exodus 12:46)

None of the meat of the Paschal sacrifice, not even a small part thereof, may be taken from the place where the group has begun to partake of it, to another group in another place. The Paschal lamb is intended to recall the miracles of the Exodus from Egypt by virtue of which we ceased to be slaves and became masters in our own right. Therefore we must partake of its flesh after the manner of free men and princes, who finish their meals in one room in their palaces and do not move their food from one place to another.

—*Sefer HaHinukh*

*   *   *   *

The Paschal lamb is to symbolize the unity of the people of Israel and thus also the Unity of God Who, as the One God, chose this one people for Himself. The Paschal sacrifice is an act performed by this one people to worship the One Sole Lord. Hence, every act connected with the Paschal sacrifice must express this unity in symbolic terms. The lamb must be roasted whole — "its head with its legs and with the inwards thereof" — and not cut into pieces, for that which is cut into pieces is no longer whole. Moreover, it must be eaten in *one* place and by *one* group only, to symbolize the unity of the people of Israel which was chosen by the One Sole God.

—*MaHaRaL*

*   *   *   *

16. *Prohibition Against Breaking Bones of the Paschal Lamb*

"Neither shall you break a bone thereof." (Exodus 12:46)

There is in the Torah an explicit prohibition against breaking the bones of the Paschal lamb. This, too, is to remind us that by virtue of our liberation from Egyptian slavery it behooves us to behave after the manner of kings and princes. Lords and rulers are not in the habit of scraping and breaking bones of their meat like famished dogs. Only the poor, and the slaves, who are perpetually hungry, are in the habit of breaking the bones of their meat in order to get at the marrow. In the season which commemorates our election as God's own holy people, a "kingdom of priests", we must act in keeping with the great new station to which we were thus raised. Symbolic acts such as these serve to impress upon us the fact of our miraculous liberation for all times to come.

—Sefer HaHinukh

*   *   *   *

Ask not why God has given us so many commandments to observe in memory of the Exodus from Egypt, or whether one commandment would not have been sufficient to keep the Exodus alive in our memories and in the memories of our descendants.

You must know that man is greatly influenced by his actions. Whatever he does affects his entire personality, so that his heart and mind are always led by the deeds he performs, both good and evil. Even an utterly depraved man whose thoughts are all evil can be led to goodness if he comes to his senses and devotes himself entirely to the study of the Torah and the observance of the commandments, though he does not do these things for their own sake, for by strength of his deeds he will be able to defeat the evil impulse within him and eventually he will do good for no other motive but its own sake. Conversely, even a completely righteous man who thinks only of studying the Torah and performing good deeds may eventually lose his righteousness and succumb to evil if he occupies himself with evil things — if, for instance, he is forced to work at an occupation that is base and sordid. Such is the influence of day-to-day activity on the heart and mind.

Therefore the Sages say: The Lord gave so many commandments to the Jewish people because He wanted to cause their merit to increase. This abundance of commandments is intended to absorb all our thoughts and actions, and we will eventually become better people as a result. For the performance of good deeds serves to make us good people.

Therefore be careful in choosing your work and your occupation, because you will not exert your influence on your pursuits, but they will surely influence you. Let not your evil impulse say to you: "As long as my own heart is steadfast in faith, what harm could it possibly do if I were to go out just this once to enjoy myself with the others, to sit in the streets and to trade small talk with the scoffers? After all, these things are not grave sins in themselves, and, besides, I am so much better than they. Why, then, should I have reason to fear that they may lead me astray?"

Do not speak thus, my son, but be careful to keep away from them, because you may be caught in their snare. Many others have been led astray before you and were forced to drain the bitter cup to its dregs. Therefore take care to guard your soul.

Once you will have considered all this you will no longer find it so difficult to understand why we have been given so many commandments just for the purpose of recalling the miracles of the Exodus from Egypt. These laws constitute a mighty pillar of our Torah, for the more we occupy ourselves with them, the more they will lead us to relive the Exodus for ourselves and thus help us become human beings who are truly free, independent and holy.

—Sefer HaHinukh

* * * *

17. The Uncircumcised are Prohibited from Partaking of the Paschal Lamb

"But no uncircumcised person shall eat thereof." (Exod. 12:48)

An uncircumcised male Jew is not permitted to partake of the Paschal lamb, even if his failure to be circumcised was due not to wilful intent to cast off the yoke of Heaven but only to the fact that he is exempt from circumcision because

486

his brothers had died of it. One who is not a full Jew because
he has not entered into the covenant of our father Abraham can
have no part in the performance of a commandment which
primarily symbolizes the entrance of the Jewish people into the
covenant with God.

—Sefer HaHinukh

* * * *

The commandment of circumcision entails the making of a
physical mark on our bodies, symbolizing the acquisition of
our bodies, as it were, by God and signifying that we are to
serve Him alone. The commandment to offer the Paschal sacrifice was given us when we went forth from the house of bondage
as free men and ceased to be slaves to the Egyptians. It should
therefore be an obvious conclusion that a man whose body has
not been marked with the physical sign which proclaims that
he is no longer a servant to flesh and blood but only to God
cannot partake of the Paschal offering which symbolizes the
complete freedom of man to serve God alone. A foreskin left
intact is utterly irreconcilable with the concept represented by
the Paschal offering.

—Orot HaMitzvot

* * * *

If a man rebels against performing one commandment, it
does not necessarily mean that he has rebelled against the entire Torah and that he is to be considered "a son of a stranger"
with regard to his partaking of the Paschal lamb. However, this is
true only if his sin is one which he has committed not while
actually partaking of the sacrifice, but before.

However, one who has rebelled against the commandment
of circumcision (and has not been circumcised) commits a
transgression with every bite he takes of the Paschal sacrifice,
for by his failure to become circumcised he shows that "his
deeds are alien to his Father in Heaven." Such an individual is

to be regarded as having rebelled outright (against God) and therefore as a "son of a stranger" in the full sense of the term.

Said the Rabbi of Lublin: "The Lord loves the Jews so much that even if, Heaven forbid, one of them should sin, He merely says: 'When will that fool cease to sin so that I will be able to love him as before?' "

But as long as he goes on sinning, neither God nor man can love him and he must be considered a "son of a stranger."

—*K'lei Hemda*

*　*　*　*

18. *The Commandment to Sanctify the First-Born*

"Sanctify unto Me all the first-born, whatever opens the womb among the Children of Israel, both of man and of beast, it is Mine." (Exodus 13:2)

We are commanded to sanctify to God all our first-born, of both man and beast. In the case of animals (unclean animals, save for the donkey, are exempt) the owner complies with this commandment by declaring that the animal is sanctified and by turning it over to a Kohanite. A first-born son must be redeemed by his father for the sum of five dollars to be paid to a Kohanite. The reason for this commandment is that the Lord desires us to accumulate more merits by fulfilling His command with our first fruits so that we may know that all things belong to the Lord and that everything man owns in this world was only allotted to him by God in His great mercy. Seeing that after having toiled so mightily until he has beheld the first fruits of his endeavors which he cherishes as the apple of his eye, he must turn them all over to the Most High, man will come to understand that he must relinquish his control over these things and place all of them under the direct control of God instead.

In addition, the performance of this commandment should recall to us the great miracle which God wrought for us in

Egypt when He smote the first-born of the Egyptians and delivered us out of their hands.

—*Sefer HaHinukh*

* * * *

The Lord has ordained that the Kohanites must devote all their lives to the study of the Law, to the performance of the Divine service and to the dissemination of the Torah among the people ("The lips of the Priest shall guard knowledge and the Torah shall be sought from his mouth"). For this reason the Lord endowed them with the "Priestly Privileges" to relieve them from the necessity of earning a livelihood so that economic concerns will not distract them from their sacred calling.

The commandment that all the first-born of both man and beast are to be given to the Kohanites means to teach us that it is incumbent upon us to give away even our best and most precious possessions, which we cherish like a first-born son, to those wise men who are constantly engaged in the study of the Law, in the performance of good deeds and in the dissemination of the Law to the people. No sacrifice must be too great for us when it comes to providing for the support of students of the Law, to free them from the necessity of earning a livelihood so that they may give all their time and energy to the sacred task which they have taken upon themselves.

—*Orot HaMitzvot*

* * * *

Let it remain impressed upon your hearts forever that all our acquisitions in the world, from Mother Earth to that life which is dearer to us than our own, the life of our children, everything belongs to God. From His hand were they given to you, and it is in His hand to let you keep them or to take them from you. If you regard everything you own in this light and treat it accordingly, then all your possessions will become verdant and blossom forth as splendid plants in the garden of God. Thus they

489

will become sacred to God as gifts from Him, given to man to use. But if man will be led in his folly to clutch these possessions with an iron hand and proclaim: "They are mine"; if he regards himself as their sole master, takes advantage of them, indulges himself with them and dissipates them to suit his whims, then they will be desecrated, their blossom will fade away and their flowering shall go down into the grave.

So it is with anything that we possess, but above all with that possession which is more precious to us than anything else — the children whom God, blessed be His Name, has given us.

You are to exert yourself to work for them. You are to regard the son whom God entrusted to you and the daughter who was born to you as possessions entrusted to your sacred charge, whom you are to bring up not for yourself but for God so that the son and the daughter may become worthy children of the Living God in the full sense of the word. If you will allow this thought to predominate in the upbringing of your children, in their physical, mental and emotional care, in their education, in their vocational training and in their complete preparation for their future living so that they will grow up to be strong and of good courage to lead a good and righteous life, then this blessing from God will bring true happiness to you and to them. Then you will always be filled with joy and contentment, seeing your children as fully Jewish men, girded with strength by God to lead a holy life as men and as Jews. If, however, you always will regard your children as "mine" and, instead of beholding them only as men and as Israelites, you will think only of your daughter's material future, if you will see her only as a future housewife or businesswoman, or as a beauty and wit, hoping that in this way she will be a source of joy and honor to you; if, instead of educating your son for the qualities which will crown him as a man and Israelite so that the title of "Jew" should be an honor and a glory to him, you will seek only a mercenary profit in your efforts in his behalf; if your greatest wish is that your son may soon earn a name for himself as a merchant, craftsman, artist or scholar, not caring whether these titles will delete the title of "Jew" from his heart, then please do not speak or think of the Divine blessing of children, of parents' reward in their children's well-being, but speak rather of the Heavenly curse and of the sin of parents who have destroyed the title of "Israelite" in the hearts of their children.

You can apply these thoughts at all times to all your possessions, from the most precious to those of least concern to you, and may the lesson of the survival of your people help you decide wisely in your choice between the curse and the blessing and to choose the blessing.

From the deliverance from Egypt you were able to see for yourself and learn that presumptuousness and perversity bring death and destruction, and that you were raised on high by God due to your way of life in that you subordinated yourself completely to God. You should proclaim this lesson aloud by patent and overt action to show that every child that is born and every possession a Jew owns is consecrated by God and is God's very own. It is only by the grace of God that you have a right to anything and so it is His will alone that should be the eternal law for you in your treatment and enjoyment of all the things that exist in this world. You can give practical expression to this thought by taking the most precious of all your possessions and (1) dedicating it to God, meaning that you withdraw it from your customary use of it and devote it entirely to such purpose as is designed so as to increase and secure reverence for God among the Jewish people, for Israel is a kingdom of priests and a holy nation, or (2) purchasing your right to use it for your own purposes by redeeming it from its original intent (as in the Redemption of the First-Born) or (3) rendering it unusable for yourself by destroying it . . .

—*Samson Raphael Hirsch, Horeb*

*   *   *   *

19. *Prohibition Against Eating Leavened Bread During Passover*

"And no leavened bread shall be eaten." (Exodus 13:3)

We are forbidden to eat leavened bread during Passover. The reason for this prohibition has already been discussed under Paragraphs 9, 11 and 12. Anyone deliberately eating even so much as one piece of leavened bread the size of an olive on Passover is subject to the extreme penalty of *kareth* (an untimely death). Anyone doing so unintentionally must make a sin-offering.

—*Sefer HaHinukh*

*   *   *   *

The phrasing of the prohibition in the passive mood ("and no leavened bread *shall be eaten"*) implies that not even several individuals together may eat of one piece of leavened bread the size of an olive. For even though the Torah imposes the penalty of *kareth* only on the eating of a piece of leavened bread the size of an olive, it prohibits even the eating of pieces of leavened bread smaller in size than an olive.

—*Maimonides, Hilkhot Hametz U-Matzah*

*   *   *   *

We already know that all prohibitions regarding food extend even to minute quantities because the Torah, in prohibiting the eating of *heleb* (abdominal fat), has explicitly stated *"all* heleb". From this the Sages infer that even a minute quantity of such forbidden food is prohibited. Still, the Torah found it necessary to be specific in its prohibition against the eating of leavened bread on Passover, for this prohibition is different from all the others in that leavened bread as such is not "forbidden food" but is prohibited only at a certain season of the year. Had the Torah not been so explicit there would be no basis for comparing the stringency of the prohibition against leavened bread on Passover with that of the ban on *heleb,* which is forbidden *per se* not only on Passover but all year round.

—*Tzlakh* and *Noda BiYehuda*

*　*　*　*

20. *Prohibition Against Allowing Leavened Bread to Be Seen In Our Dwellings*

"And no leavened bread shall be seen with thee, neither shall leaven be seen with thee in all thy borders." (Exodus 13:7)

No leavened bread may be seen in our dwellings during Passover. Though the verb "shall be seen" occurs twice in this verse, the verse should not be construed as containing two separate commandments, because both of the instructions concern the same thing. The verse speaks of "leavened bread" first and then of "leaven" in order to teach us that not only actual bread but also the leaven with which leavened bread is made is forbidden. The purpose of this prohibition has already been discussed previously in connection with other commandments and prohibitions pertaining to Passover.

—*Sefer HaHinukh*

*　*　*　*

Since the prohibition against eating leavened bread on Passover is a very strict one (any deliberate violation is subject to the penalty of *kareth*), and we see leavened bread before us all year long, the Torah explicitly commands us not even to allow leavened bread to be seen during Passover to make sure that we will not eat it inadvertently. (This is one of the rare

493

instances in which the Written Law itself provides for a separate prohibition as a safeguard to ensure the observance of another prohibition.)

—*RaN* on *Tractate Pesahim*

*   *   *   *

The Hebrew term *lakh* ("with thee") may also be interpreted to mean "thine" as in *she-lakh* (e.g. the expression *le-mi atta* is translated in Gen. 32:18 like *shel mi atta*, or "whose art thou?"). From this, the Sages infer that while it is forbidden to see "thy own leavened bread" it is not forbidden to see that belonging to others; in other words, the prohibition applies only to any leavened bread that is in one's own possession. But if this is so, why does the verse not explicitly state *she-lakh* ("thy own") rather than *lakh* ("with thee")? The answer is that, actually, no Jew can own leavened bread during Passover; indeed, he must derive no benefit or gain whatever from it during that time. Hence the Torah says "with thee" rather than "thine," implying that this leavened bread may have been his property at one time, but is so no longer.

—*HaKetav VeHaKabalah*

*   *   *   *

21. *The Commandment to Tell the Story of the Exodus from Egypt*

"And thou shalt tell it to thy son on that day, saying 'It is because of that which the Lord did for me when I came forth out of Egypt.'" (Exodus 13:8)

We are commanded to relate the story of the Exodus from Egypt on the night of the fifteenth day of Nissan, each according to his ability, and to praise the Lord for the miracles which He wrought for us at that time. The Sages explain that this commandment must be performed on the night of the fifteenth day of Nissan, the night on which we are commanded to eat unleavened bread. While the verse specifies that the story of the Exodus should be told "to thy son," one should tell it not merely to one's own children but to any and all persons present. For it is the purpose of this commandment to recall the miracles which were performed for our ancestors when they went forth from Egypt and how the Lord avenged our sufferings. Even if one happens to be observing the Seder alone and has no one to whom to tell the story of the Exodus, he is commanded to recount these events aloud for himself so that his heart should be stirred, for speech awakens the heart.

The reason for this commandment has already been stated in connection with the commandments pertaining to the Paschal sacrifice. It should not be surprising that we have been given so many commandments and prohibitions pertaining to this one historic event, for the Exodus from Egypt is one of the fundamentals of our Torah and our faith. It is for this reason, too, that we insert the phrase "in memory of the Exodus from Egypt" in our prayers and blessings. To us, the miracle of our deliverance from Egypt is a sure sign and evidence of the constant renewal of the world, a proof that there is a God Who is greater and mightier than all else, a God with a will and almighty power Who has created all things that are and Who has the power to alter the order of the world at any time according to His will even as He did in Egypt, when He suspended the laws of nature for our sake and performed great and mighty wonders in our behalf. This should silence anyone who would deny the constant renewal of the world, and should confirm the belief that God knows all things and that His power and Providence extend over all things.

—*Sefer HaHinukh*

* * * *

By merely performing the symbolic acts of the commandment to eat unleavened bread, you still have not fulfilled your obligation to show how great and solemn the movement of redemption was, to express an opinion concerning its greatness and to engrave it upon your heart as a man and a Jew. You must do it also by word. On the evening of the Passover festival you must renew each year the memory of what happened to the Jewish people at the time of the Exodus. You must recall the revelation of God's glory and the establishment of Israel as a people. You must discuss this and recount what God did to the Egyptians and what He did for His people. You must implant in the hearts and minds of your family and particularly of your young children the mighty acts of God as a foundation for their knowledge of God, to know of His mercies and His greatness so that they may understand that there is no other people which is so close to God as the Jewish people. At all times God demands of you as a father in Israel to imbue your offspring which He gave to you with that which God requires of you and of them, while they are still young; lead them at an early age to God and endow them with the desire to hold fast to the Jewish way of life and to link themselves inextricably with the destinies of their people. That night which you celebrate as the anniversary of the birth of the Jewish people — the wondrous creation which God made in the history of mankind, this is the night which God has appointed for the dedication of your little ones upon whom depends the eternity of your people and its future. By speaking to your children of these things, you cultivate the Divine plants which God planted by the redemption from Egypt for all times to come, so that they may grow up and bring forth fruit that is worthy of living. When you share the unleavened bread with them as a symbol of your link with Israel's task of self-sacrifice, let not words fail to flow from your heart, pure words which will permeate you with the spirit of the noble function of a Jewish father. Teach them the meaning of this unleavened bread; make them aware of the spirit of the festival, of the significance of this great event and of the true meaning of the title of "Israel" which our ancestors adopted when they went forth from darkness into light and from slavery to freedom.

Remember and note that the Torah never intended to have you train your children to fulfill the laws of God from mere mechanical routine, if you will not, at the same time, find the proper words with which you will teach them to understand the great significance of the *mitzvot*. See that you transmit to your children not only the external forms of Jewish living without making them understand their deeper meaning. For if you do no more than that, you have fulfilled only half of your great task as a Jewish father. If you train your children to fulfill the Law and the commandments of God, let it not be, as the Prophet puts it, just the "customary command of men" but see that they should know the true spirit of the Torah in its great splendor so that with this spirit you may influence your children and let them understand what it is that they do.

It was for this reason that the Sages have instituted, for your sake and for the sake of your children, the Seder for the night of Passover, which has existed among the people of God for thousands of years now. They ordained that you should retell the memory of the Exodus from Egypt in the circle of your family at home and they placed the *Haggadah* into your hands to serve as your guide in fulfilling this commandment.

—*Samson Raphael Hirsch, Horeb*

* * * *

22. *The Commandment to Redeem Every Firstling of a Donkey*

"And every firstling of a donkey shalt thou redeem with a lamb." (Exodus 13:13)

Every male firstling of a donkey must be redeemed with a he-lamb which the owner must turn over to a Kohanite. As al-

497

ready explained in Paragraph 18, all firstlings belong to the Lord, Who in turn has assigned them to the Kohanites. For this reason the owner redeems his firstling he-donkey by giving a he-lamb to a Kohanite. The purpose of this commandment is to have the Jews recall at all times the miracle which God performed for them at the time of the Exodus, when He smote the first-born of the Egyptians who have been likened to donkeys because of their brutish ways.

—*Sefer HaHinukh*

* * * *

Why should the donkey be distinguished from other unclean animals by requiring redemption? Because the donkeys helped the Jews at the time of the Exodus to carry the silver and the gold which they took with them from Egypt, thus helping in the fulfillment of God's promise that the Children of Israel should "go forth with great wealth."

—*Tractate Bekhorot* and *Commentary of MaHarSHa*

* * * *

Egypt has been likened to a donkey ("their flesh is like the flesh of donkeys") and the Jewish people have been likened to a lamb ("Israel is a scattered lamb"). Hence, just as the Lord redeemed the Jewish people from Egypt and took them unto Himself as His people, so we must take a lamb in place of the donkey to fulfill the Lord's command.

—*Midrash Lekah Tov*

* * * *

Although the first-born of all clean animals had to be sacrificed upon the altar, the lamb used to redeem a donkey did not have to be sacrificed but was merely turned over to the Kohanite. For it is not only impossible to use an unclean animal such as the donkey as a sacrifice but it is even forbidden to offer up to the Lord an object which once served to take the place of an unclean animal, since it is said of the Lord that "He is pure and

His servants are pure also. . . ."

—Orot HaMitzvot

*   *   *   *

23. *The Commandment to Destroy the Unredeemed First-Born He-Donkey.*

"And if thou wilt not redeem it, then thou shalt break its neck." (Exodus 13:13)

If the owner is unwilling to give up a lamb to redeem the male firstling of his donkey, he must kill the donkey by decapitating it at the neck with an axe, for the Lord ordained that anyone unwilling to redeem a firstling must not derive gain or benefit from the animal or even from the animal's carcass. The reason for this commandment has already been discussed in connection with the preceding commandment.

—Sefer HaHinukh

*   *   *   *

The Egyptians, who have been likened to donkeys (because of their brutish ways), stiffened their necks and refused to release the Children of Israel, who have been likened to lambs, and they were therefore annihilated. In the same manner, the "stiff-necked," stubborn individual who refuses to perform the symbolic act of redemption recalling the miracles of the Exodus from Egypt is punished in that the neck of his donkey must be broken because of his sin.

—RaMaH

*   *   *   *

24. *The Prohibition Against Walking Beyond a Certain Distance on the Sabbath.*

"Let no man go out of his place on the Seventh Day." (Exod. 16:29)

We are forbidden to walk beyond a certain distance on the Sabbath. According to the Oral Tradition, "his place" refers to an area equal in size to the area occupied by the encampment

of the Children of Israel in the wilderness or a total of three
Parsos, which would be equal to twenty-four thousand ells. This
means that it is not permitted to walk a distance in excess of
three *Parsos* from one's place of residence on the Sabbath. The
purpose of this prohibition is to remind us that the world is not
the First Cause but that it was made by the Creator, for, as we
are told in connection with the commandment to observe the
Sabbath, "in six days did the Lord create the heavens, the earth,
the sea and all that is therein, and on the Seventh Day He
rested." In order to remember this, we, too, are bidden to rest
"in one place" on the Sabbath, not to set out on long journeys
but to walk no further than one would on a stroll taken purely
for pleasure. To walk a distance in excess of twenty-four thousand ells would entail the sort of effort which is not in keeping
with the rest mandatory on the Sabbath.

—Sefer HaHinukh

* * * *

However, many of the earlier authorities held that the
Written Law sets no limits to the distance that may be covered
on foot on the Sabbath, and that this commandment is not one
of the 613 *mitzvot* at all but only a "safeguard" prohibition
ordained by the Rabbinical authorities who decreed that it was
not permissible to walk a distance in excess of 2,000 ells on the
Sabbath. According to this view, the statement in the Torah,
"Let no man go out of his place . . ." refers not to mere walking
but to walking with objects; i.e., it refers to the prohibition
against carrying an object from private property out into
an area of public domain on the Sabbath. The Written Law
as such sets no limits to the distance one may walk on a
Sabbath as long as one is not carrying an object.

—Sefer HaHinukh, in the name of Nachmanides

* * * *

It is a well-known fact that the Sages ordained "symbolic limits" in order to make it permissible to walk distances in excess of the "Sabbath limit." The procedure for setting up a "symbolic limit" is as follows:

On Friday, sometime before the Sabbath begins, a piece of bread is placed at the point of the two thousand-ell limit, or else the person intending to exceed the limit simply goes to that place prior to the Sabbath and declares: "This shall be the place where I will (stop and) rest (tomorrow)." With this declaration he makes that point his "dwelling place" and is permitted to walk a distance of another two thousand ells from it.

25. *The Commandment To Believe in the Existence of God and in His Unity.*

"I am the Lord thy God Who brought thee out of the land of Egypt." (Exodus 20:2)

We are commanded to believe that there is One God Who created all things that exist. All things that exist now, that have existed in the past and that are yet to come into being are derived solely from His power and might. We are commanded to believe also that it was He Who brought us forth from the land of Egypt and gave us the Law, saying "I am the Lord thy God," meaning "Thou shalt know and believe that there is One God in this world."

The statement ". . . Who brought thee out of the land of Egypt" is intended to tell us: "Do not come to regard your redemption from Egyptian servitude and the plagues with which the Egyptians were stricken as mere coincidence. You must always remember that it was I, the Lord your God, Who brought you out of the land of Egypt by My will and My Divine Providence, fulfilling the promise I made to your ancestors."

The reason for this commandment hardly requires an explanation, because it is known to all. This belief is the basic concept of our faith and he who rejects it is considered a heretic who has no portion in Judaism and no share in its merits. The main point in this belief is that the Jew must be convinced, deep within his heart, that this is the only truth and that it could not be otherwise. And if someone should question him, he should answer that he believes this deep within his heart and that he knows of no other alternative even if he were to be threatened with death on this account. For his own faith will be strengthened if he gives verbal expression to what he believes with his heart and mind. Only once a man has been privileged to grow in wisdom so that his heart can understand and his eyes can see with a perfect faith that the belief which he cherishes is obvious and true and that there can be no other truth, has he truly fulfilled this commandment.

The laws implicit in this commandment are (1) that one is duty-bound to believe in the Lord, and to believe that all power and might, greatness, strength, beauty and splendor — indeed, all prosperity and life, emanate solely from Him; (2) that we must not presume to have the ability or the wisdom to grasp or to retell His greatness and His goodness because these qualities of God can be comprehended only by God Himself and not by others; (3) that we must endeavor with all our strength to remove from Him every imperfection and everything not in keeping with His perfection; (4) that we must know that He is true perfection, that He is neither a physical entity nor a physical force, for every physical body is subject to imperfections and there can be no wrong in Him, blessed be His Name, and so forth. All these ideas and many others are clear to those who study the knowledge of God. Happy are those who are privileged to attain this level of understanding, because they are able to fulfill the commandment in all its perfection.

This is a commandment which does not depend on a fixed

time for its performance, because the Jew must remember and fulfill it all the days of his life.

—*Sefer HaHinukh*

* * * *

(1) The foundation of the Torah and the basic principle of (the Jewish) religion is the knowledge that there is One, may He be praised and magnified, Who was existed from the beginning, and Who caused all else, from the most primitive form of life to the terrestrial globe, to come into being. He created all these things, and he has shaped and perfected them.

(2) It is within the power of this Being Who has existed from the very beginning to destroy everything that exists, if He so desires, so that He alone will remain. All things that exist are dependent on Him but He is not dependent on them. Thus, while the existence of all other things is optional, His existence is a *sine qua non*.

(3) For this reason the Prophet says: "And the Lord God is truth." He is the ultimate truth and nothing in this world can even approximate the truth which is inherent in Him. Thus it is also written in the Torah that "there is none beside Him"; there is in the world no other being as true and as perceptible as He.

(4) This Being Who has existed from the very beginning is the God of the world, the Lord of the entire Universe, and He leads and guides it and all there is within it with a power that has neither end nor limit.

(5) It is an explicit commandment to know all these things, as it is written: "I am the Lord thy God." "I am" implies the existence of God; the designation "the Lord" implies that He has made and created all things that exist; "thy God" implies that He reigns supreme over all things, and that He can and does control all things according to His will. Therefore He tells us that He was the One "Who brought thee out of the

land of Egypt" — you yourself know and bear witness to all this, by reason of the great and marvelous signs and miracles and of the reversals of the laws of nature which you have beheld with your own eyes and heard with your own ears. You have felt with your own senses and with all the limbs of your body the hard labor with which the Egyptians embittered your lives, and the Lord delivered you and brought you forth into freedom and light."

The Lord did not say: "I am the Lord thy God Who created heaven and earth," for no commandment can rest on mere belief, on happenings and events that those receiving the commandment have never seen, heard or felt. He invoked, instead, the Exodus from Egypt, because then He can indeed remind us and command us to "know and remember that which you yourselves have seen, heard and felt, and then you will know, acknowledge and believe that there is indeed a God in this world."

(6) Said commandment to believe in the existence of God is the fundamental principle on which all else depends, for if there is no such Lord and Guide, all else has no validity. As the Sages put it: "A certain king entered a country (he had conquered) and the people there said to him: 'Give us commands'. But he replied: 'I cannot give you commands before you have acknowledged my sovereignty, for as long as you have not acknowledged my sovereignty, you will not carry out my commands.' "

—Yesode HaTorah, in Yad HaKetanah 81

* * * *

All that exists on earth consists of various parts. Everything must be created from elements which were previously made, and all things must have a creator who created and invented them. It is strange indeed that there should be human beings who believe that the world came into being by accident. If one holding such an opinion would hear a person voicing a similar view with regard to a water wheel that revolves in order to irrigate a portion of a field and if that person were to say that he thinks it had been set up without any intention on the part of a mechanic who labored to put it together and to adjust it, using all his tools so as to obtain this useful result, the hearer would be greatly astounded and think that the man who made such a statement is a fool. He would promptly charge him with lying and would reject his assertion. Now if he rejects such a view in regard to a small and insignificant wheel which serves only for the improvement of a small portion of the earth, how can he permit himself to harbor such a thought concerning the immense sphere which encompasses the whole earth with all the creatures in it, and which shows a wisdom so great that the minds of all living creatures . . . cannot comprehend it? How can one say that all this came into being without a mighty and wise designer who planned and conceived it? As is well known, things that come about without purpose show no trace of wisdom or power. If ink were to be poured out accidentally on a blank sheet of paper, it would be impossible that proper writing should result, legible lines such as are written with a pen. If a person were to bring us a neat piece of script that could only have been written with a pen and were to say that some ink had been spilled on the paper and that these written characters had come of themselves, we would charge him with falsehood. . . . Since this appears to us impossible even in the case of ordinary letters or characters, how can one insist that something far more fine and profound . . . could have come about without the purpose, power and wisdom of a wise and mighty designer? What we have cited . . . to demonstrate the existence of a Creator will suffice to anyone intelligent and honest enough to admit the truth that the world indeed has a Creator and Guide, may He be blessed and magnified.

—*Bachya ben Joseph Ibn Pakuda, Duties of the Heart*

* * * *

Why does the (First) Commandment read ". . . Who brought thee out of the land of Egypt and not ". . . Who created thee"? Did not the Creation precede the Exodus from Egypt?

The answer is that while God created all the nations of the world and hence His relationship with Israel in this respect was no different from His relationship with the rest of mankind, it was through the Exodus that He became the God of Israel, the God of that one people on earth which He singled out from among all the others to keep particular watch over it and to hallow it with a unique sancity.

Hence, in giving the Torah to the Jewish people, and in His choice of the Children of Israel as His own nation, He is first and foremost the God "Who brought thee out of Egypt," for this historic event was the foundation of the election of Israel as the heart, as it were, of the entire world.

—*HaKuzari*

* * * *

The three basic tenets of the faith are (1) The belief that there is in this world One God Who is the King over all creation; (2) The belief that He judges the deeds of men and that He rewards good and punishes evil; (3) The belief that He gave us a Law and commandments to show us the paths in which we must walk, and to teach us what is permitted and what forbidden.

These three tenets have been set forth as follows: "The Lord is our King; the Lord is our Judge; the Lord is our Lawgiver."

—*Sefer HaIkkarim*

* * * *

506

30. *The Prohibition Against Idolatry.*

"Thou shalt have no other gods before Me." (Exodus 20:3)

We are forbidden to believe in any god beside the Lord. This is the basic tent on which all else in the Torah depends. As the Sages put it: "He who accepts idolatry is as if he had denied the entire Torah." The reason for this prohibition is obvious. Anyone willing to accept as a god any creatures or creations on earth, even if he is willing to consider the Lord as a deity higher than they, or as ruler over them, has violated this prohibition against idolatry.

—Sefer HaHinukh

* * * *

The prohibition against idolatry warns us not to worship any creature as a god. We are forbidden to regard as deities angels, planets, stars, or any of the four elements — fire, air, earth and water — or anything deriving from these. Even an individual who, while accepting such things as deities, considers the Lord as the greatest and mightiest of these gods and has no intention of removing himself from the authority and service of the Lord, is an idolator, as long as he says that even idols have a Divine power assigned them by God and that worshipping them can bring him success or happiness, or even if he merely says that by serving such idols he fulfills the will of God because God wants men to do honor to His servants. If he has any such beliefs he is an idolator no less than if he were to regard the idols as gods in their own right, for all the honor and worship belong to God alone and to none beside Him.

—Yad HaKetana, in the name of Maimonides

* * * *

The idols are termed *"other* gods" because they are dependent on *another* source, on a source outside themselves, for their power. They have no power of their own. Only the Lord is not dependent on any other source for His power, even as the Sages said: "And there is no god beside Me, for I did not derive My sovereign power from another."

—*Bahya*

* * * *

All sorts of idolatry which at a later date took on primitive and even ridiculous forms derived primarily from an erroneous assumption that there may be a Divine force in the world other than the Lord. Maimonides writes of the devedopment of idol worship as follows:

1. In the days of Enoch, a descendant of Adam, the sons of men erred exceedingly, the counsel of the wise men of that generation was nullified and even Enoch was a victim of that folly. They erred in that they said: "Seeing that God created the stars and the planets to rule the world, that He placed them high above to share honors with them, for they are ministers serving the Lord, it is proper that we should praise, glorify and honor them, because this is the will of God, to exalt and honor those whom He exalted and honored, even as a king of flesh and blood desires to honor those who stand in his presence, for such is the honor of the king." Being of this opinion, they began to build temples in honor of the stars, to offer sacrifices to them, to praise and to glorify them in words and to bow down to them in order to do the will of God, as they thought in their error. Thus was the groundwork laid for idol worship. The first idol worshippers knew and believed that there was a Supreme Deity in the world, but they thought in their folly that it was the will of God that they should worship His ministers, the stars.

2. In the course of time there arose among men false prophets who said that God Himself had commanded them to worship one star, or all the stars, and to offer sacrifices to them, pour libations, build temples and put their image there so that all

the people, the women and the children, should bow down to them. They moreover describe for them a form which they devised and told the people that this was the image of that star which had been pointed out to them by prophecy. Thus the prophets commenced to make various images in temples, beneath trees, upon mountaintops and elevated places where they would gather together, bow down to them, and preach to the people, saying that this image had it in its power to do good or evil and that it was proper to worship it and to fear it. Their priests also said to them that by this worship they would increase and succeed, and that they should do thus and so, and not such and such. Then other frauds arose and stated that the star itself, or the planet, or the angel had told them that it or he must be worshipped in such and such a manner. In this way this thing spread throughout the world, to serve various images with varied ceremonies, to make sacrifices to them and to bow down to them. And with the passing of time, the glorious and awesome Name of God was forgotten altogether, so that they gave Him no recognition, and they, and the women and children knew of nothing beyond the image of wood or stone which they had been reared from their infancy to worship and to swear by its name. Gradually, even their wise men and their priests came to assume that there was no God except for the stars and planets for whom, and in whose likeness, those images were made, but there was no one to recognize the Creator of the world or to know Him, except a few individuals of that generation, such as Enoch, Methuselah, Noah, Shem and Eber. And the world continued on this path until the birth of that pillar of the world — our Father Abraham.

3. As soon as this spiritual giant was weaned, he began to busy his mind, and even in infancy he commenced to think day and night: "How is it possible that this planet should be

in motion all the time and have no leader to guide it? And who, indeed, causes it to revolve, since it is impossible that it should revolve of itself?" But he did not have a teacher or anyone to impart anything to him, for he was buried in Ur of the Chaldees, among the foolish worshippers of the stars, and his father and mother and all the people were star worshippers, and although he followed them in their mode of worship, he busied his heart and reflected until he came upon the path of truth. He came to understand that there was one God Who leads all things, Who created all things and that in all of creation there is no God beside Him. He realized that the entire world was in error and that the thing which had caused them to err was that their worship of the stars and the images caused them to lose the truth from their consciousness. And Abraham was forty years old when he first recognized his Creator. (According to Rabbi Abraham Ben David of Posquires, there is an Aggadah that he was three years old at the time.)

When he came to this realization and knowledge he began to engage the men of Ur of the Chaldees in debates to prove to them that they were not following the true paths. He broke all the images and made it known to the people that it was proper to worship only the One God of the Universe, and to Him alone it was right to bow down, and to offer sacrifices, so that all the creatures of earth should recognize Him; moreover, that it is right to destroy all the images so that the masses of the people not be led into error and think that there are no other gods beside these images. When he had defeated them by his arguments, the king sought to put him to death, but he was saved by a miracle and he went on to Haran. Then he again stood up and called out aloud to the whole world to let them know that there is only One God for the entire Universe and that it is proper to serve Him. And so he went on with his proclamation from city to city, and from kingdom to kingdom, until he reached the land of Canaan. When the people who gathered about him asked him about his preachments, he replied by giving knowledge to each and every one according to his mentality until he could turn him to the path of truth. Thus there gathered about him thousands, even tens of thousands, and they became the people of Abraham's household in whose heart he had implanted this great cause, concerning which he compiled books, and which he passed on to his son Isaac. And Isaac sat and gave instruction and admonition, and, in turn, imparted it to Jacob who, in turn, gave instruction and support to all who flocked to him. And Jacob instructed all his sons, but singled out Levi and appointed him head instructor and established him in a seat of learning at which to teach the paths of the Lord and the observance of the commands of Abraham. At the same time he commanded his sons not to interrupt the succession of the sons of Levi to the presidency of the Academy, so that the learning be not forgotten, so the movement advanced and grew strong among the sons of Jacob and their followers so that there came to be in the world a nation which knew God, until Israel spent a long time in Egypt and again learned the ways of the Egyptians, to worship the stars as they did, except for the tribe of Levi, which stood by the commandments of their ancestors. At no time did the tribe of Levi worship stars. Truly, in a brief space of time the root which Abraham had planted would have been uprooted, and the sons of Jacob would have lapsed again into the world-wide error and wandering. But because of the Lord's love for us, and because He keeps the vow of the covenant with our Father Abraham, he appointed our teacher Moses lord over all the prophets and made him His messenger. After our teacher Moses had been endowed with prophecy and the Lord had chosen the Children of Israel as His inheritance,

He crowned them with commandments and made known to them the way to serve Him and what would be the judgment given against star worship and all its erring followers.

—*Maimonides, Mishne Torah*

*   *   *   *

. . . Therefore the Sages say: "This is the way of the evil impulse. One day it will tell you to do thus and so, and the next day it will tell you not to do it, and so on until one day it will command you, 'Go and worship idols.' For even the slightest move away from the path of the Torah bears within it idol worship, the 'alien god who is within the body of man' and this can lead to actual idol worship in the end. Therefore man must begin the fight at the very first sign of "turning away," so that he will not come to a pass where he will 'serve other gods.' " (*"Beware lest your heart be deceived, and you turn and serve other gods. . ."* Deut. 11)

—*Sayings of Disciples of the Baal Shem Tov*

*   *   *   *

"Thou shalt have no other gods before Me." Be on your guard particularly when you stand "before Me" (says the Lord), when you are at prayer or study or in the act of performing a commandment, that you do not do it for ulterior motives, to impress others, or for the sake of honor, money or other such reward, for that would mean that your prayer or your good deed would be peformed not to serve Me but to serve others — either other people or other considerations such as glory or riches. And if you have such "other gods" when you stand "before Me", that is idolatry, for when you pray, study or fulfill a commandment you must do it solely for the sake of heaven, for the sake of the Lord alone.

—*Sefarim*

*   *   *   *

512

27. *The Prohibition Against Making Graven Images.*

"Thou shalt not make for thyself a graven image nor any manner of likeness . . ." (Exodus 20:4)

We are forbidden to make for ourselves images in order to serve them. Indeed, we are not permitted to make them even without intent to serve them, regardless of whether we make them with our own hands or whether we order another person to make them. The purpose of this prohibition is to eliminate the risk of falling into idolatry.

—*Sefer HaHinukh*

* * * *

This is so only according to Maimonides. Nachmanides holds that the prohibition against making graven images for the purpose of idol worship derives not from this verse but from Leviticus 19:4: *"Turn not unto the idols, nor make for yourselves molten gods . . ."* But this verse still deals with the worship of idols and it forms one prohibition together with the prohibition "Thou shalt have no other gods before Me." We may neither accept idolatry nor serve other gods, regardless of the form the worship may take.   —*Anon.*

* * * *

By worshipping a *pesel* (graven or hewn image), man renders himself *pasul* (defective, unfit). By serving other gods, he renders defective or "chips away at" the image of God in which he has been made and renders it impure. Therefore we are told *"Lo Taase Le'cha Pesel,"* meaning, "Do not deliberately make yourself defective by engaging in idol worship."

—*RaMaH*

* * * *

28. *The Prohibition Against Bowing Down to an Idol.*

"Thou shalt not bow down unto them." (Exodus 20:5)

We are forbidden to bow down to an idol; i.e., to any

object of worship other than the Lord. The mere act of bowing down to an idol is forbidden, even in cases when the act is not performed as a gesture of worship or when bowing down is not customarily a rite performed in the worship of that particular idol. The reason for this prohibition has already been stated before.

—Sefer HaHinukh

* * * *

Even though other rites of worship in connection with idols are forbidden only if they are rites customarily employed in the worship of these idols, the act of bowing down to any object of worship other than God is always forbidden. Also forbidden in connection with idols are such acts of worship as burned offerings, incense burning and libations, even if these acts are not customarily employed in the worship of the idols, because these rites are used in the worship of the Lord in the Holy Temple.

—Gemarah and Codifiers

* * * *

Although "bowing down" in general usage defines only an act of prostration upon the ground, the prohibition against "bowing down" to idols includes even the mere bending of the head to an idol.

—Maimonides, Hilkhot Avoda Zara (6:8)

* * * *

29. *The Prohibition Against Serving Idols.*

"*. . . Nor serve them . . .*" (Exodus 20:5)

We are not permitted to pay deference to any idol in the world in any of the ways in which they are worshipped by those who believe in them. Even if an individual does not employ one of the four ritual acts used in the worship of the Lord (i.e., burned offerings, incense burning, libation or prostration) to serve the idol, he has transgressed the prohibition if he serves the idol by acts customarily employed in the worship of that idol. Even if the ritual consists of crude or base acts such as uncovering one's body before *Peor,* or throwing a stone before the image of Mercury, or shaving off the hair of one's head in honor of Camosh, it still is a violation of the prohibition ". . . nor serve them," for it is the intent of this prohibition that we must not serve these other gods in the manner in which it is customary to worship them, whatever that mode of worship may be. The reason for this prohibition has already been stated before.

—*Sefer HaHinukh*

* * * *

30. *The Prohibition Against Taking An Oath In Vain.*

"Thou shalt not take the name of the Lord thy God in vain . . ."

We are forbidden by the Torah to take oaths when this is not absolutely necessary. This prohibition is applicable to the following four practices: (1) Swearing to an untruth; e.g., swearing that a pillar is made of gold when we know it is actually made of stone; (2) Swearing to a fact which is generally known and accepted as true; e.g., swearing that a stone is a stone, or that a piece of wood is a piece of wood; (3) Swearing to nullify a Divine commandment. Obviously, this is taking an oath in vain because it is not within the power of human beings to nullify a commandment given us by the Lord. (4) Swearing to do a thing which one is incapable of carrying out; such as not to sleep for three days in succession, to go without food for seven days in a row, and so forth.

The purpose of this prohibition is that men should know, impress it upon their souls and strengthen the belief in their hearts that the Lord, blessed be He, Who is in heaven above, lives and endures forever and that there is no one else eternal as He is. Therefore, when we make mention of His great Name in connection with our words and actions, it behooves us to do so only with awe, solemnity and trembling, and not jokingly or lightly, or in the manner of small talk, of prattle about the things of this world which pass away and do not survive. We must therefore impress upon our hearts the thought that His awe must be upon us at all times for the sake of our happiness and of our very lives. It is for this reason that we are bidden not to make mention of His holy Name unnecessarily or in vain, and he who would casually transgress this prohibition is liable to the penalty of lashes.

Derived from this same commandment is the concept of the "false oath." If one swears to do thus and so, and then fails to do it, he is guilty af having "sworn hastily," and this is explicitly forbidden in the Book of Leviticus: *"And you shall not swear by My Name falsely"* (19:12). For an individual who swears by the great Name of God in order to attest to the truth of his statement when actually he knows that his statement is not based on fact, openly shows his contempt for God. It is almost as if, Heaven forbid, he had set out to prove that God Himself is not real, and therefore the lips of such a person should be silenced. Anyone who swears to perform a certain act and then fails to fulfill his vow is counted among those who deny the truth and rebel against God, for in my opinion the meaning of an oath is that a man resolves in his heart and promises with his lips to keep the vow he has taken, and never to change his vow just as God Himself is eternal and unchanging. . . .

—*Sefer HaHinukh*

* * * *

Mentioning the Name of God is not the same as pronouncing the name of a mere king of flesh and blood. A king of flesh and blood is in no manner affected by the mere mention of his name, because his name has no bearing on his nature. But in the case of God, He and His Name are One, so that His

Name is part of His essence.

The Sages comment as follows· in the Midrash concerning the Biblical verse: "And His banner over me is love":

"He who places his hand upon the face of a king of flesh and blood would be put to death immediately, whereas many people lay their hands upon the Name of God and suffer no harm."

It was their intent to give us to understand that laying hands upon the letters of the Name of God is tantamount to laying hands upon God Himself, because wherever His Name abides, there He is also, and wherever His Name is mentioned, there He is also, as is written in the Torah: *"In every place where I cause My Name to be mentioned I will come to thee and bless thee"* (Exod. 20:21).

The above shows that when a person makes mention of God's Name it is as if he had moved the hand of God Himself and used Him for his purposes. In the case of a king of flesh and blood an individual who does an evil thing against the will of the king is not guilty to the same degree as one who moves the hand of the king for the purpose of doing evil. For in the latter instance the king says: "It is not enough that you yourself have acted contrary to my will; you have provoked me by using me for your evil purposes." The situation is much the same in the case of God. An individual who abandons Him entirely and goes forth to worship idols has· sinned less than one who uses the Name of the Lord for a false oath and mentions it for the purpose of uttering falsehood, for by so doing he has moved the hand of the Lord Himself and used Him as an instrument to perpetrate his own falsehood.

—*Alshekh HaKodosh*

*   *   *   *

517

31. *The Commandment of Sabbath Observance.*

"Remember the Sabbath Day to keep it holy." (Exodus 20:8)

At the beginning and at the end of the Sabbath we are commanded to express in appropriate words the greatness of the Day of Rest and its distinctness from all the other days of the week.

It is written: "Remember the Sabbath Day to keep it holy." This means that we must mark it as a great and holy day. The Sages explain that we must "remember it over wine"; i.e., the words of commemoration must be recited over wine. One-fourth of a *log* or more of pure or mixed wine (if mixed wine is used, the proportion must be at least one part of unprocessed good wine to three parts of water) is poured into a cup and the blessings of the Sabbath Kiddush are recited over it. When the Sabbath ends, the *Havdala* blessings must also be recited over a cup of wine.

The purpose of this commandment is to cause us to remember the greatness of the Sabbath day and to impress upon our hearts the belief in the renewal of creation and that "in six days the Lord made heaven and earth, the sea and all that is in them, and on the Seventh Day He rested." We are bidden to perform this act of commemoration over wine, because it is the nature of man to be greatly affected by wine, which has a stimulating and cheering effect on man, and we know that he is amenable to such outside stimulants in his actions.

The Gemarah states that one who likes bread better than wine is permitted to recite the Kiddush over bread because he is more likely to be put into the proper frame of mind by the food which he likes best. In the case of *Havdala,* however, the Sages make no such allowance but insist that these blessings must be recited over wine, because the Torah always goes by the ways of the majority; and it is assumed that most people prefer drink to food at the end of the Sabbath since they have

518

already eaten an ample dinner during the day in honor of the Sabbath.

It is obvious that all the pertinent ordinances of the Sages; i.e., that the cup must contain at least one-fourth of a *log* of wine, that the cup must be washed before it is filled, that no food may be eaten before the Kiddush has been recited and that the Kiddush must be recited at the same place where the dinner is to be eaten, are all intended for the same purpose; namely, they would tend to help gladden the heart of man which is the aim of the Kiddush. For instance, less than one-fourth of a *log* of wine would not have any effect on the mood of a man.

—Sefer HaHinukh

* * * *

The commandment to sanctify the Sabbath by reciting the *Kiddush* is observed by women also, despite the fact that the fulfillment of this commandment is dependent on a set time. Although, as a rule, women are exempt from a commandment of this type, they are duty-bound to fulfill this one precept, either by reciting the blessing themselves or by hearing another person recite it, because the remembrance of the Sabbath Day by verbal expression is closely bound up with the actual observance of the Day of Rest by abstaining from work (we were bidden to "keep" and to "remember" the Sabbath in a single command), so that everyone who is bidden to observe the Sabbath is thereby duty-bound also to remember it by reciting the *Kiddush*.

—Gemara and Codifiers

* * * *

The Hebrew text "Remember the Sabbath Day to keep it holy" contains five words. This implies that he who observes the Sabbath is as if he had observed the commandment of all the Five Books of the Torah.

—Baal HaTurim

519

*   *   *   *

The recital of the passage *"And the heavens and the earth were finished . . ."* prior to the *Kiddush* is a kind of testimony by the Jewish people to the unity and supremacy of God as the Creator of the world. Hence this testimony should be recited joyously and with devotion. He who recites this testimony with all his heart and mind has atoned for his sins.

—Zohar, Va-Yakhel

BIBLIOGRAPHY

NOTE: *Works* quoted in this volume but not listed in the Bibliography are either assumed to be familiar to the average Jewish reader or of unknown authorship. *Authors* not listed are those concerning whom no biographical data is available or in the case of members of Rabbinic dynasties, whose first names are unknown so that they cannot be identified as to their place in the dynasty.

BIBLIOGRAPHY

Abarbanel — Don Isaac Abarbanel, Born in Lisbon, 1437; died in Venice, 1508. Statesman, philosopher and Bible commentator, treasurer to King Ferdinand and Queen Isabella of Spain. After the expulsion of the Jews from Spain he emigrated to Italy. Author of a Bible commentary, and commentaries on such works as "The Guide for the Perplexed", Tractate Aboth, etc.

Abraham Moshe of Przysucha, see Bunehart.

Adler, Nathan ben Simeon HaKohen, (1741-1800). Talmudist and Kabbalist in Germany. He established his own Talmudical academy in Frankfort-on-the-Main, where a number of noted rabbis including Moses Sofer (Hatham Sofer) received their training.

Afikei Yehuda (The Springs of Judah) Two volumes of sermons and various topics by Rabbi Yehuda Leib of Slonim, Poland.

Agudat Ezov. Talmudic work by Rabbi Moshe Z'ev of Bialystok, Poland (d. 1830), author of a number of important Talmudic treatises and responsa.

Ahavat Yonathan (Love of Jonathan). Homiletical intrepretation of Haftarot by Rabbi Jonathan Eibeschuetz (1690-1764), Talmudist, Kabbalist, and chief rabbi of the triple community of Altona, Hamburg, and Wandsbeck (Germany). Founder and head of a prominent Talmudical academy which produced many leading Talmudic sages, he was the author of a number of Biblical and Talmudical commentaries.

Albo, Joseph — see *Baal Ha-Ikkarim.*

Aleksander, Rabbi of. See HaKohen, Hayyim Henokh.

Alshekh, Moses ben Hayyim (1507-1600). Biblical commentator and codifier of Jewish law. A disciple of Rabbi Joseph Karo, he was the author of a number of homilies and responsa. His Biblical commentary was so universally revered that be became known as *Alshekh HaKodosh* (the Saintly Alshekh.)

Alter, Isaac Meir, see *Hiddushei HaRiM.*

Ari HaKodosh. See HaAri HaKodosh.

Artzot HaHayyim (Lands of the Living). Essays and interpretations dealing with Biblical texts and sayings of the Sages. Published by Rabbi Eliakim ben Abraham of London, author of *Asara Maamarot* (Ten Statements).

Arvei Nahal. Biblical commentary by Rabbi David Solomon Eibeschuetz (d. in Safed, Palestine, 1810), preacher, codifier and author of a number of works on Jewish law and ethics.

Asifat HaKohen (Anthology by the Kohanite). Interpretations on the Bible by Rabbi Moshe Heschel of Cracow, published in 1732.

Ateret Zvi (The Crown of Zvi). Commentary on the *Zohar* by Rabbi Zvi Hirsch Eichenstein of Zidichowe. He was a famous Hassidic Rebbe, a noted Talmudist, Kabbalist, and author of novellae on Torah and Responsa. One of his disciples in Kabbala (mystic teachings) was the great Biblical commentator, Rabbi Meir Leibush (see MaLBIM).

Avnei Ezel (Guiding Stones) Planned anthology of homiletical interpretations of Biblical texts by Rabbi Alexander Zusia Friedman (see Preface). The book was never published and the notes, save for those excerpts contained in this volume, have been lost.

Avnei Nezer, see *Bornstein, Abraham.*

Avodat Yisrael. See Israel ben Shabbetai of Kozienice.

Avraham Hayyim of Zlotchov. Son-in-law and successor of Rabbi Yissokhor Ber, and author of the Biblical commentary *Orakh LeHayyim* (A Path To Life), containing his own novellae and many commentaries and interpretations of the works of great Hassidic sages. He would spend most of each day at prayer and constantly busied himself with helping others and keeping them from succumbing to temptation. *Orakh L'Hayyim* (A Way To Life) was actually a portrayal of his own saintly way of living.

Azulai, Hayyim Joseph David (known as Hida, by his initials). Born in Jerusalem, 1724; died in Leghorn, Italy, 1806. Kabbalist, bibliographer, and traveler and emissary for religious institutions in Palestine. He was the author of more than fifty volumes, including *Shem HaGedolim* ("Names of the Great"), an encyclopedic work containing the biographies of over 1,000 Jewish scholars and listing over 2,000 works and manuscripts, *Devash L'Fee* (Honey For My Mouth), *Zavrei Shalal, Nahal Kedumim* and other homiletical interpretations of *Tenakh.*

Baal Ha-Ikkarim. Rabbi Joseph Albo (c. 1380-1435). Religious philosopher in Spain. His major work *Sefer Ha-Ikkarim* (Book of Basic Principles) reduced the basis of Jewish faith to three fundamental beliefs: (1) the existence of G-d; (2) the Divine revelation of the Torah, and (3) reward and punishment.

Baal HaTurim. Rabbi Jacob ben Asher, (1270-1343). Author of the code *Arba Turim* (Four Rows) and son of Rabbi Asher ben Yechiel (*Rosh*). In addition to the classic code, Rabbi Jacob wrote a commentary on the Pentateuch based on *gematria*, or the interpretation of words in the text according to the numerical values of their letters in the Hebrew alphabet.

Baal Shem Tov, Israel ben Eliezer (1700-1760). Founder of Hassidism. His piety, kindliness, humility and his doctrine of "serving the Lord with gladness" gained him many followers. He preached that communion with G-d could be achieved by anyone through fervent prayer, and that the fundamentals of worship were religious emotion, joyous observance of the commandments, trust and love of G-d, the Law and the people of Israel.

Bachya ben Joseph Ibn Pakuda, (1050-1120). Religious philosopher. Author of *Hovot HaLevavot* (Duties of the Heart) in which "duties of the heart" and conscience such as love of G-d, humility and trust in G-d are discussed. Originally writen in Arabic, the work was translated into Hebrew by Judah Ibn Tibbon and Joseph Kimhi.

Bahya ben Asher Ibn Halawa, see *Bahya.*

Bahya — Rabbi Bahya ben Asher Ibn Halawa. Spanish Biblical commentator active during late 13th and early 14th centuries. His works include *Kad HaKemah,* a book of ethics.

Barukh of Medzibozh (1757-1810). Hassidic rabbi and grandson of the Baal Shem Tov, founder of Hassidism. His comments on Jewish law and ethics are compiled in a treatise entitled *Butzina DiNehara* ("The Shining Light").

Be'er Mayim Hayyim, see *Treor, Rabbi Hayyim.*

Benet, Mordecai. Born in Hungary, 1753; died in Karlsbad, 1829. A great Talmudic scholar, author of *Biur Mordecai,* a commentary on the work *Mordecai* by the Tosafist Rabbi Mordecai ben Hillel, and *Mogen Avos,* which deals with the laws of Sabbath, and many Rabbinic responsa, he was a fiery opponent of the Reform movement in Hungary.

Berlin, Hayyim. See *Berlin, Naftali Tzvi Judah.*

Berlin, Naftali Tzvi Judah (1817-1893). Known as *Ha-Natziv,* head of the world-famous Yeshiva of Volozhin (Lithuania) which produced many outstanding rabbis and Jewish communal leaders. In addition to his work, *HaEmek Sheelah,* a commentary on the *Sheiltot* of Aha of Shabba, Rabbi Berlin was the author of a number of Biblical and Talmudical commentaries and a volume of responsa. He was a leader of the *Hoveve Zion* movement. His two sons were Hayyim Berlin, Rabbi of Moscow, and Rabbi Meir Berlin, a leader in the Mizrachi movement.

Bet Yoseph, Commentary on the Five Books of Moses by Rabbi Joseph Karo, b. 1468 in Toledo, Spain; d. in Safed, Israel, 1555. Karo was the great codifier whose decisions have been accepted as binding in Jewish law. He is the author of *"Bet Yoseph",* an all-inclusive commentary on the *"Arba Turim"* (The Four Rows) by Rabbi Jacob ben Asher; *Kesef Mishneh,* a commentary on the works of Maimonides, *Magid Meishorim,* and the *Shulhan Arukh.* The latter is divided into four parts: *Orakh Hayyim,* containing the laws pertaining to daily life, such as blessings, prayers, phylacteries, recital of *Shema,* laws pertaining to the observance of Sabbath and holidays; *Yoreh Deah,* containing dietary laws, laws pertaining to ritual impurity, idolatry, usury, mourning; *Even HaEzer,* the code of marriage and divorce; *Hoshen Mishpat,* containing civil and criminal laws.

Bet HaLevi, see Soloveitchik, Joseph Dov HaLevi.

Beth Jacob (House of Jacob). Hassidic Biblical commentaries by Rabbi Jacob Aaron of Aleksander (Pietrkov, Poland, 1899).

Bikkurei Aviv (The Firstlings of Spring). Commentary on the weekly portions of the Bible with Hassidic interpretations by Rabbi Yaakov Aryeh of Radzimin, sage and Kabbalist (1796-1860).

Binah Le-Ittim (Insight Into the Times) Biblical commentary and anthology of holiday sermons by Rabbi Obadiah Figu (1579-1647), Talmudic scholar in Italy. Rabbi Figu is the author of *Gedulei Terumah,* a commentary on *Sefer HaTerumot* (Book of Tithes), which he wrote relying mostly on memory, for at that time Pope Julius III had ordered all copies of the Talmud to be burned. He took up secular training at Italian universities but later regretted having done so at the expense of his Talmudic studies.

Binyan Ariel, see Shaul ben Rabbi Aryeh Leib of Amsterdam.

Blacher, David (d. 1944), Rabbi of Musar, a moralist movement founded by Rabbi Israel Salanter which aimed at strengthening inner piety through moral self-criticism and the regular study of *musar* or ethical literature. Rabbi Blacher

526

founded a Musarist academy in Mezhirich. He was killed by the Nazis.

B'nei Yissokhor, see *Zvi Elimelekh, Rabbi of Dinov.*

Bornstein, Abraham. (1830-1910). The Sochatchover Rebbe. A son-in-law of Rabbi Menahem Mendele Morgenstern of Kotzk, he was the author of *Avnei Nezer* (volumes of responsa) and *Eglei Tal* (a text on the laws pertaining to the Sabbath). His son, Rabbi Shmuel Bornstein, was the author of *Shem MiShemuel,* a Bible commentary with Hassidic and Kabbalist overtones.

Bunehart, Abraham Moshe of Przyṣucha (d. 1829). Son and successor of Rabbi Bunim of Przyṣucha. He died at the age of 31.

Bunim of Otvotzk. Hassidic rebbe of the Amshinov dynasty.

Danziger, Yehiel of Aleksander (d. 1894), Hassidic Rebbe and founder of the Hassidic dynasty of Aleksander. A humble and saintly man, he requested in his will that he should not be referred to as a *Hasid, Tzadik* or *Rabbi.*

David of Lelov (1746-1814). Disciple of the *Hozeh* (Seer) of Lublin, (R. Yaakov Yitzhak HaLevi Hurwitz). He was patient and modest to a fault, helping the poor, loving his fellow-men and caring for all living things. He was loved and respected by Jews and Gentiles alike, and his saintly conduct was a source of inspiration to many of his contemporaries.

Degel Mahaneh Ephraim, see *Moshe Hayyim, Rabbi of Sadilkov.*

Derashot HaRan, see *RaN.*

Devash HaSadeh (Honey of the Field). Hassidic stories and commentaries by Rabbi Ber Meir (Bilgoray, 1908).

Devash L'Fee — see *Azulai, Hayyim Joseph David.*

Diskin, Joshua ›Leib. Born in Grodno, Poland, 1818; died in Jerusalem, 1898. Rabbi of Brisk and other communities, world-renowned Talmudist, authority on Jewish law, author of Biblical novellae and Rabbinic responsa, and opponent of the *Haskala* movement. He was the founder of the Diskin Orphan Home in Jerusalem.

Divrei Geonim (Words of the Gaonim). Anthology of Biblical commentaries from the works of various rabbinical authorities, including a sermon by Rabbi Mordecai Baneth (Podhoretz, 1899).

527

Divrei Shaarei Hayyim (Words of the Gates of Life). Anthology of Biblical commentaries by Rabbi Hayyim Sofer (Mukacevo, 1886).

Divrei Torah (Words of Torah). Anthology of treatises on ethics, morals and piety. Authorship unknown.

Dov Ber of Mezhirich (also known as *"Rebbe Reb Ber"* and *"Maggid of Mezhirich*) (c. 1710-1772). Talmudist, Kabbalist and preacher. A prominent disciple and successor of the Baal Shem Tov, he was responsible for the spread of Hassidism to the Ukraine, Lithuania and Galicia. His works include *Maggid Dvorov LeYaakov, Likute Amorim* and *Or Torah.* One of his disciples was Rabbi Shneour Zalman ben Baruch of Lyady, founder of the *Habad* movement of Hassidism.

Dubo, Maggid of, see *Kranz, Rabbi Jacob ben Wolf.*

Eger, Akiba (1761-1837). Rabbi of Posen and one of the greatest sages of his generation. He possessed a phenomenal memory, an unquenchable thirst for Torah knowledge, a sharp and deep intellect, and a noble spirit, full of humility and godliness. His decisions were accepted as universally binding. He is the author of responsa, *Shaaloth U'Teshuvoth Reb Akiva Eger,* and of novellae on the Mishnayoth, Gemara, Rambam, and Shulhan Arukh, etc. He had eight sons and eight daughters. Rabbi Moses Sofer Schreiber (see *Hatham Sofer*) was his son-in-law.

Eglei Tal, see *Bornstein, Abraham.*

Elibeschuetz, David Solomon, see *Arvei Nahal.*

Eibeschuetz, Jonathan, see *Ahavat Yonathan.*

Eliezer HaKohen of Sochatchov. Nineteenth-century Talmudist, disciple of the Hassidic Rebbe Rabbi Simha Bunim of Przysucha, the Kotzker Rebbe, and the *Hiddushe HaRIM,* and son-in-law of Rabbi Yaakov Lebarbaum of Lissa, the author of *Nesuvot Hamishpot.*

Elimelekh of Lizensk, Rabbi, see *Noam Elimelekh.*

Epstein, Kalonymos Kalman HaLevi, Eighteenth-century rabbi, d. in Cracow, Poland, 1827. He was a great Hassidic leader, Kabbalist, *Tzaddik* and a disciple of Rabbi Elimelekh of Lizensk and other Hassidic Rabbis of his generation. His work *Mo'or Vo'Shomesh* (Light and Sun) is one of the classics of Hassidic literature.

528

BIBLIOGRAPHY

Epstein, Moshe Mordecai. Head of the Yeshiva of Slobodka (Lithuania and Israel), world-renowned Talmudist and author of Talmudic novellae entitled *L'vush Mordecai* (The Garment of Mordecai). His zeal in Torah study was extraordinary. He would review fifty pages of Talmudic text every day.

Figu, Obadiah, see *Binah Le-Ittim.*

Graubart, Judah Leib. Rabbi In St. Louis, Mo., and Toronto, Canda. Author of *Devarim KiKsovom* (Words As They Were Written), an anthology of sermons (St. Louis, Mo., 1931).

Gur Aryeh — see *Judah Loew ben Bezalel.*

Gur (Ger) Rabbi of. Reb Abraham Mordecai Alter, b. Poland, 1866; d. in Jerusalem, Israel, 1948. Son of Reb Aryeh Leib Alter, the *Sefath Emeth,* and a great-grandson of the *Hiddushei HaRIM.* A great Hassidic Rebbe with tens of thousands of followers, and one of the leaders of the Agudat Israel movement, he survived the Nazi holocaust and settled in Israel after World War II.

HaAri Hakodosh, Rabbi Yitzhak ben Shlomo Luria Ashkenazi (born in Jerusalem, 1534). A great Talmudist and disciple of Rabbi Bezalel Ashkenazi, the author of *Shito Mekubetzet,* a Talmudic anthology, he later became the father of the Kabbalist movement. His mystical teachings are understood only by a few scholars. His saintly and ethical life earned him universal admiration and reverence.

HaDrash VeHaEyun. Homiletical commentary on the Books of Genesis, Exodus, Leviticus and Numbers by Rabbi Aaron Lewin of Reisha, Poland (1880-1941). One of the leaders in the Agudat Israel movement and a representative of Polish Jewry in Poland's Parliament, Rabbi Lewin defended the rights of the Jews against anti-Semitism and was an outspoken opponent of assimilation, Reform and *Haskala.* He was killed by the Nazis.

HaGahoth MaHarad. Authorship unknown.

HaKetav VeHaKabalah (Scripture and Tradition). Biblical commentary by Rabbi Jacob Zvi ben Gamliel Mecklenburg (d. 1865), Rabbi of Koenigsberg, Prussia, and prominent Biblical commentator. Rabbi Mecklenburg's commentary deduces the meanings of the Scriptures from the text itself without extraneous explanations.

HaKohen, Hayyim Henokh, see *Hashava LaTorah.*

HaKohen, Israel Meir, see *Haphetz Hayyim.*

HaKuzari (The Khazar). Book on Jewish religion and philosophy written in Arabic by Rabbi Judah Ha-Levi (born in Spain, 1075; died in Palestine, c. 1150), Hebrew poet and religious philosopher. His poetry expressed his fervent yearning for Zion. Judah Ha-Levi extolled the people of Israel as the heart of the nations of the world. Several of his poems have become part of the Jewish prayer book.

Ha-Natziv, see *Berlin, Naftali Zvi Judah.*

Hanukkat HaTorah (Dedication of the Law). Treatise containing ingenious Biblical interpretations by the world-renowned seventeenth-century scholar Rabbi Heschel ben Rabbi Yaakov, or as he was popularly called the "Rebbe Reb Heschel." It was compiled by Hanokh Henach Erzon.

Haphetz Hayyim, Rabbi Israel Meir HaKohen. Born in Zhatil, Poland, 1835; died in Radin, 1933. Author of *Haphetz Hayim*, a compendium of *Hilkhoth Loshon Hara*, a classical work explaining in detail the prohobitions against gossip and talebearing; *Mishneh Berurah*, a commentary on the *Shulhan Arukh, Orakh Hayim; Likutei Halokkhoth*, on Tractate *Kodoshim; Mahanei Israel*, a code of laws for Jewish soldiers, and many other Musarist writings and proclamations to the Jewish people. He founded the Yeshiva of Radin, where thousands of disciples were inspired by his humility, fear of G-d, and righteousness. His fame spread afar, and people from the world over turned to him for counsel and solace. He was known for his constant and active concern for the welfare of his brethren all over the world. He placed paramount stress on the training of the young in the spirit of uncompromising adherence to Jewish tradition. His volumes on *Halakhah* were accepted as universally binding in matters of Jewish law. He was one of the leaders of the Agudat Israel movement.

Hashava LeTorah. Anthology of interpretations and commentaries by Rabbi Hayyim Henokh HaKohen, Hassidic Rebbe of Aleksander, Poland (d. 1870).

Hatham Sofer, see *Schreiber, Moses.*

Havot Yair (The Villages of Yair). Rabbinic Responsa by Hayyim Yair Bachrach, Rabbi of Vermiza and Frankfort, Talmudist and author of novellae on Torah, Talmud, and Shulhan Arukh (d. 1704).

Hayyim ben Otor, see *Or Ha-Hayyim.*

Hayyim of Volozhin, see *Gaon of Vilna.*

530

BIBLIOGRAPHY

Heller, Yom Tov Lipmann (1578-1653). Rabbi in Vienna, Prague and Cracow, Talmudist and author of *Tosefos Yom Tov.* Classic commentary on the *Mishnayot; Maddanei Melekh* (Royal Morsels), a commentary on the works of Rabbi Asher ben Jehiel, etc. He took a leading part in Jewish communal affairs and was once arrested on trumped-up charges by order of Ferdinand II of Bohemia and Hungary. His personal sufferings are described in his book *Megilat Aivoh* (Scroll of Hatred). He did much to raise the prestige of the Rabbinate and of Jewish law, particularly to alleviate the plight of *agunot* (wives whose husbands' death was suspected but not proven and who therefore could not remarry according to Jewish law) left as the result of the Chmielnicki massacres of 1648-49.

Heschel, Abraham Joshua of Opatov. Descendant of prominent Talmudists, Hassidic Rebbe with thousands of disciples, and author of *Oheb Israel* (The Lover of Israel), a commentary on the Bible, and *Toras Emes.* Before his death, he requested that only one epitaph should be inscribed on his monument; namely, that he was an Oheb Yisrael (Lover of Israel).

Hida, see *Azulai, Hayyim Joseph David.*

Hiddushei Aggadot, see *MaHarSha.*

Hiddushei HaRIM (Novellae of Rabbi Isaac Meir). A commentary on the Talmud, Shulhan Arukh and Responsa by Rabbi Isaac Meir Alter (1799-1866), founder of a dynasty of Hassidic rabbis whose residence was in the town of Gur (Ger), near Warsaw, Poland.

Hildesheimer, Azriel, (1820-1899). A Talmudist who also received a secular education, he was a staunch opponent of Reform. He organized the Orthodox community and Rabbinical Seminary of Berlin, and greatly influenced the modern Orthodox movements combining traditional Jewish studies with secular education.

Hirsch, Samson Raphael. Born in Hamburg, Germany, 1808; died in Frankfort-on-the-Main, 1888. Bible commentator and leader of Orthodoxy in Germany. His basic views of Judaism are expressed in his *Nineteen Letters of Ben Uziel* and *Horeb.* His philosophy of *Torah Im Derekh Eretz;* namely that strict loyalty to Jewish law is compatible with secular education, helped stem the tide of Reform in Germany. Founder of a model "separatist" Orthodox community, including a day school, in Frankfort, he was the author of a classic commentary on the Pentateuch and commentaries on the Book of Psalms and the Prayer Book.

531

Homat Esh (Wall of Fire). Sermons on Biblical texts by Rabbi Menahem Asch, one of the leading rabbis of Hungary in the nineteenth century.

Horowitz, Isaiah, see *Shelah.*

Hurwitz, Shmuel Shmelka Halevi, (1726-1778). Talmudist, brother of Rabbi Pinkhas Hurwitz (the author of *Haflaah*), and disciple of the Rebbe Rabbi Ber of Mezhirich. He was the Rabbi of Nikolsburg and author of *Divrei Shmuel,* and *N'ziv HaShem.* His scholarship, his noble conduct, and his concern for the needy gained' him many disciples, some of whom became great Hassidic leaders in their own right.

Hurwitz, Yaakov Yitzchak HaLevi of Lublin, also known as The Seer of Lublin (1745-1814). His home became a center of Hassidism and a meeting place for students as well as *rebbes* and *tzaddikim* who came to hear his teachings and to gain inspiration from his saintliness and piety. He was the author of *Divrei Emeth* (Words of Truth) and *Zot Zikkaron* (Memorial).

Hurwitz, Yosef Josel. (1848-1920). Founder of many Talmudical academies, including the Musarist Yeshiva in Novogrodek, and other Yeshivos, and author of the work *Madregat HaAdam.* He demanded uncompromisingly high standards of ethical conduct, self-criticism, strength of character, piety and trust in God, from himself and his disciples.

Ibn Ezra, Abraham ben Meir Ezra. Born in Toledo, Spain, about 1092, died in Kalahara, Spain, about 1167. Biblical commentator, philosopher, poet, astronomer, mathematician and traveler. In his commentary he endeavors to give the plain meaning of the Scriptures with the utmost brevity and with profound insight. He also wrote several books on Hebrew grammar.

Igra De Kalla, see *Zvi Elimelekh, Rabbi of Dinov.*

Imrei Esh (Words of Fire). Novellae on Biblical texts and responsa by Rabbi Meir Asch, Talmudist and rabbi of Ungvar, Hungary, and father of Rabbi Menahem Asch (see *Homat Esh*).

Imrei Kohen (Sayings of the Kohanite). Sermons and novellae on Genesis and Exodus by Rabbi Meir Warshawick (Warsaw, 1932).

Imrei Shofar. Biblical commentary by Rabbi Solomon ben Judah Aaron Kluger (1783-1869), rabbinical scholar in Brody, Galicia, and commentator on Bible, Talmud and Shulhan Arukh. In 1854 Rabbi Kluger wrote that he had completed 136 manuscripts on the Written Law and the Oral Tradition, with each manuscript containing about 200 pages, as well as 8,000 responsa. He was greatly beloved for his efforts on behalf of his community.

532

BIBLIOGRAPHY

Imrei Tzvi (Sayings of Tzvi). Hassidic Bible interpretations by Rabbi Yerakhmiel Tzvi of Kazimir, Poland (Warsaw, 1925).

Ir Miklat (A City of Refuge). Commentary on the 613 Biblical commandments by Rabbi David Lido, head of the Beth Din (Court of Jewish Law) of Amsterdam, Talmudist and author of nine works on diverse topics of the Torah (d. Poland, 1695).

Isaac of Warka (1779-1848). Hassidic rabbi in Poland. A number of his disciples were founders of other Hassidic dynasties.

Israel ben Shabbetai of Kozienice (The Kozienicer Maggid) (c. 1737-1814). Hassidic leader and scholar in Poland. A disciple of Rabbi Levi Isaac of Berdichev and Rabbi Elimelekh of Lizensk, he wrote a number of Talmudic treatises, including *Bet Israel* (House of Israel), a commentary on several tractates of the Talmud, and *Avodat Yisrael.*

Israel of Ruzhin (The Ruzhiner Rebbe), (1798-1850). Hassidic rabbi known for his organizational skill, kindliness, and saintly conduct. Succeeding his father as *Tzaddik* in the town of Ruzhin at the age of sixteen, he held that the *Tzaddik* had to live in wealth and luxury if he was to exert influence on his disciples. After a period of imprisonment by the Russian authorities, he settled in Sadagora, Bukovina, which subsequently became a center of Hassidism. He was the founder of the rabbinic dynasty of Ruzhin.

Isserles, Moses (ReMo), (1520-1572), Rabbi of Cracow, head of a great Yeshiva and leader of Polish Jewry. He was known by the title of *Nassi* (Prince of the Law). It was thanks to his annotations that the *Shulhan Arukh* of Rabbi Joseph Karo became accepted as the Code of Laws even by the Ashkenazic (Western and Eastern European) Jews. He is the author of *Darkei Moshe* (Ways of Moses), a treatise on the *Arba Turim* (the Four Rows); *Toras Hattos,* a work dealing with the dietary laws, Rabbinic responsa entitled *Shaaloth U'Teshuvos HaRemo,* a commentary on the Book of Esther, and a philosophical work called *Torath Ha'Olah* (the Law of the Offering). His headstone bears the inscription: "From Moses to Moses there was no one like Moses," implying that since the days of Moses Maimonides there had been none like Moses Isserles.

Rabbi Jacob ben Asher, see *Baal HaTurim.*

Jacob ben Jacob Moses of Lissa (1770-1822). Prominent Talmudist and rabbinical leader in Poland. A leading opponent of the Reform movement, he was the author of a number of commentaries on the *Shulhan Arukh,* including *Nesivot Hamishpat* and *Havas Daat;* a work on religious practice entitled *Derekh HaHayyim* (Way of Life) and *Maaseh Nissim* (Tale of Miracles), a commentary on the Passover Haggadah.

Judah Ha-Levi, see *Ha-Kuzari.*

Judah HaHassid, (Judah the Pious). Twelfth-century Tosafist (d. 1217 in Germany). The head of a Yeshiva in Regensburg, he led a saintly and highly ethical life. He is the author of *Sefer Hassidim* (Book of the Pious) which contains many ethical and moral teachings, explanations of laws and customs and stories with ethical content.

Judah Loew ben Bezalel (MaHaRal). Born in Posen, 1525; died in Prague, 1609. Chief Rabbi of Moravia and rabbi in Prague and Posen. His many scholarly works include *Gur Aryeh* (a commentary on Rashi's commentary on the Pentateuch); *Nesivot Olam* (a discussion of the basic values of Judaism); *Derekh HaHayyim* on Tractate Abot; *Netzakh Israel,* and a unique commentary on the Aggadic portion of the Talmud. Active in Jewish communal life, he had many disciples, including Rabbi Yom Tov Lipman Heller (1579-1654). Legend associated the creation of the *Golem* with Rabbi Loew.

Kametz HaMinha. See Melo HaOmer.

Kanfei Nesharim (Wings of Eagles), Biblical novellae by Rabbi Isaiah Shur of Jassy, Rumania (1781-1881), Talmudist, Biblical commentator and Kabbalist.

Katz, Yitzhak, Talmudist, Rabbi of Stobnitz and Apta, and grandson of Shabsai HaKohen, author of *Sifthei Kohen* (Shakh).

Kav Hen (A Measure of Grace), Treatise by Rabbi Noah of Korav, (d. 1865), Hassidic Rebbe.

Kazimir, Yeheskel Taub of (d. 1894). Hassidic rebbe. Known widely for his saintliness and abstinence from worldly pleasures, he had thousands of disciples. He was the progenitor of the Modzitzer dynasty.

Kedushat Levi. Hassidic classic by Rabbi Levi Isaac of Berdichev (1740-1809), a disciple of Dov Ber, the Maggid of Mezhirich. Rabbi Isaac Levi was best known for his doctrine of *Ahavat Yisrael* (the brotherhood of all Jews), and his fervent prayers for God's mercy on behalf of his people.

Kehilat Yitzhak (Anthology of Issac). Compilation of *maggidic* preachings on the Torah by Rabbi Yitzhok Ben R. Nisson of Vilna.

Ketav Sofer, see *Schreiber, Abraham Samuel Benjamin.*

Khelm, Maggid of. Rabbi Moses Isaac of Khelm (1828-1900). Famed itinerant preacher in Russian Poland, known for his insistence on high standards of ethics in human relations.

K'lei Hemda (The Precious Vessel). Interpretations and novellae on the Bible by Rabbi Meir Don Plotzki, Rabbi of Ostrov (1868-1928), Talmudist, renowned leader of the rabbinate in Poland, and author of Talmudic novellae entitled *Hemdat Israel* (The Desired of Israel).

K'lei Yakar. Popular Biblical commentary by Rabbi Solomon Ephraim ben Aaron of Lunchitz (d. 1619), head of the Talmudical academy of Lvov, and rabbi of many Jewish communities. He was the author also of a novel entitled *Ollot Ephraim.*

Kluger, Solomon ben Judah Aaron, see *Imrei Shofar.*

Kodesh Yisrael. Authorship unknown.

Kokhav MiYaakov, see *Kranz, Jacob ben Wolf.*

Kol Omer Kro, see *Kro, Rabbi Joseph Hayyim.*

Kol Simcha, see *Simcha Bunim of Przysucha.*

Kometz HaMinha, see *Melo HaOmer.*

Kosnot Or. Novellae on the weekly portions of the Bible by the eighteenth-century Talmudist Rabbi Meir Ashkenazi of Eisenstadt, author also of *Ponim Meirot,* which contains Rabbinic responsa and novellae on the Talmud.

Kotzk, David of. Son of Menahem Mendel Morgenstern of Kotzk.

Kotzk, Rabbi of. See *Morgenstern, Menahem Mendel of Kotzk.*

Kranz, Jacob ben Wolf (The Maggid of Dubno). Born in Zhatil, Poland, 1740; died in Zamozh, Poland, 1804. A scholar and preacher, he traveled widely through Poland, Galicia and Volhynia, spending eighteen years in the town of Dubno. His sermons, exhorting his audiences to seek G-d and to mend their ways, were replete with epigrams and parables which have become famous. His writings were published in two volumes entitled *Ohel Yaakov* (Tent of Jacob), and *Kohav MiYaakov* (Star of Jacob), containing his commentaries on the Five Books of Moses and "Haftoros", and *Kol Dodi* (The Voice of my Beloved), a homiletic commentary on the Song of Songs.

Kro, Joseph Hayyim. Nineteenth-century rabbi of Vlatzlavek, Poland, preacher, and author of *Kol Omer Kro,* philosophical sermons on the Bible, and *Soleth*

L'Minha (Flour for a Meal Offering), a commentary on the Ethics of the Fathers.

Landau, Ezekiel of Prague, (1714-1793). One of the greatest Talmudic sages of his generation and Chief Rabbi of Prague, he was the author of Talmudic novellae entitled *Tziyun LeNefesh Hayah* (Monument to a Living Soul), and *Doresh LeZion,* a work of ethical maxims. He was the head of a renowned Yeshiva. His most famous work was *Noda BiYehuda* (Known in Judah), a two-volume classic of Rabbinic responsa. His decisions on Jewish law were accepted as universally binding. He devoted much of his time to the welfare of his people and enjoyed the respect of the Emperor Joseph II of Austria. A saintly man, he spurned even the basic comforts of life, rising before midnight to pray and study, and never sleeping in a bed until he had grown quite old. He zealously fought against any distortion or reform of Jewish law, basing his decisions and his own conduct on the traditional interpretation of the Talmudic law.

Landau, Zeev Wolf, (1807-1892). Son of Rabbi Avraham of Chekhanov. Hassidic Rabbi of Strakov, confidant and advisor to many Hassidic sages, Talmudist and author of *Zer Zahav* (Rim of Gold), *Keser Torah* (Crown of the Law) and *Amoros Tehoros* (Sayings of Purity).

Levi Isaac of Berdichev, see *Kedushat Levi.*

Lewin, Aaron, see *HaDrash VeHaEyun.*

Likutei Megodim (Gleanings of Spices). Anthology of commentaries on the Book of Proverbs by Rabbi Isaac ben Eliyahu HaLevi.

Likutei Ratzvo. Compilation of interpretations on the Bible by Zvi Hirsch ben Rabbi Abraham, Rabbi of Lazdai, Lithuania (published in 1865).

Likutei Shoshanim (Gleanings of Roses). Expositions and comments on Biblical texts, ways of serving God and ethical conduct, by Rabbi Moses Zvi of Svern (d. Poland, 1843), Talmudist, Kabbalist and a disciple and successor of Rabbi Levi Yitzhak of Berdichev.

Likutei Torah (Gleanings of Torah). Comments and Hassidic expositions on the Bible and the worship of God by Rabbi Mordecai ben Nahum of Chernobil, Hassidic Rabbi and propagator of Hassidism in the Ukraine (d. 1837).

Likutei Yekarim (Precious Gleanings). Anthology of ethical sayings, novellae on Biblical texts, Hassidic interpretations and guidelines from the great propagators of Hassidism, Rabbi Israel Baal Shem Tov, The Maggid of Mezhirich,

536

BIBLIOGRAPHY

Rabbi Menahem Mendel of Przemysl and Rabbi Yehiel Michel of Zlatchov, with preachings by Rabbi Meshulam Feivush HaLevi Heller of Zverzh, compiled by Rabbi Shmuel Segal (Lvov, 1891).

Lipkin, Israel (known as Rabbi Israel Salanter) (1810-1883). Talmudist and exponent of the *Musar* (moralist) movement. His disciples spread the *Musar* philosophy to a number of great *Yeshivos* in Eastern Europe.

Lipschitz, Yeheskiel. Rabbi of Kalisz, Poland, and Talmudist. As president of Poland's Union of Orthodox Rabbis, he headed a committee of rabbis who visited the United States after World War I to raise funds for the *yeshivot* of Poland and was received by President Calvin Coolidge. He was the author of the popular work *HaMidrash VeHaMaaseh* (Sermon and Action), an anthology of sermons and novellae on Biblical texts and Jewish law.

Lublin, Rabbi of. See Hurwitz, Yaakov Yitzhak HaLevi.

Lunchitz, Solomon Ephraim, see *K'lei Yakar.*

Maggid of Dubno, see *Kranz, Jacob ben Wolf.*

MaHaRa Yitzhaki. Rabbi Abraham ben Yitzhak HaKohen. Author of treatise *Kof HaKohen* (Palm of the Kohanite), containing Biblical commentaries, and *Zera Abraham* (Seed of Abraham), Rabbinical responsa on the Shulhan Arukh.

MaHaRaL, see *Judah Loew ben Bezalel.*

MaHaRaM Mizrachi. Dates unknown.

MaHaRaM of Amshinov. Menahem Mendel Kulish (1818-1863). Hassidic rebbe. Constantly striving for moral perfecetion, he imposed a regimen of absolute silence on himself. Two of his sons became *tzaddikim* in their own right.

MaHaRaM of Piltz. Rabbi Menahem of Piltz, Poland, Nineteenth-century Hassidic rebbe and author of Talmudic novellae. He was the brother-in-law of Rabbi Isaac Meir Alter, known as the *Hiddushei HaRiM.*

MaHarSHa, Samuel Eliezer ben Judah. Born in Cracow, 1555; died in Ostrog, 1631. Interpreter of Gemara, Rashi and Tosafot and author of Talmudic novellae entitled *Hiddushei Aggadot,* he was the head of a great Yeshiva. Many of his disciples became prominent Talmudists and Rabbinical leaders in Jewish communities.

537

MaHaRShaL of Lenchne. Rabbi Shlomo Leib of Lenchne (d. 1842). Hassidic rebbe and disciple of Hassidic leaders such as the Seer of Lublin and Yaakov Yitzhak of Przysucha.

Maimonides, see Moses ben Maimon.

MaLBIM, Meir Leibush ben Yehiel Michel. Rabbi, author, commentator, and interpreter of the Bible. Born 1809; died 1879 in Kiev, Russia. He was the author of *Artza Ha Hayyim* on Hilkhoth Tefilin; *Eretz Hemda* (homiletical interpretations on Torah) and a Biblical commentary entittled *Torah U'Mitzvah.* In this work, he demonstrates that with the proper knowledge of Hebrew grammar and syntax, all the exegesis of the Talmudic sages can be deduced from the straight Scriptural text. With his great knowledge and sharp pen, he was an articulate opponent of the *Haskala* movement and Reform Judaism.

Maoz HaDat (Fortress of Religion), Treatise on the Jewish religion and observance of Jewish law, by Rabbi Yehoshua Heller (Vilna, 1872).

Margenissa D'Reb Meir, see *Meir of Przemysl.*

Margolies, Rabbi M. Z.,

Margolith, Ephraim Zalman of Brody, (1762-1828). Talmudist, codifier, and author of works including *Beth Ephraim* (House of Ephraim), a renowned book of Rabbinic responsa; *Matteh Ephraim* (the Staff of Ephraim), which contains laws on the holidays, and *Zera Ephraim.* Although he did not occupy a Rabbinic position, he was a recognized leader of Polish Jewry.

Maskil Le-Aithon. Talmudical treatise by Rabbi Abraham (d. 1848), Talmudist and author of a number of Talmudic and Kabbalist commentaries, known by the name of his classic treatise.

Mecklenburg, Jacob Zvi ben Gamliel, see *HaKetav VeHaKabalah.*

Meir of Przemysl, (1780-1850), Tzaddik and Hassidic rabbi. Known for his love for his fellow-Jews, he was referred to as a *"Poel Yeshuot"* (Bringer of Salvation) and thousands came to seek his blessing. His sayings, and anecdotes about him are included in the work *"Or HaMeir"* (The Light that Lights), and *Margenissa D'Reb Meir* (Rabbi Meir's Diamond). He was a grandson of Rabbi Meir'l Przemyslaver, a disciple of the Baal Shem Tov.

Meir Yehiel of Ostrowicze, Meir Yehiel HaLevi Halstuch (1852-1928), Hassidic rebbe and sage. People from the world over turned to him for guidance and halakhic decisions. He fasted every day from sunup to sundown for a period of more than forty years, but this did not interfere with his daily lectures and Torah study. His Hassidic sayings are included in his work *Or Torah* (The Light of Torah). In 1892 he was proclaimed successor to the Grodzisker Rebbe.

Mekor Barukh, (The Blessed Source). Personal reminiscenses of the Epstein family and other great sages of yesteryear, commentaries on Scriptures and interpretations by Rabbi Baruch HaLevi Epstein (1860-1942), the author of *Torah Temina*, (The Complete Torah). Rabbi Baruch was shot by the German in the Ghetto of Pinsk.

Melo HaOmer, (Full Measure). Commentary on the Pentateuch and the Five Scrolls by Rabbi Aryeh Leib Zunz of Plotzk (Reb Leibush Harif; 1798-1833). The author of numerous Talmudic commentaries and Halakhic codes, Rabbi Zunz left many unpublished manuscripts with the promise that he would intercede at the Heavenly Court in behalf of anyone making possible the publication of one of these works. He is also the author of *Kometz HaMinha*, containing homiletic expositions on the Bible and the Holidays.

Menahem Mendel of Rimanov, (d. 1815). Disciple of Reb Shmelka of Nikolsburg and Reb Elimelekh of Lizensk and contemporary of the Maggid of Koznitz and the Rebbe of Lublin. He settled in the town of Rimanov, which became a great center of Hassidism. A saintly man and a miracle worker, he exerted considerate influence on his contemporaries. His Biblical expositions are included in the works *Menahem Zion, Divrei Menahem,* and *Toras Menahem.*

Meshekh Hakhmah. Biblical commentary by Simha Meir HaKohen (1845-1926), rabbi of Dwinsk (Latvia). Rabbi Simkha Meir HaKohen was the author of a Biblical commentary and *Or Sameakh*, a work tracing the sources of many Halakhic decisions by Maimonides. He also compiled a commentary on the Talmud, but except for part of Tractate *Baba Metziah,* the work has been lost.

Mevasser Tzedek, see *Yissokhor of Zlotchov.*

Midrash (Midrashic Literature). Rabbinic books containing Biblical interpretations in the spirit of the Aggadah (that part of the Oral Tradition which includes stories, chronicles, wise sayings and moral teachings, as distinct from Halakha, the actual laws to be observed in daily life).

Midrash Rabba. Anthology of Aggadic interpretations of the Pentateuch and the Five Scrolls by the Amoraim. Editorship attributed to Rabbi Hoshea Rabba.

Midrash Talpioth. Anthology of commentaries and novellae from three hundred works, arranged in Hebrew alphabetical order. Edited by Rabbi Eliyahu HaKohen, *dayan* of Izmir, Turkey.

Midrash Tanhuma. Midrashic work attributed to Rabbi Tanhuma Bar Abba (4th century Palestinian *amora*).

Mishnat R' Eliezer, (The Teachings of Rabbi Eliezer), Biblical interpretations by Eliezer Laiz, Rabbi of Altona, Hamburg and Wandsbeck, (1741-1814). A great Talmudist and endowed with a phenomenal memory, R. Eliezer knew the Bible as well as the entire Talmud by heart.

Mo'or VoShomesh, see *Epstein, Kalonymos Kalman HaLevi.*

Mordecai ben Rabbi Dov of Niskhiz (1742-1800), Hassidic Rebbe, Talmudist, and Rabbi of Kovel, Ludmir and Niskhiz. He was the author of a Biblical commentary entitled *Rishfei Esh.*

539

Morgenstern, Menahem Mendel of Kotzk. Born in Goray, Poland, 1787; died in Kotzk, Poland, 1854. A widely known Hassidic rabbi, he trained his disciples to serve G-d on a high moral level. He is noted for his wise and trenchant sayings and aphorisms.

Moses Leib of Sassov (1745-1807). Hassidic rabbi in Poland, disciple of Reb Shmuel Shmelke of Nikolsburg. A great Talmudist, he wrote novellae on many tractates of the Babylonian Talmud entitled *Likutei RaMal, Torat HaRaMal HaSholom* (The Complete Teachings of R' Moses Leib), and *Hidushei RaMal.* Rabbi Moses Leib was also known as "Father of Widows and Orphans" because of his concern for the needy. Some of his disciples like R. Menachem Mendel of Kosov, R. Zvi Hirsh of Zidichow, and Yaakov Yitzhak of Przysucha became noted Hassidic rabbis in their own right.

Moses ben Maimon (Maimonides, *RaMBaM*). Born in Cordova, Spain, 1135; died in Fostat, Egypt, 1204. Physician and greatest Jewish scholar, philosopher and codifier of the Middle Ages. His two outstanding works are *Mishne Torah,* a Hebrew compendium of the entire Halakha, which he completed in 1180 and *More Nevukhim* (Guide for the Perplexed), an exposition of the Jewish faith (completed in 1190). He is buried in Tiberias.

Moses ben Nahman (Nachmanides; *RaMBaN*). Born in Spain, c. 1194; died in Acre, Palestine, 1270. Scholar, rabbi, teacher, codifier, philosopher, and Biblical and Talmudic commentator. His Halakhic decisions have been accepted as universally binding. In 1263 he was challenged by Pablo Christiani, a Jewish convert to Christianity, to a public religious debate in the presence of King James I of Aragon in Barcelona. Tried for blasphemy, he had to leave Spain and settled in Palestine, where he infused new life into the Jewish community and wrote his popular commentary on the Bible.

Moshe Hayyim of Sadilkov, (1746-1800). Grandson of Rabbi Eliezer Baal Shem Tov, and a spiritual disciple of the founder of Hassidism. He is the author of *Degel Mahaneh Ephraim* (Banner of The Camp of Ephraim) which contains many thoughts and sayings of the Baal Shem Tov.

Moshe Zeev, Rabbi of Bialystok, see *Agudat Ezov.*

Musarists. Adherents of moralist movement initiated by outstanding nineteenth-century Talmudists (among them Rabbi Israel Salanter). The *Musar* movement preached the need for strengthening inner piety, the study of traditional ethical literature, and moral self-criticism. There were Musarist *yeshivot* in Khelm, Slobodka and Novahardok. Many other *yeshivot* in Lithuania and in the United States also came under the influence of this movement, which was considered a defense against secularism.

Nachmanides. See *Moses ben Nahman.*

Nahal Kedumim. See *Azulai, Hayyim Joseph David.*

Nathanson, Joseph Saul, see *Shoel U-Meshiv.*

Bibliography

Nehmad MiZahav (More Desirable Than Gold). Anthology containing Biblical commentaries by Rabbi Ezekiel Taub of Kazimir; *Afros Zahov* (Golden Soil) — Biblical commentaries by Rabbi Shmuel Yaakov Koppel HaKohen, and *Anaf Etz Avot* (Branch of the Ancestral Tree) (Pietrkov, 1908).

Netzakh Israel, (Eternity of Israel), see *Judah Loew ben Bezalel.*

Noam Elimelekh, (Delight of Elimelekh), Book of Hassidic thoughts by Rabbi Elimelekh of Lizensk (1717-1787), disciple of Dov Ber of Mezhirich, successor of Israel Eliezer Baal Shem Tov, and one of the founders of Hassidism in Galicia. He was widely known for his charity, humility and love for his people. A number of his disciples became noted Hassidic rabbis in their own right.

Noam Megoddim, (Sweetness of the Precious). Interpretations and novellae on the weekly portions of the Bible by Rabbi Eliezer HaLevi of Tarnigrod, published in 1807.

Noda BiYehuda, see *Landau, Ezekiel of Prague.*

Oheb Yisrael, see *Heschel, Abraham Joshua of Opatov.*

Ohel Torah (Tent of Torah). Commentary by Rabbi Menahem Mendel Morgenstern of Kotzk.

Ohel Yaakov, see *Kranz, Jacob ben Wolf.*

Olelot Ephraim, see *K'lei Yakov.*

Or HaHayyim. Biblical commentary by Rabbi Hayyim ben Oter (born in Morocco, 1696; died in Jerusalem, 1743), Talmudist and Kabbalist whose thought greatly influenced Hassidic philosophy.

Or HaMeir, see Meir of Przemysl.

Or Tzaddikim (Light of the Righteous). Sermons on the Pentateuch and the Song of Songs, by Rabbi Joseph Karo (see *Bet Yoseph*).

Orakh LeHayyim, see *Avraham Hayyim of Zlotchov.*

Orot HaMitzvot, (The Lights of the Commandments), Sermons and explanations of the commandments by Rabbi Benjamin Raphael Brandin.

Ostrowicze, Rabbi of. See *Meir Yehiel of Ostrowicze.*

541

Pardes Yosef (Orchard of Joseph). Popular anthology of interpretations of Biblical commentaries by Rashi and Nachmanides, compiled by Joseph of Piavinitz, who added ingenious annotations of his own.

Perot Levanon (Fruits of Lebanon). Anthology of homiletic interpretations of Biblical texts, by Rabbi Eliezer Lipa Weissblum, New York.

Pninim Yekarim (Precious Pearls). Hassidic anthology of interpretations and commentaries, by Rabbi Shimon Bezalel Nyman, author of *Meshiv Nefesh* (a treatise on Tractate Pesahim), who was killed by the Nazis in 1943.

Ponim Yofos. Commentary on the Pentateuch by Pinkhos Halevi Hurwitz, Rabbi of Frankfort, Germany, b. in Chortkov, Poland, 1730; d. in Frankfort, 1805. One of the greatest rabbis and Talmudists of his generation, *Haflaah,* his commentary on Tractate Ketuboth, and *Hamakneh,* his commentary on Tractate Kiddushin, are classic works studied by Talmudic scholars and Yeshiva students alike. Unlike other rabbis of his generation, he was close to the Hassidic movement and to Reb Ber of Mezhirich. His commentary on the Peutateuch represents a fusing of great scholarship with the Hassidic spirit. One of his disciples was the Hatham Sofer (Rabbi Moses Schreiber).

Proshat Derakhim, (Crossroads). Interpretations on Torah in a Talmudic vein by Rabbi Yehuda Rozanis, the author of *Mishneh L'Melekh* (Viceroy to the King), a popular commentary on Maimonides. One of the great Sephardic rabbis of his generation and Chief Rabbi of Turkey, he was greatly esteemed by Jews and Gentiles alike. He died in 1724.

Przysucha, Simcha Bunim of. See *Simcha Bunim of Przysucha.*

Przysucha, Yaakov Yitzhak. See *Yaakov Yitzhak of Przysucha.*

Rabbenu Ephraim (Our Teacher Ephraim), Rabbi Ephraim ben Rabbi Yitzhak of Regensburg, 12th century Tosafist, and composer of liturgical poetry.

RaMaH, Rabbi Menahem ben Rabbi Moshe HaBavli. Born in Bagdad in the sixteenth century, he became one of the noted sages of the Holy Land. He is the author of *Taamei HaMitzvot* (Reasons for the Commandments).

RaN (Rabbi Nissim ben Reuben Girondi). Born in the thirteenth century in Spain; died in Barcelona about 1380. One of the greatest Talmudic scholars and commentators of his generation, he wrote numerous responsa and a book of sermons known as *Derashot HaRan* (Sermons of the RaN). The most noted of his disciples and his successor was Rabbi Isaac ben Sheshet, known by his initials as RIvoSH.

Rashi (Rabbi Schlomo Yitzhaki). Born in France, 1040; died, 1105. Author of the standard commentary on the Bible and the Talmud. Through Rashi's commentary, the Torah and Talmud became an open book to student and scholar alike.

Rebbe of Kobrin, Moshe ben Rabbi Eliezer (b. Kobrin, about 1784), Hassidic Rebbe with many followers. His interpretations of Biblical texts and sayings of our Sages are recorded in the work *Amoros Tehoros* (Sayings of Purity), together with the commentaries of his grandson Rabbi Noah Naftali of Kobrin.

Rimzei D'Hokhmoso (Allusions to Wisdom). Commentaries on Torah and Jewish holiday observance by Rabbi Samuel Aryeh Zak (Warsaw, 1931).

Rishfei Esh, see *Mordecai ben Rabbi Dov of Niskhiz.*

Saadia Gaon. Born in Egypt, 892; died in Sura, Babylonia, 942. One of the outstanding personalities of Jewish history, he was head of the ancient, world-famous Talmudical academy of Sura. He was a codifier of Jewish law, commentator on the Bible, philosopher, and author of many works, such as *Emunos VeDayot* (Beliefs and Opinions). With his gifted pen and brilliant logic he effectively fought against the teachings of the Karaites and their influence in Jewish affairs.

Salanter, Israel. See *Lipkin, Israel.*

Schreiber, Abraham Samuel Benjamin (Ketav Sofer) (1815-1875). Son of Moses Schreiber (Hatham Sofer). A leader of Hungarian Orthodoxy and opponent of Reform Judaism, he is known after his collection of responsa, commentaries and glosses entitled *Ketav Sofer.*

Schreiber, Moses (Hatham Sofer) (1762-1839). Rabbi of Pressburg and world-famous *Halakhic* authority. He is known after his most distinguished work, *Hatham Sofer* (Seal of the Scribe), a six-volume collection of responsa and novellae. He founded the noted Pressburg *yeshiva.* He is also the author of *Torat Moshe,* quoted in this volume.

Schreiber, Simon (1821-1883). Son of Moses Schreiber (Hatham Sofer), rabbi in Cracow and member of the Austrian Parliament.

Sefarim. Works containing novellae and commentaries, Hassidic sayings, moral and ethical preachings.

Sefarim HaKedoshim. See *Sefarim.*

Sefat Emet, (Language of Truth). A commentary on Biblical and Talmudic literature by Rabbi Judah Aryeh Loeb Alter (1874-1905), grandson of Rabbi Isaac Meir Alter, who became head of the rabbinic dynasty of Gur at the age of eighteen.

Sefer HaHinukh, (Book of Training). Popular text in which the 613 Biblical commandments are outlined and explained. Compiled by Rabbi Aaron HaLevi of Barcelona, who lived in the early part of the fourteenth century, it is famous for the Halakhic decisions, moral teachings and rational explanations it contains. A number of commentaries (e.g. *Minhat Hinukh*) are based on this work.

Sefer HaIkkarim, see *Baal HaIkkarim.*

Sefer Shimon VaLevi (Book of Simon and Levi). Commentary on the Passover Haggadah and the mystical significance of the month of Nisan, by Rabbi Shimon ben Kayam Kaddish HaLevi.

Sforno, Obadiah ben Jacob. Born about 1475; died about 1550. Italian Torah sage, scholar, and physician. His most popular work is the Biblical commentary known as Sforno.

Shaar Bet Rabbim, Popular anthology of homiletical interpretations on Biblical and prophetic literature by Rabbi Hayyim Aryeh Leib of Yedvabno, Poland.

Shapiro, Meir of Lublin, (1887-1934). Rabbi and leader of Polish Jewry. He instituted the *Daf-Yomi,* the systematic study of one folio of the Talmud each day, a project promoting study and unity among Jews the world over. The head and founder of the famous Yeshiva of Lublin, he did much to improve the accommodations of the Yeshiva students. An eloquent orator inspired with Hassidic enthusiasm and a great Talmudist, he was one of the luminaries of Polish Jewry.

Shaul ben Rabbi Aryeh Leib of Amsterdam, Eighteenth-century Talmudist, Rabbi of Amsterdam for thirty-five years, and author of *Binyan Ariel* (Edifice of Ariel), novellae on Halakhic and Aggadic literatures.

SheLaH, (*Shnei Lukhot HaBrit* — The Two Tablets of the Law). Commentary on Jewish law, customs and ethics by Rabbi Isaiah Horowitz (born in Prague, 1556; died in Tiberias, Palestine, 1630), scholar and Kabbalist. Rabbi Horowitz served a number of communities in Poland, Lithuania and Volhynia. From 1606 to 1614 he was rabbi and head of the Talmudical academy of Frankfort-on-the-Main. From there he moved to Prague and later to Palestine where he became rabbi of the Ashkenazi community. He was well known for his ethical teachings and his own saintly way of life.

544

BIBLIOGRAPHY

Shelomo of Karlin (1747-1801). Disciple of Rab Aaron HaGodol, the *Maggid* of Mezhirich and other famous Hassidic leaders. Many of his teachings are set down in the treatise *Shem Shelomo* (The Fame of Solomon). He was killed in Lublin, Poland, by a soldier while he was reciting his prayers.

Shem MiShmuel, see *Bornstein, Abraham*.

Shem MiShimon. Novellae on tractates of the Babylonian Talmud by Rabbi Shimon Stern of Dombrova, Poland.

Shemen HaMo'or, (Oil of the Light). Preachings and commentary on morals end ethics by Rabbi Moshe Shimon HaDarshon (The Preacher), seventeenth-century scholar (father of Rabbi Hayyim Yair Bachrach, author of *Havos Yair*).

Shev Shmattso, (Seven Discourses). Profound and original novellae on Biblical texts on seven discourses by Rabbi Aryeh Leib HaKohen Heller, Talmudist and author of *Ktzos HaHoshen*.

Shir Meon. Authorship unknown.

Shmuel Shmelke of Nikolsburg (d. 1877). Rabbi in Nikolsburg, Moravia. A disciple of the *Maggid* of Mezhirich, he was the author of the treatises *Divrei Shmuel* and *Netzive HaShem*.

Sh'nei Lukhot HaBrit, see *SheLaH*.

Shoel UMeshiv. Work of Rabbinic responsa on Jewish law by Chief Rabbi Joseph Saul Nathanson, of Lvov, Poland (d. 1875). His other works include a Biblical commentary entitled *Divrei Shaul* ("Words of Saul").

Sifre. Halakhic Midrash to Books of Numbers and Deuteronomy.

Simcha Bunim of Przysucha, (1765-1827). Talmudist, merchant, pharmacist, and Hassidic rabbi. His own disciples included personalities like the Kotzker Rebbe. Some of his views and commentaries on the Bible are quoted in the works *Kol Simcha*, (The Voice of Simcha), *Hedvas Simcha*, (Joy of Simcha). and *Romosayyim Tzofim*, which were published by his disciples.

Simha Meir HaKohen. See *Meshekh Hakhma*.

Sifthei Hen (Words of Grace). Sermons by Rabbi Hayyim Nathanson (Vilna, 1899).

Sifthei Kodesh. Authorship unknown.

Sifthei Kohen, (The Lips of the Kohanite). Original Biblical commentaries containing scholarly as well as mystical interpretations, and an anthology of earlier commentaries by Rabbi Mordecai HaKohen of Safed, printed in 1610.

Sifthei Tzaddikim, Anthology of Biblical novellae by *Tzaddikim*, compiled by Rabbi Pinkhos of Dinourtz.

Soloveitchik, Joseph Dov Halevi of Brisk, (d. 1892). A great-grandson of Rabbi Hayyim of Volozhin, he was one of the heads of the Yeshiva of Volozhin and rabbi of Slutzk and Brisk. He was held in great awe and esteem by all for his ceaseless search for truth in every phase of life, in Torah study, in religious observance, and in his dealings with his fellow-men. He strove to help improve the situation of the underprivileged, rebuking the rich and influential Jews for not doing enough to help their needy brethren. He is the author of *Shaalot U'Teshuvos*, Rabbinic responsa and Talmudic novellae, and *Beis Halevi* (House of Levi), an ingenious commentary on the Bible and the works of our Sages. His son was Rabbi Hayyim of Brisk, the world-renowned scholar, who was acclaimed for his unique approach to the study of the Talmud and its commentaries.

Teshuvo MeAhavo. Novellae and responsa on Torah and Talmud by Rabbi Eliezer Fleckeles, a disciple of Rabbi Ezekiel Landau (*Noda BiYehuda*).

Tifereth Shlomo (The Glory of Solomon). Sermons and profound Hassidic interpretations on Biblical texts and Holidays by Shlomo HaKohen, Rabbi of Radomsk. He died in 1866, leaving three sons, all of whom became Tzaddikim, and many disciples who were greatly influenced by his teachings and personality.

Tifereth Shmuel (Glory of Samuel). Notes and explanations on Rashi's commentary to the Pentateuch, and sermons and novellae on Mishnayot and Gemara, by Rabbi Samuel Kaufman (New York, 1925).

Toledoth Adam (The Generations of Man). Biblical commentary by Rabbi Yehoshua of Ostrove, Poland (d. 1872).

Torat Emes, see *Heschel, Abraham Joshua of Opatov*.

Torat HaMoreh VeHaTalmud. Authorship unknown.

Torat Ha'Olah, see *Isserles, Moses*.

Torat Moshe. See Schreiber, Moses.

Tosafists, Authors of *Tosafos* (supplements to Rashi's commentary on Torah and Talmud), who were active from the 11th to the 15th century.

546

BIBLIOGRAPHY

Treor, Hayyim. Born 1770 near Buczacz; died 1813 in Safed, Israel, Rabbi of Chernowitz, disciple of the Rebbe R. Ber of Mezhirich, author and propagator of Hassidism. When the Austrian government forbade Jewish communal worship and decreed that Jewish children should be sent only to government schools, Rabbi Treor commanded the members of his community to disobey and himself led them in public worship. He was arrested, but managed to escape, and finally settled in Safed. He is the author of a number of works, including *Be'er Mayyim Hayyim,* a commentary on the Bible with Kabbalistic overtones, and *Siddurah Shel Shabbos,* a popular exposition on the sanctity of the Sabbath.

Trunk, Israel Joshua of Kutno. Born 1821, died 1893. Talmudist, author of the Halakhic work *Yeshuat Malko,* and recognized Rabbinic authority in Poland.

Tzror HaMor (Bundle of Spice). Treatise by Rabbi Moshe ben Rabbi Yaakov Shmuel Khaqiz (1672-1761), author, traveller, and strong opponent of the movement rallying around Shabbetai Zvi, the false Messiah.

Vilna, Gaon of. (Rabbi Elijah ben Rabbi Shlomo Zalman). Born in Seltz, 1720, died in Vilna, 1797. Talmudist. At the age of ten, he knew the whole Babylonian and Jerusalem Talmud by heart. His sole occupation in life was the study of Torah, and he consistently refused rabbinical positions so as not to be distracted from his studies. His diligence and dedication to study were extraordinary. He would sleep only one half hour at a time. Because of his scholarship be became known as "the Gaon" (Eminence), a title formerly given only to the heads of the academies in Babylonia. He wrote commentaries and interpretations on the Bible, Babylonian and Jerusalem Talmud, Tosefta, the Shulhan Arukh, and many work on Kabbala. His disciples testified that his writings were only a "drop in the sea" compared to the true extent of his Torah knowledge. He was an articulate opponent of Hassidism, which originated in his time. Among his many disciples was Rabbi Hayyim of Volozhin, founder of the great Yeshiva of Volozhin. He was a giant in a generation of Torah sages, and his name is still mentioned with reverence by Jewish scholars today.

Yaakov Yitzhak of Przysucha (1765-1815). Also known as *Yid Hakodosh* (The Saintly Jew). An unusually diligent Talmudist and preacher, known for his saintliness and piety, he became a devoted disciple of the *Tzaddik* Rabbi Moshe Leib of Sassov. After spending years in isolation, he became a Hassidic rebbe in his on right, with many disciples.

Yad HaKetana. Work giving sources and main laws of the 613 Biblical commandments with ethical and Musarist comments. Published anonymously at the request of the author.

Yad HaMelekh (The Hand of the King). Novellae on Maimonides' Code of Law by Eliezer Landau, Talmudist and rabbi of Brody.

Yakar MiPoz (More Precious Than Refined Gold). Hassidic commentaries on Biblical texts and Prophetic readings, by Rabbi Samuel Shapiro (Lvov, 1891).

Yalkut David (Anthology of David). Anthology of *midrashim,* commentaries and homiletical material arranged according to the portions of the Pentateuch, by Rabbi David ben Hirz Posner.

Yalkut Hadash (The New Anthology). Anthology of sermons and homiletical works arranged in Hebrew alphabetical order, by Rabbi Israel of Belz.

Yalkut HaDrush (Anthology of Sermons). Anthology of homiletical interpretations of the Books of Genesis and Exodus by Rabbi Eliezer Lipa Weissblum and Rabbi Sholom Yitzhak Levitan (New York, 1925).

Yalkut HaGershuni (The Gershuni Collection). Anthology of fine, sometimes witty Biblical and Aggadic interpretations by Rabbi Gershon Stern of Ludash, Hungary. Published in 1901.

Yalkut HaLevi (The Levite's Anthology). Anthology of essays, riddles and songs by Raphael HaLevi.

Yalkut HaUrim (Anthology of the Luminaries). Anthology of glosses and explanations relating to Biblical and Aggadic literature, by Rabbi Moshe Uri Keller of Sanz, Poland.

Yalkut Reubeni. Anthology of difficult *midrashim* from Kabbalist works, arranged according to the weekly Pentateuchal readings.

Yehiel of Aleksander. See *Hashava LaTorah.*

Yeshuat Malko, see *Trunk, Israel Joshua.*

Yesod HaTorah (Foundation of Torah). Commentary on the thirteen principles pertaining to the interpretation of Jewish Law, by Rabbi Moedecai Gumpel Schraber (Hamburg, 1741).

Yissokhor of Zlotchov, Poland; d., Safed, 1810. Talmudic disciple of the Rebbe R. Ber of Mezhirich. He was the author of Talmudic novellae entitled *"Baas Eini"* and *Mevasser Zedek* (the Messenger of Righteousness) which contains his sermons on Biblical texts written in the classical Hassidic manner.

BIBLIOGRAPHY

Zavore Shalal, see *Azulai, Hayyim Joseph David.*

Zemba, Menahem of Warsaw (1884-1943). Brilliant Talmudist, author of novellae on the Laws of Sabbath, *Totzeoth Hayyim,* and leader of Polish Jewry. Refusing an offer from the Catholic clergy to help him escape from the Warsaw Ghetto, he encouraged the Jews of the Ghetto to offer armed resistance to the Nazis. He was killed by the Nazis on the fifth day of the Warsaw Ghetto revolt. His life's work, a manuscript of over three thousand pages dealing with Maimonides, was lost in the Ghetto.

Zer Zahav, see *Landau, Zeev Wolf.*

Zohar, (Book of Splendor). Earliest work on Kabbala, a mystic commentary on the Torah and on the Books of Ruth, Lamentations, and the Song of Songs, dealing with the hidden implications of the Torah and its commandments. The author of the Zohar was the Tannaite Reb Simon ben Yohai who lived in Israel in the second century B.C.E.

Zvi Elimelekh, Rabbi of Dinov, Poland (1795-1851), Talmudist, Hassidic Rebbe, and author of novellae on diverse scholarly subjects, including *Bnei Yissoshor, Igra DeKalla, Derekh Pikudekho,* and many others. They represent an expert blending of Talmudic scholarship with Hassidic emotion.

Zunz, Aryeh Leib of Plotzk, see *Melo HaOmer.*